Jung and the Making of Modern Psychology

D1245461

Occultist, Scientist, Prophet, Charlatan – C. G. Jung has been called all these things and after decades of myth making is one of the most misunderstood figures in Western intellectual history. This book is the first comprehensive study of the formation of his psychology, as well as providing a new account of the rise of modern psychology and psychotherapy. Based on a wealth of hitherto unknown archival materials it reconstructs the reception of Jung's work in the human sciences, and its impact on the social and intellectual history of the twentieth century. This book creates a basis for all future discussion of Jung, and opens new vistas on psychology today.

SONU SHAMDASANI is a historian of psychology and a Research Associate of the Wellcome Trust Centre for the History of Medicine at University College London. His most recent book *Cult Fictions: C. G. Jung and the Founding of Analytical Psychology* won the Gradiva Prize for the best historical and biographical work from the World Association for the Advancement of Psychoanalysis.

Jung and the Making of Modern Psychology

The Dream of a Science

Sonu Shamdasani

CAMBRIDGE
UNIVERSITY PRESS

PUBLISHED BY THE PRESS SYNDICATE OF THE UNIVERSITY OF CAMBRIDGE
The Pitt Building, Trumpington Street, Cambridge, United Kingdom

CAMBRIDGE UNIVERSITY PRESS
The Edinburgh Building, Cambridge, CB2 2RU, UK
40 West 20th Street, New York, NY 10011–4211, USA
477 Williamstown Road, Port Melbourne, VIC 3207, Australia
Ruiz de Alarcón 13, 28014 Madrid, Spain
Dock House, The Waterfront, Cape Town 8001, South Africa

http://www.cambridge.org

First published 2003

Printed in the United Kingdom at the University Press, Cambridge

Typeface Plantin 10/12 pt.   *System* LATEX 2ε   [TB]

A catalogue record for this book is available from the British Library

ISBN 0 521 83145 8 hardback
ISBN 0 521 53909 9 paperback

For Maggie

Contents

Full contents

Acknowledgments

As a companion who has contributed to this book at every step along the way since its inception, I would like to thank Maggie Baron.

The book has been written alongside a series of collaborative projects with Mikkel Borch-Jacobsen. Our dialogue has continually enriched it, and shaped my thought to the extent that I am unable to quantify what I owe to him.

It was through conversations with Eugene Taylor that I began to grasp fully the significance and the possibilities of the history of psychology, and the status of Jung history as a discipline in its own right.

From the first comprehensible account of the genesis of Freud's work by Peter Swales, I glimpsed the possibility that something similar could be done for Jung.

In discussions with Ernst Falzeder, I learnt how the hidden history of psychoanalysis should be researched.

To Angela Graf-Nold, I owe clarification of Jung's psychiatric milieu, and vital support during my researches in Switzerland.

This work would be severely impoverished without conversations with Vincent Barras, John Beebe, Jacqueline Carroy, Jerry Donat, Jacques Gasser, Wolfgang Giegerich, Brett Kahr, Paul Kugler, Ruth Leys, Enrique Pardo, Jay Sherry, Richard Skues, Anthony Stadlen, Fernando Vidal, and Michael Whan.

From 1988 to his death in 1995, the late Michael Fordham provided invaluable stimulus to my work, discussing my evolving research, making many crucially important suggestions, and recalling his relations with Jung and his involvement in the world of analytical psychology since the 1930s. The list of questions I would have put to him never ceases to grow.

Since then, Ximena Roelli de Angulo has participated in a similar manner in the development of my research, and has been of continual encouragement during its travails. As a skeptical and rational onlooker, she provided invaluable recollections of Jung's circle and figures associated with it from the 1920s onwards.

For their hospitality, information, and kind assistance, I am grateful to Rudolf Conne, Lilianne Flournoy, Olivier Flournoy, Christian

Hartnibrigg, Joseph Henderson, Hélène Hoerni-Jung, Ulrich Hoerni, the late Franz Jung, Peter Jung, Pierre Keller, the late Doris Straüli-Keller, Tom Kirsch, Nomi Kluger-Nash, Peter Riklin, Leonhard Schlegel, Georg Trüb, and Ursula Trüb.

Andreas Jung, the late Franz Jung and Peter Jung graciously assisted me in consulting Jung's library on a number of occasions.

At the inception of my researches, Doris Albrecht and William McGuire provided critical assistance. James Hillman encouraged my writing at an early stage, and introduced me to Jerry Donat, who induced me to undertake a thesis at the Wellcome Institute for the History of Medicine.

My thesis would not have come about without the encouragement and support of Bill Bynum, to whom I owe a number of critical suggestions. I would like to thank Mark Micale and the late Roy Porter for their assistance with and comments on my thesis, and Chris Lawrence for instruction in the history of medicine. The Wellcome Institute for the History of Medicine, now renamed the Wellcome Trust Centre for the History of Medicine at UCL, provided a unique environment to work in, and has osmotically shaped the present work. I would like to extend my thanks to my colleagues there over the years.

This work has been made possible by sponsorship from the Wellcome Trust from 1993 to 1998, the Institut für Grenzgebiete der Psychologie from 1998 to 1999, and the Solon Foundation from 1998 to 2001. I would like to thank Eberhard Bauer, the late Yaltah Menuhin and Harald Walach for their assistance. I would like to thank the following for additional grants: the C. G. Jung Institute of New York, the Van Waveren Foundation and the Oswald Foundation, and for their assistance, Olivier Bernier, Alan Jones, Beverley Zabriskie, and Philip Zabriskie.

For assistance with the publication of this work, I am grateful to Anna Campion, Bianca Lepori, George Makari, and Michael Neve.

For assistance with transcriptions, I would like to thank Ernst Falzeder and Katerina Rowold.

For permission to cite from Jung's unpublished manuscripts and correspondences, I would like to thank Niedieck Linder AG and the Erbengemeinschaft C. G. Jung.

I would like to thank Sarah Caro, my editor at Cambridge University Press, for her enthusiastic response to this project, and for seeing it through publication.

A number of people have commented on parts or all of the manuscript. In addition to vital improvements to the text, their comments have helped me understand its significance: Mikkel Borch-Jacobsen, Ximena Roelli de Angulo, Ernst Falzeder, George Makari, Michael Neve, David Oswald, John Peck, Richard Skues, Eugene Taylor, and Fernando Vidal. Responsibility for views herein is my own.

Abbreviations

CMAC Contemporary Medical Archives, Wellcome Trust Library for the History and Understanding of Medicine, London

CML   Countway Library of Medicine, Harvard Medical School, Boston

CMS   Jung/Jaffé, *Memories, Dreams, Reflections*, editorial manuscript, Countway Library of Medicine, Harvard Medical School, Boston, original in English

CW   *The Collected Works of C. G. Jung*, edited by Sir Herbert Read, Michael Fordham, Gerhard Adler; William McGuire, executive editor; trans. R. F. C. Hull (New York and Princeton, Bollingen Series 20 and London, 1953–1983), 21 vols.

ETH   Wissenschaftshistorische Sammlungen, Eidgenössische Technische Hochschule, Zürich

FJL   *The Freud/Jung Letters*, ed. William McGuire, trans. R. Mannheim and R. F. C. Hull (Princeton, Princeton University Press; London, Hogarth Press/Routledge and Kegan Paul, 1974)

JP   Jung Papers, Wissenschaftshistorische Sammlungen, Eidgenössische Technische Hochschule, Zürich

LC   Library of Congress, Washington DC

Letters *C. G. Jung Letters*, selected and edited by Gerhard Adler in collaboration with Aniela Jaffé, trans. R. F. C. Hull, 1973, 1975 (Bollingen Series, Princeton, Princeton University Press and London, Routledge), 2 vols.

Memories *Memories, Dreams, Reflections*, C. G. Jung/Aniela Jaffé, 1963 (London, Flamingo, 1983)

MP   Protocols of Aniela Jaffé's interviews with Jung for *Memories, Dreams, Reflections*, Library of Congress, Washington DC, original in German

MZP   Minutes of the Zürich Psychoanalytical Society, Psychological Club, Zürich, original in German

SE   *The Standard Edition of the Complete Psychological Works of Sigmund Freud*, ed. James Strachey in collaboration with Anna Freud assisted by Alix Strachey and Alan Tyson, trans. J. Strachey, 24 vols. (London, The Hogarth Press and the Institute of Psychoanalysis, 1953–1974)

SFC   Sigmund Freud Copyrights, Wivenhoe

Note on translations

Unless otherwise noted, translations are my own. In Jung's *Collected Works*, a number of the titles of works were arbitrarily changed, and these have been restored to their original forms. Unless otherwise noted, the originals of unpublished letters and manuscripts of Jung are in German. In the body of the text, the titles of all works cited are given in English, with the exception of the names of journals.

Prologue: "The most cursed dilettante"

"Don't make a legend of me."

C. G. Jung, 1930.[1]

Occultist, Scientist, Prophet, Charlatan, Philosopher, Racist, Guru, Anti-Semite, Liberator of Women, Misogynist, Freudian Apostate, Gnostic, Post-Modernist, Polygamist, Healer, Poet, Con-Artist, Psychiatrist and Anti-Psychiatrist – what has C. G. Jung not been called? Mention him to someone, and you are likely to receive one of these images. For Jung is someone that people – informed or not – have opinions about. The swift reaction time indicates that people respond to Jung's life and work as if they are sufficiently known. Yet the very proliferation of "Jungs" leads one to question whether everyone could possibly be talking about the same figure.

In 1952, Jung responded to the fact that he had been variously described as a theist, an atheist, a mystic, and a materialist by noting: "When opinions over the same subject differ widely, according to my view, there is the well-founded suspicion that none of them is correct, i.e., that there is a misunderstanding."[2] Nearly fifty years later, the number of divergent views and interpretations of Jung has prodigiously multiplied. He has become a figure upon whom an endless succession of myths, legends, fantasies, and fictions continues to be draped. Travesties, distortions, and caricatures have become the norm. This process shows no signs of abating.

From early on, Jung was subject to a welter of rumors. In 1916, he wrote to his friend and colleague, Alphonse Maeder,

As to what the rumors about my person concern, I can inform you that I have been married to a female Russian student for six years (Ref. Dr. Ulrich), dressed as Dr. Frank, I have recommended immediate divorce to a woman (Ref. Frau E-Hing), two years ago I broke up the Rüff–Franck marriage, recently I made Mrs. McCormick pregnant, got rid of the child and received 1 million for this

---

[1] Jung to Margaret Flenniken, June 20, 1930, JP, original in English.
[2] "Religion and Psychology," *CW* 18, § 1500, trans. mod.

1

(Ref Dr. F. & Dr. M. In Z.), in the Club house I intern pretty young girls for homosexual use for Mrs. McCormick, I send their young men for mounting in the hotel, therefore great rewards, I am a baldheaded Jew (Ref. Dr. Stier in Rapperswyl), I am having an affair with Mrs. Oczaret, I have become crazy (Ref. Dr. M. In Z.), I am a con-man (Ref. Dr. St. in Z.), and last not least – Dr. Picht is my assistant. What is one to do? How should I behave to make such rumors impossible? I am thankful for your good advice. The auspices for analysis are bad, as you see! One must simply not do such an unattractive enterprise on one's own, if one is not to be damaged.[3]

After decades of myth making, one question becomes more insistent: who was C. G. Jung?

Once, when asked who he was, Miles Davis replied that he had changed the course of music several times in his life (1990, 371). Something similar could be said of Jung. As a psychiatrist, he played a pivotal role in the formation of the modern concept of schizophrenia, and the idea that the psychoses were of psychological origin and hence amenable to psychotherapy. During his association with Freud, he was the principal architect of the psychoanalytic movement, inaugurating the rite of training analysis, which became the dominant form of instruction in modern psychotherapy. His formulation of psychological types of introverts and extraverts with numerous sub-varieties has spawned countless questionnaires. His views on the continued relevance of myth were the seed bed for the mythic revival. His interest in Eastern thought was the harbinger of the postcolonial Easternization of the West. Intent on reconciling science and religion through psychology, his work has met with endless controversy at every turn. Alongside a professional discipline of Jungian psychology and Institutes, Societies, Clubs, and Associations still bearing his name, there is a massive counterculture that hails him as a founding figure – and the impact of his work on mainstream twentieth-century Western culture has been far wider than has yet been recognized.

The work of Freud and Jung has been taken on by the general public to a remarkable extent. For many, their names are the first which come to mind when one thinks of psychology. They have become iconic images of "the psychologist." Their names have become proper names for psychology. Like Russian dolls, they conceal many forgotten figures within them. They have come to stand in for long-standing debates in European intellectual history and transformations in Western societies from the end of the nineteenth century to the present. The plethora of positions attributed to Freud and Jung, if collectively assembled, would in both cases cover something approaching the whole spectrum of modern thought.

---

[3] October 9, 1916, Maeder papers.

The figure of "Jung" stands at the interfaces of academic psychology, psychiatry, psychotherapy, popular psychology, and New Age psychologies. The rise of these disciplines and movements is one of the decisive developments in twentieth-century Western society. It may well be its most curious legacy. The formation of modern psychology and psychotherapy took place at a time of great upheaval in Western thought and culture, in which they were deeply interwoven. Thus their reconstruction is an essential element in the comprehension of the development of modern Western societies and our present.

From psychiatric wards to pulpits, from university lecture halls to chat shows, from law courts to tabloids, from classrooms to prisons, psychology today is firmly installed. It has effected deep-seated transformations in civic life as well as in individuals' intimate perception of themselves. When so much of social reality and "common sense" have come to be pervaded by psychology, psychological ideas have been naturalized, and have taken on the aspect of immediate indubitable certitudes. They have become standards by which to judge individuals in other times and societies. An historical account of these unprecedented changes is essential if one is to arrive at a reflective distance from the installation of psychology in contemporary life.

Around 1938, Jung himself had this to say about the societal impact of psychology: "A ceaseless and limitless talk about psychology has inundated the world in the last twenty years, but it has not as yet produced a noticeable improvement of the psychological outlook and attitude."[4] Both laymen and scientists were "bewildered by the luxuriant growth of theoretical standpoints, and by a maze of unbalanced propositions" (*ibid.*). The history of psychology may offer a way into, and a way out of, this maze of bewilderment.

The advent of the new psychology

"One must be absolutely modern." (Arthur Rimbaud, *A Season in Hell*, 1873)

"Everyone seems to be publishing a Psychology in these days," wrote William James in 1893 to his friend and fellow psychologist, Théodore Flournoy.[5] Textbooks, Principles, Outlines, Introductions, Compendiums, and Almanacs of psychology poured forth. Journals, Laboratories, Professorships, Courses, Societies, Associations, and Institutes of

---

[4] Preface to a proposed English edition of Tina Keller's *L'Ame et les nerfs* [The Soul and Nerves] (JP). Original in English.
[5] December 31, 1893, ed. Le Clair, 31.

psychology were set up. A horde of witnesses was called forth and interrogated: the Madman, the Primitive, the Genius, the Degenerate, the Imbecile, the Medium, the Infant and last but not least, the White Rat. New characters entered the social stage: the Schizophrenic, the Narcissist, the Manic-Depressive, the Anal-Retentive, the Oral-Sadistic and all the "verts" – the Invert, Pervert, Introvert and Extravert. But what did all this ferment denote?

At the end of the nineteenth century, many figures in the West sought to establish a scientific psychology that would be independent of philosophy, theology, biology, anthropology, literature, medicine, and neurology, whilst taking over their traditional subject matters. The very possibility of psychology rested upon the successful negotiation of these disciplinary crossings. The larger share of the questions that psychologists took up had already been posed and elaborated in these prior disciplines. They had to prise their subjects from the preserves of other specialists. Through becoming a science, it was hoped that psychology would be able to solve questions that had vexed thinkers for centuries, and to replace superstition, folk wisdom, and metaphysical speculation with the rule of universal law.

In 1892, Flournoy was given a chair in psychology at the University of Geneva. This was the first chair of psychology in a science, as opposed to a philosophy faculty. In 1896, reflecting back on the significance of this event, Flournoy stated:

the Genevan government has implicitly recognized (perhaps without knowing it) the existence of psychology as a particular science, independent of all philosophical systems, with the same claim as physics, botany or astronomy . . . One is thus right to consider as historically accomplished, with the same authorization and the high consecration of political power, the long procession by which the study of the soul little by little detached itself, in its own fashion, from the general trunk of philosophy to constitute itself at the level of a positive science. As for knowing up to what point contemporary psychology does justice to this declaration of the majority, and has truly succeeded in freeing itself from all metaphysical tutelage of any colour, that is another question. For here not less than elsewhere the ideal should not be confounded with reality. (1)

This study unfolds within the space of Flournoy's final qualification. Proponents of the new psychology proclaimed a radical break with all prior forms of human understanding. The foundation of modern psychology was held to be nothing less than the final and most decisive act in the completion of the scientific revolution. Not only did this inform its rhetoric, but also its sense of purpose and mission. Whether it was actually ever achieved or not, this conception of an absolute break with the past became a vital element in the self-conception of psychologists, and in how they styled their works.

Flournoy's celebratory claim expresses a sentiment that was widely felt by psychologists in the 1890s. In 1892, reflecting on the "progress" of psychology, William James wrote:

When, then, we talk of 'psychology as a natural science' we must not assume that means a sort of psychology that stands at last on solid ground. It means just the reverse; it means a psychology particularly fragile, and into which the waters of metaphysical criticism leak at every joint . . . it is indeed strange to hear people talk triumphantly of 'the New Psychology', and write 'Histories of Psychology', when into the real elements and forces which the word covers not the first glimpse of clear insight exists. A string of raw facts, a little gossip and wrangle about opinions, a little classification and generalization on the mere descriptive level; a strong prejudice that we have states of mind, and that our brain conditions them: but not a single law in the sense in which physics shows us laws, not a single proposition from which any consequence can causally be deduced. We don't even know the terms between which the elementary laws would obtain if we had them. This is no science, it is only the hope of science . . . But at present psychology is in the condition of physics before Galileo and the laws of motion, of chemistry before Lavoisier and the notion that mass is preserved in all reactions. The Galileo and the Lavoisier of psychology will be famous men indeed when they come, as come they some day surely will. (468)

It is a moot point whether in the ensuing decades any such progress had indeed occurred – whether, in Flournoy's terms, the gap between the ideal and the real had lessened, or that the founding separations of psychology from theology, philosophy, literature, anthropology, biology, medicine, and neurology had successfully taken place – or whether psychology today is in any better shape than James' estimation of its standing in the 1890s (gossip, wrangle, prejudices, and so on). Nevertheless, the frequency with which psychologists were likened (or likened themselves) to Galileo, Lavoisier, and Darwin increased dramatically.[6]

Flournoy's and James' statements indicate the prospects and problems of the "new" psychology. At the outset, psychologists sought to emulate the form and formation of established prestigious sciences, such as physics and chemistry. This emulation – or simulation – took different forms. Central to it was the conception that psychology should also be a unitary discipline. Yet very quickly, the proliferation of variously styled psychologies demonstrated that there was little consensus as to what could be considered the aims and methods of psychology.

---

[6] In 1958, Alasdair McIntyre noted that "Pre-Newtonian physicists had however the advantage over contemporary experimental psychologists that they did not know that they were waiting for Newton." He likened the situation in psychology to "waiting for a theoretical Godot," 2.

In 1900, the Berlin psychologist William Stern surveyed the new psychology. Aside from an empirical tendency and the use of experimental methods, he saw little in the way of common features. There were many laboratories with researchers working on special problems, together with many textbooks, but they were all characterized by a pervasive particularism. He said that the psychological map of the day was as colorful and checkered as that of Germany in the epoch of small states, and that psychologists

often speak different languages, and the portraits that they draw up of the psyche are painted with so many different colours and with so many differently accented special strokes that it often becomes difficult to recognize the identity of the represented object. (Stern, 1900b, 415)

Psychology was faced with a welter of unresolved fundamental questions. Stern concluded: "In short: there are many new psychologies, but not yet the new psychology" (ibid.). The disunity of psychology increased exponentially by year. One wonders what images Stern would choose to illustrate the situation today.

The profusion of competing definitions of psychology was such that by 1905, the French psychologist Alfred Binet produced a typology of definitions of psychology (175). The varieties of psychologies had already become a subject for reflection for psychologists. He argued that the multiplicity of definitions which had been proffered pointed to their insufficiency. The only element of commonality underlying the different definitions was that they all happened to designate what they took to be a new field by the same name – psychology. The multiplicity of definitions of psychology also entailed a corresponding multiplicity of conceptions of why psychology was a science. Ultimately, the one common denominator was the general assumption that in the field of psychology, it was up to psychologists themselves to determine the criteria for the scientific status of their discipline.

The glaring disjunction between the disunity of psychology and its would-be status as a unitary science led to one major attempt at rectification, through an attempt to establish a common language for psychology. This took place at the international congress for experimental psychology in Geneva in 1909, under the presidency of Flournoy. In their preliminary circular, the organizers proposed that psychology had now arrived at a point of a development common to all sciences, when common unifying conceptions in terminology and technical procedures were necessary (ed. Claparède, 1910, 6). A session was devoted to this issue. The Swiss psychologist Edouard Claparède opened it by noting that there reigned a great confusion in psychology concerning the use of terms. Part of this was due to disagreements concerning the existence, nature and origin of particular processes. But he claimed that the greater part was due to the absence of a precise nomenclature. Thus, many divergences considered to be doctrinal came down to divergences of words. To rectify this situation, Claparède and the American psychologist James Mark Baldwin put forward suggestions as to how psychologists could come to agree on a common language, through agreeing upon a set of rules and procedures for the adoption of new technical terms (ed. Claparède, 1910, 480–1). Following this, René de Saussure argued that this process of unification would ultimately lead to the creation of an international language. A form of this, however, already existed, in the language of Esperanto, which was admitted at the congress as an official language (ed. Claparède, 1910, 484). In the later half of the nineteenth century, numerous international auxiliary languages were created. Esperanto had first been developed in 1887 by the Russian Ledger Ludwik Zamenhof, and attracted a great deal of attention. Auguste Forel, Rudolf Carnap, and Bertrand Russell were among figures greatly interested in it. Esperanto associations sprang up in major cities, numerous conferences were dedicated to it, and major works of literature were translated into it. De Saussure argued that Esperanto could serve in all sciences as an international language, and that in psychology in particular, it could form the basis for comparison and unification. He quickly added that he did not foresee the replacement of individual languages, but simply the creation of a supplementary means of inter-comprehension. Simply by knowing one's mother tongue and Esperanto, one would be able to communicate with everybody. Claparède, Baldwin and de Saussure were proposing a reformation of psychology based on a rectification of its language.

A heated debate followed, in which some of the congress participants spoke in Esperanto. The critical disagreements were how this unification was to be achieved. These discussions reveal the deeply felt conviction that psychology, as a science, should function as psychologists imagined other sciences to function. Like chemistry, it should have its own periodic table. The project was a total failure. Reference was already made in the discussion to the tower of Babel. Far from a unification of psychological language, a plethora of incommensurable dialects, idioms, idiolects proliferated. The relations between schools and orientations of psychology quickly became so warlike and acrimonious that even to talk about any form of collaborative unification of terminology, let alone the increasing impossibility of the task itself, would have been laughed at. The linkage with Esperanto gives some indication of the hopes that were entertained for psychology – that it would become an international auxiliary language, enabling an unprecedented level of communication and mutual understanding between psychologists, and ultimately, the general public. Was the dream of a unitary discipline of psychology, with cooperation and collaboration between coworkers, as utopian as the promotion and adoption of Esperanto? Glossolalia and private languages had come to be the order of the day, amongst psychologists themselves.

The singularity of the term "psychology" should not mislead one into thinking that such a discipline was ever successfully founded. Or that there is an essence to "psychology" that could encompass the various definitions, methodologies, practices, world-views, and institutions that have used this designation.[7] Rather it indicates the massive significance that psychologists gave to being seen to be talking about the same thing.[8] As Edmund Husserl noted, "the history of psychology is actually only a history of crises" (1937, 203). The continued reference to psychology in the singular, split up and subdivided into tendencies and schools, is an instance of what Kurt Danziger has aptly called "unification by naming". As we have just seen, it was what Claparède and Baldwin had explicitly proposed in a programmatic form. While their project was a failure, the operation of unification by naming did play a critical role in twentieth-century psychology – not through providing the ideal of univocal meaning and the possibility of effective translation and communication, but through papering over and covering up the incommensurabilities and cleavages that multiplied. This was not only important at a conceptual level, with the promotion of terms such as stimulus-response learning or the Unconscious, by which psychologists sought to bring all human experience under the rule of one universal master concept, but in the conception of the field itself. One effect of the singular conception of psychology, Danziger suggests, was that it furthered the cause of professionalization, by implying that the practically oriented branches were linked to a scientific discipline. This linkage in turn implied that the more abstruse research had practical significance (1997, 84, 133). Furthermore, by giving a distinct profile to the discipline, however conflict-ridden, unification by naming masked the epistemological anarchy that prevailed within it. The ever-increasing fractionation of

---

[7] In what follows, I shall continue to refer to "psychology," in line with the historical usage of the actors themselves. However, this is not to presuppose a unity or essence to the term.

[8] In recognition of this situation, the American psychologist Sigmund Koch has proposed that the singular designation "psychology" be dropped, and be replaced with the "psychological studies," claiming that psychology never was, nor could be, a single coherent discipline (1993). He argues: "The psychological studies must, in principle comprise many language communities speaking parochial and largely incommensurable languages" (1975, 481). I thank Eugene Taylor for drawing this article to my attention.

psychology was partially a consequence of the fact that psychology never was one thing. Rather, it was an appellation that came to be used to designate a conglomeration of diverse practices and conceptions in different domains.

Already in the 1920s and 1930s, perceptive figures who had participated in the founding of psychology expressed grave doubts as to its progress. In 1921, Stanley Hall noted that there was a growing consensus amongst "the competent" that the condition of psychology was unsatisfactory and that its inaugural promise had not been fulfilled. Morever, he thought that its state was likely to get worse (9). According to Hall,

Never in the history of the sciences has there been a stage in any of them (with the possible exception of sociology, if that can be called a science) in which along with great activity there has been such diversity of aims, such tension between groups and such persistent ignoring by one circle of workers of what is made cardinal by another (for example, the psychoanalysts and the introspectionists). (477)

For Hall, what the world needed was a "psychological Plato" to solve this situation.

A further aspect of the self-conception of psychology as a science is its evolutionary legend, the axiomatic belief that – unlike the understanding of the human condition embodied for instance in literature – psychology undergoes a process of development. As a consequence, it is widely held that we are better equipped with the theories of today than those of yesteryear through some ill-defined process of natural selection. This evolutionary legend, which passes unexamined, has lent a normative aspect to the use of contemporary Western psychological concepts, and has led to the implicit relegation of forms of psychological understanding in other cultures. Furthermore, this legend obscures the extent to which particular psychologies became dominant through historically contingent events, and, not least, through the rescripting of history.

Here we need to differentiate between various theoretical projects to found a scientific psychology, and psychologies as social formations. The latter designates the resultant disciplines, practices, and effects which arose. The projects to found psychology played an important role in legitimating the social formations. It is clear that the theoretical difficulties which beset projects for psychology did not impede the rise and "success" of psychologies as social formations. Far from it. As Nikolas Rose points out, it was precisely the lack of homogeneity and lack of a single paradigm that enabled the widespread social penetration of psychologies. They lent themselves to a variety of applications in a variety of sites. Whatever one's purposes, from brainwashing to sexual liberation, there was a psychology that offered itself as ideally suited to the task (1996, 60).

The problems posed by psychology's "will to science" are not to be solved, as some have tried to do, by simply dropping the rubric of science and declaring psychology to be an art, or hermeneutics. The critical issue is not whether a particular discipline calls itself a science or not, but the nature of its practices and institutions. Thus in science studies today, one finds that the question of the demarcation between so-called science and so-called pseudoscience has increasingly become a non-issue. This has been a consequence of the increasing realization that science, with a capital "S," never existed – in other words, that there is no atemporal essence to something one could call the scientific method.[9]

The significance of the period between the 1870s and 1930s is that the major disciplinary and theoretical forms of modern psychology and psychotherapy were established at this time. Since then, there has been massive growth in production of psychological literature, in the population of psychologists and of consumers of psychological knowledge. Psychologists have been resourceful in finding ever new markets and audiences for their knowledge. There has been an acceleration in the rate of propagation of new psychologies, which shows no sign of slowing down. One of the most common titles in psychology books this century is "the new psychology of . . ." Whether the amount of actual innovation matches the massive expansion of psychologies is another question altogether.

At the same time, despite this massive growth, there has been little change in the disciplinary forms and methods of psychologies and psychotherapies. Experimentation continues to dominate academic psychology, and the couch still forms the bedrock of psychoanalysis. When confronted with psychology today, there are several options available. One could simply attempt to ignore it, though this becomes increasingly hard to do. Alternatively, one can take up an active interest in it, install oneself into one of the already existing schools of psychology, take up an eclectic position or form a school of one's own. The majority of responses to psychology fall into one of these options. However, there is another possibility, which would be to study the psychology-making process itself. For psychology itself has now become a phenomenon of contemporary life that pressingly calls for explication.

A major difficulty in evaluating twentieth-century psychology and psychotherapy is that their conceptions of the human subject have themselves partially transformed the subject that they set out to explain. Their interpretive categories have been adopted by large-scale communities and subcultures, and have given rise to new forms of life. If there is one thing

---

[9] On recent work in science studies, see Golinski, 1998, and Latour, 1993.

that psychology and psychotherapy have demonstrated in the twentieth century, it is the malleability of individuals, who have been willing to adopt psychological concepts to view their lives (and that of others), in terms of a play of conditioned reflexes, a desire to kill one's father and sleep with one's mother, a psychomachia between the good and the bad breast, a parade of dissociated alters, a quest for self-actualization through peak experiences or contorted twists through the hoola hoops of the symbolic, imaginary, and the real. A comparative study of these varieties of psychological experience has yet to be undertaken. What is important to note is that the formation of different schools of psychology and psychotherapy, with their particular languages and dialects, has led to the rise of archipelagoes of warring communities and subcultures. Whatever the status of the entities, processes and structures that have been posited, it is clear that these have become the unquestioned assumptions of increasingly large groups of individuals. "Psychic reality" is, par excellence, the fabricated real.[10] This is but to extend William James' remarks apropos the trance state, that its most remarkable "property" was its capacity to present itself according to whatever theory one held about it.[11]

A distinctive trait of modern psychology and psychotherapy is their peculiarly historical identity. Contemporary psychoanalysis and Jungian psychology trace themselves back to Freud and Jung in a manner quite unlike other disciplines. Historical lineages and genealogies have provided important means of legitimation and authorization for current professionals, whilst these narratives themselves pass unexamined. The historian is provided with the unusual spectacle of late nineteenth-century and early twentieth-century texts being transposed and translated into novel contexts and used as the basis for diverse practices. At the same time, the names of Freud and Jung are regularly invoked as masks for conceptions and practices which have no inherent or necessary connections to their work. A new scholasticism has arisen, and their names are used to sign and underwrite an endless series of blank theoretical cheques.

Jung without Freud

In popular perception as well as in the historical field, Jung's name is so closely bound with Freud that it is hard to even consider Jung without Freud. In histories of psychiatry, psychology, and psychoanalysis, Jung's psychology is usually classed as an offshoot of psychoanalysis, as one of

---

[10] For articulations of the constitution of the fabricated real, see Borch-Jacobsen, 1997 and Latour, 1996. See also Goodman, 1978.

[11] 1890, 1, 601. On this question, see Shamdasani, forthcoming. As Nietzsche noted, "It is enough to create new names and estimations and probabilities in order to create in the long run new 'things,'" 1887, § 58.

the myriad neopsychoanalytic schools.[12] Whilst, following Henri Ellenberger, copious critical work has been done on the "Freudian Legend," nothing comparable has been done on what may be termed the "Jungian Legend" in which Jung is portrayed as the rebel heretic of psychoanalysis, who, out of the perceived shortcomings of psychoanalysis, broke away to form his own school, based on his own "discoveries." Evaluations of Jung have generally assumed this view, and differed only in how they have assessed Jung's move away from psychoanalysis – as a fall from grace or a return to something approaching sanity.

Following the logic of this location, one may surmise that as Jung's psychology was supposedly an offshoot from psychoanalysis, revisionistic scholarship on the origins of psychoanalysis, coupled with close scrutiny of the break between Freud and Jung, should be sufficient to account for the genealogy of complex psychology. Since the publication in 1974 of the Freud–Jung letters ("that accursed correspondence," as Jung termed it),[13] this has been the perspective that has generally been followed. In the plethora of studies of the Freud–Jung relation, commentators have generally been in agreement on one thing – that the period in question marked a crucial epoch in the institutional and theoretical development of psychoanalysis, and what was later to become complex psychology. With few exceptions,[14] these works have uniformly suffered from the Freudocentric frame in which they have viewed the genesis of complex psychology.

For much of the twentieth century, it was widely held that Freud discovered the unconscious, that he was the first to study dreams and sexuality scientifically and to disclose their psychological meanings to a startled public, and that he invented modern psychotherapy. Furthermore, it was maintained that these discoveries and innovations were based on his self-analysis and the analysis of his patients. Henri Ellenberger dubbed this the "Freudian legend" and demonstrated that these claims had less to do with historical actuality than with how Freudians rescripted history in their favour.[15] Since then, these claims have been subjected to decades

---

[12] To cite two early locations in this vein, in his *Contemporary Schools of Psychology*, Robert Woodworth classed Jung's analytical psychology together with Alfred Adler's individual psychology, as "modifications of psychoanalysis" (1931, 172–192). In his chapter on Jung in his *An Outline of Abnormal Psychology*, William McDougall noted: "Dr. C. G. Jung was at one time regarded as Prof. Freud's most influential lieutenant . . . But like some others of Freud's more influential followers, notably Drs. Alfred Adler and W. Stekel, he has found it increasingly impossible to accept the whole of the Freudian system, and his teaching has diverged widely from Freud's" (1926, 188).

[13] Letter to anon, April 9, 1959, cited in *Letters* 1, 19.

[14] Notably Haule, 1985, and Witzig, 1982.

[15] Ellenberger, 1970, 1993. On this question, see also Sulloway, 1979, and Borch-Jacobsen and Shamdasani, 2002.

of critical scrutiny. Historians have recontextualized the "origins of psychoanalysis" within late nineteenth-century developments in neurology, psychiatry, biology, psychotherapy, and related areas. Whilst a great deal of controversy remains concerning these issues, it is nevertheless clear that the larger share of the claims for Freud's originality have not been sustained. At the same time, Jung's derivative position with regard to psychoanalysis has not been seriously challenged. The adequacy of the Freudocentric view of Jung, in which psychoanalysis features as the key determining context for the emergence of complex psychology, has been assumed as self-evident. This represents nothing less than the complete mislocation of Jung and complex psychology in the intellectual history of the twentieth century.[16]

The Freudian legend has mystified the formation of modern psychotherapy and psychologies of the unconscious. Indeed, the terms "Freud" and "Jung" have in effect become sign-systems that refer, unknowingly, to several critical decades of debates in modern European thought. Meanwhile, many of the protagonists and issues have been completely forgotten. This has led to the curious situation today when one is faced with "answers" without the "questions" that they were purportedly addressed to. These answers have, in turn, been taken as ready-mades, *objets trouvés*, whose original design and function have been erased.

Complex psychology

How then should Jung's psychology be approached? To answer this, one first needs to consider the formation of modern psychology, and clarify what he intended his psychology to be. The current discipline of Jungian psychology as a school of psychotherapy claiming descent from Jung obscures the question of what exactly Jung set out to achieve, as it is generally assumed that it must have been the discipline bearing his name. It is important here not to confound the present profession with the discipline that he attempted to found.[17] To begin with, it does not even bear his chosen designation.

While Jung had initially used the term analytical psychology to designate his psychology, in the 1930s he renamed it "complex psychology."

---

[16] On the genesis of this legend, see Shamdasani, 1996. Eugene Taylor has presented a parallel and complementary argument, principally based upon his and my earlier work (1996b).

[17] John Peck has used Herman Melville's story *The Confidence Man* as an analogy for how some Jungians in the USA have repackaged and relabeled Jung's work (or as the case may be, passed off their own work as Jung's), 1995. This process is far from being restricted to the USA. See Wolfgang Giegerich's chapter, "Jungians: Immunity to the notion and the forfeit heritage" in Giegerich, 1998.

In the commemorative volume for his sixtieth birthday, *The Cultural Significance of Complex Psychology*, Toni Wolff noted that in recent years, Jung had come to refer to his psychology as complex psychology, especially when dealing with it from a theoretical viewpoint. By contrast, she noted that the term analytical psychology was appropriate when dealing with the practical methods of psychological analysis (1936, 7). Thus the change in term was not only stylistic, but also signalled a shift in emphasis from practical analysis to general psychology. In 1954, Jung wrote: "Complex psychology means the psychology of 'complexities' i.e. of complex psychical systems in contradistinction from relatively elementary factors."[18] C. A. Meier suggested that compared to "analytical" psychology, "complex" psychology had the value of being less restricted to the pathological associations of the consulting room (1984, xi). However, with rare exceptions, the term was not taken up by Jung's followers. One reason for this was because it was never adopted in the English-speaking world, which became the most influential sector for developments in Jungian psychology after the second world war.[19]

This startling disregard for the name Jung had chosen for his discipline gives an indication by itself of the separation of Jungian psychology from Jung. Furthermore it also gives an indication of a crucial shift in emphasis in the opposite direction, from general psychology to practical analysis. Analytical psychology today is largely a professional psychotherapeutic discipline with a problematic relation to the widespread non-professional readership of Jung. His attempt to establish a general psychology has taken a back seat, though it lingers in the background, playing a legitimating role. On a number of instances, Jung also expressed himself very critically concerning some of his followers, such as in the following statement: "There have been so many pupils of mine who have fabricated every sort of rubbish from what they took over from me."[20]

The history of analytical psychology consists in how the language that Jung developed became reformulated and taken to different ends by those around him. This process of resignification has been central to its development. In many instances, Jung's terms have come to mean radically different things. In the process, many of the issues and phenomena that he was dealing with – such as those reconstructed in this volume – have been simply forgotten or left to one side. There has been a proliferation of

---

[18] Jung's marginal annotations to Calvin Hall's "Jung's analytical theory," CLM, 12, original in English.

[19] There are thirteen instances in the Jung's *Collected Works* where the term "Komplexe Psychologie" was either translated as analytical psychology or simply omitted. In this work, I have followed Jung's actual usage throughout.

[20] Jung to Jürg Fierz, January 13, 1949, *Letters* 1, 518.

silent resignifications that seamlessly present themselves as representing Jung's theories, or faithful elaborations of them. In many instances, his signature concepts are simply employed as markers of professional identity. They have been extracted from the issues and contexts from which they arose. Consequently, they have taken on an extreme plasticity. This has opened up an endless terrain for reinventions of Jung. Analytical psychology continues to be spoken of in the singular. Descriptively speaking, it would be more accurate today to speak of an archipelago of disparate Jungian psychologies, which basically have little to do with one another, or, for that matter, with Jung. To continue to refer to Jungian psychology today in the singular – even subdivided into schools – has become an anachronism.

In the first instance, Jung did not intend to form a particular school of psychotherapy, but, in line with the unitary conceptions of psychology in the late nineteenth century, intended to establish psychology in general. In 1934, he established a Psychology Fund at the Eidgenössische Technische Hochschule (Swiss Federal Institute of Technology) in Zürich, whose initial aim was to fund a lectureship to be held at a Swiss university. His stipulations are revealing in this regard:

The treatment of psychology should in general be characterized by the principle of universality. No special theory or special subject should be propounded, but psychology should be taught in its biological, ethnological, medical, philosophical, cultural-historical and religious aspects.[21]

The aim, he continued, was to free the teaching of the human soul from the "constriction of compartments."

Jung held that psychology constituted the fundamental scientific discipline, upon which other disciplines should henceforth be based. In his view, it was the only discipline which could grasp the subjective factor that underlay other sciences. The establishment of complex psychology was to enable the reformulation of the humanities and revitalize contemporary religions. The history of Jungian psychology has in part consisted in a radical and unacknowledged diminution of Jung's goal.

When one considers the attempt of psychologists to separate their discipline from pre-existing disciplines, it becomes evident that one is not simply dealing with single episodes, as is conventionally portrayed in histories of psychology and the obligatory introductory chapters of textbooks of psychology. Rather, one is dealing with myriad attempts to achieve such ends. The mode in which these disciplinary crossings were negotiated

---

[21] Cited in Meier, 1984, x. The initial donation was 200,000 Sfr. Jung stated that this was from various sources, including Harold F. McCormick (Jung, note on ETH-Fund, JP). Previously, Jung had donated funds to the Jean-Jacques Rousseau Institute in Geneva.

gave rise to the specific form that particular psychologies took. The constitutive separations of psychology from pre-existing disciplines did not occur in one single place nor at one single time. This proposition holds even if one considers the work of a single theorist, such as Jung. Despite the overriding tendencies of nearly all presentations of his work, it did not obey a straightforward linear chronological evolution. Standard presentations of the subject, more often than not, obscure more than they reveal. Indeed, Jung went so far as to nominate this lack of linearity as the hallmark of his work. During the interviews for *Memories, Dreams, Reflections*, he said to Aniela Jaffé:

> I do not know whether the things I have told you are of value to you, and I am sorry that I repeat things. I have also done this in my books, I always consider certain things again, and always from a new angle. My thinking is, so to speak, circular. This is a method which suits me. It is in a way a new kind of peripatetics.[22]

In reading Jung's work and correspondence, one encounters two distinct modes of thinking and presentation. In the first, specific theories are advanced, established, and considered to be proven. This mode, heavily accentuated in the first generation of Jungian analysts and in numerous introductory and expository works, is the most well known.[23] Thus, "as everybody knows," he put forward theories of complexes, psychological types, and most notoriously, of the archetypes of the collective unconscious.[24] The second mode of his thinking consists in an ongoing questioning concerning the conditions of possibility of psychology. To cite but two instances of this mode, in 1929, he compared the present state of psychology to that of natural philosophy in the middle ages, in which there were only opinions about unknown facts.[25] In 1951, he wrote:

---

[22] MP, 260. See below, 23–24.

[23] There has been an endless stream of introductory anthologies of Jung's writings. Jung had severe reservations concerning this genre. In 1946, in reply to a request by W. H. Kennedy for an anthology of his writings, Jung wrote: "I must say, that the idea of an anthology does not appeal to me. I don't think one should encourage people to be satisfied with a more or less superficial extract of my ideas without getting the real substance. I know it isn't particularly easy to read such stuff as my books, but then science is not altogether easy – particularly not a pioneering attempt like my work. I consider that psychological ideas stripped of documentary evidence are worse than nothing" (Routledge papers, University of Reading), original in English.

[24] In an interview with a Finnish journalist, Nordenstreng, which was published in *Suomen Kuvalenti* in 1961, Jung is reported to have said: "the biggest disappointment of my life has been that people have not understood what I have wanted to say. They certainly know what a complex is, introvert, extrovert, they have a view of my idea that feeling and thinking do not stay in the same head, but it is something else to understand things deeper. As a superficial catchword such things are accepted by people, although every professor would say that it is all nonsense!" (McGuire papers, LC), original in English.

[25] "The significance of constitution and heredity in psychology," *CW* 8, § 223.

Our psychological experience is still too young and too little extended to enable general theories. For the time being, the researcher still needs a quantity of facts which would illuminate the essence of the soul, before we could also even think about putting up universally valid propositions.[26]

When considering Jung's strictures on the possibility of psychology and his statements about the premature status of general theories in psychology, it is important to realize that he is including his own work in this assessment. It is precisely this mode of his thinking that tends to be filtered out. These two modes thread themselves throughout his work, and their interplay is a theme throughout this book.

For many people, Jung's name is synonymous with the Archetypes and the Collective Unconscious. They constitute his signature concepts, and generally solicit instant assent or repudiation, presenting an open and shut case. Whether one accepts or repudiates them, it is generally assumed that what they designate can be considered as sufficiently well known. The reasons for this are not hard to find. Jung himself offered a plethora of definitions. In his wake, there has been no shortage of expository works setting out what these terms are. Finally, there is hardly a work of Jungian, neo-Jungian or post-Jungian inspiration that does not carry their repeated imprint.

It would be hard to characterize an author whose collected works span more than twenty volumes, by economy of expression, or by linguistic parsimony. Yet in important respects, this is precisely the case with Jung. His signature concepts contained many different ideas which attempted to resolve major debates in philosophy, psychology, sociology, biology, anthropology, comparative religion, and other fields, and enable the formation of a distinct discipline of psychology. It is precisely this combinatory operation that gives his psychology its distinctive style and substance. However, the utilization of the same terms to cover such a range of issues also generates a potential for conceptual confusion, to which any survey of the literature of analytical psychology can amply attest. This suggests that a certain caution is appropriate in assuming that these terms can indeed be considered to be sufficiently known even to be appropriately evaluated. Hence the following inquiry will not commence with definitions. Rather, it will attempt to reconstitute the debates from which Jung drew and which led to the formulation of these terms – in particular, how and why he used the same terms as solutions to distinct questions, and the significance of this combinatory operation. To grasp his signature concepts, it is critical to realize the issues and debates which

---

[26] "Fundamental problems of psychotherapy," *CW* 16, § 236, trans. mod.

he was addressing, and to which they were put forward as attempted solutions.

The study of the formation of complex psychology may be taken as a case history within the wider story of the formation of modern psychology and psychotherapy. However, this is not to suggest that it should be taken as a paradigmatic instance. For what is precisely at issue here is the impossibility of any singular encapsulation of the formation of modern psychology and psychotherapy.[27]

The new encyclopedia

For centuries, individuals have sought to draw up representative compilations of all human knowledge in the form of encyclopedias. Samuel Johnson defined an Encyclopedia as "the circle of the sciences, the round of learning," citing Glanvill, "Every science borrows from all the rest, and we cannot attain any single one without the *encyclopaedy*" (1755, 166).

Psychology, for Jung, was an encyclopedic enterprise. The fact that he was a man of encyclopedic learning has often been noted. His library, still intact in his house in Küsnacht, presents a panoramic, encyclopedic vista of human learning, without parallel in modern psychology. Jung's last major work alone, *Mysterium Coniunctionis* (1955–1956), contains over 2,300 footnotes. But what has not been sufficiently noted is the fact that this erudition was constitutive of his psychology, and significantly contributed to its form. For Jung, psychology was the discipline to unite the circle of the sciences.

In his understanding, there was no field of human endeavor that was irrelevant for psychology – as in all human affairs, psychology studied the doer of the deed. He took Terence's dictum, "nothing human is alien to me," as his duty.[28] Consequently, there was no clear delimitation of the provenance of psychology. The range of subjects that he discussed in the course of works attests to this.

In the history of encyclopedic projects, what was distinctive about Jung's was that it attempted to ground other disciplines and knowledges through psychology. This conception was made possible by the birth of the modern human sciences, from the eighteenth century to the end of the nineteenth. Correspondingly, the encyclopedic aspect of Jung's enterprise distinguishes it from other modern psychologies. This forms its signature trait. That is not to say that his psychology was systematic. Indeed, he held that the impossibility of encapsulating the soul within a

---

[27] On this issue, see Roger Smith, 1988. For the best single volume history of psychology, see Roger Smith, 1997.

[28] Jung to Herbert Read, September 2, 1960, *Letters* 2, 589.

system was dictated by its very nature, and there are many statements of his repudiating any will to system on his part.[29] The mode in which he attempted to develop his psychology ran counter to the autonomized specialization that generally held the day in psychology.

The work which marked the inauguration of this encyclopedic project was *Transformations and Symbols of the Libido*. This is not to suggest that his prior work was extraneous to this enterprise – rather, it was subsequently folded back into it. In 1913, in a letter to the editors of the newly founded *Psychoanalytic Review*, he noted:

It is beyond the powers of the individual, more particularly of physicians, to master the manifold domains of the mental sciences which should throw some light upon the comparative anatomy of the mind . . . We need not only the work of medical psychologists, but also that of philologists, historians, archaeologists, mythologists, folklore students, ethnologists, philosophers, theologians, pedagogues and biologists.[30]

This was psychology on a grand scale. The new psychological encyclopedia was an interdisciplinary enterprise which required complex realignments of existing disciplines and the carving out of a new territory from a terrain which was already occupied. Its fulfillment would require nothing less than a reformation of the Academy. The mode in which he chose to embark upon them is indicated by a letter which he wrote in 1940 to Ruth Ananda Anshen, who had invited him to collaborate in a large enterprise. He noted that through the work that he had done towards the synthesis of sciences, he had become aware of how difficult it was to achieve cooperation, given the level of specialization. He added:

It has always looked to me as if such an attempt shouldn't be made from the top, namely that specialists talk in a general way about cooperation. It rather seems to me as if one should begin at the bottom by actual scientific collaboration in the detail. Thus one could show more easily the merits of cooperation. What I mean you can clearly see, when you look into one of my books.[31]

Jung set great store by the interdisciplinary collaborations which he established with Richard Wilhelm, Wilhelm Hauer, Heinrich Zimmer, Karl Kerényi, Wolfgang Pauli, and Victor White, in the fields of sinology, indology, mythology, microphysics, and theology respectively.

One project that Jung attempted in the 1930s provides a good illustration of his encyclopedic conception of psychology. Daniel Brody, the

---

[29] E.g., Jung to Jolande Jacobi, March 13, 1956, *Letters* 2, 293.
[30] Fall 1913, *Letters* 1, 29–30.
[31] Jung to Ruth Ananda Anshen, June 10, 1940, Columbia University Archives, New York (original in English). Jung declined her invitation.

publisher of Rhein Verlag had invited him to edit a new journal, to be called *Weltanschauung*.

A few years earlier, Jung had published a paper in which he had explored the relations between analytical psychology and a Weltanschauung [world-view]. From Wilhelm Dilthey to Karl Jaspers, the topic of world-views had been much discussed in German philosophy.[32] For Jung, a world-view designated not only a conception of the world, but also the manner in which one viewed the world.[33] He argued that the past 150 years had seen a plethora of world-views, and that the basic notion of a world-view had consequently fallen into discredit. The problem of all prior world-views had been their claim to provide an objectively valid truth. In the present situation, the clamour for a new world-view had been raised, and unsuccessful attempts to establish one in the old style had been made, such as in Theosophy and Anthroposophy. A new world-view had to "abandon the superstition of its objective validity and admit that it is only a picture which we paint to please our souls, and not a magical name with which we can designate objective things."[34] In Jung's conception, analytical psychology was a science, and not a world-view. But it had a special role to play in the formation of a new world-view. Its contribution lay in the importance of the recognition of unconscious contents, and in enabling a relativistic conception of a world-view, no longer regarded as an absolute. Indeed, after Jung, it is clear that his psychology did give rise to a plethora of world-views. What he would have thought of them is another matter altogether.

The aim of the journal, *Weltanschauung*, was to bring about a synthesis of the sciences. Jung approached various scholars to see if they were interested in collaborating in it. To Zimmer, he wrote:

I have been thinking that in view of the tremendous fragmentation of the sciences today we might well have an organ that could fish out from the ocean of specialist science all the facts and knowledge that are of general interest and make them available to the educated public. Everyone who wants to find his way about nowadays has to rummage through dozens of periodicals he can't subscribe to, and thousands of books, wasting a vast amount of time until he comes to what he thinks might be helpful to him.[35]

This journal, ambitiously, was supposed to counter this situation: "It should be an instrument of synopsis and synthesis – an antidote against

---

[32] Dilthey, 1911; Jaspers, 1919.
[33] "Analytical psychology and world-view," *CW* 8, § 689.
[34] § 737, trans. mod. A similar point had been made by Oswald Spengler, *The Decline of the West*, 1918, 23.
[35] November 21, 1932, *Letters* 1,106–107.

the atomizing tendency of specialism which is one of the greatest obstacles to spiritual development" (*Letters*, 1, 107). The journal was to be aimed at the general reader, and a group of specialists would select material that would be of general interest and communicate this in an accessible manner. To Hauer, he explained how the journal would work. Questions would be put to specialists by an editorial committee. The specialists would prepare an essay, and Jung and his school would supply the psychological material, which would form "a synthesis which would make it possible to understand the living meaning of facts and ideas gathered from all times and all places."[36] The psychological viewpoint, he explained to Jolande Jacobi, was only meant to be a centre, and he had no intention of squeezing the world into a psychological straitjacket. He informed her that he had received affirmative replies from Hauer, Zimmer, and Wolfgang Pauli. He was considering inviting Erwin Rousselle for Buddhist studies, Leopold Ziegler for philosophy, his pupil Wolfgang Kranefeldt for psychotherapy and Hermann Broch for modern literature. He was still looking for contributors for "biology, astrophysics, geology, physiology, Egyptian, Assyrian-Babylonian and American archeology, and for antiquity (mysteries!)."[37] This indicates the enormous scope of Jung's undertaking. The project came to nothing, and shortly thereafter, he took over the editorship of the *Zentralblatt für Psychotherapie*, with fateful consequences.

Though this project foundered, Jung sought other means of achieving the same ends. In 1933, Olga Froebe-Kapetyn founded the annual Eranos lectures in Ascona, at which an invited group of international scholars addressed a particular theme. The conferences focused on the history of religion and culture, with a particular emphasis on the relation between the East and the West. Jung advised Froebe-Kapetyn concerning themes and speakers to invite, whilst being careful to avoid it becoming simply a vehicle for his school.[38]

In 1938, there was a project to publish a selection of these lectures in English. Jung wrote a preface for this, in which he took up again the theme of the detrimental effects of specialization. This had led, he maintained, to a narrowing of the horizon and inbreeding:

The enormous extension of knowledge exceeds the capacity of a single brain, which alone might be able to form a synthesis of the innumerable parts contributed in every department. Even the greatest genius, equipped with a fabulous power of memory, would be forced to remain an incompetent dilettante in quite a few important respects.[39]

[36] Jung to Hauer, November 14, 1932, *Letters* 1, 103.
[37] December 23, 1932, *Letters* 1, 113.   [38] On the history of Eranos, see Hakl, 2001.
[39] JP. Original in English. See ed. McGuire, 1984.

To counteract this situation, and to provide a "complete picture of our world," information from all branches of knowledge needed to be collated together. This could be attempted by finding a platform or idea common to many forms of knowledge. This was precisely what the Eranos meetings attempted.

From the foregoing, it is clear that Jung conceived the cultural role of complex psychology to be to counter the fragmentation of the sciences, and to provide a basis for a synthesis of all knowledge. This attempt to counter the increasing fragmentation and specialization of disciplines was an enormous, and ultimately insurmountable task. Towards the end of his life, surveying and assessing his work, Jung frankly stated:

> I am the most cursed dilettante that has lived. I wanted to achieve something in my science and then I was plunged in this stream of lava, and then had to classify everything. That's why I say dilettantism: I live from borrowings, I constantly borrow knowledge from others.[40]

This statement took place in the course of Jung's interviews with his secretary Aniela Jaffé that went to make *Memories, Dreams, Reflections*, and it is not surprising that it was omitted, being so far away from prevalent images of Jung. What follows is in part an explication of this dilettantism.

The incomplete works of Jung

To date, the principal sources for studies of Jung have been the *Collected Works*, *Memories, Dreams, Reflections*, *The Freud/Jung Letters*, and *C. G. Jung Letters*. This has had hitherto unsuspected consequences for how his work has been understood. To date, writings on Jung have been hampered by incomplete and unreliable textual sources. When first presented by Jack Barrett of the Bollingen Foundation with a copy of the first volume of the *Collected Works* to be published, Jung complained that it looked like a coffin.[41] The team which produced the *Collected Works* accomplished much, but the project was never finished. The *Collected Works* is far from a *Complete Works*. It by no means includes all that he published during his lifetime, and there are sufficient unpublished manuscripts to fill half a dozen volumes. Furthermore, the reproduction of Jung's texts and the editorial apparatus are not without errors, and the English translation leaves a great deal to be desired.

In 1973 and 1975, a selection of Jung's letters was published, edited by Gerhard Adler, in collaboration with Aniela Jaffé. Gerhard Adler stated

---

[40] MP, 149. On one occasion, when speaking of his work, Jung spoke of "our historical dilettantism." "Psychotherapy and world-view," *CW* 16, § 190, trans. mod.

[41] Personal communication, Ximena de Angulo.

that from 1,600 letters written by Jung between the years 1906 and 1961, over 1,000 had been selected. This gives the impression that approximately two thirds of the letters of Jung's that have survived were published in this volume. This is seriously misleading. In the Jung papers at the ETH in Zürich, there are approximately 20,000 letters, and there are many letters scattered in public and private archives around the world. It is safe to say that less than 10 percent of this has been published. This study is based on the first comprehensive study of this unpublished corpus of manuscripts and letters.

A special problem has been posed by the *Memories, Dreams, Reflections*, which has been regarded as Jung's autobiography, and hence the canonical source of information concerning his life. Its sales have far outstripped any other work by Jung. Until the researches of Alan Elms and myself, no doubts had been raised concerning its authenticity and reliability.[42] As the text still continues to be mistakenly considered as Jung's autobiography, it is necessary to clarify briefly its genesis.

The publisher Kurt Wolff had unsuccessfully tried to get Jung to write an autobiography for years. In the summer of 1956, he suggested a new project to Jung, along the lines of Eckermann's *Conversations with Goethe*. An early provisional title was *Carl Gustav Jung's Improvised Memories*. It was to be presented in the first person. Jolande Jacobi proposed Aniela Jaffé for the task, because, as Jung's secretary, it would be easier for her to ask questions concerning his life in free hours.

Jaffé undertook a series of regular interviews with Jung. In these interviews, Jung spoke about a wide range of subjects. Jaffé, with the close involvement of Kurt Wolff, selected material from these interviews and arranged it thematically. This was then organized into a series of approximately chronological chapters.

During this process, Jung wrote a manuscript at the beginning of 1958 entitled "From the earliest experiences of my life." With Jung's permission, Jaffé incorporated this manuscript into *Memories*. His request to have this clearly demarcated from the rest of the book was not followed through. Passages were also deleted and added to this by Jaffé, and further changes were made by others involved in the project. Thus there are critical differences between Jung's manuscript and the published version.[43] Jaffé also incorporated excerpted versions of some other unpublished manuscripts of Jung, such as material from his 1925 seminar, and accounts of some of his travels. Finally, Jung contributed a chapter entitled

---

[42] See Shamdasani, 1995 and 2000a, 2000b, and Elms, 1994.

[43] On one manuscript, Helen Wolff wrote in retrospect: "Revealing for changes 'toning down' Jung's original – *bowdlerised version!* Highly interesting for what was done to keep out Jung's frank and true statements about himself." (Beinecke Library, Yale University.)

"late thoughts." According to Richard Hull, parts of this were rewritten by Jaffé.

During the composition of the work, there were many disagreements between the parties involved concerning what the book should contain, its structure, the relative weighting of Jung's and Jaffé's contributions, the title, and the question of authorship. It was clear that for the publishers, an autobiography of Jung – *or something that could be made to look as much like one as possible* – held far greater sales potential than a biography by the then as yet unknown Aniela Jaffé. There were also legal wrangles between the publishers involved as to who held the rights of the book.

In 1960, a resolution was drawn up between Jung, Jaffé, and the editorial committee of his *Collected Works* which contained the following statement:

C. G. Jung has always maintained that he did not consider this book as his own enterprise but expressly as a book written by Mrs. Jaffé. The chapters written by C. G. Jung were to be considered as his contributions to the work of Mrs. Jaffé. The book was to be published in the name of Mrs. Jaffé and not in the name of C. G. Jung, because it did not represent an autobiography composed by C. G. Jung. (Shamdasani, 1995, 132–133)

Jung's attitude towards the project fluctuated. After reading the early manuscript, he criticized Aniela Jaffé's handling of the text, complaining of "auntifications" (*ibid.*, 130). Jung never saw nor approved the final manuscript, and the manuscripts he did see went through considerable editing after his death.[44]

The publication of *The Freud/Jung Letters* in 1974 marked the first work after Jung's death which was edited to a high scholarly standard, and rendered a great service to the history of the origins of the psychoanalytic movement. However, because so little of Jung's vast correspondences with other figures had been published, coupled with the fact that Jung's legendary *Red Book* remained unpublished, this only strengthened the mistaken Freudocentric perspective of the origins of Jung's work.

From 1912 onwards, Jung engaged in a process of self-experimentation which he termed a "confrontation with the unconscious." This principally consisted in provoking an extended series of waking fantasies in himself. He later called this the method of "active imagination." Drawing from these materials, he composed a work in a literary and pictorial form called the *Red Book*, which he illustrated with his own paintings. For decades, the *Red Book* has not been available for study, and has been the subject of rumour, legend, and myth-making. It could best be described as a literary

---

[44] In what follows, citations to *Memories* have been checked against the manuscripts.

work of psychology. Jung maintained that it formed the foundation of his later work. In May 2000, the heirs of C. G. Jung decided to release the work for publication, so that it would be first made available to the public in a definitive scholarly edition, to be prepared by the present author. My work on the *Red Book*, commenced in 1996, has transformed my understanding of Jung's work, and enabled me to comprehend its genesis. Whilst not explicitly cited in the present work, it has critically informed it.

There is today a great appetite for biographical works. Lives of Freud and Jung sell far better than the works of Freud and Jung. After a hundred years of psychoanalysis, we have become accustomed to regarding biography as the key to an understanding of an individual's work. Regrettably, all biographies of Jung to date have left a great deal to be desired. Jung himself had this to say about the prospect for biographies of his work: "unless the development of his thought were central to his biography it would be no more than a series of incidents, like writing the life of Kant without knowing his work."[45] This forms a fair depiction of the shortcomings of many works that have been written on Jung, and in all likelihood, of many more to come. Writing at the termination of a biographical project by Lucy Heyer, Jung expressed his distaste for biographies, and his personal unsuitability as a subject for one:

I'm quite unable to continue this funny kind of playing at a biography. You could just as well ask me to help that foolish American Radio-Company to produce myself in the form of a film. I don't go to church on Sundays with a prayer-book under my arm, nor do I wear a white coat, nor do I build hospitals, nor do I sit at the organ. So I'm not fodder for the average sentimental needs of the general public. And that will be so with my biography. There is just nothing very interesting in it.[46]

On being presented with a literature prize by the city of Zürich in 1932, he reflected on the increasing recognition that his work was receiving:

With this "I" as a public person no human individual is naturally meant, but rather my mental performance – *an idea*, whose spokesman I am. This idea is my view of psychology, my individual recognition and confession [*Er*kennen und *Be*kennen] in matters of the human soul.[47]

All too many works have collapsed these two together. Whilst the value and interest of biographical works do not need to be justified, there are critical problems if the work in question is improperly understood, and, as

[45] Cited in Bennet, 1982, 61.
[46] Jung to Cary Baynes, April 4, 1954, Cary Baynes papers.
[47] "On psychology," 1933, 22.

is the case with Jung, there is not an extensive body of informed and reliable studies to draw upon. This book thus forms an essential preliminary to any informed biography of him.

Historical cubism

This book has been envisaged as a cubist portrait, and presents a multifaceted approach to a multifaceted work. Decisive stimuli for its form and structure have also been derived from certain works of Ornette Coleman, John Coltrane and the writings of Fernando Pessoa. Its final assembly was assisted by certain compositions of Carla Bley and Charlie Haden's Liberation Music Orchestra.[48] It has more than one beginning and more than one end. Instead of presenting an over-determining context and a teleological development that can be read in reverse from an Olympian perspective, this work presents overlapping chronologies, intersecting facets and various angles. Hence no overarching coherence (or incoherence) of Jung's work has been presupposed. Consequently, the same texts and figures are discussed in more than one place, from more than one viewpoint. It is hoped that the intertwinings and interleavings thus established may illuminate the architecture of Jung's work, without reducing its complexity.

The work is divided into a series of sections which deal with major issues in Jung's work, psychology and related disciplines. These can be read in different orders, and the introduction can also be read as a conclusion. Each reconstructs the respective nineteenth and early twentieth-century backdrops for Jung's work, and situates its emergence and reception in relation to contemporaneous developments in the human and natural sciences. The interconnections between the sections show the critical linkages of diverse topics through which Jung constituted his psychology.[49]

---

[48] Finally, the means to abridge the manuscript extensively was enabled by a performance of Joe Zawinul.

[49] After completing this study, I came across the following statement by Jaime de Angulo in his introduction to his manuscript, "What is Language": "In the introduction we have called language a protean thing, and we have compared it to a kaleidoscope, ever changing with every twist of the instrument, or to an opal presenting new iridescences when viewed from different angles. For that very reason it is almost impossible to present language in an orderly sequence. To do justice to the subject the reader would have to read all the chapters simultaneously! I have tried to put in front the chapters that would catch his interest most. But it was impossible to deal for very long with the plunge into matters that demand a certain amount of close thinking. My advice to the reader is not to pay very much attention to the arrangement of the chapters in this book but to make his own choice, to jump ahead and then come back, to zigzag through the book. When some subject bores him, or he finds it too technical or subtle, let him skip lightly. It will be time to return and grasp what is meant" (De Angulo papers, UCLA, Los Angeles).

The range of issues covered is not complete, and further issues will be taken up in a future work.

This can be considered to be a book about Jung, and a book about the rise of modern psychology and psychotherapy. Both of these subjects have been focal points of my researches. The attempt to comprehend and locate Jung's work, commenced in 1981, led me to the view that, at so many critical points, Jung was dealing with broad issues concerning the conditions of possibility of psychology and the human sciences, upon which many figures in other disciplines were also engaged. His psychology was so deeply intertwined with these networks, that it simply cannot be understood in isolation. In turn, in dealing with these issues, it has been helpful to have a point of orientation to provide some minimal delimitation of the subject.

Jung's work has generated a vast literature of appraisal, commentary, and critique. Over the last two decades, I have attempted to cover as much of this as possible. However, to try to comment upon it in detail here would make the present undertaking unmanageable. Furthermore, the level of misrecognition of Jung is so high, that to straighten out the welter of fantasies, fictions, and fabrications is a more elaborate task than starting from scratch, as I have recently demonstrated.[50] Indeed, an increasingly large proportion of the work on Jung falls into the category of "History Lite" (evidence-free history).[51] Thus the approach adopted here focuses on primary source material. Whilst it reconstructs elements of the reception of Jung's work, it engages with secondary materials only when they bear directly on the issues at hand.

It is customary when reading a book to expect a thesis and a conclusion. While there are many theses explored in this book, there is no conclusion. For the aim of this work is not to conclude, but to open up new issues. One implication of this work is that no far-going attempt to evaluate Jung's psychology can avoid wider consideration of the constitution of psychology as a whole, and of the human sciences in general. As the evaluation of psychology and its effects upon society involves consideration of to what extent it was ever successful in separating itself from neighboring disciplines and establishing its own domain, it follows that the task of evaluation is necessarily a multifaceted interdisciplinary endeavor. For this to be possible, an accurate portrayal of the emergence of psychology is indispensable. This history is a contribution to this task. There has been no shortage of evaluations of Jung's work. But

---

[50] See Shamdasani, 1998a.
[51] For a characterization of this genre, see Shamdasani, 1999a.

what has hitherto been lacking has been an adequate basis for sound evaluations.

Finally, given the scope of Jung's erudition, an attempt by one individual to cover historically the selfsame terrain together with the corresponding secondary literature must inevitably succumb to the shortcomings of its own forms of dilettantism. Thus this enterprise bears more than a passing resemblance to that of Pierre Menard, the protagonist of Jorge Luis Borges' story, who set out to rewrite the *Don Quixote* of Cervantes (1939).

1   The individ[ual]

Is psychology a science? [...]king for psychologists than this. Re[...] intimately bound up with formatic [...]. A plethora of related questions imm[...] What is psychology? In what ways is [...]a should one use to adjudicate this issue? No less significant, who is a psychologist? The difficulty with approaching these questions is that while there has been no end of attempted solutions put forward in the form of psychologies and in the shape of psychologists, there has been no consensus, nor even the remote possibility of a consensus. While judgments are not lacking, there is no possibility for any forum for adjudication. However, one approach to these issues is possible. This is to reconstruct the manner in which they have been posed and "answered" historically. Psychology's "questionable" status as a science, and the variety of conceptions of its scientificity makes it important to reconstruct how different psychologists conceived of their enterprise. Furthermore, as Lorraine Daston has demonstrated, debates about the scientific standing of psychology at the end of the nineteenth century were not only significant for psychology, but also had critical impact on reshaping conceptions of science (1990).

This section commences by reconstructing debates about the scientific standing of psychology at the end of the nineteenth century. It traces how psychologists tried to establish a science of subjectivity in the form of an "individual" psychology. From this, it situates Jung's attempt to develop a critical psychology in the form of a psychological typology and the problems that this ran into. Finally, it draws together his reflections on the status of psychology, and shows how these shaped his own attempt to found psychology as the superordinate science, the only discipline supposedly capable of grasping the subjective factor that underlay all the other sciences.

In academic psychology, from the 1920s onwards, it was generally held that the use of experimentation and statistical methods formed the crucial

29

traits that ensured the scientific status of psychology. Consequently, the general attitude towards Jung's work in academic psychology has been that his early experimental studies on word associations were "scientific," ...work on psychological types presents some hypotheses which ...imentation. The rest of his work is regarded as un- ...ently been dismissed. The dominance of the ...l approaches to psychology has in turn been ...y of psychology. The overwhelming major- ...what became the dominant approaches ..., much less work has been done on al- ...gy. ..., there are few modern psychologists who ...erning the scientific status of psychology as ...s on this issue played a critical role in how he developed and reformulated his psychology. Thus his discussions of the science question form an extended meditation on the question of the possibility of psychology. In what follows, I do not take up the question of the validity of Jung's characterizations of science. In this setting, the significance of his definitions of science is how they help show what he understood psychology to be.

The personal equation: from astronomy to psychology

One of the fundamental distinctions in Western thought has been between the individual and the universal. For Aristotle, there could only be knowledge of universals, and not of particulars. The latter were the objects of practical wisdom, which was concerned with the perception of situations. At the end of the nineteenth century, many psychologists attempted to take over what for Aristotle was left to the sphere of practical wisdom. The question was, could one form a scientific psychology which dealt with individual differences and particularities, when science was traditionally conceived to be solely concerned with universals?

Jean Starobinski has eloquently demonstrated how much can be gleaned about the change in and between disciplines and social sensibilities through tracing the semantic shifts and mutations undergone by particular words or phrases (1976, 1999). The "personal equation" was first nominated to designate a calculus of observational error in astronomy. It became the hallmark of the attempt to develop an objective experimental science of psychology, and then conversely, an epistemological abyss that delimited the selfsame project. Latterly adopted by Jung, it became the leitmotif of the pretension of complex psychology to be a superordinate science, the only discipline capable of encompassing the subjective factor

held to underlie all the sciences. The genesis of the noti...
equation may be briefly narrated.

...ve period of investigation on the personal equation was in the 1860s
and 1870s, which coincided with the "birth" of physiological psychology
(1929, 146). According to Simon Schaffer, the combination of the new
technologies of time keeping, such as the invention of the Hipp chrono-
scope in 1840, which could measure time intervals down to a thousandth
of a second, combined with the social organization of the astronomical
workshop, provided psychologists with excellent models for the scrutiny
of the individual (1998, 138). This was because the astronomers had
linked time management with the measurement of the performance of
simple tasks by individuals. It was this that enabled Wilhelm Wundt to
develop means to study mental processes in a quantitative manner in his
psychological laboratory in Leipzig.

The two popes: James and Wundt

How was psychology to become a science? For many psychologists, the
answer to this question was quite simple: through experimentation. Experimentation was held to be the central and defining trait of natural
science. The assumption followed that if psychology was to be a science,
it could only lie through the adoption of experimentation. At the end
of the nineteenth century, it was often said that there were two popes
in psychology with radically counterpoised agendas: William James and
Wilhelm Wundt.

Wundt (1832–1920) studied medicine at the University of Heidelberg,
and obtained his degree in 1856. After studying for a period with the physiologist Johannes Müller, he obtained a position as a lecturer in physiology

at the University of Heidelberg. In 1873–1874, he published his *Principles of Physiological Psychology*, which attempted to establish a scientific psychology. This work drew together psychophysiology and evolutionary psychobiology, and had a major impact. In 1875, after a year at the University of Zurich, he was awarded a chair in philosophy at the University of Leipzig, where he remained right up to 1917. The first laboratory for experimental psychology was that opened by William James at Harvard in 1874. However, it was the opening of Wilhelm Wundt's laboratory at Leipzig in 1879 that came to be commemorated as the founding of modern psychology. Wundt attracted many students, and Leipzig became one of the main centres and training grounds for the new psychology. In 1881, he established a journal, *Philosophische Studien*, which published the results of his work and that of his students. It was the institutional form of Wundt's laboratory, as opposed to his own psychology, which became the dominant paradigm of the psychological laboratory. The specific model of experimentation taken over was that used in physiology. Accordingly, experimental psychology was also called physiological psychology.[1]

For Wundt, it was the adoption of experimentation that decisively segregated what he styled as empirical psychology from the previous metaphysical psychology (1902, 10). The aims of the latter had been the discovery of the fundamental laws of the mind through speculation. He held that there were two methods in natural science: experimentation and observation. The former was used wherever possible. The latter was applicable in fields such as botany and zoology with natural objects that remained relatively constant. However, as psychology dealt with processes as opposed to permanent objects, the only exact observation that was possible was experimental observation. Only with experimentation could psychical processes be started, varied and stopped at will. In the case of individual psychology, there were no permanent objects, so observation was not possible. However, there did exist mental products, such as languages, mythological ideas and customs, and the creations of communities, which could be observed. He called this branch of psychology ethnopsychology (*Völkerpsychologie*). In his map of the hierarchy of the sciences, he saw psychology as the supplementary science in relation to natural science, the fundamental science in relation to the mental sciences, and as the preparatory empirical science in relation to philosophy.

For Wundt, the astronomical experiments on the personal equation were only explicable if one assumed that the objective times of the auditory and visual impressions were not the same as the times of subjective perception, which differed in various observers (1892, 269). The

[1] See Danziger, 1990.

astronomical experiments not only demonstrated these phenomena, but they also provided the instrumental means to research them. The astronomical research on the personal equation enabled investigations of subjective experi

William James (1842-1910)

... at the sight of the book. *No* subject is wo... ...treated of in 1000 pages! Had I ten years more, I could rewrite it in 500; but as it stands it is this or nothing – a loathsome, distended, tumefied, bloated, dropsical mass, testifying to nothing but two facts: *1st*, that there is no such thing as a *science of* psychology, and *2nd*, that W. J. is an incapable.[2]

James' doubts aside, *The Principles* has been widely and justly acclaimed as one of the finest works ever written in psychology. Not least among its merits was a trenchant chapter entitled "The Methods and Snares of Psychology." In this, he depicted fallacies that psychologists were prone to, through being reporters of subjective as well as objective facts. In the formation of the new psychology, this issue was critical. One of the critical developments in the scientific revolution was a move away from the reliance on individual testimony in natural philosophy. As Stephen Shapin has argued, reliance upon individual testimony became replaced by trust in institutions. Institutions became responsible for adjudicating rival truth claims and sanctioning what could be regarded as constituting sound collective knowledge (1994). In psychology however, individual testimony was still of critical importance.

James commenced by recounting the conflicts over the use of introspection in psychology. While conceding that the method of introspection was difficult and fallible, he concluded that its drawbacks were the same for any type of observation. Consequently, the only safeguard to the method of introspection was eventual establishment of a consensus upon the object in question (1890, 1, 192). One may note in passing that it was

[2] May 9, 1890, ed. Henry James Jr., 1920, 294.

the subsequent failure of introspective methods to secure such consensus in the protracted debates concerning the existence of imageless thought that did much to discredit the use of introspection in psychology.[3]

James then dealt with the experimental method, developed by those whom he termed "prism, pendulum, and chronograph-philosophers" such as Weber, Wundt, and Fechner. While this had transformed psychology, there had as yet been little "theoretic fruit" from such labors, though he expected such to follow. Finally, he turned to the comparative method:

So it has come to pass that instincts of animals are ransacked to throw light on our own; and that the reasoning faculties of bees and ants, the minds of savages, infants, madmen, idiots, the deaf and the blind, criminals, and eccentrics, are all ransacked in support of this or that special theory about some part of our own mental life. The history of sciences, moral and political institutions, and languages, as types of mental product, are pressed into the same service. Messrs. Darwin and Galton have set the example of circulars of questions sent by the hundred to those supposed able to reply. The custom has spread, and it will be well for us in the next generation if such circulars be not ranked among the common pests of life . . . There are great sources of error in the comparative method. The interpretation of the 'psychoses' of animals, savages and infants is necessarily wild work, in which the personal equation of the investigator has things very much its own way. A savage will be reported to have no moral or religious feeling if his actions shock the observer unduly. A child will be assumed without self-consciousness because he talks of himself in the third person . . . the only thing then is to use as much sagacity as you possess and to be as candid as you can.[4]

With brilliant prescience, this passage critiques what became the pitfalls of much of twentieth-century psychology. James seizes upon the fact that while many different subjects were being proposed as the exemplary subject for psychology, at a fundamental level, they all shared the same weakness: none of them provided an objective standpoint that resolved the problem posed by the subjective variations of different psychologists. Here, the personal equation, far from being heralded as denoting a quantifiably ascertainable factor, designated the manner in which investigators manage only to see what they are led to expect by their own preconceptions. The problem was that most psychologists made their own personal peculiarities into universal rules (1890, 2, 64). The only means of escape from this epistemological solipsism and the resultant anarchy that James put forward were sagacity and candor. By themselves, these were slender

---

[3] See Danziger, 1980.

[4] James, 1890, 194. In 1927 Jung wrote "the fact that the child begins speaking of himself in the third person is in my view a clear proof of the impersonality of his psychology." "Soul and Earth," *CW* 10, § 61.

grounds to secure the scientific status of psychology. Its status was upheld only by the integrity of the psychologist. Rhetorically speaking, through using the term of the personal equation to designate this quandary, he was contesting the supposed advances made by the new experimental psychology.

James considered the misleading influence of speech to be one of the greatest sources of error in psychology. The attempt to form a distinct scientific discipline of psychology led early on to the confrontation with the problem of language. Not only was the language of psychology parasitical upon that of other disciplines, ranging from philosophy to physiology, it was also heavily reliant on everyday speech. The formation of a distinct language for psychology was seen as necessary for psychology to distinguish itself from neighboring disciplines, as well as to establish its superior analytic capacity over everyday language. There were numerous attempts to achieve these ends, such as the 1909 Geneva congress. For the most part, the means adopted was the coining of new concepts, and, in the case of borrowed terms, the attempt to rigidly and restrictively designate their range of connotation. In his *Principles of Physiological Psychology*, Wundt raised these issues. He argued that at its inception, every science was presented with certain ready-made concepts. In the case of psychology, concepts such as "mind" embodied particular metaphysical presuppositions (1874, 17). Language already presented us with concepts like "sensibility," "feeling," "reason," "understanding," against which one was powerless. Faced with this situation, psychology had to proceed like any science and establish an exact definition of concepts and systematically arrange them.

By contrast to Wundt, James claimed that language, which had not been devised by psychologists, lacked sufficient vocabulary to express subjective facts. While empiricists had emphasized the dangers of the reification of concepts, he stressed the opposite fallacy occasioned by the lack of a word for some given phenomenon, noting, "It is hard to focus our attention on the nameless" (1890, 1, 195). An even more serious defect was caused by psychology's reliance on common speech, in which, for example, "the thought of the object's recurrent identity is regarded as the identity of its recurrent thought" (197). Through this, he argued, the "continuous flow of the mental stream" (a phrase that pointed forward to his celebrated chapter on "The stream of thought") was miscognized through the atomist assumption of the existence of discrete ideational entities. By this charge, he meant to "impeach" English psychology after Locke and Hume, and German psychology after Herbart.

The manner in which James tried to circumvent this linguistic problem was markedly different from that of Wundt. Rather than attempt to provide rigidly static conceptual definitions of concepts and introduce new terminology, he sought to evoke the realm of subjective facts by stretching the evocative and metaphorical registers of language to the utmost. The language of *The Principles* sought to depict states of consciousness with the precise shadings and nuances with which they presented themselves:

Suppose we try to recall a forgotten name. The state of our consciousness is peculiar. There is gap therein; but no mere gap. It is a gap that is intensely active. A sort of wraith of the name is in it, beckoning us in a given direction, making us at moments tingle with the sense of our closeness, and then letting us sink back without the longed-for term. If wrong names are proposed to us, this singularly definite gap acts immediately so as to negate them. They do not fit into its mould. And the gap of one word does not feel like the gap of another, all empty of content as both might seem necessarily to be when described as gaps. When I vainly try to recall the name of Spalding, my consciousness is far removed from what it is when I vainly try to recall the name of Bowles . . . the feeling of an absence is *toto coelo* other than the absence of a feeling. It is an intense feeling. The rhythm of a lost word may be there without a sound to clothe it; or the evanescent sense of something which is the initial vowel or consonant may mock us fitfully, without growing more distinct. Every one must know the tantalizing effect of the blank rhythm of some forgotten verse, restlessly dancing in one's mind, striving to be filled with words. (251–252)

A few years after the publication of *The Principles*, James replied to a critique by the psychologist James Ladd. He had never claimed that psychology today was a natural science: rather, by treating it like one, he hoped to help it become one. He defined natural science as "a fragment of truth broken out from the whole mass of it for the sake of practical efficacy exclusively" (1892b, 271). He held that natural sciences aimed at prediction and control, and that this was also true for psychology (subsequent psychologists took up this phrase and repeated it like a mantra, though without reference to James). Individuals in different walks of life also felt these necessities, and what they demanded of psychology was practical rules. Psychology, like every science, had to bracket off philosophical questions. He concluded that if one was faced with a choice between a merely rational and a merely practical science of mind, "the kind of psychology which could cure a case of melancholy, or charm a chronic insane delusion away, ought to be preferred to the most seraphic insight into the nature of the soul" (277). He termed the merely rational science, structural psychology, and the practically orientated one, functional psychology.[5]

The clearest indication of how James understood the role of the personal equation in psychological observation, and attempted to delimit it,

---

[5] For more on this distinction, see below, 204–205.

is found in his 1909 study "Report on Mrs. Piper's Hodgson control."
The medium Mrs. Leonora Piper, was one of the most closely studied individuals of all time, principally by Richard Hodgson. Through his work
with Mrs. Piper, Hodgson became a convert to spiritualism. Soon after
his death, messages duly came through Mrs. Piper claiming to originate
from him. James was duly called in to authenticate these messages. James
gave full details of his involvement with Mrs. Piper, his views on her psychic phenomena, and all the factors which might bias his report. He noted
that he had given as candid an account as he could of his personal equation, and asked readers to make allowances for this (1909b, 115). Under
the rubric of the personal equation, he included the psychologist's theoretical preconceptions, the nature of their personal acquaintance with
the subjects being investigated and their "will to believe."

As we shall see, Jung adopted James' formulation of the personal equation, and viewed it as one of the most critical issues upon which the
possibility of psychology as a science of subjectivity hinged.

Human, cultural and historical sciences?

The rise of experimentation in psychology has traditionally been portrayed as an unchecked ascent. This conceals the degree of competition
between different agendas, and the level of contestation. Furthermore,
it took much longer for experimental laboratories to be established on
a large scale, and to secure financial and institutional support.[6] It was
not only psychologists who were attempting to determine and define the
status of psychology. A number of philosophers did so as well. These
philosophical debates did much to form the language and frame the issues concerning the scientific status of psychology, which were in turn
taken up by the psychologists themselves. Thus in attempting to separate
psychology from philosophy to establish psychology as an empirical science, psychologists were ironically indebted to philosophical conceptions
of science and the status of psychology.

One significant critique of experimental psychology was launched by
the German philosopher, Wilhelm Dilthey. Dilthey (1833–1911) saw the
main goal of his life work as being the establishment of a theoretical
basis for the historical understanding of life. He initially studied theology, and then turned to philosophy. After several appointments, including
a chair at the University of Basel in 1866, he obtained a chair at the University of Berlin in 1882, where he remained for the rest of his life. In
1883, he wrote an *Introduction to the Human Sciences*. The subtitle proclaimed that the work was an "an attempt to lay a foundation for the

---

[6] See Ash, 1995.

study of society and history." This foundation, according to Dilthey, was only possible through establishing a distinction between *Naturwissenschaft* and *Geisteswissenschaft*. The former, natural science, accords with what has generally been termed science in the English-speaking world. The latter has no exact equivalent, and has been translated as mental science, human science or systematic scholarship. Dilthey's distinction, while hotly contested, has proved to be very influential.

He claimed that the distinction between these disciplines was not arbitrary, but was based upon a fundamental dichotomy. Natural sciences dealt with sense-based facts, while human sciences dealt with inner experiences and historico-social reality. There was an incommensurability between material and natural processes. While natural sciences analyzed causal connections in the processes of nature, human sciences attempted to lay hold of the singular and individual, and the uniformities which shaped it. The most basic discipline of the human sciences was psychology, and its special subject was the individual. Until now, the problem was that this central position "has been occupied only by the vague generalizations of experience of life, creations of poets, descriptions of character and destinies by men of the world, and by indefinite truths which the historian weaves into his narrative" (1883, 95). Psychology was to replace these, and hence provide a firm basis for the human sciences in general.

Dilthey's proposal that there existed two different types of sciences, and that psychology belonged to the human sciences, was directly opposed by the experimental psychologists. For the latter, psychology could become a science through applying the experimental procedures and explanatory methods of the natural sciences to the human subject. The ascendancy of experimental psychology led him to embark upon a critique of this tendency. In 1894, he contrasted explanatory psychology with descriptive or analytic psychology (using the term "analytische Psychologie"[7]). The former attempted to establish a causal system that explained the life of the soul through the combination of its component parts. It consisted in analysis, that is, the discovery of the elements of psychic phenomena, and synthesis or construction – how these elements come together. The basic problem of explanatory psychology was the unwarranted misapplication of the methods of the natural sciences to psychic life and history. Inner experience could not be compared to processes in nature. Whereas one *explained* nature, he claimed that one *understands* psychic life. Understanding (Verstehen) had pride of place. Rather than following the constructive method, he held that psychology had to begin from the

[7] 1894, 182 and 239, German edition, 64 and 119, English edition.

evolved psychic life, as opposed to attempting to derive it from elementary processes. He critiqued the reductionism of explanatory psychology. Evolved psychic life could not be explained as a mere combination of its constituent parts, as the combination of psychic elements produced new qualitative properties not contained in the elements themselves. It was precisely this aspect which was creative. Psychic life was characterized by an inner purposiveness, rather than being conditioned by an external goal. He used the following analogy to illustrate his argument: "Analysis, has at first to do, so to speak, with the architectonic articulation of the finished edifice; it does not first concern itself with the stones, the mortar, nor the hands which work them, but the inner coherence of the parts" (58). Dilthey's distinction between natural and human sciences, while influential, did not go uncontested. In 1894, Hermann Windelband, a prominent neo-Kantian philosopher, presented a rectorate address at the University of Strasbourg, "History and Natural Science." Windelband challenged Dilthey's dichotomy. He used the case of psychology to highlight its insufficiency, as such an important science could not, on Dilthey's criteria, be unambiguously classed as a natural or human science. Windelband held that from the perspective of its subject matter, it could only be a human science, and could in a certain sense be described as the foundation for the other human sciences. However, its methodology belonged to the natural sciences. As an alternative, he proposed a distinction between sciences which aimed at establishing general laws, and sciences which inquired into specific historical facts. The first were nomothetic sciences, and the second, idiographic sciences. Psychology was a nomothetic science, as it tried to establish general laws. Idiographic sciences, by contrast, attempted to provide a complete and exhaustive description of a single process within a unique temporally defined domain of reality. While general propositions were necessary in the idiographic sciences, they did not aim to establish general laws. For Windelband, unlike Dilthey, the same subject could be the object of both types of investigations.

Windelband's philosophy of science was developed by the philosopher Heinrich Rickert (1863–1936). Rickert did his dissertation under Windelband, and held a chair at the University of Freiburg. In 1899, he published an essay entitled "Natural sciences and cultural sciences (Kulturwissenschaft)." Rickert stated that unlike Windelband, he distinguished between individualizing and generalizing sciences. Between these sciences, he saw a relative difference, as opposed to an antithesis. The paradigmatic cultural science was history, as it attempted to study the "nonrepeatable event in its particularity and individuality" (14). Whilst psychology had not yet arrived at a generally recognized theory, the method it used was the generalizing method of the natural sciences.[8] In 1902, he enlarged upon these distinctions, and used them to launch a critique upon the exclusive domination of the natural sciences, and against the attempt to construct a world view upon them.

Rickert maintained that concepts in the natural sciences were abstract, and were formed through the purging of empirical perception. As soon as an empirical reality was conceived in natural scientific terms, its uniqueness was lost. The distinguishing trait of empirical reality was that it was situated in time and space. Thus this could only be adequately approached via a historical science. Meanwhile, psychologists were trying to approach the unique and individual from quite different angles.

Individual psychology

In 1890, James noted that it had been generally supposed by philosophers that there was a typical mind of which all individual minds were like (1890, 2, 49). Recently, however, the fallaciousness of this axiom had been demonstrated by a series of studies that had begun to demonstrate the range and extent of differences between individual minds. In this regard, he held that a new era in descriptive psychology had been inaugurated by Francis Galton's (1822–1911) investigations into mental imagery. Galton was a multifaceted figure who contributed to a number of different fields. His studies were collected together in 1883 under the title *Inquiries into Human Faculty and its Development* and had an important impact in fostering the psychological study of individual differences.

The issue of the different capacity for mental imagery in individuals and the desirability of a statistical study of this subject had been raised in 1860 by Gustav Fechner in his *Psychophysics*. David Burbridge suggests that Galton may have been prompted to undertake such an inquiry through his reading of Fechner (1994, 446). Galton prepared a questionnaire inquiring into the strength and nature of mental imagery. Between 1879 and 1880, he circulated several hundred copies of this around. He first questioned men of science, as he held that they were most likely to give accurate answers. His list of respondents reads like a who's who of British science (*ibid.*, 450–452). To his surprise, his results indicated the very low incidence of mental imagery among men of science. The general conclusion that he drew was that there was a great variation in the capacity for mental imagery in different individuals, and that it was possible to gain statistical insights into other people's minds.

---

[8] 1928, 157. According to Rickert, psychology was far from being a "real science" due to its fundamental lack of methodological clarity.

While he focused on the preponderance of visual imagery, some of his observations were taken up and extended by the leading French neurologist Jean-Martin Charcot in his work on aphasia. Charcot (1825–1893) held a chair at the University of Paris, and in 1882 opened a neurological clinic at the Salpêtrière hospital. He became one of the most renowned neurologists in Europe. Through his work on aphasia, he elaborated a theory of four physiological types. These were classified according to the centres of partial memory of words which predominated in the representation of words: auditive, visual, motor, or indifferent.[9] While Charcot had focused on cases of aphasia, in 1886, Alfred Binet (1857–1911), a young psychologist working at the Salpêtrière, took Charcot's observations as the basis for a general model of four different sensory types of individual: the visual type, the auditory type, the motor type, and the indifferent type. These types were widely taken up.[10] Binet initially studied law, which he gave up in 1878 to study with Charcot. After working for a number of years at the Salpêtrière, he took up a position in 1891 at a laboratory of physiological psychology at the Sorbonne which had just been established by Henri Beaunis in 1889. In 1894, he became the director there, and he remained till his death.

In 1895 Binet and Victor Henri put forward a programmatic statement in the newly founded journal, L'Année psychologique, edited by Binet in conjunction with Henri Beaunis, for a new branch of psychology – individual psychology. As John Carson notes, Binet's work at the Sorbonne during this period was profoundly affected by the Wundtian vision of psychology as an experimentally based science (1994, 226). In their article, Binet and Henri stated that while general psychology, which had hitherto prevailed, studied the general properties of psychic processes, the aim of individual psychology was to study the individual differences of such processes (1895, 411). In this respect, they were parting company with the Wundtian agenda, which had concentrated on attempting to study general, as opposed to particular human capacities. Unlike Wundt, Binet and Henri claimed that higher mental processes such as memory, reasoning and imagination were also amenable to experimentation. They argued that individual psychology was faced with two tasks: to identify the variable properties of these processes and to determine their variation between individuals; and to study the relation within an individual of these various processes, to determine whether any particular ones predominated, and to study their level of mutual dependency (412). The result of

[9] See Gasser, 1995.
[10] See Binet, 1886, James, 1890, 2, ch. 18. Théodule Ribot noted that there also existed an affective type, characterized by the easy revivification of affective representations (1896, 166). On Ribot, see below, 185–186.

such an analysis would be a precise scientific account of the "character" of an individual. It was clear that individual psychology was intended to replace the "prescientific" study of temperaments, characters, humors, etc., together with the manifold means that had hitherto been deployed to describe human diversity.

The determination of the dominant processes within an individual took the form of typologies. In a subsequent follow-up article, Binet described experiments that they had conducted on a group of school children. The procedure they had devised was to present their subjects with a picture for two minutes, after which they had ten minutes to describe what they saw in as detailed a manner as possible. Their aim was to study the different psychic processes that the same object gave rise to (Binet, 1897, 299). The results of their experiments led them to distinguish between five intellectual and moral types: the describer type, the observer type, the emotional type, the erudite type, and the imaginative and poetic type.

Throughout his career, Binet equivocated on the role of experimental methods in psychology. As Carson notes, Binet, while being one of the most active in founding experimental psychology in France, was also one of its sternest critics (1994, 242). He shared this trait with Théodore Flournoy in Switzerland and William James in America. Significantly, in each case, experimental methods were unfavorably contrasted with the detailed study of individual lives in natural settings, and each one held that such studies were intended to yield results of greater practical utility than laboratory-based work.

In 1903, in his *Experimental Study of Intelligence*, Binet gave extended descriptions of the observer type and the imaginative type in the form of his study of his daughters, Madeleine and Alice, for whom he gave the pseudonyms Marguerite and Armande. He subjected them to a series of tests, such as soliciting associations to given words. The results showed two distinct typical forms of reaction. He argued that objectivism, the tendency to live in the outer world, and subjectivism, the tendency to enclose oneself in one's own consciousness, characterized different mental types (297). Binet advocated the in-depth investigation of individuals, particularly those one already knew well.

The utilization of in-depth clinical investigation as the mode of exploring typological differences easily enabled a transition to utilizing psychotherapy as the methodological means for the study of individual differences, which is precisely what Jung subsequently attempted.

Differential psychology

In 1900, William Stern (1871–1938) a lecturer in philosophy at the University of Breslau and former student of the experimental psychologist

Herman Ebbinghaus, commenced his *On the Psychology of Individual Differences (Ideas for a "Differential Psychology")* by boldly proclaiming that individuality was to be *the* problem of the twentieth century.[11] While the new experimental psychology had been pre-eminently concerned with establishing the general laws of mental functioning, Stern argued that the task confronting psychology was the discovery of the principles of individual differences. As he understood the task of psychology to consist in the establishment of laws, the task confronting a differential psychology became one of determining the respective types of individuals.

In his consideration of method, Stern considered the problems of introspection. Introspection alone could not determine whether a given psychic phenomenon was individual or not. He noted the problem posed by the individual peculiarities of the psychologist, "A psychologist born blind can never understand the constitution of the visual type" (22). He claimed that these difficulties could be overcome through observation of others, pre-eminently through experimentation.

Amongst the types that he described were the objective and subjective judgment types. In the case of the former, judgments were primarily determined by the outer stimulus; in the latter, by the state of the subject. In 1935, while commenting on types of character, he returned to his distinction. He noted that he had distinguished the "objective" and "subjective" types in 1900 and that Jung's terms "introverted" and "extraverted" had more recently come into use (1938, 434–435). This reference suggests that Stern was making a priority claim.

In his autobiography, Stern claimed that even at the time when he wrote this work, he saw the limitations of differential psychology. He argued that real individuality could not be reached by differential psychology. This was because differential psychology dissected the unity of mental life, and because, like any other science, it generalizes. Here, he adopted Rickert's conception of psychology as a generalizing science. A concept of a type, he argued, was a general functional rule: "the relegation of an individual to a type or to several types can never do justice to the ineffable particularity of his individuality" (1930, 347). In his work on psychological typology, Jung would subsequently find himself confronted with such dilemmas.

By the turn of the century, as John Carson notes, individual psychology was fragmenting into a host of unrelated research programmes (1994, 300). Part of the problem was that there seemed to be as many typologies as there were investigators, with little common vocabulary, let alone consensus. It is hard to dispel the impression that the different conceptual models were in part put forward to justify the introduction of new

[11] 1900, foreword. Jung possessed a copy of this book.

terminology to replace that of other psychologists, and hence to relegate their work to a secondary position. Thus when Jung took up these issues, it can fairly be said that they had reached an impasse.

Becoming a psychiatrist

To Aniela Jaffé, Jung said that his life had been interwoven and drawn together by one work: how to penetrate into the secret of the personality.[12] In *Memories*, Jung recounted that his growing scientific interests in his adolescence led him to decide to study science at university. The choice of medicine – which he saw as an established science – was a secondary compromise to enable a livelihood (104–106). As to his specialization, he saw the choice as being between surgery and internal medicine. If he had had the funds, he would have opted for the former.

Psychiatric textbooks are not renowned for leading to revelations. However, such seems to have been the case with Jung. Towards the end of his medical studies, Friedrich von Müller, who was in charge of the medical clinic at the University of Basel, invited him to accompany him to Munich as his assistant. He would have taken up this invitation and devoted himself to internal medicine, had he not started reading Krafft-Ebing's *Textbook of Psychiatry* in preparation for his state exams. He recalled:

> I thus read in the preface: "It is probably due to the peculiarity of the subject and the incompleteness of its elaboration that psychiatric textbooks are stamped with a more or less subjective character." A few lines further on, the author called the psychoses "diseases of the person" . . . it had become clear to me in a flash of illumination, that there could be no other goal for me than psychiatry . . . Here was the empirical field common to biological and spiritual facts, which I had everywhere sought and nowhere found . . . My violent reaction set in when I read Krafft-Ebing on the "subjective character" of psychiatric textbooks. So, I thought, the textbook is in part the subjective confession of the author, who with his prejudice, with the totality of his being, stands behind the objectivity of his experiences and responds to the "disease of the person" with the whole of his own personality. (*Ibid.*, 129–30, trans. mod.)[13]

His reading of Krafft-Ebing's preface is curious. Following the first sentence that he cited, Krafft-Ebing wrote that his work presented disease-portraits based upon thirty-three years' work. The general correspondence between his experience and that of other observers guaranteed that

---

[12] MP, 14.

[13] Jung had the fourth edition of 1890, signed and dated 1899. To Ingaret Gifford, Jung said: "The real reason why I took up psychology was that when I was a child, I always noticed that I didn't understand people – they were incomprehensible to me" (interview with Ingaret Gifford, July 20, 1955, JP, original in English).

he had been correct, and that there were fixed laws which enabled the establishment of distinct disease-portraits (1879–1880, iii). Thus Krafft-Ebing presents his own textbook as having achieved a level of objectivity, and overcome the drawbacks of previous psychiatric textbooks. Similarly, in the final sentence, he states that *despite* the variety of manifestations of diseases of the person, he has been able to establish distinct disease pictures, due to their lawfulness.

Jung understood Krafft-Ebing's preface as posing the question, how could psychiatry be a science, given its inescapable subjective character? When Jung came to designate his work as psychology, it was this question that he repeatedly posed of psychology. The series of solutions that he proposed at various stages significantly gave shape to what has become his most renowned work, which hitherto has not been viewed from this perspective.

Differences in associations

In 1903 the Genevan psychologist Édouard Claparède observed that out of the interest in recent years in individual psychology, the question as to whether individual coefficients marked the process of association had grown increasingly prominent.[14] In the long-standing associationist tradition in philosophy and psychology, association was seen as the defining characteristic of the mind. Thus if there existed distinct mental types, it would be reasonable to assume that such types would reveal themselves by different forms of associative reactions. Second, from Wundt onwards, associations had been subject to a great deal of experimental research, as they seemed to provide a ready means of a quantitative approach to mental processes, easily amenable to laboratory investigation.

In December 1900, after finishing his medical studies, Jung took up a post of assistant doctor at the Burghölzli asylum in Zürich, which was a university clinic. In an important passage omitted from *Memories*, Jung related to Aniela Jaffé that he had initially been interested in anatomical brain research, and worked in the laboratory at the Burghölzli preparing brain dissections. The laboratory was directed by Alexander von Muralt, who became a close friend of Jung's during this period. Jung gave courses in histology. He recalled that on occasion, he asked von Muralt what one was really doing in brain anatomy, and what one really saw in the brain of the dementia praecox patient. To this, von Muralt answered, that one saw nothing, and that there was no real reason for doing it. One day, von

---

[14] 201. Jung cites from this work frequently in his association studies. On Claparède, see below, 206–207.

Muralt stopped attending the laboratory, and Jung asked him why. Von Muralt replied that he had now taken up photography. Jung asked him if this had anything to do with brain dissection, and he replied that it was just a sport. This led Jung to realize that brain dissection was also a sport, and this led him to turn to the associations experiment.[15] Von Muralt was also important for Jung's career in another respect. In 1905, he contracted tuberculosis, and went to Davos. Von Muralt had been the first "Oberarzt," which meant that he was second in command after Bleuler. As a consequence, his post became vacant, and Jung filled it.

It was his work on the associations experiment that established Jung's reputation as one of the rising stars in international psychiatry. In this context, I plan to take up a few aspects of this research, which was carried out at the psychological laboratory of the Burghölzli. In these experiments, subjects were requested to respond to a list of one hundred words which were read out in turn with the first word that occurred to them. The experiment had been initially devised by Galton, and then taken up and developed by Wundt to study reaction times.

The initial aim of the experiments at the Burghölzli was to provide a tool for the differential diagnosis of mental disorders. This project collapsed, and the investigators found that they were unable even to differentiate genders on the basis of the experiment. However, the research took a new turn, and attention was redirected to disturbances of response. Jung and his principal co-worker Franz Riklin argued that the disturbances of response were due to the associations that had been triggered in the subject's mind by the stimulus word. The words evoked what they termed emotionally stressed complexes.

Jung and Riklin also claimed that they had determined two typical forms of reactions. Certain subjects showed a tendency to express subjective judgments and construct relations to their ego (1904, *CW* 2 § 97). This form of reaction showed itself in the process of association. It followed from this that the associations experiment could be used to determine experimentally an individual's reaction type in a quantifiable manner – for instance, by calculating the number of self-referential or egocentric reactions in a given test. Jung and Riklin claimed that there existed two well-characterized types. With the first type, subjective and often emotionally charged experiences were present in their reactions. With the second, the reactions showed an objective and impersonal disposition (§ 412).

---

[15] To Aniela Jaffé, Jung recalled that von Muralt later told him that he and other doctors at the Burghölzli had wondered whether Jung could be psychically abnormal, as during the first six months in which he was at the Burghölzli, he never went out once (MP, 326).

Jung was in effect fusing the Wundtian experimental methodology of the study of reaction times and word associations with the project of individual or differential psychology, as established by Binet and Stern, and combining this with the clinical approach of the French psychology of the subconscious.[16] In such a manner, he was attempting to develop a clinic-experimental method, which he termed experimental psychopathology. The appearance this gave of being able to conduct psychotherapy in a supposedly scientific manner, through adopting some of the procedures of the experimental laboratory, did much to ensure the popularity of Jung's associations research, particularly in America. The leading psychiatrist Adolf Meyer hailed Jung and Riklin's co-authored paper in laudatory terms: "This remarkable piece of work and its continuation are no doubt the best single contribution to psychopathology during the past year."[17] In his review of subsequent studies on the associations experiment by Jung, Meyer described Jung's achievement in the following manner: "it is so far the nearest approach of an experimental test to the combination of a qualitative and quantitative inquiry into the stream of mental activity and its most frequent disturbers" (1906, 280).

However, this combination of qualitative and quantitative inquiry, or of experimental and clinical methods made for an uneasy alliance, as some critics, notably Binet, Janet and Stern realized.

Critical responses

In the winter of 1902 Jung went to Paris to attend Pierre Janet's lectures at the Collège de France. At that time, Jung considered the French to be the "leaders in psychiatry."[18] Jung also revealed a further motive for his trip to Paris. He stated that before he went to Paris, he had discovered the emotionally charged complex, and his original intention was to work on this with Binet. Binet warmly welcomed Jung, but the plans were abandoned due to the fact that the experiments would have had to have been conducted in French (317).

There may have been further reasons for Jung's abandonment of his proposed research with Binet. In *The Experimental Study of Intelligence*, while describing his method of getting subjects to write down twenty words as fast as possible, Binet criticized the use of the associations experiment. He claimed that his method was far superior. Instead of resulting in single associations, his method led to a continuous chain of twenty. This had the advantage of being far closer to natural conditions.

---

[16] See Shamdasani, 1996.
[17] 1905, 242. On Meyer and Jung, see Leys, 1985.   [18] CMS, 311.

Furthermore, the subject was freer and more spontaneous than in the associations experiment, which constrained one to give artificial associations (1903, 59–60). For Binet, Jung's artificial method would simply lead to the production of experimental artifacts, as it did not adequately deal with the problem of suggestion. It is possible that Binet expressed a similar sentiment to Jung, when the latter approached him concerning collaborative research on the associations experiment. Jung never replied to this criticism.

Ellenberger noted the close parallel between Binet's types of "introspection" and "extrospection" and Jung's "introversion" and "extraversion." He suggested that as Binet's book appeared when Jung was in Paris, he might have read it and then forgotten it. This would make it another instance of what Flournoy called cryptomnesia, the spontaneous revival of forgotten memories (Ellenberger, 1970, 703). Binet's typology is cited neither in Jung's work on the associations experiment, nor in any of his subsequent work on psychological typology. It is possible that this lack of citation may have had something to do with the circumstances surrounding the abandonment of Jung's proposed research project with Binet.

Similar criticisms of Jung's associations experiments to those of Binet were made by Janet, who expressed a sharp critique of Jung's work at the International Congress of Medicine in London in 1913, where Jung also presented. After criticizing Freud's method of free association, Janet stated that Jung had proposed a more interesting method, through reviving an old experimental procedure (1914–15, 12–13). Janet's judgment of Jung's method, however, was no more positive than his appraisal of psychoanalysis. With suitable and interested subjects whose fixed ideas were already known to the experimenter, suitable lists of words could be prepared. He had tried this, and shown that prolonged and abnormal reactions could be obtained to words linked with the subject's fixed ideas. However, he wondered if this was the case if the subject's fixed ideas were not already known, or when they did not represent memories which played a powerful role. Furthermore, he held that there would be many clinical errors if one attempted to use this method as a tool for diagnosis. Long reaction times could simply be induced by introducing words such as "shit" or "your cunt." Moreover many subjects did not like being experimented on, and this factor could easily have more effect on the experiment than their emotional memories.

For Janet, Jung's associations experiment collapsed through an elementary failure in experimental methodology. Its confirmatory value for the psychoanalytic theory of repression was nullified, as it also confirmed Janet's theory of subconscious fixed ideas. Its diagnostic value was dismissed out of court. And finally its clinical value was reduced to a species of iatrogenesis, as its use would lead to the postulation of traumatic memories where none existed.

In 1905 Stern wrote a review of Jung's "On the behaviour of reaction times in the associations experiment," which had been published the same year. Stern focused on an example that Jung gave of a married lady in which he claimed to detect a pregnancy-complex – namely, the fact that she feared that her pregnancy might lead her husband to be estranged from her. Stern argued that Jung's practice of asking for retrospective clarifications could easily lead one astray, since, solely on the basis of the subject's self-observation, the investigator projected a relation of underlying representations between previously isolated acts of association that may not have in fact been effective in each moment. Due to this, the purported explanations turn into interpolations (1905, 440).

In his reply, Jung conceded that his method was difficult and dangerous, particularly for inexperienced investigators. However, in a manner reminiscent of Binet, he noted it was for this reason that he chose as test persons individuals who were well known to him, were psychological, and were experienced in observing associations (1905, *CW* 2, § 761). In this, he was following Wundt's practice of using trained observers as subjects. Jung could be said to have known the first subject, which Stern singled out for his remarks, rather well – as it appears to have been his wife, who was pregnant for most of 1904 and 1905 with their first two children. As to the charge of interpolation, Jung stated: "even Freud has been accused of interpreting into a subject's statement more than is in it" (1905, *CW* 2). He added that when a subject was asked to report what came to mind in connection with an idea, they were of course likely to reply with a "canalized" rather than a spontaneous association; this applied to any form of retrospective elucidation. However, this hardly replied to Stern's charge: for if any form of retrospective elucidation had such a directing effect on the explanation, retrospective elucidation would be insufficient to establish that the various associations were in fact due to the activation of a particular complex, which Jung required of it.

Jung never gave an explicit account of why he stopped working on the associations experiment during this period. His student, the analytical psychologist H. G. Baynes, gives indication that Jung's realization of the significance of the personal equation may have played a critical role in this. According to Baynes, Jung found that the personality and sex of the experimenter "introduced an incalculable factor of variation" (1927, 108). On one occasion, he conducted an associations experiment with a colleague using a galvanometer. When he asked his colleague to think of something disagreeable, there was only a slight deflection of the galvanometer reading. He then asked him if he was thinking of an incident which had occurred in the hospital that morning, which led to a violent oscillation of the needle. While the content had been the same in both instances, the reaction to it had varied dramatically. According to Baynes, he deduced from this that contents that were known or shared by another had a different "energic value" from one that wasn't shared, and furthermore, the individual with whom it was shared was another significant factor. Hence it was impossible to exclude the personal equation.

The personal equation in psychoanalysis

The correspondence between Freud and Jung is hard to outclass in terms of the incidence of invective and vitriol that they dished out to their psychological and psychiatric colleagues, and finally, to each other. One of the reasons for this is the employment of a particular style of ad hominem psychological critique, which simply stated, took the form of asserting that a given individual's theorizing was fallacious, as the individual was neurotic, psychotic, or worse (the only remedy being psychoanalysis). What is significant concerning this is that it embodied a particular understanding of the relation of the subjectivity of a psychologist to his theories.

In what follows, this issue will be taken up in terms of the final phase of the relation between Freud and Jung, where it is most markedly prominent. On November 15, 1912, Jung commented to Ernest Jones,

Freud is convinced that I am thinking under the domination of a father complex against him and then all is complex-nonsense . . . He already ceased being my friend, understanding my whole work as a personal resistance against himself and sexuality. Against this insinuation I am completely helpless . . . If Freud understands each attempt to think in a new way about the problems of psychoanalysis as a personal resistance, things become impossible.[19]

A few weeks later, this issue openly broke out in the correspondence between Freud and Jung. On November 29, 1912, Freud explained his prior fainting fit in Jung's presence by appealing to "A bit of neurosis, that I still should take care of" (*FJL*, 524, trans. mod.). Jung seized upon this admission in his reply, and stated that it ought to be taken seriously. He claimed that it was this factor that prevented Freud from grasping his recent work. Hence Jung's answer to what he took to be Freud's judgment on his work was simply to diagnose Freud in kind. Jung highlighted the fact that Freud began *The Interpretation of Dreams* with "the mournful admission

---

[19] SFC, original in English.

of your own neurosis – the dream of Irma's injection – identification with the neurotic in need of treatment, which is very significant."[20] This wasn't simply a personal shortcoming of Freud's, but one that, through a quasi-degenerationist inheritance, afflicted psychoanalysis as a whole:

I am forced to the painful conclusion that the majority of psychoanalysts misuse psychoanalysis for the purpose of devaluing others and their progress by the well known insinuations of complexes . . . A particularly preposterous bit of nonsense went around, which says, that I wrote my libido theory as the result of anal eroticism. When I consider *who* cooked up this "theory," then I become fearful for the future of analysis. (*Ibid.*, trans. mod.)

He concluded that in this respect, psychoanalysts were as dependent upon psychoanalysis as their opponents were upon authority, and that this protective function of psychoanalysis needed to be unmasked. Freud's counter was to draw attention to a slip of the pen that Jung had written, which provoked an outraged response from the latter. Jung stated that this revealed Freud's general tactics, which was to sniff out symptomatic actions in those around him, hence reducing them to the status of sons and daughters. As for himself, he stated: "I am namely not in the least neurotic – touch wood! I have namely *lege artis et tout humblement* let myself be analysed, which has been very good for me."[21] He claimed that as Freud had only conducted a self-analysis as opposed to having had an analysis, he had been unable to escape from his neurosis. On receiving this letter, Freud wrote to Ernest Jones:

As regards Jung he seems all out of his wits, he is behaving quite crazy . . . I directed his attention to a certain Verschreiben in his letter . . . It was after this that he broke loose furiously proclaiming that he was not neurotic at all, having passed through a psychoanalytic treatment (with the Moltzer? I suppose you may imagine what the treatment was).[22]

Freud enclosed a copy of Jung's letter to Ferenczi, and commented that Jung was clearly attempting to provoke Freud, so that the responsibility for the break would be with him. He added: "he is behaving like a florid

[20] December 3, *ibid.*, 526, trans. mod. Jung's copy of the 1909 edition of Freud's *Interpretation of Dreams* has many underlinings and annotations around Freud's Irma dream, and his copy of the 1911 edition has some further annotations. At the end of the interpretation, in the 1909 edition, Jung wrote: "No wish-fulfillment but admonition."
[21] December 18, 1912, 535.
[22] Freud to Jones, December 26, 1912, ed. Paskauskas, 1993, 186. Jung's pupil, Jolande Jacobi recalled that "I heard from others, about the time before he [Jung] met Toni Wolff, that he had a love affair there in the Burghölzli with a girl – what was her name? Moltzer." Jolande Jacobi interview, 110, CLM. She practiced as an analyst, and worked closely with Jung as his assistant. Further research has indicated that there was an intimate relation between them at a later date. On Moltzer, see below, 70–72, 306, and Shamdasani 1998a, 1998b.

fool and the brutal fellow that he is. The master that analyzed him could only have been Fräulein Moltzer, and he is so foolish as to be proud of this work of a woman with whom he is having an affair."[23] In private, Jung's theoretical developments were simply dismissed through being attributed to neurotic origins. In 1913, Jones wrote to Adolf Meyer apropos Jung:

> In my opinion he has shown grave signs of defective balance, and there must be something wrong. His new scientific views constitute of course another matter, which must be judged on their merits, but even here they seem to have a suspiciously subjective origin.[24]

In these transactions, the mutual accusations between Freud and Jung are symmetrical: both sought to invalidate the other's theoretical position by reducing it to being nothing other than the expression of personal psychopathology. While fully engaging within this dynamic, Jung at the same time attempted to distance himself from it. In 1913 he wrote to Jones: "It is an extremely difficult and even unfair standpoint to reduce a different view to personal complexes. This is the psychology of the 'nothing but.' It removes all seriousness and human consideration and replaces it with personal gossip and suspicion."[25]

It is important to consider the event which led to the final termination of relations between Freud and Jung. On September 21, after the Munich congress, Freud wrote to Jung's Swiss colleague Alphonse Maeder that the congress had shown the uselessness of all discussion, and criticized Jung's "clumsy and incorrect management." He wrote: "I can predict that your way will soon lead you out of psychoanalysis and you will not find the way back. Whether you will feel comfortable in the labyrinth of the mystical, where Jung steers, I do not know. I no longer believe in his bona fides."[26] After receiving this letter, Maeder wrote to the American psychiatrist Smith Ely Jeliffe that the Munich congress had shown the impossibility of the Viennese to understand those from Zürich. Between the two, there lay a difference in world-views. The Viennese thought that those from Zürich had abandoned psychoanalysis and got lost in mysticism due to negative father complexes.[27] On being informed of Freud's comments by Maeder, Jung informed Freud that he resigned from the *Jahrbuch für psychoanalytische und psychopathologische Forschungen*.

---

[23] December 23, 1912, ed. Falzeder, 1993, 446.
[24] Meyer papers, Johns Hopkins University.
[25] November 25, 1913, SFC, As Eugene Taylor pointed out original in English, the use of the phrase "nothing but," in this sense, was a favorite of William James, from whom Jung appears to have adopted it (1980, 165).
[26] September 21, 1913, Freud papers, LC. I thank Ernst Falzeder for suppling a copy of this letter.
[27] Maeder to Jeliffe, September 26, 1913, Jeliffe papers, LC.

Referring to Freud's comments to Maeder, Jung wrote "since this is the gravest reproach that one can level at a man, you have with this made further collaboration with you impossible for me."[28] On November 7, Jung communicated Freud's letter to Maeder to the Zürich psychoanalytical society. He said that he had wanted to resign his editorship of the *Jahrbuch*, but that the publisher, Deuticke, replied that he would prefer to cause Freud to resign, and continue the *Jarhbuch* with Jung. Thus the *Jahrbuch* would become the organ of the Zürich school. To this, Maeder said: "So the separation is prepared, which we all expected, and with which we are in agreement." Jung replied: "We of Zürich must now strive especially, so that we may replace with the quality of work, what we lack in quantity. We stand before a cultural task, that will give us the necessary impulse."[29]

The following year, in his history of the psychoanalytic movement, Freud wrote of Jung that for Freud's sake, he had given up "certain racial prejudices which he had previously permitted himself." Freud described him as someone "incapable of tolerating the authority of another, but who was still less capable of wielding it himself, and whose energies were relentlessly devoted to the furtherance of his own interests" (*SE* 14, 43).

There are several interlinked problems that Jung was grappling with. As he understood it, the distinguishing trait of psychoanalysis was its total reliance upon the personal equation. In 1911, he wrote that psychoanalysis demanded a sacrifice beyond that of any other science: merciless self-knowledge. This was because the practical and theoretical understanding of "analytical psychology" was a function of analytical self-knowledge.[30]

Hence it became axiomatic that the scientific status of a psychological theory could be safeguarded only if the theorist was not neurotic. In this context, freedom from neurosis seemed to designate the fact that one had a "successful" analysis (whatever that was). Second, even if one was a non-neurotic theoretician (as Jung here claims to be), there was little likelihood of having one's theory generally recognized, as the neurosis of analysts not only impeded them from producing genuine scientific theories, but also from being able to recognize them. While James could appeal to an ethical code as the final court of appeal, no such recourse was possible for psychoanalysis, as it considered itself beyond good and evil, and hence in a superordinate position to all ethical codes.

---

[28] October 27, 1913, *FJL*, 550, trans. mod. To William Alonson White, Jung wrote: "Freud discredited me personally in a letter to Dr. Maeder. And I had to withdraw from the Jahrbuch therefore. Fr. is working with nice means against all those who don't strictly believe in the dogma" (November 10, 1913, White papers, LC.) English in the original.

[29] MZP.

[30] "Morton Prince, 'The mechanism and interpretation of dreams': A critical review," *CW* 4, § 156, trans. mod.

Hence the possibility of theoretical debate within psychoanalysis had, by these terms, collapsed into mutual diagnosis. Significantly enough, it was at this juncture that Jung put forward the proposal that every analyst had to have a training analysis, which subsequently became adopted not only by psychoanalysis, but by the myriad schools of psychotherapy.[31]

It was with the adoption of the practice of training analysis that psychoanalysis differentiated itself from rival forms of psychotherapy, and ultimately ensured its continuance. Jung appears to have been the first to have set up this practice. In part, this seems to have arisen out of the particular set of working circumstances at the Burghölzli. During the period of the experimental research into word associations, the staff subjected each other to tests. At the same time, mutual dream analysis was practiced. Abraham Brill recalls that at the Burghölzli, when one wanted to analyze one's dreams, one usually asked someone already proficient in dream analysis. Thus his dreams "were analysed mostly by Jung, some by Bleuler, and later by Freud and Ferenczi" (1945, 42). In 1907, Sándor Ferenczi visited Jung at the Burghölzli. Towards the end of his life, Jung recalled that he "trained" Ferenczi in psychoanalysis, but that unfortunately, Ferenczi "remained stuck with Freud."[32]

In 1912, in his lectures at Fordham University, Jung argued that success in analysis depended upon how far the analyst had been analyzed himself. To be analyzed was the only solution. There were analysts, he noted, who thought they could get by solely with a self-analysis. He called this "Münchausen" psychology, and added that they would remain stuck (*CW* 4, § 449). Jung compared this necessity with the formal requirements of surgical training. Just as a surgeon required, in addition to technical knowledge, "a skilled hand, courage, presence of mind, and power of decision," consequently, an analyst required a serious and thorough "psychoanalytic training of his own personality" (§ 450). Jung's suggestion was quickly seconded by Freud. The same year, in "Recommendations to physicians practising psycho-analysis," Freud stated that he counted it as "one of the many merits of the Zurich school" that they had increasingly emphasized this demand, and embodied it (*SE* 12, 116).

In terms of current practices in psychiatry and psychotherapy, this was a striking departure. Accounts of individuals commencing the practice of hypnotic and suggestive practices often take the form of visiting Bernheim and Liébeault, learning induction techniques, watching them work and doing likewise.[33] It would have been unthinkable to have established the hypnotic treatment of the physician as an essential training requirement.

---

[31] On the genesis of this practice, see Falzeder, 1994, 2000, and Shamdasani, 2002.
[32] MP, 331.   [33] See for example Forel, 1937, 166–167.

Indeed, on his return from the psychoanalytic congress at Weimar in 1911, the American neurologist James Jackson Putnam stated in a talk:

Then I learned, to my surprise and interest, that a large part of these investigators had subjected themselves, more or less systematically, to the same sort of searching character-analysis to which their patients were being subjected at their hands. It is fast getting to be felt that an initiation of this sort is an indispensable condition of good work.[34]

It was with the adoption of the practice of training analysis that psychoanalysis differentiated itself from rival forms of psychotherapy, and ultimately ensured its continuance.[35]

What is not realized is that the proposal to establish training analysis was in part put forward to resolve the epistemological problem of the personal equation in psychoanalysis. The training analysis was the only means of assuring the transmission of analytic knowledge, through making sure that the "self-knowledge" of the prospective analyst developed along the prescribed lines. The financial benefits of this practice should also not be underestimated. Training analysis played a critical role in enabling private practice psychoanalysis to be a viable enterprise.

The issue of the range of permissible theoretical divergence in psychoanalysis came up with the dispute between Freud and Alfred Adler, which became significant for Jung. Adler (1870–1937) was a Viennese medical doctor. In 1902, Adler, together with Max Kahane, Rudolf Reitler, and Wilhelm Stekel began meeting regularly with Freud on Wednesday evenings. This formed the nucleus of what became the Vienna Psycho-Analytical Society. In 1910, he became the chairman of this society, and in 1911, he became the co-editor, together with Wilhelm Stekel, of the *Zentralblatt für Psychotherapie*. That year, his increasing divergence from Freud's theories became the issue of debate in heated sessions of the Vienna Psycho-Analytical Society. This led to his resignation from it, together with a number of supporters. They formed a Society for Free Psychoanalysis, which was later renamed the Society for Individual Psychology, Adler's new designation for his work. This formed the first major schism in psychoanalysis (see Handelbauer, 1998). In 1912 Adler published his work *On the Nervous Character*. On August 2, 1912, Jung informed Freud that he intended to scrutinize Adler's book critically and "underline its improprieties" (*FJL*, 512). A few months later, Jung informed Freud, "I have succeeded in descending into its depths, where I found some delightful things that deserve to be hung aloft."[36]

---

[34] "What is Psychoanalysis?" Putnam papers, CLM.
[35] See Falzeder, 1994, 2000, Shamdasani, 2002.   [36] December 7, 1912, 531.

Jung never published his review of Adler's work. However, a handwritten manuscript of it exists, entitled "On the theory of psychoanalysis: review of a few new works." He took this opportunity to criticize current styles of review. This was a response to the psychoanalytic criticisms of his recent works. What he was attempting was a psychology of the review process, the factors that hindered productive discussion of innovative works in psychology, and the attitudes required to foster such discussion. His comments still ring true today.

In many cases, reviewers failed to deal with the essence of a work, and overcompensated for their lack of competence through irrelevant and unjust criticism. In the cases where reviews were written by people of larger scientific horizons, there was the danger of apodictic judgment and authoritarian rejection. Individuals who had already achieved something in the same field do not consider that anyone else knows as much as they. Consequently, "One arms oneself against new ideas as against the evil enemy and reads each line *only* with the aim of finding the supposed weak point."[37] Due to this, one picked up on trifles such as errors in citations, grammatical errors, etc., without seriously engaging with the work. What was required was that "the competent person has to read the new book *with the feeling that he himself has possibly up to now done wrong*, and that now somebody will show him how things are really to be grasped" (*JP*, 2). Such an attitude was the sole condition of intellectual progress. If a reviewer failed to do this, the author was justified in judging his reviewer to be incompetent.

Turning to Adler's work, he stated that he had to apply the above considerations to himself. Contrary to his comments concerning Adler's work in his letters to Freud, Jung treated it sympathetically. Adler's work, he wrote, with its new terminology and approach, had presented him with a heavy endurance test. The work forced everyone who wanted to understand it to completely renounce their current views. The difficulty of this explained why the work had found no understanding with Freud's pupils Jung wrote and crossed out "and with Freud himself" (3). Adler had renounced the psychoanalytic movement, "as if a dogma ruled in the psychoanalytic movement, requiring steadfast loyalty" (4). This was a prejudice (it would not be long before Jung would radically reverse this judgment). Adler's action "makes one believe that the whole movement rests on a belief and – *Adler has another belief*" (*JP*, 2). Jung added: "If we thus want to renounce seeing a single truth in each scientific opinion we must say, that Adler offers us a new version of a theoretical approach to psychoanalytic results"(*JP*, 2). What was lacking was sufficient comparison

---

[37] "On the theory of psychoanalysis: review of a few new works," JP, 2.

with what Freud had already put forward. While Adler presented his work as an entirely new conception of the neuroses, this was deceptive, as the work really belonged to the psychoanalytic school, as a divergence. At this time, Jung was envisaging psychoanalysis as a pluralistic discipline capable of containing divergent viewpoints and approaches within it.

As to the work itself, in Jung's view, Adler's overall approach was finalistic. This Jung claimed, was as philosophically permissible as the causal standpoint. While such a standpoint wasn't completely lacking in psychoanalysis, it was inadequately considered, and Adler's work fulfilled an important gap. Here, Jung turned from philosophical considerations to psychological ones. He claimed that the preference for the final or the causal standpoint was temperamental, as James had "very beautifully" shown apropos the "tough-minded" and "tender-minded" in philosophy. This applied to the disputes in psychoanalysis: "We find between Freud and Adler a similar opposition, which is very strongly founded in personal disposition" (7). While Adler's perspective corresponded to the "tender-minded" viewpoint, Freud's corresponded to the "toughminded." In conclusion, he claimed that what was at work in the Adler–Freud opposition was a clash of unconscious world views.

In the autumn of 1912, Jung added a preface to his New York lectures on psychoanalysis, in which he noted that he became aware of Adler's work after the preparation of his lectures, and saw that they had reached similar conclusions on a number of points (*CW* 4, § 87).

A number of years later, Jung wrote a brief tribute to Adler, which he also did not publish. Here, he remarked that what was meaningful about Adler's work was that it confronted Freud's "overworked" concept of sexuality with equally important "individual urge for significance." From the biological perspective, this corresponded to the drive for the preservation of the species on the one hand, and of the individual on the other. Adler's other contribution was his illumination of the social context of neuroses.[38]

Jung and James

We have seen that Jung turned to James' typology as an attempt to understand the theoretical conflicts in psychoanalysis. They had met at Clark University in 1909. James took to Jung, and wrote to Flournoy that while Jung "professed great esteem for you and made a very pleasant

---

[38] "On Alfred Adler" (Jaffé, 1979, 63–64). On Jung, Adler wrote: "We owe a particular advance in the use of the concept of complex to the not very original psychologist Jung, whose own complex seems to be that of the fellow traveller" (Adler, 1935, 72–73).

impression," Freud "made on me personally the impression of a man obsessed with fixed ideas."[39]

In the draft of *Memories*, there was a chapter on James that was cut out of the published version. In this chapter, Jung gives an account of their contact, and attempts to spell out his intellectual debt to James. He recounts his meeting with James in 1909, and recalls that he paid him a visit the following year. He said that James was one of the most outstanding persons that he had ever met. He found him aristocratic, the image of a gentleman, yet free of airs and graces. He spoke to Jung without looking down on him, and Jung felt that they had an excellent rapport. He felt that it was only with Flournoy and James that he could talk easily, and that he revered his memory, and that he was a model for Jung. He found that both of them were receptive and of assistance with his doubts and difficulties, which he never found again. He esteemed James' openness and vision, which was particularly marked in his psychical research, which they discussed in detail. He saw the far-reaching significance of psychical research as a means of access to the psychology of the unconscious. Jung said that he was also very influenced by James' work on the psychology of religion, which also became for him a model, in particular, the way he managed to accept and let things stand, without forcing them into a theoretical bias. Jung said that he was very interested in James' pragmatic philosophy, which was of great importance for psychology.[40] To Kurt Wolff, Jung wrote of James, "aside from Théodore Flournoy he was the only outstanding mind with whom I could conduct an uncomplicated conversation. I therefore honour his memory and have always remembered the example he set me."[41] Of Flournoy and James, he also wrote, "I owe it mainly to these two researchers that I learnt to understand the essence of psychic disturbances within the setting of the human soul as a whole."[42] Thus by Jung's own admission, the effect of James' work upon his own was widespread and far-reaching.[43] Here I will consider three aspects of James' late work that became important for Jung: pragmatism, pluralism, and typology.

In his *Principles of Psychology*, in keeping with the general tendency of psychologists, James ventured to set aside metaphysical questions. What differentiated him from other psychologists was that rather than abandoning such questions, he subsequently took them up explicitly. Until recently, it has been a commonplace of James commentary that after

---

[39] 28 September 1909, ed. Le Clair, 1966, 224.   [40] CMS.
[41] 17 June 1958, *Letters* 2, 452.
[42] "Concerning the archetypes, with special reference to the anima concept" (1936), *CW* 9, pt. 1, § 113, trans. mod.
[43] On James and Jung, see Taylor, 1980.

1890 he progressively abandoned psychology for philosophy. By contrast, Eugene Taylor has argued with great cogency that far from abandoning psychology, James' philosophy of radical empiricism should also be considered as a critique of the metaphysical assumptions of the new psychology (including that of *The Principles*).[44] As such, radical empiricism was intended to pave the way for the development of psychology. This did not take place. In part, this was due to the ascendance of behaviorism and psychoanalysis, and to the fact that James left no school behind him. Just after James' death, Flournoy thought that the latter was because schools were no longer characteristic of the epoch, and because James didn't put forward a system "that has the rigid formulae and the complicated deductive adornments which are required to attract a crowd of awe-struck and disputatious disciples" (1911, 211). Flournoy was correct on the last point, but widely off the mark on the first, as psychology was soon set to enter what has been called the "era of the schools." However, James' late work did have a critical impact on Jung.

James' *Pragmatism* had appeared in 1907. It opened with a chapter on "The present dilemma in philosophy." This was the realization that up till now, the history of philosophy had largely been a clash of human temperaments (19). James claimed that the temperament of a philosopher formed their fundamental presupposition and final court of appeal. In adopting such a position, he was echoing a view advanced by Nietzsche in *Beyond Good and Evil*: "It has gradually become clear to me what every great philosophy has hitherto been: a confession on the part of its author and a kind of involuntary and unconscious memoir."[45] While Nietzsche was assiduously read by Jung, his work was not taken up by James. Nietzsche's approach to this question of the subjectivity of philosophy was through reformulating his conception of the subject in terms of a struggle for supremacy of conflicting drives.[46]

The particular temperamental difference that James singled out was that familiar in the history of philosophy as the contrast between rationalists and empiricists. He dubbed them tender-minded and tough-minded respectively. The former were rationalistic, intellectualistic, idealistic, optimistic, religious, freewillist, monistic, and dogmatical; the latter were empiricist, sensationalistic, materialistic, pessimistic, irreligious,

[44] See below, 177–178. Taylor, 1996a.
[45] 1886, 19. On Nietzsche's conception of philosophy as autobiography, see Parkes, 1994, 8–14. In 1794, Fichte had argued that "What sort of philosophy one chooses depends, therefore, on what sort of man one is; for a philosophical system is not a dead piece of furniture that we can reject or accept as we wish; it is rather a thing animated by the soul of the person who holds it," 1794, 16.
[46] See below, 192–194.

fatalistic, pluralistic, and skeptical. In addition to philosophy, these temperamental biases had great significance in government, art, religion, literature, and manners.

The conglomeration of traits was meant to designate the extreme ends of each spectrum. He was not only arguing that such temperamental differences existed, but that they were the ultimate factor in philosophy: "What the system pretends to be is a picture of the great universe of God. What it is, – and oh so flagrantly! – is the revelation of how intensely odd the personal flavour of some fellow creature is" (1907, 35). Philosophical systems, which purported to portray the constitution of the world, were in fact involuntary confessions of the psychological peculiarities of their authors. This was a reformulation of the notion of the personal equation. The new element that he was adding here was that this equation took on typical forms, such as tough or tender-minded. He was not, however, proposing a vast reductionist psychological taxonomy of culture. His solution to this problem was itself epistemological, and he proposed pragmatism as a philosophy that could satisfy both types. Age old philosophical conundrums could be resolved in each given concrete instance simply through invoking the pragmatic rule and by weighing up the resultant practical implications of each position.

In his 1907 account, James presented pragmatism as a means of resolving interminable philosophical impasses. For Peirce, as James read him, to attain clarity in our thoughts about an object, we have to consider the practical effects that they might have. Philosophical conflicts could be resolved by weighing up the concrete consequences of competing conceptions. One needed, as James put it, to extract the cash value from ideas. James considered all theories as instrumental. They were "mental modes of *adaptation* to reality" (127). Consequently, he held that "The truth of an idea is not a stagnant property inherent in it. Truth *happens* to an idea. It *becomes* true, is *made* true by events" (133). Ideas became true through enabling individuals to get into satisfactory relation to other parts of experience. In James' conception, pragmatism was intimately bound up with his late philosophy of radical empiricism in several important respects. The metaphysical attempt to construct an all-encompassing system that could function as a mirror image of the world, represented par excellence by Hegel's philosophy, was doomed to failure. Such systems failed to grasp the fact that the world as James put it, was unfinished, and still in the making. The abandonment of this task led to the critique of monism and intellectualism and the advocacy of pluralism. The pluralistic viewpoint, "is willing to believe there may ultimately never be an all-form at all, that the substance of reality may never get totally collected" (1909a, 34). Reality was a concatenation of singulars that could not be encompassed within a conceptual system. He concluded that "The word 'and' trails along after every sentence. Something always escapes. 'Ever not quite' has to be said of the best attempts made anywhere in the universe at attaining allinclusiveness" (321).

In September and October, Jung had been in America principally to deliver a course of lectures at Fordham University. In his foreword to the printed version of these lectures, dated autumn 1912, Jung stated that he had taken as his guiding principle, James' "pragmatic rule." Jung's copy of James' *Pragmatism* is inscribed "New York Oct 1912."[47]

Fundamental mentalities

At the beginning of 1913, discussions were held in the Zürich Psychoanalytical Society on Jung's new theories. Alphonse Maeder gave a paper in which he discussed the differences between Freud and Jung. In his abstract, Maeder noted that in the history of any science, there are usually two counterposed currents, which had been described in terms of different mentalities, such as Ostwald's distinction between classical and romantic researchers. Maeder asserted that such a distinction existed between Freud and Jung (1913, 622). In the ensuing discussion, Jung "left the question open as to which type of researcher he belonged to. James differentiated the materialist, agnostic, etc. tough minded, and the philosophical world-fearing tender minded. Freud [is] perhaps the first, Adler the last."[48] Maeder was claiming that the theoretical differences between Freud and Jung masked a more fundamental difference of mentalities, akin to Ostwald's discrimination of the romantic and classical types. While Jung had viewed the opposition of Adler and Freud in such a perspective, Maeder extended it to encompass the opposition between Freud and Jung.

Jung took up this line of thought at the Munich Psycho-Analytical Congress, which took place on September 7–8, 1913, where he spoke on psychological types. In retrospect, Jung stated that the origin of his work on psychological types was an attempt to grapple with the relative validity of the views of Freud and Adler, and to establish a position of his own

---

[47] Jung's copy of *Pragmatism* has numerous underlinings. The passage Jung cited here was the following: "You must bring out of each word its practical cash-value, set it at work within the stream of your experience. It appears less as a solution then, than as a program for more work, and more particularly as an indication of the ways in which existing realities may be changed. *Theories thus become instruments, not answers to enigmas, in which we can rest.* We don't lie back on them, we move forward, and, on occasion, make nature over again by their aid." There is a line in the margin of Jung's copy by this passage (86).

[48] MZP.

(Freeman, 1959, 389–390). At the same time it is also clear that he was taking up an issue that did not belong to the established subject matter of psychoanalysis, but rather to the tradition of individual or differential psychology.

At the outset, Jung contrasted the clinical portraits of hysteria and schizophrenia. He summed up the difference by stating that the former consisted in a centrifugal movement of the libido, while the latter consisted in a centripetal one. This centrifugal movement, in which the subject's interest was predominantly directed towards the outer world, he termed extraversion. The centripetal movement, in which the subject's interest was directed towards himself, he termed introversion.

Jung had first introduced the term introversion in 1909. In commenting on the fantasies in his case (which in private to Freud, he revealed to be that of his own daughter – a fact that brings it into line with Binet's procedure), he stated that the reveries of the child expressed the fact that part of the love that formerly belonged to a real object is now "introverted." This resulted in an increase of fantasy activity.[49] Introversion denoted an inner-directed movement of the libido. Whilst Jung broadened his conception of the libido, he maintained this view of introversion.

Returning to his 1913 presentation, Jung argued that the existence of disturbances such as schizophrenia and hysteria in which either extraversion or introversion predominated led to the question as to whether there existed "normal human types." He stated that the best observations along this line were by William James, and that James's descriptions showed that the difference between the types stemmed from different localizations of the libido. Jung added further parallels, such as Wilhelm Ostwald's division of men into classics and romantics, Wilhelm Worringer's differentiation of the processes of abstraction and empathy, Nietzsche's contrast between the Apollonian and the Dionysian, Franz Finck's contrast between transitive and intransitive verbs, and Otto Gross' distinction between two types of psychopathic inferiority. Descriptively speaking, there was little new about Jung's classification. However, with his libido theory, he claimed to be in a position to give an account for the mechanism that gave rise to such typological differences.

Finally, Jung took up his application of James' categories to Freud and Adler in his draft review of Adler's work, but now reframed this in terms of his own terminology. In contrast to Maeder, who had presented Freud and Jung as counterpoised types, Jung argued that Freud's work presented an example of an extraverted theory, and that Adler's work represented an example of an introverted theory. He concluded: "The difficult task of

---

[49] "On the conflict of the infantile soul," *CW* 17, § 13.

the future will be to create a psychology, which will be equally fair to both types."[50] Such a psychology would be able to surpass the conflict between introverted and extraverted theories, through presenting a theory that was not shaped by a typological bias, and hence resolve the problem of the personal equation.

"Our laboratory is the world"

In 1909, Jung gave up his post at the Burghölzli asylum, and turned to private practice psychotherapy. In 1910, he became the first president of the International Psychoanalytic Association. He held this position until his resignation in 1914, when he also gave up his post as a lecturer at the University of Zürich. It wasn't until 1933 that he held another academic position, when he was awarded a professorship at the Swiss Federal Institute of Technology in Zürich, and began to lecture there. It was during this twenty-year period that Jung elaborated his major theories, a period of institutional independence from the psychiatric hospital and the university, which became the main operative bases of psychiatry and psychology respectively.

The question of the status of psychology and its standing as a science became important for Jung around the time of his break with Freud. It plays a critical role in his separation from the psychoanalytic movement, and in how he came to formulate his psychology. In 1912, he published a paper entitled "New paths in psychology." He commenced this with a short account of the history of modern psychology. It was doctors, and in particular, neurologists [Nervenarzt] who had need of psychological knowledge if they wanted to help their patients, due to the fact that nervous disorders were of psychic [seelischer] origin. In this respect, psychiatric text books were of no help, and neither was experimental psychology, as "He who wants to get to know the human soul will find out next to nothing from experimental psychology" (*CW* 7, § 409, trans. mod.). He recommended that one

hang up exact science and put away the scholar's gown, to say farewell to his study and wander with human heart through the world, through the horror of prisons, mad houses and hospitals, through drab suburban pubs, in brothels and gambling den, through the salons of elegant society, the stock exchanges, the socialist meetings, the churches, the revivals and ecstasies of the sects, to experience love, hate and passion in every form in one's body. (*CW* 7, § 409)

---

[50] *CW* 6, § 882, trans. mod. Sándor Ferenczi contested this characterization of the typological differences between Freud and Jung, and contrastingly stated that the critical difference was between a psychology of the unconscious and a psychology of consciousness respectively (Ferenczi, 1914, 66–67).

This was an impassioned plea for the psychologist to experience life to the full, with images evocative of Zola and Dostoevsky. There was a great gulf between what daily life expected of psychology, and what science called psychology. This gulf, he claimed, was what led to the development of psychoanalysis. His position was close to James' advocacy of functional psychology over structural psychology. What was required was a psychology that was of practical use. In 1924, he contended that for analytical psychology, the laboratory was the world. Its purpose was the "better adaptation of human behavior," and abstract science was merely its by-product.[51]

In 1914, he presented a paper before the Psycho-Medical Society in London, "On psychological understanding," in which he contrasted Freud's analytic-reductive method with the constructive method of the Zürich school. The former method was based on causality, and thus was in line with the contemporary understanding of scientific explanation as being causal. He questioned this equation, especially in the field of psychology. The shortcoming of the analytic-reductive mode of understanding, through tracing back to antecedent elements, was that it only dealt with half of the picture, and failed to grasp the living meaning of phenomena. Someone who attempted to understand Goethe's *Faust* in such a manner would be like someone who tried to understand a Gothic cathedral by considering its mineralogical aspect.[52] The living meaning "only lives when we experience it in and through ourselves" (§ 398). In as much as life was essentially new, it could not be understood merely retrospectively. "The constructive standpoint asks how, out of this present psyche, a bridge can be built into its own future".[53] He called causal explanations "objective understanding," and contrasted this with subjective understanding. The handwritten manuscript, written in English, contains the following statement which was deleted from the published version, "the worth and the worthlessness of modern experimental psychology and of Freud's psychoanalysis reposes on objective understanding."[54]

There was one element that the constructive method shared with the reductive method: it too sought to arrive at types. At this date, he held that constructive method did not produce anything like a scientific theory.

---

[51] "Analytical psychology and education," *CW* 17, §§ 171–172.
[52] *CW* 3, § 396. In his Fordham lectures, Jung had used the same analogy in critiquing Freud's sexual terminology: "Such a terminology would be tantamount to treating Cologne cathedral in a text-book of mineralogy, on the ground that it consisted very largely of stones," *CW* 4, § 279. The analogy that Jung used here was very close to that employed by Dilthey to make the same point.
[53] *Ibid.*, § 399, trans. mod.   [54] "On psychological understanding," JP.

However, the antiquity of the concepts it used testified to their usefulness. The constructive method needed to produce many more experiences, before a scientific theory of lines of psychological development could be produced (§ 424). Thus while a scientific theory remained an ultimate goal, the time for this had not yet arrived. The value of the constructive method was that it gave rise to concepts which were practically useful. In the manuscript, he wrote apropos the idealistic standpoint that no one knew whether it was true or not: "But it doesn't matter: it works. That is the criterion for its truth."[55] This indicates the extent to which he had adopted James' pragmatic rule as a means of resolving the issue of the scientific standing of psychology.

Jung also termed the constructive method "synthetic." In 1917, he noted that "just as analysis (the causally reductive procedure) disintegrates the symbol into its components, so the synthetic procedure synthesises the symbol into a universal and comprehensible expression."[56] The notion that analysis must be followed by synthesis was a common refrain in psychology. For example, in 1884, the British psychologist James Sully argued that analysis, which resolved psychical phenomena into their constituent parts, needed to be supplemented by "a synthetic reconstruction of the process of mental formation or development" (8). In 1900, the French psychologist Théodule Ribot argued that "analysis has to be completed by synthesis. All imaginative creation, small or large, is organic, and requires a principle of unity: thus there is also a synthetic factor which it will be necessary to determine" (9).

In 1916, Jung continued his reflections on the scientific status of psychology in "The structure of the unconscious," a paper published originally in French in Flournoy's journal, the *Archives de Psychologie*. Despite the fact that it ran against the grain of the scientific spirit, psychology had to recognize a plurality of principles. Only by doing this could the "sinking of psychology be avoided." Here, psychology was indebted to the preparatory work of James. He commented on the predicament of individual psychology:

With regard to the individual psychology, science must give itself up. To speak of a scientific individual psychology is "contradictio in adjecto." It is necessarily always only the collective part of an individual psychology which can be an object of science, for the individual is according to its definition the unique and incomparable . . . Every individual psychology must have its own textbook, for the general textbook contains only collective psychology. (*CW* 7, § 484, trans. mod.)

---

[55] "On psychological understanding," JP.
[56] "The psychology of the unconscious processes," 1917b, 418.

As science dealt with the universal, only the common or collective elements of individuals could be subject to science. Due to the limitless variation of individuals, there was much that could not be circumscribed by science. However, these elements, and in particular, certain lines of psychological development, were of great practical significance in psychotherapy. These lines of development were partially individual and partially collective. Consequently, their correctness could not be proved by science. Their validity was shown by their value for life.

Such a view, while unacceptable to those for whom science was a superordinate principle, was acceptable to those who viewed science as a means "to corroborate the data of their inner experiences and help them achieve general validity" (§ 494, trans. mod.). This statement is critical. Not only does it enunciate what he was attempting to achieve in his psychology, it also articulates precisely how so many individuals have continued to read him: as a means of corroborating and validating their inner experiences.

These statements indicate that Jung had adopted James' pragmatism as a critical part of his methodology, as well as acknowledging pluralism as a basic necessity for psychology. In both of these respects, James' epistemology provided theoretical ground for some of the issues at stake in Jung's conflict with Freud, and the basis for his own radically different methodology.

The Zürich school

In 1926 Maeder wrote that psychoanalysis had become a dogmatic international school centered around a leader, and that it had issued from a Judeo-German spirit. When transplanted to Switzerland, and Zürich in particular, it had taken on a democratic form, corresponding to the Swiss mentality (577–579). In this regard, Jung had written to Maeder in 1915 that "despite the independence of individual persons [Köpfe] in our circle we must appear united to the outside, according to the principle of Switzerland."[57]

The work of the Zürich school has subsequently been regarded as stemming solely from Jung. This portrait was enhanced by the account in *Memories*, where he stated that after his break with Freud, he had lost his friends and acquaintances, with the exception of Riklin and Maeder (190). Freud himself admitted that most of his followers had come to him by way of Zürich (*SE* 14, 27). The larger share of these figures, except those in Switzerland, remained with Freud. On July 10, 1914, the

---

[57] December 4, 1915, Maeder papers.

Zürich Psychoanalytical Society voted by fifteen to one to cede from the International Psychoanalytical Association.

During the discussion, it was agreed that in Freud's *History of the Psychoanalytical Movement*, psychoanalysis was bound to the teaching of one individual in a manner which the Zürich group considered incompatible with the principle of free research.[58] In 1914, the now renamed Association for Analytical Psychology had thirty-eight members, and in 1916 when the Psychological Club was formed, it had over sixty members. Thus in Zürich itself, Jung had significant support.

The tendency to view Jung as the founder of a school of psychology has obscured the extent to which his work was a collaborative enterprise, and the nature of the contributions made by others to it. This tendency is particularly marked in the case of Jung's work on psychological types, and was encouraged by some of his retrospective accounts, such as the following:

> I saw first the introverted and extraverted attitudes, then the functional aspects, then which of the four functions is predominant . . . it took me quite a long time to discover that there is another type than the thinking type . . . There are, for instance, feeling types. And after a while I discovered that there are intuitive types. They gave me much trouble . . . And the last, and the most unexpected, were the sensation type. And only later I saw that these are naturally the four aspects of conscious orientation.[59]

There are several ways to view this situation (the genesis of types is by no means the only example). First, one could view it simply as a failure to supply full acknowledgment of individual contributions of co-workers and predecessors. In his 1925 seminar, while giving an account of the subjective aspects of the development of his book on *Types*, Jung candidly stated

> I could perfectly well say that this is the way the book came about and make an end of it there. But there is another side, a weaving about among mistakes, impure thinking, etc., etc., which is always difficult for a man to make public. He likes to give you the finished product of his directed thinking and have you understand that so it was born in his mind, free of his weakness. (32)

He went on to compare a thinker's attitude to his intellectual life to that of a woman to her erotic life. In a similar way, a man "does not want to tell of the secret alliances, the *faux pas* of his mind . . . He thinks that if he tells the truth in this field it is equivalent to turning over the keys

---

[58] MZP.

[59] Evans, 1957, 320. In an undated manuscript entitled "Notice on the origin of psychological types," (JP) Jung gave the following sequence of discovery: "First thinking and feeling, then sensation ("fonction du réel") and finally intuition."

of his citadel to the enemy" (32). From this perspective, his subsequent
accounts would simply be further examples of this all too human tendency
of the thinking man.

A decade later, in his lectures on psychological typology at the Swiss
Federal Institute of Technology, he commented on Wilhelm Ostwald's
statement that the classic type (which corresponded to Jung's introvert)
destroyed the traces so that one couldn't see how he arrived at his conclusions. According to Jung, the introverted thinker:

does not know exactly where his ideas originate and is afraid of being mortally
wounded. The Extravert is always willing to speak of his thoughts and their origin,
but the Introvert is more introspective, he knows more about this and is more
careful even if his idea can be traced to the outside, he thinks that [they] probably
came from the inside, and he has a mysterious feeling that these thoughts are in
some way illegitimate, so he washes out their traces.[60]

Thus the introverted thinker covers his tracks, for fear of the illegiti-
macy of his ideas. From Jung's own perspective, it would be legitimate to
view his thinking as an example of such introverted thinking. The consequences for anyone studying his work are immense. He went on to
say:

The pupil can find no way of approaching him for he has destroyed his footsteps,
there is no historical approach. If someone can really get into this process he
will realise how difficult it is to see the origin of these things, and to know how
introverted thinking works. (*Ibid.*)

The third way in which one could view this policy is to see it as part of
his encyclopedic conception of psychology. In an encyclopedia, individual
contributions are generally subordinated.

Whatever the reasons for this policy, its effects are nevertheless clear,
particularly when coupled with the ahistorical manner in which psychology has been taught and studied. Jung's psychological types – and indeed,
much of his work as a whole – have been viewed as a solitary creation,
rather than arising of out a tradition of research and collaborative work.

Types in dialogue

It is important then to grasp that Jung's work on psychological types represented the summation of collective research. Jung's pupil C. A. Meier
gave the following account of the respective contributions of Jung's colleagues. He stated that Hans Schmid showed Jung that extraversion was
not necessarily correlated with feeling; Toni Wolff was instrumental in

[60] *Notes of Jung's 1935/1936 ETH Lectures*, May 22, 1936, 6.

introducing the functions of sensation and intuition; and finally intuition was dealt with critically by Emil Medtner.[61] According to Jung's son, Franz Jung, Jung met on a regular basis with a sort of committee consisting of Emil Medtner, Toni Wolff, Adolf Keller, and some theologians, which worked together in the preparation of *Psychological Types*, particularly focusing on the issue of terminology.[62] In a circular letter to members of the Association for Analytical Psychology, Jung suggested that they should hold meetings "to establish unanimity in theoretical basic viewpoints, and especially in the definition and application of technical terms."[63]

Jung had conducted a lengthy correspondence with his colleague Hans Schmid on the type problem, which was initially planned for publication.[64] By 1913, Jung had put forward the existence of two types, which represented the extremes of tendencies present in everyone. The characteristics of each type and how they related to one another needed filling out, and this was the subject of Jung's correspondence with Schmid.

Schmid (1881–1932), a Swiss psychiatrist, first met Jung in 1911. He subsequently went to Zürich to study with Jung and became a member of the Zürich group of the International Psycho-Analytical Association. In 1913 he started a psychiatric practice in Basel, and was among those who sided with Jung when he broke with Freud. Jung's correspondence with Schmid reveals that not only much of the substance of Jung's own letters but of Schmid's as well found their way into *Psychological Types*.

In his work on the type problem, Jung was attempting to formulate a metalanguage of psychological interaction that would account for why individuals agreed and why they differed. In the correspondence, the types are strongly delineated: one is either one or the other. Jung identified himself as an introvert, and Schmid identified himself as an extravert. In the course of their correspondence, it quickly became apparent how difficult it was to provide a detailed description of the types, and their relation to each other, that both would assent to. In the language of their correspondence, the introvert did not assent to the extravert's account of

---

[61] 1986, 244–245. Medtner gave a series of lectures on intuition to the Psychological Club in 1919, which he subsequently published (1923). In dealing with intuition, Medtner noted that he was not sure if what he had to say was connected with "analytical psychotypology" or not (22–23). His emphasis was on another typology of types of thinking, for which he took Schiller as his point of departure. He introduced three contrasts: intuitive-discursive, which he termed a gnoseological [related to the theory of knowledge] opposition, intuitive-instinctive – a psychological opposition, and intuitive-speculative – a thinking typological opposition (33). In the discussion following this lecture, Jung spoke of another contrast, intuitive-perceptive, which he made for his own use (49). On Medtner, see Ljunggren, 1994.
[62] Personal communication.   [63] Reproduced in Shamdasani, 1998a, 38–39.
[64] Personal communication, Franz Jung.

introversion and extraversion, and vice versa. At one point, Jung stated, "the Archimedean point outside psychology, with the help of which we could lift psychology off its hinges, is hardly to be found."[65] The debate on types between Jung and Schmid did not seem to make for mutual understanding – in fact it seemed to have the opposite effect, of creating an ever widening gulf of misunderstanding. In his final letter to Schmid, Jung wrote: "Your letter has confirmed in me the conviction, that agreement on fundamental principles is impossible."[66] He summed up the basic problem in the following way:

It seems to me that one can agree scientifically about the general principles of the types, but not about the more subtle details. For that, language is not absolutely sufficient. Under the verbal signs of concepts, each thinks just what he understands.[67]

In this statement, the failure of agreement is put down to the nature of language. For Jung at this juncture, to parody Wittgenstein, there could be nothing other than a plurality of private languages. In his introduction to *Psychological Types*, he acknowledged that he owed a great deal of clarification to his correspondence with Schmid, and much of it had entered his book in a revised form. He had decided not to publish the correspondence, as it would generate confusion.[68]

Moltzer's intuition

During this period, one of Jung's closest associates was Maria Moltzer. Jung's writings contain one solitary acknowledgment of her. Concerning the intuitive type, Jung stated: "The credit for having discovered the existence of this type belongs to M. Moltzer" (*CW* 6, § 773). There exist manuscripts of talks that she presented in 1916 to Jung's Psychological Club in Zürich. One of these sheds remarkable light on how the problem of psychological types was pursued during this period. Moltzer stated:

In my opinion a misuse has been made within the last years of the not yet fully developed conceptions of types. Oblivious of the enormous difficulties with which this question is of necessity bound up, all people were forced into one of the two categories and judged according to this very superficial diagnosis. One was extraverted and must therefore think thus and so. This seemed to me a very rough

---

[65] Ed. Iselin, 1982, April 4, 1915, 40.   [66] *Ibid.*, September 6, 1915, 106.

[67] 109. The breakdown of the dialogue with Schmid seems to have been part of a wider problem that Jung had with collegiality. Schmid's daughter recalls, "my father was one of a very few who stood up against him. Mrs. Jung used to say that she was really sorry that Jung didn't have any real friends." Interview with Jeanne Boller-Schmid, CLM, 8.

[68] Jung and Schmid remained friends, and Jung would refer patients to him (Jung to Henry Murray, May 2, 1925, Murray papers).

abuse of the personality . . . It would mean a neglect in the stage of development to treat the patient only from the point of view of type. Then it must be added that a personality is not only conditioned by its type . . . To look only at the type means as much as obliterating the personality and identifying it entirely with its type. The solving of personal problems is difficult and there are many patients who are only too glad to find a way of escape from their tasks, and feel themselves justified in taking refuge in a new collectivity through the identification with their type . . . Just as the Vienna school reduced practically everything to sexuality, after it had discovered its value, – so in the last years has the Zürich school reduced everything to types. We must guard against this danger as centralizing on two types leads to the reduction to formula of all psychic life, – which threatens to annihilate the new life of the introduction of the libido-theory.[69]

This statement demonstrates the extent to which typology was a central research topic in the Zürich school as a whole during this period, and indicates that its utilization played a dominant role in the analyses that were conducted. Moltzer's judgment on the therapeutic validity of its utilization was resoundingly negative. In 1916, there could have been few more powerful indictments of the Zürich school, from one of its leading members, than to be likened to its much derided foe, psychoanalysis.

To rectify this situation, she stated that there were "various mixed types, with more or less developed introverted and extraverted attitudes." In addition, she recalled the fact that at the last meeting of the Club she had introduced the existence of a third type – the intuitive type. Intuition, which stood at the threshold of the unconscious, "registers the impressions received (in the unconscious) and brings the compensating tendency over into the conscious." Intuition was a phylogenetically earlier mode of adaptation, from which the other functions of thinking and sensation had been differentiated. It was the origin of religion. There were three categories in this type – those inclined to thinking, those inclined to action, and artists. This type had its characteristic neurosis in compulsion-neurosis, and some forms of mania and manic depression as its psychosis.

Her new model replaced Jung's – his types were sublated as derivatives of the more primordial intuitive type. He had linked hysteria to extraversion, and schizophrenia to introversion. From a nosological point of view, this raised the question of what became of the other diagnostic categories. She neatly followed this with her designation of the corresponding neuroses and psychoses of the intuitive type. In 1918, she resigned from the Club, and went her separate way.

The details of Moltzer's psychobiological tracing of the genesis of intuition and its relation to thinking and feeling were not taken on by Jung.

[69] Reproduced in Shamdasani 1998b, 113–114.

However, the existence of the intuitive type was taken up by Jung in a reworked form.

Psychology's relativity problem

From around 1915 onwards, the schisms in the Freudian school, principally those of Adler and Jung, were seized upon by critics of psychoanalysis as refutation of the claims of each school. It was commonly argued that their claims were mutually contradictory, and that there was no means of adjudicating between them – the parting of ways and mutual recriminations were taken as graphic proof of this.

A clear example of this kind is provided by Stern. Though from a later period, it exemplifies a common criticism. In 1935, Stern criticized Jung together with Freud and Adler. The common element of their work was that "The 'Unconscious' is elevated into a kind of mythical force that sets up a secret despotism in the individual" (37). The limitations of this internal dualism within the personality or divided subject was that the basic urge was conceived of differently by each school. He objected to the obstinacy and monotony in which adherents of these schools explained everything using the same schemas of interpretation. He held that this had nothing to do with science. The shortcomings of each of these schools lay in their proclivity for what he termed monosymptomatic explanations. By their very nature, these could not do justice to the complexity of individuals, for which pluralistic explanations were prerequisites. Hence the internal division between the various schools of depth psychology relativized the truth claims of each of them. He concluded that while in a therapeutic or pedagogical context the adherence to such truths might help to bring about a state of suggestibility, they were valueless as psychological theory. This was a snide way of saying that the practical utility of such psychological theories for psychotherapists lay solely in their ability to foster hypnotic induction, while denying that this was the case.

Jung's next public statement on the type problem came in 1917 in his *The Psychology of the Unconscious Processes: An Overview of the Modern Theory and Method of Analytical Psychology*. Here, he attempted to deal with the problem posed by the schism in the psychoanalytic movement and the relativity of the claims of each school. He commenced by presenting a case and providing a cogent interpretation of it from a Freudian perspective, and then an equally cogent interpretation of the same case from an Adlerian perspective. In this example, he was exploring the consequences which followed from allowing a plurality of explanatory principles in psychology to exist. As to the question as to which of these contradictory theories was correct, the answer one gave depended upon the relative value one placed upon love or power in one's scheme of values.[70] Those who gave higher significance to love would favour Freud's explanation, while those who gave higher significance to power would favour Adler's. The difference between Freud's and Adler's theories was the outcome of their typological differences.[71] Both theories were partially true (when appropriately applied to individuals of the corresponding psychological type). Their error lay in their generalization. He noted: "The relative rightness of the two hostile theories is explained by the fact that each one draws its material from cases that prove the correctness of the theory."[72] Thus the criteria for assessing the adequacy of a psychological theory no longer lay in the fact that it was able to cite empirical evidence in its favour, nor appeal to therapeutic efficacy. That would be too easy. Rather, for a psychological theory to achieve universal validity, it had ultimately to provide an explanation for the differences between psychological theories, and account for how such contradictory theories could arise. In other words, what was required was a psychology of psychology. The first "subject" of psychology was psychology itself, and psychology had to study the psychology-making process.

While up till now Jung's presentations of psychological typology had consisted of static portrayals of individual temperament, in this text this was augmented with a dynamic portrait in a section entitled, "The development of the types of introversion and extraversion in the analytical process." In the process of analysis, the contrary (hitherto unconscious) function developed, which led "beyond the type over to individuation, and thereby to a new relation to the world and spirit" (440–441, trans. mod.). He characterized individuation as consisting in the transit from a one-sided typological orientation to a state in which one's capacities for introversion, here equated with thinking, and extraversion, here equated with feeling, became equipotentially developed. An extreme one-sided orientation was seen as the hallmark of neurosis. This implicitly presented a new solution to the personal equation: the magnitude of subjective bias

---

[70] 1917b, 391, trans. mod. The psychiatrist Ernst Kretschmer agreed with this (1934, 261).

[71] 392. This was criticized by William McDougall: "Could anything be more unfortunate? Freud with his lifelong intense interest in the inner life of man and his highly elaborated system, is classed with those who are not interested in the inner life and cannot make a system. Adler, who has a large popular following and whose voluminous writings are peculiarly lacking in system and order, with those who cannot exert personal influence and who are paralysed by their self-criticism and produce work of finished perfection" (1929, 293). On McDougall, see below 196, 268.

[72] Freud wrote to Karl Abraham that Jung "seems not to have gone beyond the crude conversion into theory of the fact that he came across myself and Adler. We meet in the 'archaic'" (July 13, 1917, ed. Falzeder, 2002, 353). I thank Ernst Falzeder for drawing my attention to this.

was equated with the degree of lack of personality development. It was only through the process of individuation that one could minimize the subjective bias, and attain what he later termed psychic objectivity. He further refined his views on the paradoxical position of psychology. His psychology had two sides: one that was entirely practical, and another that was entirely theoretical. On the one hand, it constituted a method of treatment or education, and on the other, it was a scientific theory, related to other sciences. This division was one that he maintained throughout his subsequent career. What he had yet to do was to articulate how these parts related.

The theory of attitudes

"Bouvard drew his arguments from La Mettrie, Locke, Helvétius; Pécuchet from Monsieur Cousin, Thomas Reid and Gérando. The former gave his allegiance to experience, the ideal was everything for the latter. There was something of Aristotle in the one, of Plato in the other, and they had discussions." Gustave Flaubert, *Bouvard and Pécuchet*, 203

In 1919, Jung wrote to André Tridon that he was writing a book on the "problem of Attitude and Types of Attitude." The aim of this book was to reconcile the contradictory views of the psychoanalytic schools through "a theory of attitude and a different appreciation of symbolism."[73] The work appeared in 1921, entitled *Psychological Types*.

Jung's description of the psychological types passed over into general usage. It is his only work to have given rise to a continued outpouring of experimental studies, by means of questionnaires and statistical tests (part of the curse that James predicted!). *Psychological Types* presented a wealth of erudition.[74]

---

[73] Cited in Tridon, 1919, 9. Jung told James Kirsch that "he was very busy with patients at that time and just did not find the time to write, although he felt great pressure to express his new ideas. In this conflict between his duty to his patients and to that of the general public, the unconscious hit him with an illness. He came down with whooping-cough, a condition in which people feel quite well in the daytime but suffer coughing-attacks at night. Since it was an infectious disease, he had to cancel all his appointments with patients. He asked a secretary, who had had whooping-cough herself and therefore was immune, to take dictation from him. He dictated all day every day and completed the first 583 pages in the six weeks of his quarantine" (Kirsch, 1975, 59–60). The absence of a handwritten manuscript for *Psychological Types* lends credence to this.

[74] It is possible that Jung had some assistance concerning the historical aspects of the question, which made up the larger share of the book. In an interview, Ernst Harms recalls that he was analyzed by Jung for no fee, and that Jung questioned him about sources on aspects of typology, and made notes of the information that Harms provided. Interview with Ernst Harms, CLM, 8. However, Harms does not make clear precisely when these discussions took place. Elsewhere, he refers to his "contact with Jung since the early twenties" (1967, ix), which would suggest that they took place after Jung published *Psychological Types*.

He commenced his work with some reflections on the history of psychology. While there had always been psychology, "objective psychology" was only a recent development. The general consensus that observation and experience were sufficient to provide the basis for an objective psychology was fallacious. This was because the aim of science went beyond description, to the establishment of laws. Through the use of concepts, the empirical was transcended. This was because conceptions "will always be a product of the subjective psychological constellation of the investigator" (*CW* 6, §9). He designated this as the personal equation, which showed itself already in observation: "*One sees what one can best see oneself*" (*ibid.*). This effect was even stronger in the presentation of observations, and in their interpretation. The ideal of objectivity was an impossibility: all one could hope for was that one didn't view things *too* subjectively. Recognizing the effects of the personal equation, which constituted the subjective determination of knowledge, constituted the precondition for the scientific appraisal of other individuals. This required a high degree of self-knowledge on the part of the investigator.

The possibility of an objective scientific psychology hinged not only upon the recognition of the significance of the personal equation, but of finding a means of evading the infinite regress and relativity that it potentially led to. If all knowledge, if all psychology, is determined by one's personal equation, what chance is there of any objectivity, of any means of adjudicating between the claims of rival theories, or any possibility of a unified science of psychology? Jung's attempted solution was to provide a theory of the subjective determinants of the personal equation. Not only would this secure the scientific and objective status of psychology, psychology itself would be a superordinate science, as it alone could provide an explanation of the subjective determinants of all knowledge. Its success or failure hinged upon whether, in its own terms, it could provide a theory of the personal equation that attained to a level of objectivity. This issue was predominant in his treatment of previous typological systems, which takes up the bulk of *Psychological Types*.[75] In his formulation here, the personal equation was principally conditioned not by biographical experiences, but by an innate disposition – that is, one's type. Thus if one's psychology constituted one's subjective confession, as Jung held, this was not because it consisted in the transformation of details of one's biography into theoretical terms: rather, it designated the fact that one was constrained to view the world from a particular mind set.

Jung took up this issue in his discussion of the German poet and dramatist Friedrich Schiller's work on the type problem. As Schiller belonged to

---

[75] To Aniela Jaffé, he stated that the psychologist must depend upon historical and literary parallels to exclude the worst errors of personal bias (*Memories*, 222). This indicates why *Psychological Types* was above all a historical study.

a type, he was compelled to give a one-sided description. In this respect, the example of Schiller was exemplary of a wider problem:

> The limitations of our conceptions and knowledge become nowhere so apparent than in psychological presentations, where it is almost impossible for us to depict any other picture than the one whose main outlines lie marked out in our own soul. (§ 102, trans. mod.)

The limitations of Schiller's treatment of the subject stemmed from his own typology. Jung argued that the same was true of Nietzsche, James and previous typologists. In this passage, the problem of the personal equation takes the form of a psychological solipsism. By what means is it possible for the statements of a psychologist to refer primarily to anything other than themselves? In addition, it raises the question, by what criteria can one differentiate Jung's typology from those that preceded it.

His historical presentation of the subject embodied a position concerning the status of psychology. He considered the treatment of the type problem in theology, poetry, aesthetics, philosophy, biography, psychiatry, and philosophy, and while finding useful descriptions and examples, ultimately finds them all insufficient. It is only after this survey of the redundancy of previous thinking on the subject in all these disciplines that he provided his own general description of the types. What is striking is that he gives scant account of prior and noticeably similar typological differentiations in psychology. Thus there is no mention of the typologies of Charcot, Binet or Stern. In his introduction to the first edition, he stated that this historical approach was adopted due to the conviction that the psychological views put forward were of a wide significance and potential application. Thus this approach served to demonstrate the pre-eminence of psychology, and its almost unlimited range.

The narrative voice of the book is of someone who has surmounted the type problem, and is able to survey human history from an Olympian standpoint, and provide an understanding of the hitherto unresolvable conflicts through the new standpoint of a psychological typology. It is precisely this tone that the publication of the Schmid letters would have disrupted. In *Psychological Types*, Jung refrained from mentioning his own psychological type, which, given the thesis of the book, is a significant lacuna.[76] Consequently, the reader is not provided with a key to read

---

[76] Iselin, ed., 1982, 39. In his correspondence with Schmid, Jung designates himself as an introvert. When posed the question as to his psychological type by John Freeman, Jung replied that his superior functions were those of thinking and intuition (Freeman, 1959, 390). C. A. Meier commented, "With his typology book, Jung, in keeping with his own introversion, is attempting a sort of apologia for this attitude." Meier attempted to justify this temperamental bias, by stating that it served to balance the predominant extraversion of Western civilization (1989, 92).

his "personal equation." In this respect, his procedure markedly differed from that of James.

The development of Jung's work on psychological types was accompanied with a growing distance from pragmatism. In 1915, he had written to Hans Schmid that he had needed the viewpoints of the pragmatic tendency of modern philosophy. He added, "although I make no secret of my unbounded admiration for Schiller and William James, I cannot help admitting also that pragmatism leaves me with a rather barren feeling. I can't help myself: it is too 'business like.'"[77] It was Henri Bergson's concept of the irrational which had freed him from the barrenness of pragmatism.[78]

In his extended discussion of James's types in *Psychological Types*, he characterized pragmatism as nothing but a makeshift, which "presupposes too great a resignation and almost unavoidably leads to a drying of creativeness" (§ 541). He held that the solution to the problem of opposites could not be solved through pragmatism, but only through a positive act of creation which assimilated the opposites, and that it was Nietzsche as opposed to James or Bergson who pointed the way forward in this respect. While it is not clear from this passage what such a creative act might consist in, it is clear that Jung found the relativistic approach of pragmatism to opposed conceptions unsatisfactory.

In *Psychological Types*, the issue of the personal equation was linked also to that of pluralism. Jung described the assumption that there was only one psychology, or fundamental psychological principle, as an "intolerable tyranny." Prime examples of such psychologies were those of Freud and Adler. Their psychologies were equally one-sided, and the expression of their own type. What was required was the recognition of the existence of a multiplicity of individuals, each with their own particular psychologies. At the same time, it was critical that the level of variation was not limitless: otherwise, there was little that could be encompassed with the span of a scientific psychology, as a science was supposed to deal with the collective and universal. Thus Jung developed a schema of eight main types. These fell into two main groups – introverts and extraverts. Each of these was further subdivided into four sub groups, characterized by the main function of the individual.

The elegance of this model was that it reconciled the aim of developing a universal model of psychological functioning: on the one hand, the attitudes of introversion and extraversion, and the functions of thinking, feeling, intuition and sensation were present in everyone. As such, it

---

[77] "Business like" is in English in the original. The Schiller here is the English philosopher and colleague of James, F. C. S. Schiller.
[78] See below, 207–210.

followed the traditional conventions of the psychology of the personality and the philosophy of mind. On the other hand, the preponderance of a particular function enabled him to account for the variation of individuals and their corresponding psychologies. The one-sidedness of Freud and Adler was replaced with an eightfold model of different psychological profiles. Otherwise put, psychology would henceforth be written in eight keys. Hence *Psychological Types* critically both allowed for, and limited, the level of variation of individuals. Jung had drawn back from the extreme position that he had put forward a few years earlier, in which each individual required his own textbook.

He maintained that the problem with psychological theories to date was that they had presupposed the uniformity of human psychology, in an analogous way to which natural science assumes one and the same nature as a basis. It follows from this assumption that the process of theory-making would be the same in different individuals. The existence of diverse theories of the essence of psychic processes demonstrated that this was not the case. Each investigator naturally presumes that his own theory is the only correct one, as "he does not realize that the psychology he sees is his psychology, and on top of that is the psychology of his type" (§ 849). As a result, the different psychologies corresponding to the seven other types is not taken into consideration. At best, such a theory would correspond to one eighth of the truth. The success of particular theories was not purely due to the effects of mass suggestion. Rather it was because those who assented to it found in it something they could understand and appreciate.[79] The fact that other individuals supported a theory indicated that it was not purely idiosyncratic, but corresponded to a typical attitude.

He was not denying the existence of a uniformity of human psychology – it was precisely this, he noted, that had led him to the hypothesis of a collective unconscious. But alongside this homogeneity, there lay an "equally great" heterogeneity of the conscious psyche. This point is worth stressing, as Jung is traditionally associated only with the former point of view. It was only at the foundations of consciousness that homogeneity existed. But a theory based only on this aspect ignored the historical and individual differentiation of the psyche. His depiction of the results of this process was a critique of the current state of psychology:

I reduce man as it were to his phylogenetic prototype, or I dissolve him into his elementary processes; and when I try to reconstruct him again from this reduction, in the former case an ape will emerge, and in the latter a welter

---

[79] This position is closely linked with Jung's understanding of suggestion, as he held a suggestion was only accepted if it was agreeable to the subject. See Shamdasani, 2001a.

of elementary processes engaged in aimless and meaningless reciprocal activity. (§ 852, trans. mod.)

However, this heterogeneity was not limitless. The existence of the psychological types provided a delimitation of the range of individual variations. In his view, there were two options available to the psychologist: either to accept the fact that several contradictory theories of the same process could exist side by side, or to make the hopeless attempt to form a sect, claiming the only correct and true theory.

It was the final section of Jung's book, the general description of the types, which had the greatest impact. His descriptions of the types became detached from the historical, philosophical, and psychological issues that he had embedded them in. The types he described were "Galtonesque family portraits" which drew together the typical and common characters, while effacing the individual features (§666). The reference was to Francis Galton's technique of composite photographs. Galton had superimposed photographs of different individuals, such as those in the same family, to arrive at representative faces. As he put it, "The effect of composite portraiture is to bring into evidence all the traits in which there is agreement, and to leave but a ghost of a trace of individual peculiarities" (Galton, 1883, 7). The effectiveness of Jung's composite portraits of the types was that they were recognizable as individuals. Readers could easily recognize themselves and others in Jung's portraits, and were drawn into matching their traits with those of the various types. A great deal of the success of his typology was due to the success of his literary technique in this chapter.

He concluded *Psychological Types* with an extensive dictionary of concepts. Wide divergences in the meaning of words had led to great misunderstandings in psychology. The experimental method in psychology had limited itself to "elementary facts." He claimed that outside of its purview, the role played in experimental psychology by quantification was played by precision of the concept. Given the current state of psychology, a generally agreed lexicon was not a possibility. Hence it was incumbent upon each psychologist to define his concepts with "fixity and precision" (§ 674). In this instance, his linguistic project bore resemblance to that of Wundt.[80] One can see it as derived from the programme of the linguistic reformation of the language of psychology set out at the Geneva congress in 1909, which he attended. He added a disclaimer that his definitions were meant only to designate his own personal use of the concepts, and that "I would in no way want to say, that this use should have been

---

[80] Jung's subsequent work, in particular, his work on alchemy, articulated a markedly different approach to language.

in all circumstances the only possible one or the absolutely right one" (§ 675, trans. mod.). However, despite this disclaimer, his dictionary was a bold undertaking, for it amounted to establishing a complete conceptual lexicon. Alongside redefinitions of general concepts, such as affect, attitude, fantasy, feeling, symbol, and so on, he added definitions of his own concepts, such as archetype, individuation, persona, anima, animus. It is important to note that in the first edition, Jung's signature concepts did not have entries of their own, but were found in the definitions of more general terms, such as soul, symbol, and image. This indicates that at this stage, these terms did not have the significance that would later be attributed to them as the keywords to Jung's psychology. However, far from facilitating communication with other psychologists, his lexicon and linguistic project inadvertently had the opposite effect: it served to demarcate analytical psychology as a distinct dialect, and tended to encourage either wholesale adoption or rejection. This mirrored the disciplinary separation of analytical psychology from academic psychology. It is ironic that in respect of introversion and extraversion, when the terms became taken up by the psychological community and the general public, they were detached from his conceptual definitions of them.

The languages that psychologies have developed have had a profound impact on twentieth-century psychology. A hundred years ago, James could state that ordinary language lacked sufficient vocabulary to express subjective facts. Subsequent psychologists have been far from mute in their coining of concepts to fill this lacuna. Regardless of whether what these concepts refer to exists or not, they have undoubtedly transformed subjective experience through reshaping the language used to talk about it, and created new forms of sensibility. The language of psychological typology – as with psychological conceptions in general – has come to be the idiom in which large numbers of individuals have come to identify themselves and frame their own experiences, as well as that of others.

Within *Psychological Types* itself, there was a tension between this conception of psychological language, and another, which became increasingly predominant in Jung's later works. While discussing mythological and religious symbols, he noted that when one was dealing with unconscious processes, one scientifically had the greatest difficulty in coming out of the "image language" (Bildersprache) to reach the image language of the other sciences. In the end, the effect of psychological explanations was to do nothing other than to create new symbols for age-old riddles. Thus while "our science is also an image language," its advantage was that it was "more suitable in practical respects than the old mythological hypothesis" (§ 428, trans. mod.). This suitability lay in the fact that psychology employed a language that appeared to be more in keeping with scientific modernity.

Schism in the Jungian school?

In 1922, Jung's most prominent advocate in the United States, Beatrice Hinkle, published a lengthy article, "A Study of Psychological Types." Hinkle, a medical doctor, had opened a psychotherapeutic clinic in America at Cornell Medical College. She had been analyzed by Jung in 1911, and thereafter translated his *Transformations and Symbols of the Libido* into English.

Though her article appeared after Jung's book on types, it had been written prior to reading his work. Her study represented a detailed elaboration of his 1913 paper on the subject. Hinkle stated that as time went on, the need for more differentiated distinctions had become apparent, and she criticized aspects of Jung's formulations. To remedy this situation, she claimed that the introverts and extraverts were each further split into three categories: objective, simple, and subjective. The simple types corresponded to Jung's original classification, but the two other groups made up the majority of persons. Hinkle's model was significantly different from Jung's.

Thus in 1922, there were two divergent and fully elaborated Jungian systems of psychological types. From Jung's epistemology in *Psychological Types*, the only way to understand the difference between these two systems was by appealing to the psychological type of the author. But in this case, should one use Hinkle's types or Jung's? Whereas in his work, Jung had been able to relegate earlier type systems to a prepsychological phase, this was not possible in this instance, and furthermore, Hinkle's study presented itself as a development of his earlier work. Her study drew an enthusiastic response from her Jungian colleague Constance Long (1922). Hinkle's and Jung's typologies were compared by William McDougall. He critiqued Jung's system of the four functions, which to his mind, smacked of faculty psychology, and concluded that Hinkle's typology was better.[81] Hinkle's and Jung's typologies were also compared by the American psychologist A. A. Roback, who used them to mutually cancel each other out. He expressed his sense that writers on typology made distinctions according to their likes and dislikes. While Jung seemed to favor the introvert, Hinkle seemed to favor the extravert (927, 292).

---

[81] 1926, 450. On McDougall, see below 196, 268.

Another attempt to construct a typology based on, but diverging from Jung's, was put forward by J. van der Hoop, a Dutch psychiatrist, and president of the Netherlands Society for Psychotherapy, who had gone to Zürich to be analyzed by Jung in 1913. In his 1937 work, *Types of Consciousness and their Relation to Psychopathology*, he argued that while Jung's typology was an advance on previous typologies, he differed from Jung in his understanding of the functions, and their interrelation. Van der Hoop finished his book with a chapter entitled, "The Personal Equation." Arguing that one's orientation took the form of typical attitudes, he claimed that these attitudes made themselves felt in the different schools of psychology. He focused upon Freud and Jung as his prime exemplars. After explaining what he termed the peculiarities of Freud and psychoanalysis through the fact that Freud was an intuitive extravert, he turned to Jung. He stated that Jung described himself as a "thinking-introvert" and gave a lengthy typological analysis of Jung, attributing the strengths and weaknesses of his work to his type. Van der Hoop was trying to portray Jung's personal equation (1937, 327–328). The tables were reversed, and the analyst found himself analyzed by his former analysand, in what reads like a parody of Jung's own interpretations of individuals in *Psychological Types*. Whereas Jung chose Freud and Adler as his examples to show the manner in which the personal equation resulted in a one-sided and partial theoretical perspective, van der Hoop pointedly chose Freud and Jung, to demonstrate the same lesson. And worse still, Jung's personal peculiarities were identified as the reason for the shortcomings of his typological system.

In the 1920s and 1930s, characterology and typology were popular subjects in Germany. The most prominent works were those of Ludwig Klages, Ernst Kretschmer, Eduard Spranger and Philip Lersch.[82] Jung's typology did not meet with much success in this sphere, and these writers did not draw upon his work. In the sixth edition of *The Science of Character*, Klages, a prominent figure in characterology and the founder of modern graphology, noted that in the first edition of 1910, he had introduced the distinction between the outward and inward-looking mind. Subsequently, "two foreign words, extraverted and introverted, were employed by medical men, and an attempt was made to make this a supreme principle for classifying all characters in general. The result, to put it most politely, was nil" (1929, 280). The target of his criticism was plainly Jung.

---

[82] Ulfried Geuter gives a detailed analysis of the extent to which the work of the characterologists was shaped by the Wehrmacht, which was the largest employer of psychologists in Germany. There was little take up of their work in Wehrmacht psychology, as "The Nazis had ways of selecting people other than characterological or psychotechnical" (1992, 121).

Jung's typology, as an epistemological attempt to halt the infinite regress threatened by the personal equation, through the establishment of a psychology of psychologies, did not meet with any general acceptance. The reasons for this are not hard to find. Psychologists were reluctant to view the theories which they had claimed had universal validity as merely the expression of their type, and correspondingly relativized.

Critical psychology or characterology?

In the English-speaking world, the translation of *Psychological Types* was greeted with widespread press reviews.[83] It received a long and glowing review in *The New York Times*, where the review hailed it as a "splendid" and "great" contribution to psychology which had marvelously revealed the "kingdom of the soul" (Isham, 1923). The book received a glowing review in the *Times Literary Supplement*, which hailed Jung as a great writer, comparing him to Dostoevsky, Shakespeare, and Tolstoy (Anon, TLS, 1923, 448). In *The New Republic*, the book was taken to task by J. B. Watson. Behaviorism was then strongly on the rise, and on the way to becoming the most dominant tendency in modern psychology. As Watson's review of Jung was the most prominent treatment of his work by a behaviorist, it is worth dwelling on, particularly as it articulates what became the dominant attitude towards his work in academic psychology. Watson began by noting that psychoanalysis started to make headway in the United States after Freud, Jung, and "other continental authorities" lectured at Clark University. Recounting the mutual antipathy of the analysts and the psychologists, he remarked that "in print and in conversation the psychologist was told that until he had been analysed he could not even understand this difficult subject, much less criticise it" (1923, 287). However, dialogue began to increase, as newer analysts realized that they were behavior diagnosticians and teachers, instead of magicians. According to Watson, Jung did not belong to one of these, and he took him to task for ignoring "nearly all of twentieth-century psychology" in his book. To anyone who had read *The Psychology of the Unconscious*, this work would come as no surprise, as it had the same lack of clarity and obscurity. Watson conjectured whether the whole aim of the book was one of justifying Jung's obscurity by appeal to type. He wrote: "One cannot go into a criticism of Jung's psychology. It is the kind the religious mystic must write in order to find justification for certain factors his training has forced him to believe must exist" (*ibid.*).[84] Jung's stress on

---

[83] On its reception in anthropology, see below 334–337.

[84] This was a charge that was frequently made against Jung. In a draft manuscript written in the 1950's, "Jung's analytical theory," the American psychologist Calvin Hall had

the innateness of typology evoked Watson's scorn. This was not surprising, given the extreme environmentalism that the behaviorists espoused. Jung's book, far from aiding psychology, "confuses it by unjustifiable and unsupported assumptions." Furthermore, Watson held that it didn't contribute to analysis, but rather "it seems to be but another justification of life's failures and to give one more shoulder upon which the weakling may lean" (288). In conclusion, he stated that there were as many types as individuals, which was in accord with both modern psychology and common sense.

Jung did not reply to Watson's review. It was, however, responded to by James Oppenheim, an early popularizer of Jung's work in the United States. Oppenheim argued that the difference between Watson and Jung lay in the fact that the former was an extraverted thinker, while the latter was an introverted thinker. Correcting Watson's claim that according to Jung, an individual could not change his type, Oppenheim wrote: "Dr. Jung himself is an excellent example of an introvert who has developed the extraverted side" (1923). It was precisely for this reason that he was able to develop a system that did justice to both extraversion and introversion, and consequently, was fairer to Watson and his psychology than vice versa. In reference to behaviorism, Jung made a few passing remarks, describing it as a "psychology without man" and an "unsound philosophical prejudice."[85]

Despite Watson's critique, psychological types was the one aspect of Jung's work that found its way on to the agenda of academic psychology, and it was the only aspect of his work that was accorded any serious and not purely dismissive attention by psychologists. In 1937, the American psychologist Gordon Allport noted concerning the terms extraversion and introversion, that over the past twenty years psychologists had accorded more interest to these traits than to any others, and that they had found their way into common speech. He wrote: "it was Jung's terms with their transparent etymology that held the day."[86] However, the manner in which psychologists engaged with Jung's typology transformed it beyond

---

written that "Jung has far less appeal than Freud because there is such a strong flavour of occultism, mysticism and religion in Jung's writing and this repels many psychologists." By the first clause, Jung wrote "Are such phenomena unknown in America?" After "many psychologists" Jung added "who don't want to see the world as it is. There is such a thing as religion, even in Russia" (CLM, 45).

[85] Jung to Henry Murray, July 2, 1948, *Letters* 1, 504, and Jung to Charles Aldrich, January 5, 1931, *Letters* 1, 80.

[86] 1937, 419. Given the success of Jung's terminology, it is interesting that in 1915 he was considering replacing the "introversion-type" and "extraversion-type" with "abstraction-type" and "empathy-type" respectively (Jung to Maeder, December 4, 1915, Maeder papers).

all recognition. Jung's historical, clinical, and epistemological concerns were completely left to one side, and were replaced by the experimental and statistical methods that held sway in psychology, in the course of which his theoretical understanding of the types was discarded. One is left with the impression that little other than the terms that Jung coined – introversion and extraversion – were left of his work when it was taken up by academic psychologists. Isabel Myers Briggs and her daughter Katherine used Jung's work as the basis for the "Myers-Briggs Type Indicator" – which is the most widely used personality test in the United States today.[87]

In response to such research, attempts were made to develop psychological type tests and to provide experimental and statistical validation of Jung's work. However, even here, the process of accommodation to the methodology and concerns of the academic psychological community made itself felt.[88] In 1945 Horace Gray and Joseph Wheelwright, who played a prominent part in the development of psychological type testing, noted of the reception of Jung's type theory that "Psychologists . . . have eagerly sought to grasp its intriguing implications, but have blurred the original proposer's specifications" (266–267). They set out to correct the misinterpretations that Jung's specifications had been subject to, down to correcting spelling: extraversion, and not extroversion, they chided. Gray and Wheelwright developed a questionnaire for typological assessment, which was widely used. Significantly, they noted: "we have avoided as far as possible entanglement with [Jung's] other psychological principles which may be unacceptable to other schools of depth psychology" (268). The outcome of this statement was that not only was Jung's type theory dissociated from the rest of his work, it was dissociated from itself. Of the eleven chapters of the book, ten were effectively discarded, leaving only the chapter on the general description of the types. Even that chapter was reworked to fit in with methodological assumptions then prevalent in academic psychology. It was, as they say in psychology, "operationalized." Not surprisingly, the lengthiest section concerning practical applications of the test concerned military uses in personnel selection.

C. A. Meier, who was analyzed by Jung during this period, claims that after the publication of *Psychological Types*, "In actual analytical sessions, typological problems were seldom discussed, yet it was still important to him as the *compass*" (1995, 69). Joseph Wheelwright also notes that

---

[87] Personal communication, John Beebe.
[88] For instance, C. A. Meier stated, "statistics are the closest we can come to truth in psychology . . . Academic psychologists are right in wanting things shown to them statistically, and it is we Jungians who have the *onus* of showing them that our ideas stand their tests" (1986, 252).

Jung "left types behind" (1972, 214). It is possible that this indicates Jung's dissatisfaction with what he had achieved with his typological project. Typology, however, was widely taken up in the Jungian community (and beyond) in the twenties and thirties. In part, it filled the lacuna created by the rejection of the reductive personalistic psychologies of Freud and Adler. For many, the language of typology provided a means for individual differences to be acknowledged and respected. However, there are grounds for suggesting that this was not Jung's sole or primary interest in the subject. In 1932, Jung informed his pupil Wolfgang Kranefeldt:

I have generally never occupied myself with the so-called character. My intentions and interests are also in no way directed to characterology, but in complete contrast, to typology. But not in the sense that I have established types in order to classify people with, but to have a schema with which I can order psychological material.[89]

The following year, he qualified his typology to Kranefeldt again. He noted that it was a "critical psychology," which meant "a critical apparatus for the sifting of the empirical material," and not "a pigeon-hole in which single individuals can be locked up without further questioning." The term "critical psychology" seems to be an analogue to Kant's designation of a "critical philosophy." Likewise, correctly understood, the theory of the functions was concerned with "types of psychological occurrences, and not typification as characters."[90] In the same year he indicated to Hans Schäffer how his typology had been misunderstood:

Nor was it ever my intention to characterize personalities, for which reason I did not put my description of the types at the beginning of the book; rather I tried to produce a clear conceptual scheme based on empirically demonstrable factors. Hence my typology aims, not at characterizing personalities, but at classifying the empirical material in relatively simple and clear categories, just as it is presented to a practising psychologist and therapist. I have never thought of my typology as a characterological method and have never applied it in this sense. For any such application it would be much too general and therefore too scanty. As you rightly observe, one needs 27 categories and probably a few more besides in order to give an adequate characterization of mentally differentiated persons. For the psychologist, who has to deal with people in practical terms, a characterological diagnosis of the patient is of secondary importance; for him it is far more important to have a terminology in which at least the crassest differences between individuals can be formulated . . . My typology aims at elucidating conceptually the empirical psychological material presented by any one individual and thus subordinating it to general points of view. This intention of mine has often been misunderstood.[91]

[89] October 20, 1932 (JP).   [90] October 24, 1933 (JP).
[91] October 27, 1933, *Letters* 1, 129–130.

The ironic paradox of the situation is that it is precisely this misunderstanding of Jung's typology as a characterology, which has been responsible for its "success." The following year, he again responded to reception of his work in his foreword to the Argentine edition. There, after stating that the task of the book was a critical psychology, he wrote:

This fundamental tendency in my work has often been overlooked, and far too many readers have succumbed to the error of thinking that chapter X ("General Description of the Types") represents the essential content and purpose of the book, in the sense that it provides a system for classification and a practical guide to a good judgment of human character . . . This regrettable misunderstanding completely ignores the fact that this kind of classification is nothing but a childish parlour game, every bit as futile as the division of mankind into brachycephalics and doliocephalics . . . My typology . . . is not a physiognomy and not an anthropological system, but a critical psychology dealing with the organization and delimitation of psychic processes that can be shown to be typical. (*CW* 6, xiv–xv)

In 1935, Jung gave a series of lectures on his typology at the Swiss Federal Institute for Technology in Zürich. If much of the popular success of his typology was due to the ease with which individuals could identify with his portrait of the types, it was precisely such identification that he cautioned against. The theory of types, he stated, was a theoretical function "without muscle or flesh, and if you identify with it you identify with a corpse" (1935, 2). In describing the introvert, he cautioned that the type of which he was about to speak was not a human being but an abstraction which could not physically exist: "I speak of the extract we should get if you put 10,000 introverts into a retort. I say this to warn you against identification" (5–6). Finally, in his undated manuscript on the origin of psychological types, Jung wrote that the value of the typology for psychotherapists was as a critical system of orientation. He added that "it does not serve as a superficial aprioristic classification of types of men. Here Kretschmer's physiological-psychiatric typology is much more suitable."[92] Reiterating that his typology was not a characterology, he added that it was only interesting for practical psychologists, and the lay people could not use it correctly.

Psychology and the science question

If psychological typology did not manage to resolve the problem of the personal equation in psychology, Jung continued to grapple with this question, and the issue of the relation of the individual to the universal in psychology, and the status of psychology. The theory of the archetypes was critical in this regard. According to this theory, the "personal" was

---

[92] "Notice on the origin of psychological types" (JP).

viewed as being built up of innate universal structures. While the theory of the collective unconscious is generally dismissed as being non-scientific, one of the reasons that he advanced it was precisely to secure the scientificity of psychology, through positing a level of universality in the personality which underlay individual differences. As such, it constituted another attempt to resolve the problem of the personal equation.

On two subsequent occasions, he gave papers on the topic of psychological types, in which he gave further reflections on the state of psychology and its need for linguistic reformation. In a lecture delivered to a congress of Swiss psychiatrists in Zürich in 1928, entitled "Psychological typology," he stated that as psychology was the youngest of the sciences, it suffered the most from preconceived opinions. Up till then psychology had been a "fantastic arbitrary product" like natural science in the middle ages. The fact that we ourselves were the psyche led to the assumption that we knew it, and this led to the situation that "everyone has not only his opinions about psychology, but also the conviction that he naturally knows it better" (1929, *CW* 6, § 919, trans. mod.). Thus the personal equation was an effect of the general tendency to assume that one's experience was the template of human psychology in general.

The problem with psychology was that it lacked the concepts and definitions with which to grasp facts, which it had a superabundance of. Unlike sciences such as botany, even the task of description was difficult when it came to psychology:

with an empirical-descriptive standpoint we are only caught in the incessant stream of our own subjective psychic (seelisch) happenings, and when any sort of summarizing general concept emerges from this bustle, it is usually nothing but a symptom. Because we ourselves are souls, it is almost inevitable that when we give free rein to psychic (seelisch) happenings, we become dissolved in them and in this way robbed of the ability of recognizing distinctions and making comparisons. (§ 920, trans. mod.)

If this difficulty wasn't bad enough, the non-spatialness of the soul meant that exact measurement was impossible, which made it difficult to establish facts. As a result of this situation, psychology was: "still little other than a chaos of arbitrary dogmas, produced for the most part in the study or consulting room by spontaneous generation from an isolated and consequently Zeus-like brain of a scholar, with complete lack of agreement" (§ 945, trans. mod.). In the chaos of contemporary psychology, there were no sound criteria. These had first to be created. Psychology was a "virgin territory, and its terminology has still to be fixed" (§ 952). The following year, he stated:

We in applied psychology today must be modest and allow an apparent plurality of contradictory opinions to be valid, for we are still far from knowing anything fundamental concerning the most distinguished object of the science, the human soul itself. For the present we only have merely more or less plausible opinions that are still nowhere satisfactory.[93]

Two years later in "The basic problems of contemporary psychology" he expressed himself in striking terms: "the natural history of the mind finds itself today in a position which can be compared to the position of natural science in the thirteenth century."[94] It is critical to note that by this date, Jung had introduced all of his key signature concepts. These statements indicate the provisionality with which he viewed them, and how far short from his own vision of the possibilities of psychology he held them to be. Eight years later, in his final paper on psychological typology, he concluded in a similar vein:

Limited definitions in some form will sooner or later in the field of our still young science be absolutely necessary, since psychologists must one day come to agreement on principles removed from certain arbitrary interpretations, if their psychology is not to remain an unscientific chance conglomeration of individual opinions. (*CW* 6, § 987, trans. mod.)

These statements emphasize the fact that his prime intention was not to set up a school of psychology or psychotherapy, claiming that it alone had the truth, but of contributing to the establishment of a general psychology, analogous to how he conceived the other sciences to be. Hence *Psychological Types* was an attempt to enable psychology as a whole to escape from the impasse of the chaos it had resulted in. Rather than establishing general laws, psychology had simply led to the proliferation of contradictory opinions. Nearly seventy years later, psychologists today are even further from any possibility of agreement than they were then. The chaos has simply increased.

If psychological typology did not manage to resolve the problem of the personal equation in psychology, Jung continued to grapple with this question, and the issue of the relation of the individual to the universal in psychology, and the status of psychology itself.

In 1928, in a lecture in Vienna, he argued that a fundamental question for psychology was whether the soul could be recognized through itself. All psychological theories were subjective confessions, and "the founder of a psychological theory must get accustomed to the thought that he is

---

[93] "The aims of psychotherapy," *CW* 16, § 71, trans. mod.
[94] "The basic problems of contemporary psychotherapy," *CW* 8, § 687, trans. mod.

not only its founder, but also its sacrifice."[95] In this stark statement, to make a psychological theory was a form of self-sacrifice.

In a paper in 1929 on "The Freud–Jung opposition," he took up the theme of the subjectivity of psychology. He nominated the recognition of this factor as the critical dividing line between Freud and himself. His critique of the contemporary status of psychology had led him to advocate a radical solution: "I will for our psychological use first completely renounce the thought that we men of today are in general in a position to make out something "true" or "correct" about the essence of the soul. The best that we can produce is *true expression*" (*CW* 4, § 771, trans. mod.). True expression, Jung defined as an open avowal and description of everything subjectively noted. Present day psychology, he held, was simply "a more or less successfully formulated confession of a few individuals" (§ 772). If the aim of modern psychology was to surpass the reliance on individual testimony as the sole guarantor of truth, it had come a complete circle. The sole factor which gave these confessions any validity was the fact that each psychologist belonged to a type, and consequently, his testimony had some validity for those of the same type. Addressing this question in the course of his lectures in London at the Institute for Medical Psychology in 1935, Jung stated that what Freud had said agreed with many people, so they presumably had the type of psychology he described. The same held true for Adler, and by extension, with himself:

I consider my contribution to psychology to be my subjective confession. It is my personal psychology, my prejudice that I see things in such and such a way. But I expect Freud and Adler to do the same and confess that their ideas are their subjective point of view. So far as we admit our personal prejudice, we are really contributing towards an objective psychology.[96]

The one difference then, between his own work and that of Freud and Adler, was that he at least admitted this was a subjective confession. This extreme formulation of the personal equation had critical consequences. For if the theories of complex psychology held true only for those with

---

[95] Jung, "The structure of the soul," Vienna lecture (JP). A different version of this essay was published (see *CW* 8).

[96] *CW* 18, § 275. Joseph Wheelwright wrote: "One of the high spots of that evening was a reply to a psychologist who asked for some explanation of his psychology in relation to Freud's. He spoke then of psychology as being a personal confession, & that his psychology differed from Freud's especially because he hadn't that psychology nor that of Adler. He said 'I have always enjoyed myself and I have always been successful, therefore I never was interested in infantile psychology or will to power, though I admit many people have such a psychology & I treat them accordingly.' It really was an extraordinarily convincing confession of faith – with that huge smile on his face nobody could resist it" (Joseph Wheelwright to Cary Baynes, undated, 1935 Cary Baynes papers).

a particular psychology, what was one to make of its claim to have discovered universal structures and processes? Did only some people have complexes, animas and animuses, shadows, personas, archetypes, and an unconscious, personal or collective? Were these theories valid for some people only? How could one reconcile this extreme form of personal equation, with the claim to the universal validity of his theories that Jung presented at the same time?

One way of understanding this paradox is in terms of the notion of the two types of thinking in Jung's work put forward in the preface. From this perspective, it is possible to say that on the one hand, Jung was putting forward theories and hypotheses in a conventional manner. On the other hand, he was engaged in a reflection on the very possibility of psychology.

As we have seen, the Freud–Jung relation collapsed into mutual diagnosis. For Jung, it was on the issue of the personal equation that psychoanalysis collapsed. This was not only because it did not have a theoretical role in psychoanalysis, but primarily because of the effect of Freud's personality upon his theories. In *Memories,* commenting on the fact that Freud had a neurosis with highly troublesome symptoms, he stated: "Apparently, neither Freud nor his disciples could understand what it meant for the theory and practice of psychoanalysis if not even the master could deal with his own neurosis" (*Memories,* 191). For Jung, it was precisely Freud's neurosis which limited psychoanalysis: "I cannot see how Freud can ever get beyond his own psychology and relieve the patient of a suffering from which the doctor himself still suffers."[97] In a foreword to Kranefeldt's book, he wrote: "Freudian psychoanalysis . . . is a psychic symptom which, as the facts show, has proved to be more powerful than the analytic art of the master himself."[98] To John Billinsky, Jung spoke at greater length concerning Freud's neurosis. Referring to his trip with Freud to America in 1909, Jung stated:

> During the trip Freud developed severe neuroses, and I had to do limited analysis with him. He had psychosomatic troubles and had difficulties in controlling his bladder. I suggested to Freud that he should have a complete analysis but he rebelled against the idea because he would have to deal with problems that were closely related to his theories. If Freud could have consciously understood the triangle, he would have been much, much better off. (Billinsky, 1967, 42)

The implication of this statement is that Freud's theories, and presumably, those concerning the role of incest and the Oedipus complex, were intimately connected with his triangular relations with his wife and sister-in-law.[99]

---

[97] "The Freud–Jung opposition," *CW* 4, § 774.   [98] 1930, *CW* 4, § 747, trans. mod.
[99] On this issue, see Peter Swales, 1982, 1983b, 1998.

Such statements allow one to differentiate two forms of the personal equation in Jung. In the first, such as in these statements above, a neurotic theorist inevitably theorizes neurotically, or encodes their neurosis into their theories. It is hard to see how this form is different from the reductive "nothing but" that Jung himself critiqued on many occasions. In the second, the personal equation is the expression of a typical attitude or orientation of consciousness, and not biographically determined. In this form, Freud's theories were the expression of an extraverted attitude.

It was Jung's statements in 1934 in "The state of psychotherapy today" that Freud's and Adler's psychologies were specifically Jewish, and therefore not legitimate for Aryans, that created a controversy which has not died down (CW 10). It is critical to see such statements in the context of the problem of the personal equation. Jung was suggesting that this was also racially conditioned. Thus in his reply to the Swiss psychotherapist Gustave Bally in 1934, who had taken exception to his statements, he reiterated his statement that every psychology should be criticized in the first instance as a subjective confession (CW 10, § 1025).

Around 1936, Jung wrote an unpublished paper entitled "The Schism in the Freudian School." It was a reply to a paper by Mauerhofer in a Swiss journal, Bund, commemorating Freud's eightieth birthday. He commented that he found it regrettable when a scientific discussion descended to the level of personal motives. He considered it questionable to explain divergent theoretical standpoints from the moral dubiousness of the opponent. This was precisely what Freud had done when he had considered Jung's criticism of his theory to be the product of antisemitism. Even if he was an antisemite, his objections to Freud's theory, which others shared, would have to be considered. His so-called antisemitism consisted in recognizing that Jews, as the descendants of a nearly two-thousand-year-old people, had a different psychology. He was not the first to claim this, and Jewish writers such as Rosenzweig had done so.[100] The problem with the Freudian school was that they had never tried to consider the legitimacy of other conceptions. Freudian doctrine only recognized personal motives, and regarded objective criticism only as a proof of its own truth. Its one-sidedness was "the first step towards the Muscovite paradise of idiots."[101]

Jung wrote that he was quite aware of what he had to thank Freud for, and he was one of his first supporters. It was through the Zürich school

---

[100] The reference is presumably to Franz Rosenzweig's *The Star of Redemption* (1921).

[101] JP. To James Kirsch, he wrote, "I have not invented the whole complication of the soul, and neither has Freud succeeded in doing away with it" (July 12, 1951, JP, ETH, trans. James Kirsch).

under Bleuler that Freud achieved world-renown, which they have never been thanked for. Freud's failing was that he could never see beyond his own conception, which he took to be universal. As a result of this, he could only view Jung's separation from him as a "personal apostasy." Correcting the Freudocentric view of his work, he stated: "I in no way exclusively stem from Freud. I had my scientific attitude and the theory of complexes before I met Freud. The teachers, that influenced me above all are Bleuler, Pierre Janet, and Theodore Flournoy" (*ibid.*). In Switzerland, there was a tendency only to value what had been imported. One needed to remember that "Freud had important contemporaries, whose importance is not less, because they are Swiss"(*ibid.*).

A number of years later, Jung wrote a letter to Hans Illing which provided some further reflections on these issues: "Freud is in this respect 'profoundly Jewish' as he never undertook a personal analysis, but despite this claimed that his psychoanalytic judgment was valid for all others. This corresponds to the Jewish representation of God."[102] He added that Freud had accused him of antisemitism, "because I gave him as an association in a personal dream analysis, that I disliked the Jewish milieu in Vienna. This was an indiscretion on his part" (*ibid.*).[103]

In 1935, he reflected on the problem of the individual and the universal in psychology in "fundamentals of practical psychotherapy." He noted that if individuals were absolutely unique, psychology could not be a science, because there would simply be a chaos of subjective opinions. However, human individuality was only relative, and there existed areas of general conformity. This enabled scientific statements to be made. These statements "relate only to those parts of the psychic system which conform, and are consequently comparable, hence statistically ascertainable; they do not relate to the individual, which means the uniqueness of the system" (*CW* 16, § 1, trans. mod.). In this formulation, psychology, as a science, could only deal with the areas of typicality and commonality in individuals.

In 1945, he revised his talks on analytical psychology and education, and added some reflections on the status of psychology. As if echoing James' comments concerning the snares of psychology, he wrote:

[102] October 20, 1955 (JP). "Profoundly Jewish" is in English in the original.
[103] *Ibid.*, Jung informed Michael Fordham that "The story of my anti-semitism and Nazi-sympathies originally started with the holy father Freud himself. When I disagreed with him he had to find a reason for my most incomprehensible disagreement and found that I must be an anti-semite" (April 18, 1946, original in English, CMAC). In an undated text on antisemitism, he also remarked that the accusation of antisemitism "originates with Prof. Freud and his disciples, who have obviously failed to understand what reasons could have moved me to adopt a different scientific view to that taught by their master" ("On antisemitism," original in English, JP).

Nowhere do prejudices, misinterpretations, value-judgments, idiosyncrasies, and projections offer themselves more easily and more unashamedly than just in this field . . . Nowhere does the observer disturb the experiment more than in psychology. Because of this one can, so to speak, never establish the facts sufficiently. (*CW* 17, § 160, trans. mod.)

Psychology had the dubious distinction of being the most error-prone field imaginable. Therein lay its specificity. The cardinal problem was how to surmount this situation. In all other natural sciences, physical processes were observed by psychical processes. The difference in psychology, with the exception of psychophysiology, was that the psyche observed itself. This, he noted, reminded one of the story of Baron Münchausen, and led one "to doubt whether psychological knowledge is possible at all" (*ibid.*, trans. mod.). The problem with the psyche was that there was "no knowledge *about* the psychical, but only *in* the psychical" (*ibid.*, trans. mod.). As the medical psychologist held to an empirical and phenomenological approach, he worked within the framework of natural science. However, he departed from it, through attempting to explain the medium in the selfsame medium. Its principle was *"ignotum per ignotus"* (the unknown by the unknown). It was as if

the physicist were unable to do anything except repeat the physical process (with all possible variations), without "Theoria." But every psychical process, so far as it can be observed as such, is in itself already "Theoria," that is to say, *presentation*; and its reconstruction is at best only a *variant of the same presentation.* (§ 162)

Consequently, while psychology used the methods and form of verification of natural science, it stood outside it. Psychology could also claim to be one of the human sciences. Even here, it occupied an exceptional position. He claimed that other human sciences, such as law, history, philosophy, and theology, were characterized and limited by their subject matters. In the case of psychology, its subject was not a mental product but a natural phenomenon. While for Dilthey, psychology was the pre-eminent human science, Jung held, by contrast, "In respect of its natural object and method, modern empirical psychology belongs to the natural sciences, but in respect of its method of explanation it belongs to the human sciences."[104] His view of psychology as straddling the distinction

[104] § 166, trans. mod. Jung referred to Toni Wolff's discussion of the scientific status of complex psychology in her 1935 paper, "Einführung in die Grundlagen der Komplexen Psychologie." Wolff drew from Rickert, and found in his work the methodological basis for a clarification of the principles of complex psychology. She took up Rickert's distinction between natural sciences and cultural sciences. For Wolff, complex psychology had two sides: on the one hand it constituted a scientific theory, and on the other it was a psychological analysis of the individual. When it dealt with general psychic elements or aspects of the individual and when it researched general structures and functions of the psyche such as typology, the collective unconscious and the concept of energy, it used a generalising method. When it dealt with the concept and process of individuation, individualising experience comes into operation (24).

between the natural and human sciences came very close to that of Windelband. In conclusion, he stated that it was hard to see where the solution lay to the problem of the relation of psychology to the natural sciences. The one discipline which had found itself in a similar predicament was atomic physics. Increasingly, it was through bringing psychology in relation with the latter, principally through a collaboration with the Nobel prize winning physicist Wolfgang Pauli, that Jung tried to solve the issue of the personal equation in psychology.

The following year, in a paper initially presented at the Eranos conference and later revised as "theoretical reflections on the essence of the psychical," he continued his reflections on this issue. At the outset of his work, he had thought that he was working on the best natural scientific lines, only to find that he had entangled himself "in a network of reflections which extend far beyond natural science and ramify into the fields of philosophy, theology, comparative religion, and the history of the mind in general."[105] He reiterated the point he had made earlier, that psychology could only translate itself back into its own language. Consequently, psychology merged with the psychic process itself. However, he now put a positive reading to this situation. If psychology could no longer be considered an explanation of psychical processes, it was through psychology that psychical processes "came to consciousness." Thus psychology represented a collective coming to consciousness of the unconscious. The result of this process was that psychology "must as a science sublate itself, and therein precisely it reaches its scientific goal" (§ 429, trans. mod.). In a sense, this process represented the consummation of the other sciences, as the object of psychology was "the inside subject of every science"(ibid.). Thus only through psychology could the other sciences reach their culmination.

In twentieth-century psychology, the two touchstones of science in mainstream academic psychology have been experimentation and statistics. What could not be the subject of an experiment, or treated statistically, was held to be outside the purview of psychology. In the 1950s, Jung undertook a critique of these positions. In so doing, he was challenging the two dogmas of academic psychology.

In 1952, in his paper on synchronicity, he critiqued the artificial limitations of experimentation. The problem with experimentation was that it consisted in formulating definite questions and excluding anything extraneous. This imposed conditions upon "nature" which "forces it to give an answer orientated to the human question" (CW 8, § 821, trans. mod.). This prevented nature from "answering out of the fullness of its

---

[105] CW 8, § 421, trans. mod. Here, the problem of the personal equation became linked with Heisenberg's principle of indeterminacy.

possibilities"(§ 864). The very mode of posing a question determined and limited the form of the answer. Consequently, the results were always a mixed product or amalgam, neither totally natural nor totally constructed. Thus the laboratory was an artificially restricted situation, which excluded the unrestricted wholeness of the workings of nature. The only means of approaching nature without these limitations would be to have "a formulation of questions which imposes the fewest possible conditions, or if possible no conditions at all" (§ 821, trans. mod.).

He went on to indicate what he meant more specifically. The manner in which questions were formulated in natural science aimed at regularity, and in experiments, at reproducible events. What this left out of account were unique or rare events. As a consequence, the natural scientific world view could only be a "psychologically prejudiced partial view" as it left out of account the aspects and features of the world which could not be subjected to statistics.

If one wanted to grasp the unique, one was left with individual descriptions. While descriptive natural sciences such as biology dealt with unique specimens, the critical factor was that they could be viewed by different individuals. This was often not the case in psychology, where one had to deal with ephemeral events which had only left traces in memories, which brought one back to the problem of the unreliability of individual testimony. This led him to state that absolutely unique or ephemeral events, of which there was no means of affirming or denying the existence, could not be the subject of an empirical science. However, "rare" events could be, if there were sufficient reliable observations.

A few years later in *Present and Future*, he continued these reflections. The text began with the theme of the plight of the individual in modern society. Addressing the problem of how an individual gained self-knowledge, he noted that theories were of little help, as self-knowledge was a question of individual facts. In fact, "The more such a claim to general validity rises, the less capable it is of doing justice to individual facts" (*CW* 10, § 493, trans. mod.). Here, he sets up an opposition between the claims for general validity of a theory, and its capacity to do justice to individual facts. He held that theories based on experience were necessarily statistical, which meant that they disregarded exceptions. While giving an aspect of reality, statistical methods and theories based on them could falsify the truth. This was because

Real facts display themselves through their individuality. To exaggerate, one might say that the real picture consists of nothing but exceptions to the rule so to speak, and that, in consequence, absolute reality has predominantly the character of *irregularity*. (§ 494, trans. mod.)

He had previously maintained that there were two parts to human nature, what was held in common, and hence could be the subject of a science, and what was individual, and lay outside. He now appeared to be altering the ratio in favor of individuality and irregularity. In so doing, he was radically delimiting the purview and significance of theories in psychology.

He noted that these reflections were critical in considering whether theories could serve as guides for self-knowledge, as "there is not and cannot be any self-knowledge based on theoretical assumptions" (§ 495, trans. mod.). This was because it was not the universal and regular that characterized the individual, but the unique. In the last analysis, the individual could not be known or compared with anything else. At the same time man could and had to be described as a statistical unit – or else nothing general could be said about him. This led to a universally valid anthropology or psychology, with all the individual features removed. However, it was precisely these features which were critical when it came to the understanding of man (§ 496). Jung's use of "understanding" (Verstehen) in this context had strong echoes of Dilthey. As Jung saw it, understanding, which was concerned with the individual and unique, was opposed to knowledge, with was concerned with the general.

His discussion here also closely echoed Rickert's discussion of individualising and generalising sciences, both in theme and in language.[106] In particular, Rickert's statements concerning the incapacity of the generalizing method of the natural sciences to grasp the unique, particular and non-repeatable character of individual reality are reiterated by Jung. The one difference is that Rickert affirmed the capacity of historical sciences to deal with these aspects.

Jung argued that when it came to understanding an individual, theoretical assumptions and scientific knowledge had to be left to one side. If the psychologist happened to be a doctor, who wants to understand his patient as well as to classify him scientifically, this was a difficult sacrifice. As he saw it, the only possibility was to develop a two-track way of thinking, and of being able to do the one without losing sight of the other. Taking up his analysis of experimentation from his synchronicity essay, he specified how this form of thinking operated. Whereas in experimental psychology, the experimenter had full freedom in the choice of questions he posed, in medical psychology, it was the object that posed

---

[106] There is one reference to Rickert in Jung's work. In contrast to Rickert and other philosophers and psychologists, Jung stated that he held that "everyone thinks as *he* thinks and sees as *he* sees," *CW* 18, § 1732. Jung had a copy of the 3rd edition of Rickert's *Der Gegenstand der Erkenntnis* [The Object of Knowledge].

the question, and not the experimenter. It was the sickness of the patient that posed the critical questions. Consequently, it was nature which experimented with the doctor, and expected an answer from him. While the doctor commences with using principles based on general experience, he soon finds these inadequate. The more he begins to understand his patient, the more general principles, and consequently objective knowledge falls away. Taken to the limit, this held the danger that "an ideal understanding would ultimately result in a knowledgeless going along with and witnessing, combined with the most complete subjectivity and lack of social responsibility" (§532, trans. mod.). Thus it was important that understanding was not carried too far, but that a balance between understanding and knowledge was reached. This was the critical practical task of the psychologist. How this balance was to be achieved was not made clear. These texts presented a radical delimitation of theoretical psychology.

His final discussion occurred in the course of a correspondence with his friend and colleague, the British psychiatrist E. A. Bennet. In a review of a work of Jung in May 1960, Bennet had written apropos Jung's hypothesis of a collective unconscious that while it lacked a scientific foundation, it presented the most satisfactory explanation for certain psychological facts. Jung took offense at the statement that his hypothesis lacked a scientific foundation. A correspondence ensued in which he defended the scientific status of his theories. He wrote to Bennet that the only proof of a scientific theory was its applicability. He claimed that he had given ample evidence of the applicability of his hypothesis in his works. It was up to someone else to show how his ideas weren't applicable, and to show what other ideas were more applicable.[107] In reply, Bennet maintained that the applicability of a theory didn't constitute scientific proof.[108] This led Jung to specify that by applicability, he didn't mean the practical application of a theory in therapy, but "its application as a principle of understanding and a heuristic means to an end as it is characteristic of each scientific theory."[109] Thus the only proof he could conceive of a theory was that it gave an adequate or satisfactory explanation and had a heuristic value. This emphasis on the heuristic value of theories attests to the abiding significance of pragmatism for Jung. Bennet countered this by indicating that he meant by scientific proof "an explanation of phenomena capable of being checked and observed by others and found to possess an unchanging and predictable order."[110] Consequently this required general agreement, which was lacking in psychology. As an example, he pointed

---

[107] May 22, 1960 in Bennet, 1961, 95–96.
[108] May 27, 1960, 96.   [109] June 3, 1960, 97–98.   [110] June 8, 1960, 99.

out that the facts on which Jung based his archetype theory had been differently explained in terms of recapitulation and psychoanalysis. In reply, Jung stated that what Bennet had in mind concerning scientific evidence was something analogous to chemical or physical proof. One had to take into consideration the commensurability of evidence, and the fact that the way of proving a fact was different in different disciplines. Consequently, "the question ought to be formulated: what is physical, biological, psychological, legal and philosophical evidence?"[111] In his final letter, Jung added that while he had frequently been charged with being unscientific, no one had pointed out why this was the case. He claimed to have followed exactly what Bennet took to be the scientific method: "I observe, I classify, I establish relations and sequences between the observed data, and I even show the possibility of prediction."[112] He added that part of the disagreement stemmed from the restriction in the Anglo-Saxon realm of what science meant to physics and chemistry, and pointed the wider use of the term on the continent. However, in his earlier statements about psychology, Jung had not been content simply to class psychology as one of the human sciences, but had also stressed that it was connected to the natural sciences. Jung concluded: "Psyche is the mother of all our attempts to understand Nature, but in contradistinction to all others it tries to understand itself by itself, a great disadvantage in one way and an equally great prerogative in the other!" (*ibid.*). Thus the problems that beset psychology were ultimately of concern for all other scientific disciplines, for they too stemmed from the psyche. The question was not simply one of whether psychology was possible as a science: rather, the sciences themselves ultimately rested on psychology. The attempt to found a scientific psychology had come a full circle.

[111] June 11, 1960, 100–101.   [112] June 23, 1960, 102.

2   Night and day

Our entire history is only the history of waking men; no one has yet
thought of a history of sleeping men.

G. C. Lichtenberg.[1]

Dream cultures

While dreaming is seen to be a universal phenomenon, conceptions of
dreams vary in different cultures and at different times. Several decades
of historical and anthropological inquiry have indicated that in any given
culture, conceptions of dreams are intimately linked with their place in
cosmologies; theological, medical, aesthetic, and philosophical theories
about them; individual, therapeutic, and ritual practices accompanying
them; and with conceptions of individuality and language.[2] They have
also indicated that it is impossible to dissociate dreams from their particular dream cultures.

By contrast, contemporary psychological and neuroscientific theories
claim to be in a position to determine the universal essence of the dream as
an unchanging entity. At the same time, such theories, while purporting to
be independent of their surrounding dream cultures, have been a powerful
force in the creation of new dream subcultures. The dream has been
utilized to generate new configurations of the personality and the brain,
together with new rituals of dream recording, sharing, and retrospective
divination, which have been adopted by large social groupings.

In modern Western societies, the cultural location of dreams has been
decisively shaped by Freud and Jung. This has taken place through the
utilization of dreams in psychotherapy as an interpretative practice, and
through the dissemination of Freudian and Jungian dream theories in
intellectual circles and popular culture. Whether as wishfulfillments or

---

[1] Cited in Tomlinson, 1992, 781.
[2] For anthropological works on dreams see Tedlock, ed., 1992, and Shulman and Stroumsa,
eds., 1999.

as compensations, dreams are widely understood to be revelations of the personality that stem from the unconscious, and this view is seen to be the legacy of Freud and Jung. They have played a decisive role in giving rise to our contemporary dream cultures.

Freud's estimation of his achievement is encapsulated in his statement in a letter to Wilhelm Fliess of June 12, 1900, asking whether a plaque would one day be put on the house where he dreamt his famous specimen dream, the Irma dream, bearing the inscription: "In this House, on July 24th, 1895 the Secret of Dreams was Revealed to Dr. Sigm. Freud" (Masson edn., 1985, 417). The epochality of Freud's discovery was proudly proclaimed by protagonists of psychoanalysis.

The Freudian legend would have us assume that the changes wrought in the cultural understanding of dreams since the beginning of the twentieth century have been brought about through the advent of psychoanalysis, and that before Freud, there is no significant story to tell, other than a tale of superstition and error. The historical account of the transformation of the understanding of dreams in Western culture would then take the form of cultural histories of the psychoanalytic movement. Indeed, the impression one gleans from such works as Nathan Hale and Elisabeth Roudinesco's respective two-volume tomes on the history of psychoanalysis in America and France is that the broadscale cultural transformations in psychological understanding should be viewed as the derivatives of the saga of the Freudian dynasty.[3]

In the public imagination, Jung is primarily associated with the subject of dreams. A large measure of the public interest in Jung stems from his approach to dreams. The reason for this is that under the guise of a modern scientific psychological theory, he valorized the prophetic and mysterious powers of the dream, to a greater extent than any other modern psychologist.

In 1935, while in London to give a series of lectures at the Institute of Medical Psychology, Jung gave an interview to the *Evening Standard*, which was titled, "HE PROBES MAN'S DREAMS: Professor Jung Says He is a Practical Psychologist," which commenced with the following admonition:

"Tell your practical English readers that I am a practical man, not a mystic full of crazy theories," said Professor Jung, the famous Swiss psychologist, to me in his London Hotel. As an example of his practical outlook, he stated: "The great way to see a man's unconscious mind is through his dreams. What a man dreams may be something that happened in the past or something that will happen in the

---

[3] Hale, 1971, 1995; Roudinesco, 1986, 1990; Schwartz, 1999.

future" . . . I quoted to him the case of the racing journalist who recently dreamed of the correct result of a big race, and published his result in a newspaper the day before the race. "Undoubtedly it was a prevision of the future," he declared. "I could give you a thousand such examples . . ." (Barker, 1935)

This sums up the paradox of Jung's approach to dreams: how could an empirical scientific psychologist validate the prophetic qualities of dreams, and fail to be simply regarded as having fallen prey to super-stition?

Among psychotherapists, Jungians are widely considered to place the most emphasis on dreams. Within the Freudian tradition, when not being surreptitiously plundered, Jung's work on dreams is viewed as a reversion to superstition. Within the Jungian tradition, Jung's work on dreams is accorded a secondary place to that of Freud. While Freud, it is claimed, discovered that dreams had a meaning, it was Jung who discovered what their meaning really was. In this respect, the Jungian legend is a branch grafted onto the Freudian legend. From both perspectives, the question of the sources of Jung's understanding of dreams has not arisen, as it has been answered in advance with a one-word answer: Freud.

In the following, this assumption will be eschewed. By contrast, I will claim that it is only through understanding the transformations of dream theories in the nineteenth century that one is in a position to grasp the comparative sources of Freud's and Jung's dream theories, their respective reception, and consequently, their role in shaping contemporary dream cultures.

One of the first to question the originality of Freud's dream theory and its relation to prior dream theories was Freud's great rival Pierre Janet. In 1919 he noted that in contrast to previous researchers, Freud had not concerned himself with the disorders of memory, through which dreams were transformed, nor with how individuals systematized their dreams on waking (vol. 1, 605). Citing Alfred Maury's statement that in dreams, passions and desires found freer expression than in the waking state and Alphonse Daudet's description of the dream as a safety valve, Janet commented, "for these authors, the principle to which they referred was merely a particular law applicable to certain dreams and not to all. Freud has transformed this partial hypothesis into a general principle" (606). Thus for Janet, Freud had simply taken what were held to be characteris-tic of certain dreams, and unrestrictedly applied them to all dreams. This statement was in line with Janet's general evaluation of psychoanalysis, namely, that it had turned partial truths into general errors.

In 1926, through a lengthy study of the dream in the French tradi-tion, Raymond de Saussure concluded that the issues that Freud took up concerning the dream had been long established before him, and that there was nothing thematically new in Freud's work. He argued that what Freud had done was to synthesize and limit the work of previous dream researchers. This was because his interest was not the dream per se, but what it could reveal about the affective life of the subject.[4] De Saussure's work made no impact. More notice was taken of Henri Ellenberger's briefer reiteration of de Saussure's point, almost fifty years later, in *The Discovery of the Unconscious*.[5] Despite such works, the epochality of Freud's work on dreams continues to be proclaimed. Part of the problem of placing *The Interpretation of Dreams* is the fact that Freud commenced it with a literature review, which continues to be taken uncritically by scholars.[6] What is clearly needed is a general history of dream theories, which would enable an account of how the dream was utilized to establish psychologies of the unconscious in the last quarter of the nineteenth century, and how Freud's and Jung's dream theories were constituted on this basis. Such an account would contribute to understanding the creation of the modern dream cultures, and how psychology has transformed sensibilities.[7]

There exists an undated manuscript of Jung's consisting of a list of 78 writers on the subject of dreams.[8] Many of these have page references to specific texts indicated. The following are among the authors cited:

Bleuler, Blobbs, Burdach, Carus, Delage, Delboeuf, Erdman, Eschenmayer, Fechner, I. H. Fichte, Frazer, Freud, Garbe, Gassendi, Kant, Lélut, Lemoine, M. Wagner, Maudsley, Maury, Michelet, Mourley Vold, Rabier, Radestock, Rasmunsen, Scherner, Schleiermacher, Schopenhauer, Schubert, Seafield, Siebeck, Spitta, Steffens, Stekel, Strumpell, Sully, Thurnwald, Tissié, Troxler, Ulrici, Vaschide, Volkelt, Weygandt, Wundt.

---

[4] 1926, 58–59. In his review of Freud's *Interpretation of Dreams*, Théodore Flournoy perceptively stated: "Mr. Freud's ideas can be readily understood and that their *raison d'être* and correctness can be perceived much better when one does not lose sight of the special terrain that is both the point of departure and the point of application of his research on the dream: to understand psychopathological processes, in particular the subconscious phenomena of hysteria" (in Kiell, ed., 1988, 167).

[5] 1970, 303–311. Stephen Kern also argued that almost every element of Freud's dream theory had been put forward before him (1975, 83). Kern gave examples of Freud's tendentious citation of authors in his opening chapters, how in several instances, he omitted to cite precisely those aspects that were closest to his theories, such as Hildebrandt's claim that dreams reveal our "unconscious disposition" and raised the question, "Who is really the master in our house?" (85) – a phrase which was subsequently used by Freud and Jung to indicate the radicality of the advent of the psychology of the unconscious.

[6] For example, Decker, 1975. For one corrective, see Lavie and Hobson, 1986.

[7] For reasons of space, the one major area not considered here is articulations of dreams in literature. See Béguin, 1967, and James, 1995.

[8] "Dream problem" (JP). Also found with this manuscript is a letter of reply to Jung from one of his colleagues, the Indologist Emil Abegg, giving him details of Indian dream interpretation (January 16, 1922).

This list attests to a detailed and comprehensive study of the dream liter-ature of the eighteenth and nineteenth centuries. It is like a fragment of a vast unfinished and unrealized work on the history of dreams. It is unclear as to how many of these works Jung was familiar with prior to putting forward his own dream theories. In 1925, he gave a seminar at Swan-age, in Dorset on dream interpretation in antiquity. He considered the modern revival of dream interpretation, and particularly as practiced by the Zürich school, as a "revival of this antique science" (Crow, 1925, 1). In the late 1930s he gave a seminar at the Swiss Federal Institute of Technology on old books on dream interpretation from the Greeks to the present. The seminar took the form of formal presentations of selected texts by members of his seminar group. He did not publish anything con-cerning this research. To answer the question as to why the history of dreams may have held such fascination and interest for him, one has to enter into this nocturnal labyrinth oneself. Moreover, tracing the ques-tion of how the dream has been considered in Western societies from the eighteenth century to the present opens up the possibility of compre-hending the constitution of our modern dream cultures, and indicating their relativity.

The philosophy of sleep

In 1923 in *The Ego and the Id*, Freud claimed that most people educated in philosophy simply could not conceive of anything psychical which was also not conscious. This, he contended, was because they had never stud-ied dreams and hypnotism (*SE* 19, 13). This statement would lead one to conclude that a study of dreams and hypnosis would lead one to grasp what had been unthinkable by the philosophical tradition, and that psy-choanalysis had consequently overturned the philosophical tradition.[9] However, contrary to the impression given by this passage, philosophers had long pondered the subject of dreams, and written about them at length. Indeed, the topic of dreams properly belonged to philosophy, be-fore it was annexed by the emergent psychological disciplines in the later half of the nineteenth century, psychoanalysis among them. As a back-drop for looking at the transformation of dream theories in the eighteenth and nineteenth centuries, it is useful to consider briefly the philosophical background.

---

[9] On this question, see Borch-Jacobsen, 1991b. Through a study of the concepts of the cerebral unconscious in nineteenth-century psychophysiology, Marcel Gauchet concludes that Freud's claim that prior to psychoanalysis it was the rule to equate the psychical with the conscious is "rigorously false" (1992, 32).

René Descartes' *Meditations on First Philosophy* (1641), traditionally considered to be the inaugural moment of modern philosophy, commences with a consideration of dreams. Setting out to doubt all that could be doubted, Descartes (1596–1690) pondered the fact that in one's dreams one often had the same experiences that madmen had while awake, and often mistakenly takes one's self to be in particular material surroundings. This led him to the conclusion that there are no clear signs to distinguish being awake from dreaming. Dreams thus figure as the exemplars of the lack of the very certitude that Descartes sets out to establish in the *Meditations*. This culminated in his speculation that the external world was a dream delusion devised by a malicious demon to ensnare our judgment. As Georges Lanteri Laura noted, for Descartes, the dream was principally used as an argument that destroyed the authority of sense experience, as opposed to forming an object of research in its own right (1968, 26). However, while he claimed to have been able to differentiate waking thought from the dream, the precise relations between the two continued to vex subsequent philosophers and psychologists.[10]

For the Cartesians, dreams were viewed as the form that thinking took in sleep. Their axiom of the continuity of thought led to the positing of the notion of the continuity of dreaming during sleep. While subsequent philosophers put forward multifarious understandings of dreams, this position was generally held. For instance, in *The Principles of Human Understanding* (1671), the English philosopher John Locke (1623–1704) stated: "The *dreams* of sleeping men *are*, as I take it, all *made up of the waking man's* ideas, though for the most part oddly put together" (41). Locke put forward a subtractive model of the dream, considering dreaming to be having ideas not suggested by external objects. Thus the dream was generally considered to consist of waking thought, minus some particular factor. This accounted for its lesser epistemological status.

In the eighteenth century, the continuity thesis and the subtractive model were generally adhered to. Waking thought and thinking in dreams were generally seen to be subject to the same mechanisms. Towards the end of the eighteenth century, thinkers such as Borsch, Mendelssohn, and Nudow distinguished between the objective associations of waking and the totally subjective associations of the dream, in which the laws of similarity and analogy took the place of the real relations between things. Dreaming was seen as a secondary form: both in valuation, and in derivation. The key question was one of determining the difference

---

[10] Lanteri Laura noted that for Voltaire, contrastingly, "The phenomena of the dream . . . shows the precariousness of this pretension of human thought to be sufficient to itself and thus destroys the Cartesian desire for a knowledge founded on the autarchy of reflexive thought," *ibid.*, 29.

between the two states. This took the form of determining the causes, which, in weakened consciousness, troubled the regular functioning of association.[11]

An example of such an approach was the Scottish philosopher, Dugald Stewart (1753–1828). In his *Elements of the Philosophy of the Human Mind* (1792), he began his consideration of dreams by stating that the best means of ascertaining the state of the mind in sleep was to consider its condition just prior to sleep. The principal characteristic of this state was the suspension of volitional activities. In order to sleep, we brought our body and mind close to the state in which they would continue in sleep (283). He took this absence of volition to be the principal characteristic of dreaming. Hence all mental operations which were independent of the will could continue during sleep. Through explaining dreaming by analogy to the state of mind just prior to sleep, the latter took on an epistemological priority. Stewart argued that the peculiarity of dreams could be simply explained by the fact that in dreams, the association of ideas took place minus the factor of volition. In dreams, the operation of thoughts depended solely on the power of association, while in waking life, it depended on the power of association together with waking exertion. The absence of volition also served to explain why the scenes and occurrences which presented themselves in dreams were most frequently those of childhood and youth, when the facility of association was much stronger. He concluded that understanding the function of dreaming had the value of shedding light not only on the state of mind in sleep, but on the general functioning of the mind, as it would illuminate the relations between the different parts of our constitution. The dream was thus the royal road to the mind.

In the nineteenth century, the associationist approach to dreams was carried over by psychology, and constituted one of the major components of the understanding of dreams. Dream dictionaries, or dream keys flourished.[12] While their basic format was a direct continuity from antiquity, their interpretations were updated to reflect contemporary social values. The very antiquity of the genre was appealed to as witness to the veracity of dream symbolism. Benedetto Gentile commenced his 1882 *Book of Dreams or Oneiroscopy* by citing the belief in dream divination held by the Egyptians, the Chaldeans, the Greeks, and the Romans (6). The dream keys took the form of classificatory schemata of dream images. The following is a series of examples from Gentile:

---

[11] This paragraph is based on Béguin, 1967, 5–7.

[12] The following three paragraphs are based on Ripa, 1988, coupled with a survey of nineteenth-century dream keys.

To wash one's hands, denotes work.
To look at one's hands, denotes infirmity.
To see a house burn, denotes scandal.
To see a house established, denotes war. (98)

The dream keys gave the signification of particular images, portraying the fate connected to them. Images were often arrayed in complex relations. In Raphael's work, one learns that:

ANCHOR – To dream of an anchor in water is a bad omen; it implies disappointment in your wishes and endeavours. To dream of an anchor part in water and part out, foretells that you will speedily have a voyage. For a young woman to dream of an anchor [indicates] she will have a sailor for a husband. To dream you see an anchor difficult to weigh is a good sign, denoting your abiding prosperity. (1886, 109)

The symbolism they used often drew upon astrological, numerological, and Kabbalistic traditions.[13] In the dream keys, images were seen as revelatory of the personality. The dream was attributed a moral and protective function. Particular dreams were seen as critiques of the dreamer's attitude, and as indicating correctives. Rules were laid down as to the interpretation of dreams, such as the reversal of signification: that dreams announced the opposite of what they seemed to indicate. For example, Raphael described dreaming of gallows as "a dream of contrary. You will be lucky in all ways – much trade, much money, much honour, a high position" (139). The keys were predominantly conservative and traditionalistic in their formulations.

The interpretation of dreams took place outside of any professional relation. The book laid bare the secret of dreams, and made their decipherment available to all. Thus the dream keys promoted an auto-interpretive dream practice. Alongside this, individuals practiced as dream interpreters.

Within the philosophical and medical approaches to dreams in the eighteenth and early nineteenth centuries, attempts were made to provide naturalistic explanations of dreams, which freed them from spiritual interpretations, and in particular, from what were regarded as the superstitions of the dream keys. The scientific explanations were written against the dream keys, which were frequently not explicitly mentioned. However, the relation between these traditions was not simply one of straightforward opposition, as the scientific approach to dreams often covertly drew upon the keys of dreams.

---

[13] For an astrological dream book, see Raphael, 1886; for a dream book drawing from astrology and numerology, see D'Albumazar De Carpenteri, 1822; for a dream book drawing on the Kabbalah, see Gentile, 1822.

While in philosophy dreams were principally viewed as mental states, in medicine dreams were conceived in physiological terms. For example, the French physician Pierre Cabanis (1757–1808) stated in 1802 that the characteristics of dreams stemmed from the fact that the action of the external senses was suspended. This had the effect of withdrawing nervous energy to the cerebral organ, which was abandoned to its own impressions or those from "internal sentient extremities," without these being corrected by impressions from external objects (5). This served to explain the content of dreams: "The compression of the diaphragm, the work of the digestion, the action of the genital organs often bring back old events, or persons, or reasonings, or images of places one had entirely lost from sight" (625). The continuity of mental activity in dreams served also to provide a rational explanation of phenomena that were seized upon by the superstitious. He cited the example of Benjamin Franklin, who claimed that he had been instructed on matters that concerned him in his dreams. Cabanis contended that Franklin hadn't paid sufficient attention to the fact that his prudence and wisdom still operated while asleep, and that the "mind may continue its own research in dreams" (626). He also highlighted the "constant and definite relations" between dreams and delirium, which he attributed to the Scottish physician William Cullen (602). This relation came to play a prominent role in the psychiatric understanding of dreams in the nineteenth century.

In 1809 the French philosopher Maine de Biran (1766–1824) stated in his "New considerations on sleep, dreams and somnambulism," that the exploration of dreams should be properly seen as a part of physiology. He upheld the subtractive view of dreaming. Dreams and somnambulism were characterized by an absence of judgment, reflection, and controlled attention (85). This led him to equate dreams with insanity. Even in such physiological accounts, room was given for what would later be termed psychological factors. Thus he noted in dreams the "return of images connected to primitive affections," such as the memories of youth (101). The attempt to establish the physiological mechanisms of the dream had the effect of desacralizing the dream, and was aimed against the continued popular belief in the prophetic and symbolic powers of the dream. However, as we shall see, there were other developments that set out to reverse these developments.

The hidden language of the soul

The subtractive model of dreaming, and the view of the dream as a secondary phenomenon, were overturned in German Romanticism. In the place of the subtractive models, positive views were put forward that stressed the poetic qualities of the dream, and its status as a deeper revelation of the essence of being than waking consciousness. What took place was a reversal of hierarchy between sleep and waking. Rather than seeing the dream as a lower, derivative condition of waking consciousness, it was viewed as a higher state. The philosopher-physician Ignaz Troxler (1780–1866), considered the dream to be the "revelation of the very essence of man."[14] The most prominent study of dreams was Gotthilf Heinrich von Schubert's *The Symbolism of Dreams* (1814). Schubert (1780–1860) had studied with Schelling, whom he nominated as the most influential figure in his life.[15] Schubert stated that in the dream, the soul spoke another language than in waking life, a universal hieroglyphic picture language of symbols. The soul expressed itself more fully in dreams. The language of dreams was more appropriate to its nature than natural language, and infinitely more expressive (1814, 35). Dreams stemmed from the "poet hidden in us," and their language was poetic and metaphorical. Consequently, a translation of the language of dreams into the language of waking was necessary. The oneiric language was a natural activity of the soul. Schubert's valorization of the language of dreams was also reflected in his ideas concerning the history of language. While poetry was the original language of the people, prose was a later invention. Poetry was infinitely more expressive, more powerful and more magical than prose. He highlighted the protective function of dreams. A large part of our oneiric images seemed to be the product of a good spirit protecting us. The association of ideas of the conscience in dreams was other than that of waking thought, and opposed to it:

One of the two faces of Janus of our double-sided nature seems to laugh when the other cries, or sleeps and only speaks in dreams when the other is the most awake and speaks loudly. When the outer man gives himself freely and joyously to all the pleasures, a voice expresses an inner aversion and a profound sadness comes to trouble our drunkenness . . . The more the outer man triumphs with a robust energy, the more the inner man weakens and seeks refuge in the world of obscure sentiments and dreams. (83–84)

The symbolism of dreams intersected with the findings of archeology in important ways:

Finally, this hieroglyphic image language which has been particularly observed in the ancient Egyptian monuments and on the strange figures of ancient idols of the oriental peoples present a striking kinship with the image language of the dream. Through the aid of this kinship, we can perhaps succeed in finding the lost key which would give us access to part of the sign language of nature not elucidated up to now; thanks to this key, we could obtain much more than a simple enlargement of our archeological and mythological knowledge. (46)

---

[14] Cited in Béguin, 1967, 93.
[15] Roelke, 1994, 128. On Schelling, see below, 171–173.

While the philosophical and physiological tradition had been at pains to set aside and to explain away the popular prophetic and symbolic interest in dreams, as represented by the dream keys, he thought that a great deal of the content of the dream keys was founded on pertinent observations. He affirmed the prophetic quality of dreams, and took such dreams as paradigmatic of the nature of dreaming. Thus he could be said to have validated the popular dream keys through providing them with a metaphysics. His work was widely read. However, it did not play a significant role in psychiatry (Marx, 1991, 22).

Dreams were also given importance in the tradition of animal magnetism, or mesmerism. This was due to the filiation of dreams with somnambulism, or artificial sleep. The following are the principal faculties that were attributed to states of somnambulism: the ability to estimate the time, the insensibility to the exterior, the exaltation of the imagination, the development of intellectual faculties, the instinct of remedies, prevision, the communication of the symptoms of the sick, the communication of thoughts, seeing without the help of the senses, the possibility of an influence exercised by a somnambulist on their own organization, the power of seeing into the future and the exaltation of memory (Bertrand, 1826, 408–417). It was held that the dreams that occurred in states of somnambulism were identical to those that occurred in sleep. Through analogy, the properties attributed to states of somnambulism were likewise attributed to dreams. Thus Alexandre Bertrand (1795–1831) noted that in somnambulism, there was an absence of self-reflection, attention and the ability to turn back upon oneself to know the state in which one found oneself. This was comparable to dreams, in which one was affected by a multitude of bizarre and incoherent sensations, which caused us a great deal of surprise in the waking state, but not while we were dreaming (425). In dreams and somnambulism, ideas were independent of the will (426), and ideas in magnetic crises came about in the same way as in dreams, in which one found oneself dreaming of the person whom one thought of on going to sleep (1823, 468). Hence "somnambulism . . . hardly merits to be distinguished from dreams, and constitutes not much other than a *dream in action*" (*ibid.*, 468). This connection was later elaborated by the German philosopher Arthur Schopenhauer (1788–1860), who stated in 1851:

the dream becomes the connecting link, the bridge, between somnambulistic and waking consciousness. According to this, we must, therefore, first attribute prophetic dreams to the fact that in deep sleeping dreaming is enhanced to a somnambulistic clairvoyance.[16]

---

[16] 1851, 254–255. On Schopenhauer, see below, 173–174.

The linkage between dreams and somnambulism was subsequently carried over into the linkage between dreams and hypnosis. August Forel (1848–1931), who played a pivotal role in introducing hypnotic suggestion into Switzerland claimed that the three main characteristics of the dream were the same as those of hypnotic consciousness. These were: "hallucinations of perception, exaggerated feeling and reflex action of the same, and dissociation of the organic logical associations of the engram complexes."[17] In dreams, the stimuli of the senses rarely called forth normal perception. In this respect, the dreamer resembled the hypnotized individual, with the proviso that when the hypnotizer was present, the former was conscious of his influences (86).

Diagnostic dreams

Since antiquity, the principal use of dreams in medical practice was as diagnostic tools. Dreams were taken as disclosive of bodily states. This approach remained prominent in the nineteenth century, and was presented in 1830 by Robert Macnish (1802–1837) in his popular *Philosophy of Sleep*. He held to the subtractive view of dreaming. The essential conditions for dreaming were a suspension of judgment coupled with an active state of memory and imagination (50). Dreams had an important mnemonic function, of being able to recall to mind events which had been forgotten "and restoring them with all the force of their original impression" (116). This took on a moral dimension, under the form of conscience. In waking life, individuals might seek to evade the "memory of their wickedness" and to silence "the still small voice" of conscience. In sleep however, their crimes appeared "in naked and horrible deformity" (94–95). Dreams also had a diagnostic and prognostic function: "Violent and impetuous dreams occurring in fevers generally indicate approaching delirium; those of a gloomy terrific nature give strong grounds to apprehend danger; while dreams of a pleasant cast may be looked upon as harbingers of recovery" (68). Particular diseases gave particular characters to dreams: "jaundice tinges the objects beheld, with its own yellow and sickly hue; hunger induces dreams of eating agreeable food" (69).

A similar position was put forward towards the end of the nineteenth century, by Philippe Tissié, a French physician in Bordeaux, in his *Dreams: Physiology and Pathology*. He maintained that our organs created dreams, which meant that dreams could enable the early detection of a disease:

---

[17] 1906, 84. On Forel, see below, 186–187.

Affections of the circulatory apparatus are generally revealed by a sentiment of fear, anxiety, breathless anguish; by visual hallucinations, by short, frightening, tragic dreams, by ideas of impending death, by scenes of dying, by carnage, by visions of objects in flames, by sensations of falling, by receiving a wound. Waking is brought about with a start. (1898, 201)

Similarly, the physician Maurice Macario argued that the incubation of a disease could provoke dreams. In a case of heart disease, one might find dreams of being pierced in the heart by a sword (1857, 86–87). Dreams varied with each type of madness: in "expansive" monomania, dreams were happy and laughing; in mania they were strange, bizarre and disordered. Following from this, one could use dreams to monitor an individual's state of health (88–90).

While such works made no mention of the popular keys of dreams, in drawing symbolic connections between specific imagery and bodily conditions, they were clearly reliant upon them. Yannick Ripa observed:

The symbolism of the body takes the relay of the symbolism of the keys . . . Do the keys not give, through the function of the purport of dreams, veritable diagnostics? . . . It is certainly right to ask if the adoption of the medical views was not largely facilitated by the striking resemblances. (1988, 150)

There are some indications in nineteenth-century psychiatry that dreams were also seen as disclosive of psychological states. In his *Principles of Medical Psychology* (1845) the German psychiatrist Ernst von Feuchtersleben (1806–1849) considered dreams as "the occupation of the mind in sleep with the pictorial world of fancy" (315). Following the German philosopher Immanuel Kant (1724–1804), von Feuchtersleben attributed a teleological function to dreams. In his *Critique of Judgment* (1790), Kant had speculated that dreams had the purpose of stimulating the vital organs by means of imagination. He suggested that without this stimulation and the psychophysical agitation that it led to, sleep would amount to a complete extinction of life.[18] Von Feuchtersleben denied any prophetic quality to dreams. However, they could provide a form of retrospective understanding, through their mnemonic function:

dreams may give a man historical information respecting himself, and hence, according to a favourite expression, 'he may divine like a prophet looking backwards.' As when the sun has gone down, the countless stars, not visible in daytime, appear on the dark ground of the firmament, so, at the call of fancy, the forgotten images of bygone days rise up and show the mind its former shape. (1845, 315)

---

[18] 29. On Kant, see below, 168–171.

He advocated the clinical investigation of dreams. Dreams as the "unconscious language of the coenaesthesis," showed the state of the patient. Hence physicians should study the interpretation of dreams (198–199). It is not clear what influence von Feuchtersleben's recommendations had, nor to what extent such "divining backwards" – which was to become the predominant mode of modern psychotherapy – had already become established in psychiatric practice at this stage. Nevertheless, his discussion of dreams indicates that the theoretical presuppositions for the clinical utilization of dreams as a means of memory retrieval had been established before 1850.

Dreams and madness

Analogies between dreams, insanity and what were regarded as kindred states, such as somnambulism and intoxication, played significant roles in the nineteenth century. The strength of these analogies was differently conceived: at times a phenomenon was likened to another phenomenon, declared identical to it, or subsumed as a subspecies of it. The significance of these analogies was that they enabled the understanding of one phenomenon via another, even though the precise relations were rarely specified. Further, these analogical chains had the significance that the reconceptualization of some particular phenomena often had a knock-on effect all along the chain. This analogical form of reasoning about dreams has survived intact, right up to the present day.[19]

The German physician Johann Reil (1759–1813), who was the first to coin the term "psychiatry," considered dreams as analogous to madness:

In dreams we always wander in appearances of spaces, time and our person. We spring from one part of the world to another, from one century over to another and play each role from king to beggar, that the magical fantasy grants us. Precisely this occurs in madness, which is a dream while awake. (1803, 87)

He argued that the character of dreams stemmed from the fact that they were "a product of a partial wakening of the nervous system" (92). They shared this characteristic with madness. In dreams, fantasy was present, either alone, or in conjunction with an individual sense organ. He also remarked upon the "peculiar art" of the dream – that the dreamer seemed only to take on roles connected with their personality. He cited Lichtenberg, who had called this a dramatized reflection (93–94). The likeness of dreams to insanity precluded their therapeutic utilization.

[19] On the linkage between intoxication and dreams, see James, 1995, 98–129.

In the middle half of the nineteenth century, one of the best-known psychiatric textbooks was the German psychiatrist Wilhelm Griesinger's *Mental Pathology and Therapeutics*. This text was one of the prime representatives of what was characterized as the somaticist approach in psychiatry. Griesinger (1817–1868) claimed that our knowledge of insanity was increased through consideration of analogous states, one of which was the dream. In the insane, there occurred states of sensation and motion that resembled dreams. Sometimes in insanity, as in dreams, the sense of time was absent. This analogy was most marked in dreams occurring in the half-waking state. Dreams received their fundamental tone from the governing disposition. He drew an analogy between one's conduct in dreams, and that of the insane:

The dreamer, like the insane, accepts all, even the most adventurous and foolish, representations as possibilities without particular astonishment, and the veriest absurdity becomes the most unquestionable truth, if the masses of perception which can rectify it remain dormant. (1867, 108)

Ravishing dreams were rare in states of health, and frequent in states of ill-health. Ideas suppressed in waking life came forth in dreams. To troubled individuals, dreams realized what reality had refused. Thus he stated that in dreams and in insanity, one often found the imaginary fulfillment of wishes, and the reversal of disappointments.[20] However, in his section on therapeutics, there was no mention of the subject of dreams, which seems to indicate that they were not therapeutically utilized.[21]

[20] In *The Interpretation of Dreams*, Freud paraphrased Griesinger's views on dreams and psychoses as being wishfulfillments and concluded, "My own researches have taught me that in this fact lies the key to a psychological theory of both dreams and psychoses" (*SE* 4, 91).

[21] One of the most persistent analogies was that between dreams and hallucinations. In 1832, the French psychiatrist Jean-Étienne-Dominique Esquirol described hallucinations as waking dreams (2). In 1867 Hervey de Saint-Denys stated: "Hallucinations are nothing but the dreams of a waking man" (141). Following in this vein, Freud posited that dreams have a hallucinatory character: "we shall be in agreement with every authority on the subject in asserting that dreams *hallucinate* – that they replace thoughts by hallucinations" (*SE* 4, 114). Janet challenged this analogy: "it is a grave mistake to confound the dream with suggestion and hallucination" (1919, 287). He claimed that what was distinctive about an hallucination was not, as commonly thought, that a subject saw or heard something that was not actually present, but that a subject acted impulsively: i.e., that the subject behaved as if he or she had been signaled, or as if he or she had heard abusive language. Without these behavioral manifestations, a hallucination would be something incommunicable, and hence unknowable. Contrastingly, he thought that dreams were marked by the absence of such outward actions. While a hallucination was "a tendency activated by a high degree of tension," a dream was "a tendency which is not activated at all" (*ibid.*).

The psychologization of the dream

The next period, from the mid-century onwards, was marked by the major dream investigators, such as Karl Scherner, Alfred Maury, and Hervey de Saint-Denys. According to Havelock Ellis, it was Maury in 1861 who inaugurated the modern study of dreams (1911, vi). André Breton described him as "one of the finest observers and experimenters ever to have appeared during the nineteenth century" (1932, 12). These investigators left to one side the romantic views on dreams, together with the continuing public interest in the prophetic capacity of dreams. The main method of investigation used was introspection. Psychology became increasingly used as a self appellation for such research, which was mainly geared towards establishing taxonomies of the different types of dreams, providing explanations of their respective causes, and putting forward physiological explanations of dreaming.

Ian Dowbiggen argues that during this period in France, dreams were charged with cultural and political significance, owing to Romantic exaltation of the dream as a source of creativity and revelation that gave access to truths which were inaccessible in waking states (1990, 277). For Maury, dreams enabled the understanding of cognate irrational phenomena, such as mesmerism and somnambulism. While the magnetists had employed the analogy between somnambulism and dreams to valorize the latter, he used it in the other direction, to devalue states of somnambulism and to discredit the practices of mesmerism. The analogy between dreams and madness took the form of likening dreams to hallucinations (1861, 124).

Maurice Macario classified dreams into the following types: sensory dreams, dream-hallucinations, dream-illusions, affective dreams, intellectual dreams, prodromic dreams, symptomatic dreams, morbid dreams (1857). The classificatory systems of the psychologists did not simply impose order on a previously uncharted terrain; rather, they replaced the already established systems of classifications in the dream keys. The latter consisted in classificatory systems of dreams, embedding dream images within a vast semantic network of personal, familial, societal, and cosmic significations. By contrast, the classificatory systems of the dream investigators extracted the dream from this semantic network and isolated it as a discrete epistemological object located within the interior of the subject. The dream investigators attempted to purge the dream of this vast social, religious, and cosmic network of signification. While the dream keys had focused upon the dream scene as the key identifying factor of the dream, the dream investigators shifted their emphasis to the type of the dream. They attempted to provide explanations not of particular dreams, but of classes of dreams through explaining their function. The relegation of the practice of dream interpretation was an aspect of this endeavor. Through the psychologization of the dream, the dream became increasingly viewed as disclosive of hidden subjectivity. For Maury:

In the dream, man is thus entirely revealed to himself in his nudity and his native misery. Since it suspends the action of his will, he becomes the plaything of all the passions, against which, in the waking state, conscience, the sentiment of honour, and fear defends us. (1861, 88)

Hence in dreams "we attribute thoughts and speeches to different personages which are nothing other than our own" (115). He highlighted the mnemonic quality of dreams, and denied any prophetic quality to dreams. Thus if dreams were revelatory of the subject, it was a revelation purged of any transcendent dimension.

Ripa argued that the dream studies affected how individuals viewed their dreams during this period. Through a study of nineteenth-century French journals, Ripa noted:

In the large part of the cases, the dream is recounted in the journal, as an account heard, without its begetter commenting on it. The more one advances in this century, and thus in the physiological or psychological discovery of the mechanisms of the dream, the more the annotations multiply: the diarists, whatever their cultural level, take note that the dream is a magnifying mirror of this self which they pursued through words. (1988, 115)

In the latter half of the nineteenth century, the psychogenesis of dreams was reached through different angles. One route was through a delimitation to the psychological components of the dream studied in the physiological tradition. The Belgian philosopher-psychologist Joseph Delboeuf (1831–1896) noted that he would limit himself to the purely psychological aspects of the dream (1880, 130). This epistemological delimitation was closely paralleled by the concurrent attempts to establish psychology as an independent discipline.

Delboeuf set out to study dreams from the double aspect of certitude and memory. He set to one side the "vulgar superstitious" belief in prophetic dreams, and claimed that dreams were solely made of past events, and shed no light on the future (647). After a critical review of recent works on dreams, he recounted the first dream he recorded after deciding to write on the topic of dreams. This dream featured two lizards, and a plant that he saw on a wall, an *asplenium ruta muralis*. On waking, he assumed that he had made up the name of this plant. However, he was informed that there existed a fern, called the *asplenium ruta muraria*, which grew on walls, though it looked different. Two years later, he discovered the source of this image. While visiting a friend, he saw a copy of a herbarium album. He recalled that in 1860, he had written, at the dictation of a botanist, the family and class of each plant beside the name. In this album, he found a picture of the *asplenium*. The following year, he was leafing through a copy of the *Tour du monde* at his parents' home, when he came across an engraving of lizards which was the exact representation of the second part of his dream. The journal was dated 1861 (133–134). He utilized this dream to draw a general conclusion concerning the permanence of memory traces: "one is authorized to infer that all impressions, even the most insignificant, leave an unalterable trace, indefinitely susceptible to come back to light."[22]

With the expansion of concepts of memory and inheritance, the way was open to conceiving dreams as representing the revivification of cultural or ancestral memories. In 1876, the British psychophysiologist Thomas Laycock (1812–1876) argued that in dreams we reverted beyond our immediate ancestors to "substrate of the race acquired during savage life in long-distant ages."[23] In a similar vein, Friedrich Nietzsche drew a far reaching evolutionary connection between dreams and history in *Human, all too Human*:

in our sleep and dreams, we go through the work of earlier mankind once more . . . I think that man still draws conclusions in his dreams as mankind once did *in a waking state*, through many thousands of years: the first *causa* that needed explaining sufficed and was taken for truth . . . This old aspect of humanity lives on in us in our dreams, for it is the basis upon which higher reason developed, and is still developing, in every human: the dream gives us a means by which to understand them better. Dream thought is so easy for us now, because, during mankind's immense periods of development, we have been so well drilled in just this form of fantastic and cheap explanation from the first, best idea. In this way dreaming is recuperation for a brain which must satisfy by day the stricter demands made on thought by higher culture. (1880, 20–21)

Thus the transition from sleep to waking could be considered to be a recapitulation of the course of cultural history. For Nietzsche, this analogy between dreams and history designated the formal similarity between the form of thinking in dreams and that prevalent in antiquity. Rather than seeing the thinking in dreams as simply a secondary derivation of waking thought, he saw the latter as an evolutionary development of the former.

---

[22] 136. On the significance of this conception in the development of memory theories, see below, 189. François Duckyearts notes the striking structural similarities between Delboeuf's work and Freud's *Interpretation of Dreams*, arguing that Freud's work was self-consciously modeled on Delboeuf's (1993, 241).

[23] 179. See below, 185.

Symbolism and associationism

The dream had been purged of a large part of its signification through being reconceptualized as a subjective psychological component of the dreamer. However, it recovered a range of personal signification through attempts to establish a restricted symbology of the dream and through associationist psychology. In 1861 Karl Albert Scherner, a philosopher at the University of Breslau, published a study entitled *The Life of the Dream*.[24] In 1917 Freud hailed Scherner as "the true discoverer of symbolism in dreams" (*SE* 15, 152) – which is an odd statement, given the longevity of the tradition of symbolic dream interpretation represented by the dream keys. Scherner argued that the psychic activity in dreams expressed itself via symbolic language, and that it was possible to interpret this. While asleep, the dreamer possessed a greater sensitivity to bodily sensations. These sensations translated themselves into dream images. Hence the greater part of this symbolism was related to the human body. He emphasized the significance of the disguised sexual symbolism in dreams. His restricted code of dream symbolism can be seen as an attempt to free the symbolizing activity of dreams from the metaphysical cosmology represented in the dream keys.

The arrogation of the authority to designate the symbolic code of dreams had the significance that psychologists, in the form of a science shorn of superstition, were now in a position to create new symbologies for the culture at large. In the twentieth century, it was principally the work of Freud, Jung, and their followers which had this effect.

The symbolic understanding of dreams, in whatever form, tended to the establishment of general meanings. Paralleling such transformations of the symbolic understanding of dreams was the significance accorded the multifarious and individual sources of dream imagery, through the tradition of associationist psychology. In 1893, the English psychologist James Sully (1824–1923) stated that in waking states, the paths of the association of ideas were not visible due to the force of sense impressions and volitional control. As these were withdrawn in dreams, the threads of association "made known their hidden force" (1893a, 158). The apparent unintelligibility of the dream was due to the fact that it laid bare the underlying associative process, which was partially masked in a waking state. He drew from this the following conclusion:

It will be possible, I think, after a habit of analysing one's dreams in the light of preceding experience has been formed, to discover in a good proportion of cases

---

[24] On Scherner, see Massey, 1990, and Hauser, 1992. Hauser translated a chapter of Scherner's book under the title "The sexual stimulation dream."

some hidden force of association which draws together the seemingly fortuitous concourse of dream-atoms. (160)

There are signs that among psychologists, such a practice was not uncommon. On March 12, 1880, Francis Galton wrote to Sully:

some months ago I was quite troubled with over vivid dreams that I confused with fact; indeed I became rather frightened about it . . . [?] told me he went to stay at a house in the North. He went to bed and had an extraordinary dream full of lizards & snakes & got up in the morning full of wonderment about it. Going downstairs he saw a dish of [table]ware with these things on it (you know the dishes I mean) & at once recollected that he had seen it, but had not attended to it, when he went to bed & that the dream was based on it. He is sure that the existence of the dish would have wholly faded from his memory if he had not seen it in the morning, but the memory of the dream might well have endured and its incidents have become the origin of associations connecting the [?] with reptiles.[25]

The same year, Sully published another study of dreams, entitled, "The Dream as Revelation." He commenced by noting that in history, there were two opposing views of dreams: the one seeing in them a degree of insight and intelligence far outstripping waking consciousness, reaching supernatural revelation, and the other dismissing them as simply phantastic by-products of an idle brain. The modern scientific study of dreaming could reconcile these two ideas, as it accounted for the irrational side of dream life, viewing it as an extension of human experience and a revelation of what would otherwise be unknown (1893b, 355). There were three main ways in which the dream could be considered a revelation. First, the simplification of the "mature complex pattern of consciousness" brought into prominence forces and tendencies which were usually hidden, such as "nascent and instantly inhibited impulses" of waking life. He illustrated this with examples that designated the manner in which certain dreams could be considered as the culmination of "a vague fugitive wish of the waking mind" (357–358). The dream "strips the ego of its artificial wrappings and exposes it in its rude native nudity. It brings up from the dim depths of our subconscious life the primal, instinctive impulses" (358). Secondly, he drew an analogy between the phenomena of double or alternate personality, the hypnotic trance and dreams. Utilizing a notion of the multiplicity of the self strongly reminiscent of William James' model in *The Principles of Psychology*, he argued that dreams were means of preserving these successive personalities. In sleep, we reverted to old ways of thinking and feeling about things. It was the dream then, that

---

[25] Sully Papers, University College London. Question marks in square brackets indicate indecipherable words. On Galton, see above, 40.

placed one *in statu nascendi*. Thirdly, he claimed that dreams gave freer rein to individual characteristics and tendencies. In social life, much of our deepest and most vital traits were "repressed and atrophied" (363). He held that it was precisely such aspects that were revealed in dreams. Sully concluded that dreams could be considered as an intrapsychic message:

> Like some letter in a cipher, the dream-inscription when scrutinised closely loses its first look of balderdash and takes on the aspect of a serious, intelligible message . . . we may say that, like some palimpsest, the dream discloses beneath its worthless surface-characters traces of an old and precious communication. (364)

From dreams to the unconscious

Towards the end of the nineteenth century, concepts of the unconscious increasingly became invoked to explain the phenomena of dreams. One influential place where this occurred was in the work of the English physiologist William Carpenter, through his concept of unconscious cerebration. In a study of the cerebral unconscious, Marcel Gauchet studied the development of concepts of the unconscious in nineteenth-century neurology and physiology. He argues that it was due to the concept of the cerebral unconscious that the traditional pre-eminence of the will was called into question and subverted (1992, 24). In his 1874 *Principles of Mental Physiology*, Carpenter commenced his consideration of unconscious cerebration by stating that to affirm that the cerebrum (the uppermost portion of the brain) could act upon impressions and produce intellectual results without any consciousness on our part was held by metaphysicians, especially in Britain, to be impossible (515). Through extending the notion of reflex action, he claimed that a large proportion of mental activity took place automatically, and that this automatic action was unconscious. Under the plane of consciousness, mental actions took place, of whose results we only subsequently became conscious. In support of this view, he cited the example of the forgetting of a name:

> when we have been *trying to recollect* some name, phrase, occurrence, & c., – and, after vainly employing all the expedients we can think of for bringing the desiderated idea to our minds, have abandoned the attempt as useless, – it will often occur *spontaneously* a little while afterwards. (519)

In such instances, the detachment of attention enabled the cerebrum to work by itself, undisturbed by the conscious attempt at recollection. In such circumstances, "two distinct trains of Mental action are carried on simultaneously, – one *consciously*, the other *unconsciously*;" (562). In dreams, which were principally characterized by the suspension of volition, the current of thought flowed automatically. Thus reasoning processes could continue in sleep with vigour and success, and the imagination could develop new forms of beauty. Consequently, he thought that a great part of dreams consisted in the automatic activity of the constructive imagination.[26]

The application of notions of the unconscious to explain dreams did not only stem from physiological psychology, but also from idealist philosophy.[27] In 1875, the German philosopher Johannes Volkelt produced a study entitled *The Dream Phantasy*. Freud cited Volkelt several times in *The Interpretation of Dreams*, and drew upon his account of the work of Karl Scherner. Freud claimed that though Volkelt had penetrated into the nature of the symbolizing imagination, his work was hard to understand for a non-philosopher.[28] In his study, Volkelt articulated a relation between dreams and the unconscious, which Freud made no mention of. Following Scherner, Volkelt stated that there were two groups of dreams, those that stemmed from the body, and those that stemmed from a mood (86). In the reproductive phantasy of dreams, the unconscious creative power of the mind showed itself. The dream phantasy, which operated in the unconscious, seized upon the presenting physical or psychic forms, and remodeled them (167, 157). The dream world and the dream body were both seen as the product of the unconscious dream phantasy. The dream was not the only product of the unconscious: "also in waking consciousness numerous unconscious processes occur – sudden notions, witty aperçus and all kinds of moods" (158). Thus the explication of the dream presented itself as paradigmatic for the explication of kindred processes: "the dream . . . has itself confirmed, that penetrating understanding will first be possible through the concept of the unconscious" (167). In conclusion, he postulated that the age-old problems of philosophy could finally be solved through a consideration of dreams:

The riddle of the world, for whose solution philosophers have for a long time often futilely struggled, the dream practically solves every night . . . in the dream we are near the innermost world: admittedly not with what we experience through the dream images, but with what we unconsciously do and are in the dream forming process. (208)

---

[26] On British psychophysiology see Danziger, 1990b.

[27] On the development of concepts of the unconscious in philosophy, see below, 168–179.

[28] Freud, *SE* 4, 86–87. André Breton accused Freud of plagiarizing Volkelt, which produced some agitated letters from Freud, of which Breton commented: "Freud's manifest agitation on this topic (he writes me two letters a few hours apart, excuses himself profusely, passes off his own apparent wrong on someone who is no longer among his friends . . . only to end by pleading in favor of the latter an unmotivated omission!) is not likely to make me change my mind" (1932, 154).

Tell me your dreams

The term psycho-therapeutics was coined by the English psychiatrist Daniel Hack Tuke in 1872 (Tuke, 1872). It became quickly taken up and used as a synonym for the hypnotic and suggestive therapeutics principally associated with Hyppolite Bernheim (1840–1919) and the Nancy school.

In the 1880s and 1890s, the practice of hypnotic and suggestive therapeutics became increasingly publicly contested, after which it fell into discredit. Several reasons have been put forward for this, principally the dispute between the Nancy and Salpêtrière schools (Janet, Ellenberger) and the forensic battles (Laurence and Perry, Harris).[29] Within texts of this period, one also finds strong concerns articulated around the levels of susceptibility of hypnosis in the population and the appropriateness of authoritarian suggestion at different social levels. Taken together, these strands generated an increasing tendency to develop modes of psychotherapy that were more generally applicable, and that obviated recourse to deep states of trance. A clear articulation of these concerns is found in the Dutch psychotherapist Frederick van Eeden's 1893 paper "Principles of psychotherapy," in which he put forward the maxim that one should seek to use suggestion while exalting suggestion as little as possible. The increasing turn towards memory retrieval made the therapeutic investigation of dreams an obvious choice. For one, dreams were ready at hand, occurring in (or at least, being recalled by) most of the population. Second, not only had dreams become strongly associated with the revivification of past events, principally from childhood, they were also linked to the retrieval of forgotten or "unconscious" impressions, as Delboeuf eloquently argued.

A significant figure in this respect, who took up the therapeutic investigation of dreams, was Pierre Janet (1857–1947). He initially trained in philosophy. From 1883 to 1889, he taught at Le Havre. Under the influence of Dr. Gibert, he commenced studying hypnosis and suggestion (see Carroy, 1999). Janet's investigations resulted in a series of landmark articles, culminating in 1889 in his book *Psychological Automatism*. Continuing his research under the leading French neurologist Jean-Martin Charcot at the Salpêtrière hospital in Paris, he completed his medical studies. In 1893 he presented his medical dissertation, *The Mental States of Hysterics*. That year, Charcot opened a psychological laboratory at the

---

[29] Janet, 1919, 180–207; Ellenberger, 1970, 85–101; and Jean-Roch Laurence and Campbell Perry, 1988, 179–262; Harris, 1989, 155–242.

Salpêtrière, which he entrusted to Janet. In 1902, he succeeded Théodule Ribot in his post at the Collège de France.

In *Psychological Automatism*, Janet considered dreams from the aspect of spontaneous modifications of the personality. Every night, one had a particular mental life that was distinct from one's waking consciousness. While the ideas of dreams were nearly always borrowed from one's normal life, they are presented and arranged differently (1889, 118). Thus dreams represented a group of psychological phenomena isolated from the great mass of ideas of our normal life. These ideas were sufficiently grouped together to form a simple personality. For most individuals, this tendency to form a memory and secondary personality remained rudimentary. However, if one augmented the activity of the dream, one would arrive at a distinct and independent psychological state, akin to a state of somnambulism. Thus the dream and somnambulism were seen as being on a continuum. The latter was seen as a continued or augmented dream. This enabled the explication of one via the other. He utilized Maury's statements concerning the presence of passion in dreams to explain the relation between somnambulistic states and the waking state. Janet claimed that in both states the passions were unfettered, and dormant impulses regained their previous strength (211). In 1893, before Freud had compared the dream to an hysterical symptom, Janet extended this analogy to encompass hysteria: "Hystericals are not content to dream constantly at night; they dream all day long" (1893, 201). The therapeutic significance of dreams was that they often revealed the pathogenic event. He claimed that dreams brought to light subconscious fixed ideas (1898, 326). He also held that dreams enabled one to monitor the state of the rapport between the patient and doctor.

He utilized dreams to extend his notion of the scope and extent of subconscious mental activity, through his notion of subconscious reveries. Such reveries developed independently of our consciousness and volition and played a considerable role in our lives (392). His description of these resembles Carpenter's description of unconscious cerebration. In these reveries, one often finds "curious psychological work which takes place in us without our knowledge. It is thanks to this subconscious work that we find problems completely resolved which a little time before we did not understand" (393). These reveries were scarcely conscious, and we only retained vague memories of them. He used their relative preponderance as a diagnostic indicator, as in the sick, they became completely involuntary, and the person was unable to stop or modify them. The reveries became more subconscious. The subconscious was considered as a kind of continued dream. Rosemarie Sand argues that Janet, Charcot, and Krafft-Ebing

> were conversant with ideas that later emerged as essential concepts in Freud's dream theory: Jean-Martin Charcot assumed that the psychological trauma that precipitated a hysterical symptom, such as paralysis, often appeared in the patient's dreams; Pierre Janet believed that the causes of hysteria often were depicted in dreams, and he used dreams to monitor the therapeutic relationship with himself; Richard von Krafft-Ebing thought that unconscious sexual wishes could be detected in dreams. (1992, 215)

Sand's argument further demonstrates the widespread interest in dreams in psychology and psychiatry at the end of the nineteenth century. Interestingly enough, the significance of Janet and Charcot's work on dreams was drawn attention to by Jung in a seminar he gave in 1925. He stated that after the Romantic dream literature, the significance of dream interpretation was neglected. Subsequently, he claimed, "it came up again, to some extent, with Charcot and Janet, and then, especially with Freud" (Crow, 1925, 6).

Dreams in psychical research and subliminal psychology

The psychogenesis of dreams was also arrived at through the psychological investigation of spiritualistic phenomena. In 1885, the German philosopher and spiritualist Carl du Prel (1839–1899) stated that the question for psychology was ". . . whether our Ego is wholly embraced in self-consciousness" (vol. 1, xxiii). Behind the phenomenal ego of self-consciousness, lay a transcendental ego of neo-Kantian lineage, which especially revealed itself in somnambulism and dreams. Dreams revealed the transcendental constitution of subjectivity. They established the atemporal and aspatial existence of the soul. He sought to demonstrate the fallacy of the contemporary opinion that dreams were nonsensical:

> . . . the dream has not merely a scientific importance in general, but one peculiar to itself, and that it fills a vacuum, so that analysis of waking consciousness cannot be substituted for it. It will further be shown that metaphysically, also, the dream has a real value, and is a door through which we can penetrate into the obscurity of the human enigma. In dreams are exhibited other forces of the human Psyche, and other relations of the Psyche to the whole of Nature, than in waking life . . . To judge dream-life merely by its analogies with waking life is an actual contradiction, for the foundation of the former is an entire negation of the consciousness and self-consciousness which are the basis of the latter. (vol. 1, 54–55)

The dream presented *cogitationes* without a *cogito*, and hence could not be understood as a secondary derivative of consciousness. On the relation of dreams to waking life, he wrote:

If we analyse our dreams, at first sight, certainly, they seem to contain merely the materials of the waking life thrown together in a disconnected, irregular state, and only the waking life which holds together its rationally-combined representations seems decentralized in dream. But, with closer observation, it is easy to see that dream also has its positive sides, for as it is connected with the displacement of the threshold of sensibility, the sleeper then first experiences influences, formerly remaining below the threshold, from his own interior bodily sphere; his consciousness thus obtains a new content. On these influences the Psyche reacts with faculties latent in waking life; thus the self-consciousness also receives a new content. (vol. 1, 151–152)

He conceived of dreams as symbolic self-representations of the psyche. In these statements, one finds a reversal of the hierarchy between sleep and waking, akin to that established within German Romanticism, such as in Schubert. As with German Romanticism, it was the dream, as opposed to consciousness, which was regarded as truly disclosive of the soul. However, this thesis was now expressed within the language of psychology as opposed to a poetic metaphysics.

Du Prel highlighted two aspects of dreams: their dramatic form, and their healing capacity. The dream was "a completely accentuated drama" (vol. 1, 102). Hence all the figures in dreams represented facets of the dreamer's personality: ". . . every dream may be described as a dramatic sundering of the Ego; and the dialogues we seem to carry on in them are in truth monologues" (vol. 1, 112). The analogy between dreams and drama had already been made by Lichtenberg and Coleridge.[30] With du Prel, this analogy became elevated to forming the basis of his understanding of dreams. In regard to the healing aspect of dreams he noted that in dreams one found a "curative instinct" at work.

Another attempt to utilize a psychological approach to dreams as a means of resacralization was put forward in 1886 by the British psychical researchers Frederic Myers, Edmund Gurney, and Frank Podmore in *Phantasms of the Living*. In this book (principally the work of Edmund Gurney), they studied death-bed apparitions and dreams. In an important appendix entitled "Note on a suggested mode of psychic interaction," Myers (1843–1901) attempted to put forward a psychological interpretation of such phenomena. As opposed to seeing these as ghosts, he argued that they were the result of telepathic transmissions via the unconscious. Telepathy was negatively defined as communication other than through the known channels of the senses. The significance of telepathy for these investigators was that it was meant to furnish a mechanism

---

[30] Lichtenberg referred to dreams as consisting in dramatized self-reflection; Tomlinson, 1992, 778. On Coleridge, see Ford's section, "dreams, drama and dreamatis personae" (the latter was the term that Coleridge used to refer to the figures in dreams), 1994, 40–49.

that could ultimately explain the disembodied communications from the dead.[31] In respect to the understanding of dreams, the telepathic dream had the significance of maintaining that the representations of figures in dreams had an objective external signification, and that dreams contained a level of knowledge outstripping our mental capacities.[32]

In 1892 in a study of "Hypermnesic dreams" Myers extended his examination of dreams. He considered dreams ". . . in their aspect as indications of the structure of our personality, and as agencies which tend to its modification."[33] Their value resided in the fact that they more accurately revealed the psyche than waking consciousness:

> One may even say that with the first touch of sleep the superficial unity of consciousness disappears, and that the dream world gives us a truer representation than the waking world of the real fractionation or multiplicity existing beneath that delusive simplicity which the glare of waking consciousness imposes upon the mental field of view. (59)

The notion that the dream offered a truer representation was coupled with a new form of continuity thesis – rather than see the dream purely as a discrete nocturnal phenomenon, he speculated that beneath the surface of our waking or supraliminal consciousness, dreams are going on all the time: "the dreaming state . . . is nevertheless the form our mentation most readily and habitually assumes. Dreams of a kind are probably going on within us both by night and by day, unchecked by any degree of tension of waking thought" (58). In the philosophical tradition, dreams, the "thoughts of sleep," were generally regarded as representing the continuation of normal mental activities under the altered state of sleep. Here, Myers radically bifurcated the dream from waking consciousness, and suggested that the dream stems from another level altogether, which he nominated the subliminal. This led to "a shifting of gravity from the conscious to the sub-conscious or subliminal strata of [man's] being" (1893, 35). This brought with it the reformulation of the task of psychology as the exploration of the subliminal; the psychology of consciousness was to be upbuilt from this basis. To use a term that Myers appears to have coined, dreams, and cognate phenomena such as automatic writing, crystal vision, and post-hypnotic suggestion were seen as psychoscopes, which were to have as revolutionary effects at revealing the hidden and

---

[31] On Myers, see Shamdasani, 1993. On telepathy, see Shamdasani, 2001b.

[32] While Freud was not averse to accepting the existence of telepathy, he could not accept the existence of the telepathic dream, for to do so would signal the complete collapse of his theory of dreams, as they would represent a species of dreams that were not wishfulfillments, nor subject to distortion and condensation. "Dreams and Telepathy" (1921), *SE* 18.

[33] Reproduced in 1903, 57.

unseen dimensions of the psyche, as the telescope and the microscope respectively. He gave the following description of the subliminal consciousness:

> I suggest that the stream of consciousness in which we habitually live is not the only consciousness which exists . . . Our habitual or empirical consciousness may consist of a mere selection of thoughts and sensations, of which some at least are equally conscious with those we empirically know. I accord no primacy to my ordinary waking self, except that among my potential selves this one has shown itself the fittest to meet the needs of common life. I hold that it has established no further claim, and that it is perfectly possible that other thoughts, feelings, and memories, either isolated or in continuous connection, may now be actively conscious, as we say, 'within me', – in some kind of coordination with my organism, and forming some part of my total individuality. I conceive it possible that at some future time, under changed conditions, I may recollect all; I may assume the various personalities under one single consciousness, in which ultimate and complete consciousness, the empirical consciousness which at the moment directs my hand, may be only one element out of many. (1891, 301–302)

He added that all of this psychical action was conscious, and that it was misleading to call it unconscious or subconscious.

From India to the planet Mars

Like Janet, the Swiss psychologist Théodore Flournoy (1854–1920) had the benefit of both a medical and a philosophical formation.[34] In 1878 he received his MD from the University of Strasbourg. He then went to Leipzig where he studied experimental psychology with Wilhelm Wundt for two years. Fortuitously, this coincided with Wundt's founding of the psychological laboratory at the University of Leipzig. In 1891 he was appointed a professor of psychophysiology at the University of Geneva. In an almost identical manner to his lifelong friend William James, Flournoy quickly became disaffected by the limitations of laboratory psychology. He passed the running of his laboratory over to his younger cousin Edouard Claparède.[35] For Flournoy, as for James and Myers, for psychology to be a science, it could not omit to study any human phenomenon. Considering that the fields of hypnotism and suggestion had already become part of official science, he turned to the study of religious and mediumistic phenomena.

Indication of his early interest in dreams is provided by his diary, which contains notations of his dreams.[36] The diary mainly covers the period

[34] On Flournoy, see Shamdasani, 1994.
[35] On Claparède, see below, 206–207.   [36] Flournoy papers, Geneva.

between 1891 and 1896. In noting his dreams, Flournoy traced back the sources of dream imagery to prior waking experience. In commenting on one dream, he wrote: "In short, my dream contains a crowd of elements which occupied me while awake" (September 2, 1891). It would be interesting to establish how widespread such a practice was among psychologists, as it would certainly recontextualize Freud's supposedly unique self-analysis through dreams. It appears that by the 1890s, dreams had become firmly associated with the retrieval of forgotten memories, and viewed as disclosive of hidden subjectivity.

At the close of 1899, Freud published *The Interpretation of Dreams*. It had the misfortune of appearing at the same time as Flournoy published *From India to the Planet Mars*, a study of a spiritualistic medium. The latter work, despite being around twice the size, sold more copies in three months than the former in six years, and swiftly became a best seller. Flournoy's medium, whom he dubbed Hélène Smith, claimed to be the reincarnation of Marie Antoinette, the Hindu princess Simandini and a frequent visitor to Mars. As well as Martian, he spoke what purported to be Sanskrit. Linguists such as Ferdinand de Saussure and Victor Henry were fascinated by her linguistic productions, and the latter even wrote a whole book on her Martian language. Flournoy claimed that her spiritualistic romances were analogous to dreams. He explained their formation through a notion of subconscious incubation. Their content consisted of cryptomnesias, a term that he coined to indicate the fact that "certain forgotten memories reappear in the subject to see in them something new" (1900/1994, 8). Delboeuf's asplenium dream would be an example of such a phenomenon.[37] Such memories often appeared in a disfigured and elaborated form, as they had been subjected to the work of the subliminal imagination. Developing Janet's notion of subconscious reveries, he claimed that beneath the surface of consciousness, such memories were constantly being elaborated, and that the productions of the medium simply represented the momentary eruption into consciousness of a latent subliminal dream. Such fantasies served two functions: they were compensations for one's difficulties in life, and they had a teleological function. He designated this latter function by the term, teleological automatisms, by which he meant helpful, protective impulses that prepared the future. Significantly, dreams were not seen as solely concerned with the past, but possessed a futural dimension as well.

In the work of Myers and Flournoy, one finds a shift from viewing dreams as a discrete regional phenomenon to viewing the psyche as a continuous dream. In this manner, before Freud and Jung, the dream

---

[37] As would an episode discussed by Samuel Taylor Coleridge below, 182–183.

was taken as the paradigm for a general psychology of the unconscious. The role of the dream in the constitution of psychologies of the unconscious was pointed out by the French philosopher Henri Bergson (1859–1941).[38] The constitutive elements of this lay in the reversal of the hierarchy of sleep and waking, coupled with the formulation of dreams as stemming or taking place in the unconscious. He described the former shift in the following manner:

> . . . the dream-state will then be seen . . . to be the substratum of our normal state . . . [the] reality of the waking state is gained by limitation, by concentration and by tension of a diffuse psychical life, which is the dream-life. In a sense, the perception and memory we exercise in the dream-state are more natural than those in the waking state . . . it is the awake-state, rather than the dream-state, which requires explanation.[39]

The significance of the study of dreams for psychology was due to their relation to the unconscious: "To explore the unconscious, to labour in the subsoil of mind with appropriate methods, will be the principal task of psychology in the century which is opening" (1901, 103). However, this very elevation of the dream into the psychoscope for psychologies of the unconscious paradoxically led to a lessening of interest in the dream itself – the prime interest was no longer the charting and classifying of the multifarious forms of dreams, but one of seeing through the dream, to its invisible substrate: the unconscious.

By looking at the transformations in dream theories between the eighteenth and nineteenth centuries, one is in a better position to locate and appraise the work of Freud and Jung. Indeed one can see that the basis for the transformations which are commonly attributed to their work had already been established by the end of the nineteenth century.

The interpretation of dreams

In 1914 Freud claimed that he "did not know of any outside influence" which drew his attention to dreams, and added that he had established the significance of the symbolism of dreams prior to reading Scherner's work (*SE* 14, 19). The following year, he remarked that when he took up the study of dreams, the subject was generally held in contempt (*SE*, 15, 85). In 1925 he stated that

---

[38] On Bergson, see below, 207–210.

[39] Henri Bergson, 1908, 126–127. In his Lowell lectures of 1896, James put forward two primary characteristics of dreams: "A 'narrowing' of the field of consciousness, which is a 'negative' quality; and a 'vividness' of the contents that remain, which is 'positive'." Taylor, 1984, 17.

psychoanalysis succeeded in achieving one thing which appeared to be of no practical importance but which in fact necessarily led to a totally fresh attitude and fresh scale of values in scientific thought. It became possible to prove that *dreams* have a meaning, and to discover it . . . modern science would have nothing to do with them. It seemed inconceivable that anyone who had done serious scientific work could make his appearance as an 'interpreter of dreams.' (*SE* 20, 43)

He added that it fell to psychoanalysis to disregard the "excommunication" which had been pronounced upon dreams. The tendentiousness of such statements has already been demonstrated. In the latter half of the nineteenth century, rather than being excommunicated, dreams were one of the most written about subjects in psychology. In addition to works explicitly on dreams, a great deal of general works of physiology, psychiatry, and philosophy contained sections on dreams. In the first decade of the twentieth century, more interest was promoted in the subject of dreams in psychiatry and psychology by the treatment of dreams in works such as those by Flournoy, Janet, and Krafft-Ebing. Compared to other theorists, what is striking about Freud's theory of dreams was that it was monocausal.[40]

It is also important to note that while there may have been little interest in Freud's *Interpretation of Dreams*, there was a great deal of continued public interest in the subject of dreams. Dream keys continued to be published. Some incorporated elements of the physiological and psychological study of dreams.[41] Ripa noted that by the beginning of the first world war, the key of dreams of Lacinius, which was first published in 1874, had gone through six editions and sold ten thousand copies (1988, 67). Indeed, it rather seems that the *Interpretation of Dreams* was a text that was retrospectively perceived as having been an epochal work, by which time the text had been vastly expanded, and that this perception was in no small measure a result of the proselytizing efforts of the members of the psychoanalytic movement.[42] For example, in 1913, Isador Coriat claimed that Freud's psychology of dreams was one of the greatest advances in the knowledge of the mind ever made. He claimed that psychologists had previously held that the dream was a senseless group of ideas, and dreams were regarded as "not worthy of study by any serious

---

[40] In his 1901 review of *The Interpretation of Dreams*, Flournoy wrote: "Some will find that he is sometimes too ingenious and that his interpretation of such and such a dream has been procured as though pulled by the hair. In addition, we must admit that the universality he gives his thesis leaves us perplexed. Without a doubt many of our dreams, under close examination, are only, in effect, 'the disguised fulfillment of a repressed desire'; but that they all are – that is more difficult to concede." In Kiell, 1988, 166.

[41] See for instance Madame de Thèbes, 1908.

[42] On the critical changes between editions of this book, see Marinelli and Mayer, 2000.

individual" (8–9). Then came Freud who "showed for the first time that the dream was of great importance psychologically and was really the first link in the chain of normal and abnormal psychic structures" (9–10). Coriat compared the significance of *The Interpretation of Dreams* to Darwin's *Origin of Species*.

In *The Interpretation of Dreams*, one sees the confluence of the associative and the symbolic traditions. As the dream was made up from the association of given elements, it followed that the practice of soliciting associations would eventually lead back to the basic elements of the dream. The interpretation reversed the process of dream formation. This procedure was generally taken up in psychotherapy, though it increasingly became separated from its theoretical rationale in associationist psychology. Second, he made use of a restricted symbolics. In his *Introductory Lectures*, he stated that "we obtain constant translations for a number of dream-elements – just as popular 'dream-books' provide them for *everything* that appears in dreams" (*SE* 15, 150). The separate epistemological basis for the associative and symbolic approach led at times to their separation. Thus the Viennese analyst, Wilhelm Stekel, who placed great emphasis on the symbolic approach, largely dispensed with soliciting associations, and directly interpreted the dream symbols (Stekel, 1943).

In the first half of the twentieth century, the classificatory project in dream research, together with physiological research into dreams went into a demise. Part of the reason for this was the discrediting of the use of introspection in psychology, and the ascendancy of behaviorism. The dream – as the epitome of a private, subjective, unobservable phenomenon – was the behaviorist's nightmare. A further reason for the demise of classificatory and physiological research into the dream was the ascendance of psychoanalysis. If psychoanalysis preserved a level of interest in the dream, it was insofar as it could be utilized as a therapeutic tool. Here again, the introspective study of dreams gave way to their clinical investigation. For Freud, the psychogenic understanding of dreams not only separated them from physiology, but also from metaphysics, spiritualism, and religion. As we shall see, for Jung, it was precisely these areas that the psychogenic understanding of dreams recovered.

A career in dreams

In 1958, Jung wrote a manuscript entitled "From the initial experiences of my life," which was subsequently incorporated in a heavily edited form in *Memories*. Here, he recounted the significant role that dreams played in his childhood. It was due to two dreams that he opted for a scientific career. In the first dream he found himself in a wood, digging in a burial mound, when he found the bones of prehistorical animals. After this dream he realized that he wanted to study nature. In the second dream he again found himself in a wood and saw a giant radiolarian in a pool. These two dreams led him to choose natural science (104–105). Up till then, he had understood that such experiences came from God, but now he had taken in so much critique of knowledge that he doubted this (108). In an entry for December 1898 in his diary (by which time he had read the work of du Prel), we find the following statement:

> My situation is mirrored in my dreams. Often glorious, portentous glimpses of flowery landscapes, infinite blue skies, sunny coasts, but often, too, images of unknown roads shrouded in night, of friends who take leave of me to stride towards a brighter fate, of myself alone on barren paths facing impenetrable darkness. (Cited in Jaffé, 1979, 27)

Here, dreams are seen as disclosive of psychic states. In a discussion following a presentation by a fellow student called Grote on sleep in 1899 at the Basel Zofingia Society, the Swiss student fraternity, he stated his view that in dreams we were our wishes, and at the same time, different performers.[43] This indicates the influence of the work of du Prel.

At first, Jung seems to have believed in the observations of the spiritualists, and it was only subsequently, under the influence of Myers and Flournoy, that he came to a more psychological evaluation of the phenomena. By the time of his reading of Freud, he was familiar with the understanding of dreams present in the works of du Prel, Myers, and Flournoy as well as Janet, and possibly the German Romantics. He would have been sympathetic to the manner in which their psychological understanding of the dream valorized its traditional prophetic and spiritual aspects in a modern guise, as it was congruent with his own value system. Indeed, one can pose the question, to what extent did Jung ever really adhere to Freud's theory of dreams? This question may be approached by closely looking at Jung's statements on the dream in the first decade of his career.

In 1925, Jung stated that he read Freud's *Interpretation of Dreams* in 1900, and that he put it aside, as he did not grasp its significance. He returned to it in 1903, seeing a connection in it to his own theories (1925, 8). In a report on Freud's monograph, *On Dreams* in January 1901, Jung concluded that Freud's approach to dreams was somewhat one-sided, as the cause of a dream could equally be an undisguised repressed fear, as well as a wish (*CW* 18, § 869).

Jung's 1902 dissertation, *On the Psychology and Psychopathology of so called Occult Phenomena*, was a study of the mediumistic productions of

---

[43] Protocols of the Zofingia Society, 1899, Staatsarchiv, Basel, 86.

his cousin Hélène, closely modeled after Flournoy's *From India to the Planet Mars*. It contained several passages discussing dreams and Freud's dream theory. While Jung regarded dreams as disclosive of the personality, contrary to Freud, he didn't think they utilized censorship: "dreams suddenly present to consciousness, in more or less transparent symbolism, things one has never admitted to oneself clearly and openly" (*CW* 1, § 97). Citing Janet and Binet, he drew attention to the relation between dreams and the level of dissociation, stating that the greater the dissociation of consciousness, the greater the plasticity of dream situations (§ 117). He explained his medium's dreams by stating that they consisted in emotionally stressed ideas which had only briefly occupied her consciousness, and referred to Flournoy's similar explanations of Hélène Smith's reveries. Referring to Janet, he added that hysterical forgetfulness played a significant part in the genesis of dreams – meaning that unimportant ideas continued working in the unconscious through dissociation and reappeared in dreams. He designated budding sexuality as the cause of her dreams, which represented sexual wishfulfillments (§ 120). His position differed from Freud's as the sexual wish in question was an adolescent one, as opposed to an infantile one.

By 1902, Jung had read Freud's *Interpretation of Dreams* and *On Dreams*, and expressed his differences: dreams were not always wishfulfillments, they were frequently undisguised, the content of dreams was related to the state of consciousness, and if dreams presented wishfulfillments, these were by no means always infantile. These are among the precise charges that he would level against Freud's dream theories, from around 1912 onwards, and represented positions from which he never subsequently moved away.

His next significant study of dreams took place in 1906 in a paper entitled "Association, dream and hysterical symptom," which consisted in a case study. He described dreams as symbolic expressions of the complexes. The complexes revealed in the associations experiment also constellated dreams (*CW* 2, § 844). In his analysis of his case, he traced back her dreams to a sexual complex. Any complex, which could date from any age, could be revealed in a dream, and not all complexes involved wishes.

The psychology of madness

Dreams, and in particular, their analogy to madness, played a significant role in Jung's 1907 *On the Psychology of Dementia Praecox*. Jung discussed Madeleine Pelletier's linkage between daydreams and mania and stated that the "manic" did not resemble the dreamer. By contrast, he argued that the analogy was most appropriate with dementia praecox, and cited Reil's analogies between dreams and insanity (*CW* 3, § 22). Jung phrased this analogy in a manner that followed on from a long line of psychiatric theorizing: "Let the dreamer walk about and act like a person awake, and we have the clinical picture of dementia praecox" (§ 174). Rather than using this analogy to demonstrate the unintelligibility of the dream, he utilized it to demonstrate the intelligibility of dementia praecox, through applying to it the psychogenic interpretation of dreams. This transfer was made possible through the increasing psychologization of the dream in the last quarter of the nineteenth century. To effect this, he principally drew upon Flournoy, Freud, and Kraepelin.

Jung stated that "Freud, as is known, has at last put dream analysis onto the right track."[44] Jung gave the example of a dream analysis. The dreamer was a friend whose personal and family circumstances were well known to him. The dream featured horses being hoisted up cables. A horse fell, but galloped away dragging a log. A rider on another horse rode in front of it. The dreamer feared that the frightened horse would run over the rider, until a cab came in front of the rider, which slowed down the frightened horse. He then gave an account of his analysis of the dream and the dreamer, which ran for several pages.

He argued that the dream dealt with the problem of the dreamer's wife's pregnancy and the problem of too many children, which restrained the husband. Through presenting the restraint as accomplished, the dream represented a wish, as well as disclosing an "extremely personal matter" (§ 132). In a letter to Freud, Jung revealed that the dreamer was himself.[45] While in his associations experiments, Jung presented the tests of individuals that were well known to him, such as his wife, without disclosing their identity, this appears to be the first time in which he presented a fictionalized account based on an analysis of his own material.

As Siegfried Bernfeld and Peter Swales have established, Freud had utilized such a technique on numerous occasions, such as in his "Screen Memories" paper, and in his Aliquis analysis in *The Psychopathology of Everyday Life*.[46] Swales has argued that the ingeniousness with which Freud laid bare the hidden secrets of his fictionalized alter ego in the latter instance significantly contributed to what became the prevalent image of Freud, as a psychological sleuth. One may see a further significance to these disguised self revelations. In the nineteenth-century dream literature, the predominant pattern was the presentation and introspective analyses of one's own dreams. With the increasing psychologization of

---

[44] § 122 [literally, "on a green branch"].
[45] December 29, 1906, *FJL*, 1974, 14.   [46] Bernfeld, 1946; Swales, 1998.

dreams, coupled with the notion that dreams were disclosive of hidden secrets of which the dreamer was unconscious, one finds a corresponding decline in the first-person reportage of dreams. In the psychoanalytic literature, the dreams reported became almost invariably dreams of patients.[47]

Jung regarded dreams as the symbolic expression of complexes (*CW* 3, § 140). As to the formation of dreams from complexes, he noted: "Flournoy has pointed out the roots of the complexes in the dreams of the well known Hélène Smith. *I regard knowledge of these phenomena as indispensable for the understanding of the problems here discussed*" (§ 298, trans. mod.).

The centerpiece of the book was his analysis of a case of paranoid dementia, the case of Babette Staub. Jung subjected her to associations experiments, and then got her to associate to the neologisms that she produced. He stated that she spoke as if in a dream, and that he conducted the analysis just like a dream analysis. Three major complexes lay behind her delusions: the complex of grandeur, the complex of injury, and the sexual complex. Her conscious psychic activity was taken up with creating wishfulfillments as "a substitute for a life of toil and privation and for the depressing experiences of a wretched family milieu" (§, 299). In regarding such wishfulfillments as compensations, Jung was following Flournoy's interpretations of Hélène Smith's spiritualistic romances.

The third major source that Jung utilized was the work of the leading German psychiatrist Emil Kraepelin (1856–1926). In 1906 Kraepelin published a study of speech disorders in dreams. He noted that the changes of mental life in dreaming had long been a favorite topic of introspection (Heynick, 1993, 65). His study was principally based upon his own dreams. He tried to establish a taxonomic classification of the various forms of speech disturbances in dreams, and to draw comparisons with similar occurrences elsewhere. In his view, the linguistic disturbances in dreams differed in degree, but less in kind than those found in waking (115). Among the conditions of waking life that Kraepelin singled out for comparison were slips of the pen. Most significant was his comparison with forms of insanity, noting remarkable similarities with cases of dementia praecox. These similarities had the significance of opening up a reciprocal clarification of the nature of dreams and dementia praecox. Kraepelin held that the study of one's dreams was particularly valuable, because it enabled one introspectively to study analogous conditions to insanity (129). He employed the results of his analysis of his dreams to understand the speech of his patients. This led him to conjecture that

---

[47] On this question, see Shamdasani, 1999b.

patients with speech confusion also believed themselves to be speaking intelligibly, as we do in dreams (125).

Jung made several citations to Kraepelin's work on dreams in *On the Psychology of Dementia Praecox*. He referred to Kraepelin's statement that speech disturbances in dreams were connected with a clouding of consciousness and a reduction of the clarity of ideas, stating that his remarks "suggest that he is not so far from the view we have outlined here" (*CW* 3, § 50). He then affirmed that dreams "show the special speech-condensations consisting of the contamination of whole sentences and situations. Kraepelin, too, was struck by the resemblance between the language of dreams and that of dementia praecox" (*ibid.*). Jung cited Kraepelin's view that in dreams, the formulation of a thought was often frustrated by a subsidiary association, noting, "on this point, Kraepelin's views come very close to Freud's" (§, 135n). Kraepelin's linkage between the language disorders of dreams and dementia praecox was utilized by Jung to extend his study of the linguistic expressions of complexes in the associations experiment to dreams and dementia praecox.

The year 1907 marked the advent of Jung's formal affiliation with the psychoanalytic movement, with the founding of a Freud society in Zürich. In 1909 he wrote a didactic presentation of Freud's dream theories, entitled "The analysis of dreams" (*CW* 4). The following year he published a paper entitled "A contribution to the knowledge of number dreams" (*CW* 4). In this he stated that as the significance of number symbolism had been established by Freud, Adler and Stekel, he intended simply to provide some further examples. One of these is interesting as regards Jung's mode of interpretation. A woman had a dream that consisted simply in the line: "Luke 137" (§ 146). After exhausting the patient's associations concerning the numbers, Jung turned to the Bible. He stated that as the woman was not religious or well versed in the Bible, it was pointless to rely on associations. He looked up Luke 1:37, 13:7 and 7:13, and connected each of them to the psychology of the dreamer. Luke 13:7 narrated a parable in which a man had a fig tree planted which bore no fruit, after which he requested that it be cut down. He stated that the fig tree was "since ancient times" a symbol of the male genitals, and that it represented her husband's unfruitful organ, and that the wish to cut it down accorded with her sadistic fantasies. He claimed that the appearance of "Luke 137" in the dream must be regarded as a cryptomnesia, citing Flournoy's work and his own (§§ 148–152).

The following year saw his most stridently Freudian piece on dreams, a critical review of the Boston psychologist Morton Prince's "The Mechanism and interpretation of dreams" (*CW* 4). Prince (1854–1929) presented the results of his dream analyses and claimed that they demonstrated that each dream contained an intelligent motive. He put this forward as a partial confirmation of Freud's work. However, Prince claimed that not every dream was the fulfillment of a wish – that some seemed to be the fulfillment of a fear or anxiety. Jung reanalyzed Prince's dreams, and claimed that Prince's conclusions stemmed from the fact that he had not analyzed the dreams thoroughly enough. When the analysis was carried through, all the dreams could be shown to be wishfulfillments. What is curious about this piece is that Prince's position, that not all dreams are wishfulfillments, represents what was in fact Jung's position in his published writings from 1901–1907, and from 1912 onwards. Thus there are good grounds for suggesting that Jung's positions during this brief hiatus were a result of his political involvement with the psychoanalytic movement.

Dreams, myths, and the collective unconscious

In 1909, Jung, together with Freud and a host of other figures were invited to the thirty-year celebrations at Clark University in Worcester, Massachusetts. Jung received an honorary doctorate of law. His speech of thanks represented the highpoint of his identification with the psychoanalytic movement, "my work is identical with the scientific movement inaugurated by Professor Freud, whose servant I have the honour to be."[48] On the ship returning to Europe, Jung had the following dream:

I dreamed I was in a medieval house, a big complicated house with many rooms, passages and stairways. I came in from the street and went down into a vaulted Gothic room, and from there into a cellar. I thought to myself that now I was at the bottom, but then I found a square hole. With a lantern in my hand I peeped down this hole, and saw stairs leading further down, and down these I climbed. They were dusty stairs, very much worn, and the air was sticky, the whole atmosphere very uncanny. I came to another cellar, this one of very ancient structure, perhaps Roman, and again there was a hole through which I could look down into a tomb filled with prehistoric pottery, bones and skulls; as the dust was undisturbed, I thought I had made a great discovery. (Jung, 1925, 23)

Jung stated that Freud's interpretation was that there were individuals connected with Jung that he wanted dead, which he did not agree with. He thought that the cellar represented the unconscious, but could not make out what the medieval house represented. He then proceeded to make fantasies concerning the dream. Over thirty years later, to his friend the British psychiatrist E. A. Bennet, he recalled more details concerning this dream. In reply to Freud's statement that the dream represented a

---

[48] Jung, "Speech of thanks" [Dankesrede], JP.

death wish, he suggested his wife, to which Freud replied, "Yes . . . it could be that. And the most likely meaning is that you want to get rid of your wife and bury her under two cellars."[49] Jung was unsatisfied with this interpretation in personal terms. Bennet noted that "Jung felt that Freud's handling of the dream showed a tendency to make the facts fit his theory" (88). Bennet added that as Jung reflected on the dream, he saw the house as representing the exterior of his personality, and the inside of the house, the interior of his personality, containing historical layers. Thus the house possibly represented the stages of culture. To Bennet, he said "It was then, at that moment, I got the idea of the collective unconscious"(88). In his discussion of this dream in the protocols of his interviews with Aniela Jaffé, there occur statements that weren't reproduced in *Memories*. There, he stated that after the dream, he had an idea that it meant a way of portrayal of the psyche, which he didn't tell Freud. He further added that the house seemed to come from a previous generation. The ground floor felt uninhabited and museumlike, and the cellar was empty. He was in the second floor, which felt lived in. The first floor had a historical reference. He recalled he had then been impressed by "the historical formulation in Freud, so the Oedipus-Complex, the Pompeian phantasy of the villa of mysteries, Jensen's Gradiva," and that this dream "was the first sign against which Freud was completely helpless."[50] It was at this moment that he came to a completely other conception of dreams than Freud, namely that the dream was nature:[51] "The unconscious has a natural function, which consciousness is completely dependent on. I had long thought this before I got to know Freud" (108).

If one draws these accounts together, it appears that he took this dream as indicating that dreams revealed not only personal but also cultural memories. The dream could be considered as the *via regia* into cultural history.

---

[49] Bennet, 1961. In Aniela Jaffé's account in *Memories*, Jung gave his wife and his sister-in-law as the subjects of his putative death wish, 183.

[50] Jung/Jaffé protocols, 107. The significance of this dream is also indicated by the following description Jung gave in 1927 of the structure of the psyche: "Perhaps I may be allowed a comparison: it is as though we had to describe and explain a building whose upper storey was erected in the nineteenth century, the ground floor dates back to the sixteenth century, and careful examination of the masonry reveals that it was constructed in the eleventh century. In the cellar we come upon Roman foundations, and under the cellar a choked-up cave with neolithic tools and remnants of fauna from the same period in the lower layers. That would be the picture of our psychic structure." "Soul and Earth," *CW* 12, § 54.

[51] If this was in fact the case, Jung certainly kept quiet about his new ideas about the dream in his stridently Freudian critique on Morton Prince's paper on dreams, discussed earlier.

From around 1907 onwards, many psychoanalysts took up the psychological interpretation of cultural history, and mythology in particular. Jung recalled that subsequent to Freud's having drawn parallels between the Oedipus legend and infantile psychology, the "real working out of mythological material was then taken up by my pupils," citing works by Maeder, Riklin, and Abraham.[52] Throughout these works, the analogy between dreams and myths came to play a prominent role. While for Nietzsche, the analogy simply held between the characteristic forms of thinking of each, the psychoanalysts claimed to be in a position to specify further what this thought consisted in.[53]

There were two broad trends in the psychoanalytic investigation of mythology. The first consisted in applying to the field of mythology the same interpretive models that had been utilized on the individual. Thus in his 1908 "Wishfulfillment and symbolism in fairytales" Jung's colleague, the Swiss psychiatrist Franz Riklin argued that fairytales were the spontaneous inventions of the primitive human soul and the general tendency to Wishfulfillment (Riklin, 1908, 95). In a similar vein, in his "Dreams and myths: a study in ethnopsychology" of the following year, the psychoanalyst Karl Abraham (1877–1925) described myths as the fantasies of a people, and set out to demonstrate that they could be understood through applying Freud's doctrines (1909, 154). Abraham attempted to explain the analogy between myths and dreams by stating that myths were survivals from the infancy of a people. Myths were fragments of the infantile psychic life of peoples, which contained their prehistoric infantile wishes in a veiled form (180). Thus myths could be considered as the dreams of a people.

In 1910 the Viennese psychoanalyst Herbert Silberer (1882–1922) extended these investigations in a study entitled "Phantasy and Mythos." While Abraham sought to apply the principles of psychoanalysis to the province of ethnopsychology, Silberer's study began calling into question some of the basic assumptions of psychoanalysis. He commenced with a section on what he termed functional or autosymbolic phenomena. This referred to the manner in which fantasies represented symbolic autorepresentations of the state of the psyche, which played an important part in dreams.[54] He argued that the connecting point between individual and ethnopsychology was provided by the analogy between myth and dreams: "Myth is the dream of the people – the dream is the myth of the

---

[52] Jung, "The psychology of the child archetype," 1940, *CW* 9,1, § 259n.
[53] See above, 117.
[54] 1910, 108. Jung had a number of Silberer's articles, bearing dedications.

individual" (118). Silberer cited the German biologist Ernst Haeckel's statement in *The Riddle of the Universe* that the biogenetic law held for psychology as for morphology, as support of this argument.[55] Utilizing his view of the significance of functional phenomena in dreams, he argued by analogy that they also played an important role in myths and fairy tales.

In 1912, in a study of the formation of symbols, he expanded his conception of the role of functional phenomena in dreams. Citing Havelock Ellis on the dramatic aspect of dreams, he argued that the functional aspect of dreams should be described as "dramatizing."[56] Dreams were a kind of "soul's conversation with itself" (Selbstgespräch der Seele). All of the forms that appeared in dreams were parts of ourselves. The actors into whom we were split in dreams stood in for and personified our tendencies, opinions and drives (623).

Jung and his students Johann Honegger, Jan Nelken, and Sabina Spielrein sought to apply the study of myth and cultural history to individual psychology. In 1911/1912 in *Transformations and Symbols of the Libido* Jung cited the passage from Nietzsche on dreams in *Human all too Human* (cited above) in support of his view that in psychology, the biogenetic law held, and that infantile thought and the dream were simply re-echoes of the thought of antiquity.[57] He attempted to demonstrate that one could find clear indications of the presence of myths in dreams and further, that this took place without the subject's prior acquaintance with the myths in question. He made his strongest statement for the endogenous origins of myth: "should it happen that all traditions in the world were cut off with a single blow, the whole mythology and history of religion would begin again from the beginning with the next generation" (§ 41, trans. mod). It seems that only the near destruction of the world could provide a test for this claim of Jung's.

The dream problem

On November 16, 1907, Flournoy presented a paper on the purpose of dreams in Geneva.[58] He gave an account of the general trends in dream theories since antiquity to the present day. He developed his critique of Freud's dream theory and put forward one of his own. Flournoy claimed that the former was simply "too narrow," as dreams expressed all tendencies as opposed to simply desires, and that these needn't be repressed.

[55] Haeckel, 1900, 117. On Haeckel, see below, 183–184.
[56] Silberer, 1912, 621.   [57] *CW* B, § 36. See below, 299–300.
[58] The following account has been reconstructed from Flournoy's lecture notes, Flournoy papers.

As an example, he cited the fact that during the three years in which he had been preoccupied with spiritualism, he had often dreamed of producing the physical phenomena of spiritualism, or of finding a medium who did. He added that this desire was perfectly avowed by his conscious personality. Opposed to this, he put forward his theory based upon the creative imagination. Below conscious mental functioning, there was an imaginative functioning that created fictive situations. He put forward several explanations to explain this functioning, and the ones that he favored were the teleological and polypsychic explanations. The process of selection assured the survival of individuals who had developed "this faculty of imagining the possible," who found themselves adapted to the possibilities that arose.

We also each possessed many latent individualities, hereditary tendencies, and atavisms, and different circumstances brought these into action. The dream could have a purposive and teleological role in developing latent faculties. It derived this from the special significance that Flournoy attached to the creative imagination. This faculty was "the foundation of our being." It was stimulated by reality, to which it applied itself through acting to transform it. As a result, "the human soul is a machine to transform the real." This lecture was never published. In Jung's late tribute to Flournoy, he stated that Flournoy helped him to see where Freud's weaknesses were, that Flournoy was the only figure with whom he could discuss the psychological issues that preoccupied him, and that he "adopted" Flournoy's concept of the creative imagination.[59]

In a series of publications from 1909 onwards Jung's colleague Alphonse Maeder put forward a new view of the dream, which was to play a crucial role in the split between the Vienna and Zürich schools. After studying medicine, he worked for a few years under Hans Driesch from 1903, during which time he became interested in neovitalism. After a spell in Berlin, he decided in 1906 to become a psychiatrist. He took up a post at the Burghölzli. Psychoanalysis offered him an alternative to the sterility of speculative academic psychology and experimental psychophysical research. In retrospect, he described Jung as the "first really significant person" whom he had met (1956a, 191). He was struck by Jung's "profound and worldwide knowledge and the instinctive certainty with which he went after depth psychological problems." He described Jung as a "superior brother" and noted that a certain rivalry developed when his own originality emerged (191).

In an article in 1912, Maeder gave an historical overview of Freud's work and then continued the story up to the present day with an

[59] Jung, in Flournoy (1900/94), ix.

account of the recent developments by the Zürich school. He claimed that the examination of numerous dreams showed the importance of a factor other than wishfulfillment, which he described as follows: "The dream has in effect a cathartic action. It gives us a sort of compensation and facilitates up to a certain point the return to a state of affective equilibrium (1912a, 415). He added that the observation of series of dreams by individuals demonstrated that all the dreams dealt with the same subject, and attempted to provide a solution to the individual's moral conflicts. He was attributing to dreams a wholly other function than that accorded by Freud. Dreams informed the analyst of the attitude of the unconscious towards conflicts and problems. If for Freud, dreams were the royal road to the unconscious, Maeder was providing a new interpretation of dreams in which they led to a new conception of the unconscious, and one which did not merely consist of repressed infantile wishes. He claimed that the dream did not merely point to the past, but prepared the way for the future. Such a teleological conception was shared by other automatisms, and he specially cited Flournoy's anti-suicidal teleological automatisms. In retrospect, he acknowledged Flournoy's paper as the first stimulus to this new conception, which led him to the assumption that it was necessary to add a finalistic mode of consideration as a correlate to Freud's causal mode (1956a, 194). Referring to the biologist Karl Groos' theory that the play of children had a teleological function in preparing for future activities, he argued that the dream had two of the key characteristics of play, namely "the cathartic action and the exercise which prepare certain complex activities" (1912a, 416). The imagination had a compensatory function; it gave the individual what was refused by reality, but also prepared the future and created new possibilities. As to the source of this theory, he noted:

I have just received the beautiful book of Professor Flournoy, *Spirits and Mediums*. The author names precisely his theory: playful or theatrical theory of mediumship. His point of view towards the manifestations of the unconscious presents a grand analogy with those developed in these lines. His work, *From India to the Planet Mars* is equally a beautiful illustration of that which was said above of fantasies. (417)

Maeder had rerouted the "royal road," and argued that rather than starting from Freud in Vienna, it started in Geneva with Flournoy, and its destination was Zürich. Later that year, Maeder published a fuller account of his dream theory (1912b).

In 1912 in Vienna itself Alfred Adler wrote a paper on dreams that opened with a question that indicated what was at stake in the new conceptions of the dream, namely, can one see into the future? Adler

(1870–1937) had recently broken from Freud, developing his own "individual psychology." He argued that in everyday life, one commonly acted as if one had knowledge of the future and that the body often made preparations as if it knew the future, which remained in the unconscious. Claiming that Freud's view that the dream was a wishfulfillment was untenable, he thought that one could discern in dreams an anticipatory, prescient function.[60] Dreams attempted to give the solution to the problems that were confronting the dreamer, as well as indicating what the dreamer intended to do. Hence the study of dreams leads to a knowledge of a man's lifeline "that unconscious life-line by means of which he strives to dominate the pressure of life and his own feeling of uncertainty" (222).

The same year, Jung also expressed his divergence from Freud's theory of dreams. In his lectures on psychoanalysis in July, he argued that dreams varied according to the personality of the dreamer. While some dreams contained wishfulfillments, this was by no means true of all of them. Dreams contained subliminal thought which was too weak to come to expression in consciousness.[61] They showed the "thoughts of the unconscious" in a symbolic form. Noting the connections between infantile thought and myth, he argued that dreams expressed "the most ancient thoughts."[62] In his lectures a few months later in New York, he noted that Freud's procedure with dreams was predominantly analytical. While this was of indisputable value, it was important not to overlook the teleological significance of dreams which Maeder had stressed (*CW* 4, § 452).

After Maeder published his paper on dreams in the *Jahrbuch für psychoanalytische und psychopathologische Forschungen*, Adler accused him of plagiarism. In 1913, Maeder responded to this charge. He noted that there was a general agreement between Adler and himself concerning the function of dreams. He had had the idea that dreams prepared the solution of a conflict in 1908, and pointed this out in a paper published in 1909, of which he wrote an abstract in the *Jahrbuch* in 1910. That year, he became aware of the parallel with Groos' play function, and discussed this with the Genevan psychologist Edouard Claparède, who was in agreement. He presented his paper at the Zürich Psychoanalytical Society in May 1911, and submitted it to the *Jahrbuch* at the end of the year. Thus he had presented and published his theory before Adler (1913a).

---

[60] 1912b, 217. On Adler, see above, 55–57. Jung's library contains a bound collection of offprints by Adler entitled, *Traumdeutung und andere Aufsätze*, with "from the author" embossed in the front. Adler's paper on dreams cited here contains a few marks in the margin.

[61] Fanny Bowditch Katz notes, Jung's lectures on *Psychoanalysis*, July 14, 1912, CLM.

[62] *Ibid.*, July 23, 1912.

The following year, Wilhelm Stekel accused both Adler and Maeder of plagiarizing his ideas concerning dreams.[63]

For Jung and Maeder, the alteration of the conception of the dream brought with it an alteration of all other phenomena associated with the unconscious. In the Zürich Psychoanalytical Society there was discussion of the subject of dreams. Following a presentation by Maeder on January 31 on Jung's libido theory, Jung argued "the dream gives the answer through symbols which one should understand. But one should not only see wishfulfillments in it, or else the analyst simply joins in with the phantasies of the neurotic."[64] In a discussion on May 2, Jung stated that dreams were not egocentric. Nature always expressed the aims of the species, and the neurotic suffered because of his egocentricity. Consequently, the dream functioned as a biological correction, and represented the "biological morality" (ibid.).

In a discussion on dreams on January 30, 1914, Jung stated that the difference between the Freudian conception and the Zürich conception lay in the fact that Freud's standpoint was very concretistic. Instead of this "a subject- and object-level had to be adopted." He argued that:

> the dream images do not give the relations between the dream and the person seen there, but they are the expression of the tendencies in the dreamer. When I possess a tendency in myself, which characterises me, it arises from a type of biological corrective as a compensation for the unbalanced consciousness from the subliminal . . . The dream is a clear tendency to hand over the material which balances the morality.[65]

Further indication of the changes in Freud's dream theory that Jung was proposing is provided by manuscript notes of a talk that he gave entitled "The dream problem," dated February 12, 1914.[66] He argued that Freud completely neglected the manifest dream content, which was a questionable procedure. In consciousness, a sentence contained its meaning within it; by analogy, Jung claimed that the same was true for the

---

[63] Stekel claimed that Maeder's likening of the dream to a work of art expressed what he (Stekel) had written in 1909 in "Dichtung und Neurose"; that in 1908 in *Nervöse Angstzustände* he had shown dreams are often warnings or prophecies; that he gave many examples of prospective dreams in his *Die Sprache des Traumes* of 1911, and also laid emphasis there on the manifest content of the dream, to which the Zürich school had then protested. He claimed that Adler "cribbed" his method of interpreting dreams without soliciting associations, and that in his *Die Sprache des Traumes* he had pointed out that the patient's leading aims had to be taken into account in dream interpretation (1943, 57–58). A few years later, Claparède wrote to Maeder "I would much like sometime to remind you that from 1905 I defended the ludic theory of dreams. I often had dreams which prepared my conduct the following day, and often determined it" (September 25, 1915, Maeder papers, original in French).
[64] MZP.   [65] MZP.   [66] JP.

"unconscious sentence" (1). Rather than having the purpose of expelling incompatibilities, he claimed that Freud's "censor" represented the effort to find a suitable expression. Similarly, he argued that Freud's "work of condensation" was actually the selection and construction of the fitting expression for a particular content: "when a new psychic [seelischer] element seeks to gain expression, then we refer to nearby analogous material and select the fitting analogy, to find a right or possibly exact expression" (1). Jung claimed that dreams took many of their analogies from the sexual sphere, as this provided fitting comparisons for the actual meaning, which he defined as the meaning of the manifest dream content. Whereas for Freud, an incompatible wish attempted to break through in the dream, for Jung, the dream attempted to represent a meaning, which was expressed through an analogy with an infantile content. Whereas for Freud, the symbolizing activity of the dream served to mask an incompatible wish, for Jung, it was an analogical description of a not clearly given meaning. This later could even express itself via an incompatible wish. While Freud claimed that the origin of the dream lay in an incompatible wish of the previous day, Jung contended that it lay in an unsolved problem of the previous day. He then turned to the actual meaning of the dream, which he claimed was the symbolically outlined solution to a problem. This he described in the widest possible terms, stating that "the future is dark," and the question was one of deciding which of different possibilities was the best. The dream often simply presented a problem or a symbolic allusion to it if one was unable to grasp the problem itself. Insofar as the dream brought subliminal material to consciousness, it had a compensating function, and insofar as it symbolically indicated a solution, it had a finalistic function. Finally, he gave a series of examples of typical dream symbols indicating how Freud would interpret them and how he would.

In this talk, it appears that Jung was attempting a point-by-point replacement of Freud's dream theory with a new conception which would render the former completely obsolete. Jung had attempted to reinterpret the function of all the Freudian mechanisms of dream formation. However, there were clearly problems in this attempt. For instance, while he claimed that the actual meaning seized upon infantile and erotic situations as analogies, for Freud, the infantile erotic wish was not visible in the manifest content of the dream, but only emerged through interpretation of the latent content.

On March 13, Jung presented a talk on dream psychology, in which he attempted to provide alternative explanations for Freud's understanding of typical dream symbols. Here are a few examples:

Nakedness motif in dream: For Freud, wishfulfillment, for Jung, attitude, as if one is incompletely dressed = insufficiently equipped.

Anxiety dream. Freud: wishfulfillment disguised in anxiety. Jung: real danger, which exists or will exist.

Climbing stairs. Freud: sexual act. Jung: literally to go into the heights, to be from the lower, or as if one could only go up, instead of also down.[67]

From this, one gets the impression of two competing dream keys, vying for hermeneutic authority.

Also in 1914, Jung prepared a talk on "The psychology of dreams" for the Berne Medical Congress which was postponed due to the outbreak of the war, which was subsequently published in 1916 (Jung, 1917). Here, Jung stated that dreams, like all psychic phenomena, had to be looked at both from a causal-retrospective perspective (Freud) and a prospective-finalistic perspective. In commenting on a dream from this latter perspective he stated:

In this dream we can discern a balancing function of the unconscious, consisting in the fact that those thoughts, propensities, and tendencies of the human person-ality, which in conscious life are seldom shown to advantage, come into operation in the form of hints in the sleeping state, when to a large extent the conscious process is disconnected . . . It is evident that this function of dreams signifies a psychological balancing, which is absolutely required for ordered action. (311, trans. mod.)

From this perspective, he argued that Freud's thesis that dreams were wishfulfillments was of limited validity, and that rather than simply having the function of concealment of inadmissible wishes, dreams actively prepared the way for the psychological development of the individual. Thus in some instances, dreams could be seen to perform a moral function. He ended this paper with some reflections on the significance of typical themes in dreams. The typical themes of mythology were found in dreams, with the same significance, which confirmed Nietzsche's statements that from a phylogenetic perspective, the dream was an older mode of thought. He concluded:

the psychology of dreams opens up for us the way to a general comparative psy-chology, from which we hope to attain the same sort of understanding of the development and structure of the human soul, as comparative anatomy has given us concerning the human body. (*Ibid.*, trans. mod.)

The dream was the psychoscope for a general psychology of the uncon-scious. The psychology of the dream led to a dream psychology, the phrase

---

[67] MZP.

that was used the following year by Jung's disciple Maurice Nicoll, in the first didactic presentation of Jung's psychology (Nicoll, 1917).

Jung's statements in this paper on the prospective, compensatory function of the dream reproduced the position that had previously been put forward by Maeder. Aside from passing references to Nietzsche and Saint Augustine, the only reference was to Freud. The historical perspective this suggested was – first Freud, then Jung. If Freud had been the first to understand that dreams had a meaning, Jung was supposedly the first to understand their true significance.

Crucially, this mode of presentation – first Freud's views, then Jung's criticisms of Freud, then Jung's views – was one that Jung now came to predominantly employ in presenting his new concepts. It also had the effect of lending credence to the view that the origin of Jung's concepts could be found in psychoanalysis and that there was no other significant source for his ideas. His rhetorical mode of presentation was mistaken as indicating the genealogy of his ideas.

What Maeder, Adler, and Jung were proposing was a psychological version of the prophetic and diagnostic dream. While they presented their new conceptions as revisions and corrections of psychoanalysis, their views were a great deal closer to those of German Romanticism, du Prel, and the subliminal psychology of Myers and Flournoy. Indeed, in the case of the latter, Maeder admitted as much. Not only did this other tradition present the basis of the new conceptions of the dream, it also presented the basis for a critique of Freud's theory of dreams. In the case of Jung, one can argue that this shift in effect represented a return to his intellectual roots. This had the additional effect of bringing his dream theories into much greater proximity with the popular conception of dreams and the continued valuation of their prophetic and symbolic power. Rather than presenting his psychology as the unmasker of popular superstitions as Freud had done, Jung began to present it as validating them, through presenting psychological mechanisms that could go some way towards explaining them.

Neither Maeder nor Jung explicitly cited the conception of the dream in German Romanticism. In a seminar in 1925 Jung stated:

Interest in dreams revived with the psychology of the nineteenth century. One of the best students of the subject was Schubert, who had a very advanced point of view, and a very correct idea of the symbolism of dreams. He rightly maintained that dreams express the most essential things in man, and deal with the most intimate things of life. (Crow, 1925, 5–6)

In 1917, he published his *Psychology of the Unconscious Processes*, where, as an attempt to resolve the problematic of the personal equation, he attempted to develop a relativistic standpoint in psychology.[68] In terms of dream theory, he no longer attempted to present his theory as a complete replacement of Freud's, as he had attempted in his talk "The dream problem," but to incorporate it within a wider synthesis. After presenting a dream which he analyzed in a traditional Freudian manner he noted that when the analytical or causal-reductive interpretation no longer brought anything new, it was time to use another method of interpretation.[69] He then introduced a distinction between interpretation on the objective level in which dream objects were treated as representations of real objects, and interpretation on the subjective level in which every element concerns the dreamers themselves.[70] In the case of interpretation on the objective level the dream figures may be taken as objective references to people. Such a perspective had also been taken in the nineteenth-century dream literature. Philippe Tissié gave an example of an occasion where after an argument with his sister in which he had been alternatively soft and severe, she dreamed that she had two brothers who resembled one another and who both carried his name, one being friendly, the other bad. Tissié stated that his sister had doubled his character and objectivized it into two persons (1898, 45). As in much nineteenth-century dream literature this was an anecdote that was not used to set up a theory of dreams. The objective level of interpretation is also prefigured in Myers, Gurney, and Podmore's study of the telepathic dream in *Phantasms of the Living*. In the case of such apparitions it was taken that the dream figures did not represent a facet of the dreamer's own personality, but objectively referred to an external person.

What Jung called the synthetic method consisted in the utilization of a symbolic mode of interpretation. The only means of truly elucidating the meaning of the dream images was by tracking down analogies in the field of comparative mythology and religion – a method which he termed amplification. In his example of such a procedure in his paper on the analysis of number dreams, he had claimed that the biblical passage had been reproduced by a process of cryptomnesia. Now, by contrast, Jung took the view that in many instances what was at issue was the spontaneous emergence of archetypic contents.[71] The difficulty with this position was

---

[68] See above, 72–74.

[69] 1917, 420–421. Concerning this idea, Freud wrote to Karl Abraham on December 15, 1919 that he considered it "a superfluous addition that is to the understanding of dreams. Naturally one destroys the father only because he is the 'inner' father, that is, has significance for one's own mental life" (ed. Falzeder, 2002, 411).

[70] As we have seen, Jung had already presented this distinction in discussions at the Zürich Psychoanalytical Society. In 1913, Maeder referred to Jung's "excellent expression" of the "objective level" and the "subjective level" (1913c, 657–658).

[71] While the word "archetypal" has become one of the most heavily used in Jungian psychology, Jung preferred the word "archetypic," and hence I have used this throughout.

that in any given case, to rule out any possibility of cryptomnesia was a theoretical impossibility.

Jung came to revise his paper "The psychology of dreams" in 1928 and 1948. Through these changes the essay doubled in length, though the original essay was preserved as the first section. In his 1928 revision he elaborated his distinction between dream interpretation on the subjective and objective level. He described the former as follows: "The whole dream creation is in essence subjective, and the dream is that theatre in which the dreamer is the scene, the player, the prompter, the producer, the author, the public and the critic."[72] Here, Jung was presenting a dramatic theory of the dream. Such a view had been put forward by du Prel as the basis of his dream theory.[73] Subsequently, he went on to argue that not only was the basic structure of the dream dramatic, but so also its narrative sequence. In 1945, in "The essence of dreams" he stated that most dreams have the following structure: statement of place, development of the plot, culmination or peripeteia, then solution or lysis (*CW* 8, § 561–563). His comments concerning telepathy in this paper would certainly have pleased Myers, Gurney, and Podmore:

The general reality of this phenomenon is nowadays no longer to be doubted. Understandably, it is very easy to deny the existence of the phenomena without the proof of the existing evidence, but that is unscientific behaviour, that in no way deserves observation. (1928, *CW* 8, § 503, trans. mod.)

In his 1928 revision of "The psychology of dreams" he also added the following reference to Maeder: "Maeder energetically called attention to the prospective-final significance of dreams in the sense of a purposive unconscious function which prepares the solution of actual conflicts and problems and seeks to portray it through gropingly chosen symbols" (*ibid.*, § 491, trans. mod.). Further on, while discussing the manner in which the compensatory function can become a purposive, guiding function, he added that Maeder had shown this with success. Contrary to Freud's thesis that dreams were wishfulfillments, he and Maeder considered the dream as "*a spontaneous self-portrayal, in symbolic form, of the actual condition of the unconscious,*" and that their view coincided with Silberer.[74]

To his translator, Richard Hull, he wrote: "Concerning 'archetypal' I was not sure how much this rather unwarrantable ending 'al' has been accepted" (October 2, 1958, LC) original in English.

[72] "General standpoints on the psychology of dreams," *CW* 8, § 509, trans. mod. In a note, Jung added that Maeder had given examples of this.

[73] The one citation of du Prel in Jung's work occurs in 1924. Describing the psyche as pre-existent and transcendent to consciousness, he wrote: "we could therefore describe [it], with du Prel, as the transcendental subject." "Analytical psychology and education," *CW* 17, § 169.

[74] *Ibid.*, § 505, trans. mod. A few lines further on, while noting researches "expressly referred to by Maeder" that the sexual language of dreams need not be interpreted concretistically, Jung added in a note: "at this point we meet with agreement from Adler," § 506.

These belated acknowledgments that Maeder had expressed the theory of dreams that Jung in his 1916 article put forward as his own suggests, reading between the lines, that a priority dispute may have occurred, and that the references to Maeder may have been added as a correction. Intriguingly enough, in a letter to Ellenberger in which he discusses his relation with and subsequent estrangement from Jung, Maeder raised the issue of the citation and lack of citation of his work in Jung's writings:

Jung was, in his manner, as authoritarian as Freud . . . He did not practice exchanges of viewpoint with his collaborators.[75] He was very soon surrounded by admirers; finally he only had women around him, total admirers. It was he who created the isolation of which you speak . . . he couldn't accept my independence of spirit. In the first years he cited me often (for example in *Energetik-Seele*), then finally I disappeared totally from his publications.[76]

In Maeder's view, these failings were not particular to Jung, but afflicted the modern psychotherapy movement. In retrospect, he reflected on the isolation of the psychotherapeutic schools, such as the gulf between the Adlerians, Freudians, and Jungians. In each of these schools, he thought that the person of the founder and the party name had been overstressed by the followers. The absolutism, and ultimately the totalitarian pretension of each school was a compensation for inner uncertainty. The worship of the master resembled the characteristic hero worship of our age, which he saw as a substitute for a lost relation to God. In their dealings with one another, psychotherapists lacked the spirit of understanding and tolerance which was so necessary in working with patients, and the quarrels between psychotherapists had become just like those between theologians (1956b).

We have seen that Maeder explicitly traced his theory of dreams back to Flournoy. However, in the very revision in which Jung belatedly credited Maeder's work, he attempted to establish his priority over Flournoy: "I had already in 1906 drawn attention to the compensatory relation between consciousness and the split-off complexes and also emphasized their purposive character. Flournoy had done likewise, independently of

[75] In retrospect, Maeder recalled that Jung "said to me after these discussions (where I had to hold his line against every one), he said something like, 'Yes, what was best was that you told you had newly analyzed a dream of Freud better than Freud!' But of the principal thing, he didn't mention a word. That was in some ways strange for me, and that I saw he was a bit similar to Freud. He could not really bear the independence of his collaborators; basically he had the same faults for which he reproached Freud" (Maeder interview, CLM, 5).

[76] Maeder to Ellenberger, February 15, 1964, Ellenberger archives, Paris. It was in *Über die Energetik der Seele* (1928) that Jung revised his essay on dreams, and in which the citations above are found.

my designs."[77] However, the compensatory and purposive character of the teleological automatisms featured prominently in Flournoy's 1900 *From India to the Planet Mars*, which Jung cited extensively from in his dissertation in 1902.

Jung's next published statement on dreams came in 1931, with a paper delivered to the 6th General Medical Congress for Psychotherapy in Dresden, "The practical use of dream analysis." He stated that the possibility of dream analysis stands or falls with the hypothesis of the unconscious as the aim of dream analysis was to reveal unconscious contents (*CW* 16, § 294). The significance of dreams lay in the fact that they revealed the inner situation of the dreamer, and used a medical analogy to indicate their significance: "I have therefore made it a rule to regard dreams as I regard physiological facts: if sugar appears in the urine, then the urine contains sugar, and not albumen or urobin."[78] While Jung's theory of dreams was far removed from physiological theories of dreams, in this analogy, he was attempting to appropriate something of the authority and supposed certainty of physiological analysis. From several examples that he presented, he argued that dreams presented not only the aetiology of a neurosis, but also its prognosis, demonstrating that they were futural as well as retrospective. This was especially so as regards the initial dreams in psychotherapy (a position that had earlier been put forward by Wilhelm Stekel): "It frequently happens at the very beginning of treatment that a dream will reveal to the doctor, in broad perspective, the whole programme of the unconscious" (§ 343).

On a practical level Jung held that the main problem of dream analysis was that of suggestion. When interpretations were based on a preconceived theory or opinion the therapeutic results were due to suggestion (§ 315). A fundamental problem for Jung was how to demonstrate that his theories were anything but the results of suggestion. In his view the analytical approach was superior to suggestive approaches as it made ethical demands upon the patient. He claimed that to avoid suggestion, the doctor should set aside theoretical assumptions and regard any dream interpretation as invalid until it won the assent of the patient: "It should be completely self-evident that he should at that time give up every theoretical assumption and be willing in every single case to discover a completely new dream theory, since an immeasurable field for pioneer work stands

---

[77] *CW* 8, § 488, trans. mod. In his footnote, Jung referred to his *On the Psychology of Dementia Praecox* of 1907 and Flournoy's "Automatisme téléologique antisuicide" of 1908.

[78] § 304. Jung used similar medical analogies on several occasions. In his *Dream Analysis* seminar in 1928, he stated, "Just as a serious technique is required to make a diagnosis of heart, liver, kidneys, etc., so we had to work out a serious technique in order to read the impartial facts of dreams" (4).

open here" (§ 317, trans. mod.). In 1933, he expressed himself in even stronger terms:

It is, indeed, good that no valid method [of dream interpretation] exists, for otherwise the meaning of the dreams would already be limited in advance and would lose precisely that virtue which makes them so especially valuable for psychological purposes – namely their ability to give a new point of view.[79]

Aside from the axiomatic assumption that dreams added something to one's conscious knowledge, all other hypotheses should be regarded as merely rules of thumb (1931, *CW* 16, § 318). Due to the fact that dreams revealed the compensatory function of the unconscious, every dream was "an organ of information and control," and consequently dreams were "the most effective aid for building up the personality" (§ 332, trans. mod.).

One manner in which dreams could be an organ of control was through their classical function of providing a means of nocturnal diagnosis. In 1935, T. M. Davie reported a patient's dream in a paper in the *British Medical Journal* entitled, "Comments upon a case of 'periventricular epilepsy.'" Davie submitted this dream to Jung for his opinion and reported that Jung,

had no hesitation in saying that it indicated some organic disturbance, and that the illness was not primarily a psychological one, although there were numerous psychological derivatives in the dream. The drainage of the pond he interpreted as the damming up of the cerebrospinal fluid circulation. (Cited in *CW* 18, 135n)

In the discussion following one of Jung's lectures at the Institute of Medical Psychology in London in 1936, the psychoanalyst Wilfred Bion asked Jung to comment upon this case. In reply he stated that the dream clearly represented an organic disorder, and cited the fact that such a view was held by doctors in antiquity and the Middle Ages (*CW* 18, 136). With the rise of modern medicine the diagnostic dream had disappeared from general medical practice – that is, apart from the practice of Jung and his followers. His attempt to effect a return to traditional medical practice in this regard was connected to his study of alchemy and iatrochemistry during this period, and in particular, with his detailed study of Paracelsus, which attempted to call into question the presuppositions of modern scientific medicine.

The proof is in dreams

In 1916, Jung had used the term archetype to designate the phylogenetic mythological images that, following Jakob Burckhardt, he had termed

---

[79] "The meaning of psychology for the present," *CW* 10, § 319, trans. mod.

primordial images in 1911.[80] These images resided in the suprapersonal or collective unconscious. In addition to positing a prospective or future orientated function of the unconscious, he claimed that this led to a process of individual development which broadly took typical forms. This he termed the process of individuation, and he claimed that it underlay the process of personality transformation in religious and mystical traditions. Dreams were taken as furnishing the main evidence for the existence of such a process. Dreams were Jung's principal psychoscope. Because they were the most frequent and normal expression of the unconscious, they supplied the bulk of the material for its investigation.[81]

In his published writings, he claimed that it was the study of series of dreams that revealed the individuation process, a general and universal process of personality development which was simply quickened by analysis:

It is therefore possible that the motifs accompanying the individuation process appear mainly only in the first place in dream-series, received within the analytic process, whereas in "extra-analytical" dream-series they perhaps occur only at much greater intervals of time. ("The essence of dreams," *CW* 8, § 552, trans. mod.)

If we look at the dreams that Jung published we find that in the main, he presented dreams as illustrations of his theoretical arguments. He did not publish any lengthy detailed case studies from his therapeutic practice. Indeed, his lengthiest published studies of dreams were by individuals whom he either had not met, or was not dealing with directly. He adopted this procedure to obviate the charge of suggestion.[82] In his seminars, he did present much lengthier dream analyses, where they were put forward for pedagogical purposes.

His major presentation of the archetypic nature of dreams was in "Dream symbols of the individuation process," a paper initially presented at the Eranos conference in Ascona and also at a seminar in Bailey Island, Maine, USA, and then subsequently enlarged and published as the first part of *Psychology and Alchemy*. The accounts that he gave of the case in his seminar differ significantly from that in the latter.

In the published version of "Dream symbols of the individuation process," he stated that to exclude the factor of his own personal influence, the patient was treated by a woman pupil of his. It was later revealed that the patient was none other than the Nobel prize-winning physicist, Wolfgang Pauli. Of the four hundred dreams that he studied, only the last forty-five took place under his personal observation. He added that

---

[80] See below, 297–298.
[81] "The essence of dreams," 1945, *CW* 8, § 544.   [82] See Shamdasani, 2001.

no interpretations were given, because the dreamer, having an excellent scientific training, did not need help with this.[83] In the Bailey Island seminar, Jung stated that the man:

is a highly educated person with an extraordinary development of his intellect, which was, of course, the origin of his trouble; he was just too one-sidedly intellectual and scientific . . . The reason he consulted me was that he had completely disintegrated on account of this very one-sidedness.[84]

His account of what ensued demonstrates his unusual procedures as a psychotherapist:

I saw him at first for only twenty minutes. I instantly perceived that he was in a way a master mind, and I decided not to touch his intellect. I therefore proposed to him to go to my then most recent pupil, a woman who knew very little about my work. She was right in the beginning of her own analysis; but she had a good instinctive mind. She was not a fool, but had a good deal of common sense, and was, of course, highly surprised when I told her that I was going to send such a fellow to her. Naturally I had to do some explaining. I told her why I was doing it and also suggested to her how to deal with him. I told her I had instructed him to present his dreams to her; that he must write them out very carefully, and that she should listen and nod her head; and, in case she was astonished or puzzled, should say so. She should not, however, try to understand or analyze these dreams. Now she was, of course, quite glad that she had to play a more or less passive role, and astonishingly enough that man incidentally saw the point too. He understood what I told him. I said, "I don't want to influence your own mind, which is valuable. If I should do it for you, you would never be convinced, therefore I shall not even try. You go to this woman doctor and she will listen to your dreams." (7)

Such procedures would seem the opposite of non-interventative, non-suggestive therapy, and indeed, read like a skillful example of Milton Erickson's use of direct and indirect suggestion. The man in question was clearly directed to note his dreams and tell them to his analyst, who was directed not to analyze them, and how she should react, down to physical cues. In the ensuing discussion, the question was raised by one of the members of the seminar group as to what role the woman doctor played, and whether the same processes would have occurred if he had simply been keeping a record of his dreams. Jung replied:

Of course it is quite certain that the presence of that doctor was important and the same development would probably have not taken place if the dreamer had not felt the presence of a sympathetic audience . . . the role of that doctor was in

---

[83] Jung, 1939, 97. On Jung's collaboration with Pauli, see H. Atmanspracher, H. Primas and E. Wertenschlag-Birkhäuser, eds., 1995, and Meier, ed., 2001.
[84] *Dream Symbols of the Individuation Process, Bailey Island*, 1936, 6.

a way very important, as was the fact that she was a woman. She produced that substance or that secret which is characteristic of women, namely, a productive force, a pregnancy force. (37–38)

In his published version of this paper, Jung stated that the dreams had been abbreviated, for reasons of length and discretion – "personal allusions and complications" having been removed. He added that he applied a similar discretion in deliberately overlooking certain passages in the dreams. In addition to truncating the material in such a manner, he omitted the context of the dreams, and therefore noted that "I treat the dreams to a certain extent as if I had had them myself and were for that reason able on my own part to supply the context" (1936/1939, 100). This procedure was admissible due to the fact that he was dealing with several interconnected series of dreams, which were their own context. While the dreams were being dreamt the dreamer was not informed of Jung's interpretations. Though he had taken such precautions, he added that he thought that the possibility of influencing such a process was generally exaggerated, as "the objective psyche . . . is independent in the highest degree" (101). Thus the precautions were not primarily taken to obviate suggestive influence, but to obviate the *accusation* of suggestive influence.

These statements and the procedure that Jung followed were predicated upon the assumption that there existed an archetypic layer to the psyche which revealed itself in dreams independently of the personal psychology of the dreamer, to such an extent that one was entitled to regard another's dreams as one's own. Such a mode of exposition was unlikely to convince a skeptical critic, particularly as the material he was omitting would have been used by psychologists of other persuasions to interpret the dreams.[85] Thus the material served as an illustration, rather than proof.

Another instance where he privately acknowledged the active effects of the agency of the therapist, and critically, the relation of dreams to their social context, was in a letter to his student, the analytical psychologist James Kirsch:

With regard to your patient, it is quite correct that her dreams are occasioned by *you*. The feminine mind is the earth waiting for the seed. That is the meaning of the transference. Always the more unconscious person gets spiritually fecundated by the more conscious one. Hence the guru in India. This is an age-old truth. As soon as certain patients come to me for treatment, the type of dream changes. In the deepest sense we all dream not *out of ourselves but* of what lies *between us and the other*. (*Letters* 1, September 29, 1934, 172)

---

[85] However, in his account in the Bailey Island seminar, Jung did go into much more personal detail concerning his subject. From the impersonality of the published version, some have taken a misleading impression of Jung's procedure in actual practice.

In the twentieth century, the ascendancy of Freud's theory of dreams
had the effect of privatizing the dream, which was seen to be solely concerned with the intimate sphere of subjectivity, and its all too human
concerns. Jennifer Ford noted that in the eighteenth and early nineteenth
centuries, "At dinner parties, and at philosophical gatherings, dreams
were substantial topics for conversations, precisely because they were not
confined to the personal" (Ford, 1994, 7). In the case of Jung, notions
such as "interpretation on the subjective level" – in which all the figures in
dreams are seen to stand for aspects of the dreamer's personality – clearly
contributed to this development. However, his notion that some dreams
had a suprapersonal source in the collective unconscious, together with
his validation of the view that they could be a source of guidance, wisdom,
and ultimately religious experience, recovered the religious and metaphysical significance that had traditionally been assigned to the dream.
These conceptions served to deprivatize or collectivize the dream.

In 1937, Jung again utilized some of Pauli's dreams in his Terry lectures
on psychology and religion at Yale University. He presented a historical
survey of the attitude of the medieval church towards dreams, considering the views of Benedictus Pererius, Gregory the Great, Athanasius, and
Kaspar Peucer. He concluded: "In spite of the Church's recognition that
certain dreams are sent by God, she is disinclined, and even averse, to any
serious concern with dreams" (*CW* 11, § 32). He then presented some
of Pauli's dreams, and claimed that they represented the spontaneous
emergence of religious symbols, unknown to the dreamer, which demonstrated that the unconscious had a naturally religious function. Dreams
then, could lead to a direct religious experience, freed of creed and denomination. The recovery of the traditional spiritual significance, in a
modern psychological guise, was complete. In commenting on a dream,
he sought to justify his utilization of dreams as evidence for existence of
such a natural religious function:

I hold that our dream is really speaking of religion and that it intends to do so.
Since the dream has a coherent and well-designed structure, it suggests a certain
logic and a certain intention, that is, it has a meaningful motivation which finds
direct expression in the dream-content. (§ 41)

Thus if dreams spoke of religion, they should be taken literally. Elsewhere,
he suggested that when dreams spoke of UFOs, they were really speaking
about symbols of the Self.[86] Ultimately, the criterion to which he appealed
to validate religious experiences – and hence the possibility of regarding
dreams as a legitimate source of religious conceptions – was pragmatic:

---

[86] *A Modern Myth: Of Things, that have been seen in the Skies*, 1958, *CW* 10.

"And if such experiences help to make life healthier, more beautiful, more complete and satisfactory to yourself and to those you love, you may safely say: 'This was the grace of God.'"[87]

Children's dreams

It is curious, given the centrality of dreams for Jung, that he did not publish a comprehensive work explicitly on dreams. In 1929 he wrote to Cary Baynes: "I have not yet begun, to write about dreams. I imagine I am not up to such an enterprise yet. I know what you think about such a statement, so you don't need to give me your mind about it."[88] However, in the late thirties, he commenced an extensive seminar dealing with the subject of children's dreams and the history of dreams at the Swiss Federal Institute of Technology. He instructed members of his seminar to collect accounts of children's dreams, and the earliest remembered dreams of adults. The seminars were based on discussions of the cases that members of the group presented. At this stage in his career this mode of delegating specific research tasks to his students became more common.

There exists a handwritten manuscript of a questionnaire that Jung evidently wrote in preparation for this seminar.[89] In his view of development, consciousness developed out of the collective unconscious. Due to the child's proximity to the collective unconscious and undeveloped personal identity, he held that in children's dreams one found the clearest examples of the spontaneous emergence of archetypes. This constituted a critical test for the existence of the collective unconscious for Jung: for if archetypic motifs were only found in the dreams of adults, then the claim that they had an endogenous *a priori* source would become somewhat tenuous. He claimed not only that the archetypes but also the prospective tendency of the unconscious were clearly revealed in children's dreams. He stated, "These early dreams are most important, and it is not unusual for them to give a prophetic picture of a person's whole life."[90] What is striking about this seminar is that contrary to the widely

---

[87] *CW* 11, § 167. In this regard, he was closely following William James' position in *The Varieties of Religious Experience*. On Jung's relation to pragmatism, see above, 57–61.

[88] Jung to Cary Baynes, April 5, 1929 (CFB).

[89] Jung, "Dream problem" (JP). Among the questions asked were: what is the earliest childhood dream you remember? Did you have this dream again in later life? Does the dream have a new meaning in terms of subsequent life developments? Have you had precognitive dreams, dreams of a cosmic character, dreams in relation to the death of others?

[90] *Psychological Interpretation of Children's Dreams*, 1938–1939, 1.

held stereotype (even among Jungians) that Jung neglected childhood, he conducted considerably more direct research on childhood than Freud.

Dreams and race

Early on the field of anthropology became a contested ground for the proof of the universality of psychoanalysis. In Jung's case the anthropology of dreams took on a particular significance, not only to provide proof for the universality of his theories of the dream: for what was crucial was not only the dream, but what it revealed – the archetypes and the collective unconscious.

In his positing of a phylogenetic layer to the unconscious, a critical question for Jung was to what extent this phylogenetic layer was identical in different races. In 1912, Jung visited St. Elizabeth's Hospital in Washington DC for three days at the invitation of William Alonson White. While there, Jung conducted some clinical investigations of "negroes," which convinced him that collective patterns were not only racially inherited, but were universal. It was the presence of obscure motifs from classical mythology in their dreams that struck Jung. On the basis of such instances, he claimed that the apparent cross-cultural similarity of motifs in dreams was evidence for a universally human layer of the unconscious, the collective unconscious, which was the source of such images.[91]

Jung's trip to Kenya and Uganda in 1925 had important effects on his conception of dreams. From the Elgonyi, he learnt that there were two types of dreams, the ordinary dreams, which most people had, and the "big" dreams that the medicine man or chief had. These dreams had great importance for the tribe as a whole. The medicine man of the Elgonyi informed Jung, with much regret, that he had stopped having such dreams since the British came. The function of guidance that the dreams provided had now been filled by the District Commissioner.[92] Jung argued that while such a conception of dreams had been absent in the West since Roman times, such dreams still occurred (1928–1930, 5). Such dreams stemmed from the collective unconscious, and did not only have a significance for the dreamer, but also for society at large.[93] One immediately recognized them by their sense of significance, and felt impelled to communicate them.[94]

[91] See below, 311–313.
[92] "The Symbolic Life" 1939, CW 18, § 673.
[93] "The meaning of psychology for the present," 1933, CW 10, § 324.
[94] "The relations between the ego and the unconscious," 1927, CW 7, § 276.

One of the earliest extensive anthropological studies of dreams was Stewart Lincoln's 1935 *The Dream in Primitive Culture*. Lincoln, who had attended some of Jung's seminars, attempted to apply psychoanalytic understanding of dreams to primitive cultures. He discussed Jung's distinction between the individual and "big" dreams of primitives. He dismissed Jung's invocation of the collective unconscious to explain the latter class of dreams, which Lincoln redubbed culture-pattern dreams. Jung had failed to point out that "the images of the great cultural visions are collective only for a given culture and not for all mankind" (1935, 24). The fact that these visions disappeared when a culture broke down demonstrated that their existence depended on cultural traditions, as opposed to racial memories. Hence they were culturally specific symbols. Any cross-cultural similarity between such images could be explained by reference to the similarity of the cultural traditions that gave rise to them. Lincoln's critique enunciates a position that was widely held by Jung's critics, not just in anthropology, but in many other disciplines. A few years later, Jung attempted to rebut Lincoln's argument in detail in a seminar.

He commenced by stating that he knew Lincoln, and described him as being an amateur who had an insufficient knowledge and experience of psychology. He stated: "One cannot know what a primitive means by 'a great dream,' for instance, if one has not oneself had such an experience."[95] He countered Lincoln's claims with anecdotes of his own encounters with primitives, noting: "One must feel one's way into the inner life of primitives if one wants to understand them. Theoretical ideas are of little use there" (*ibid.*). Yet at the same time, he cautioned, "Our own cultural conditions can in no way be applied, as Lincoln has done, to interpret those of the primitives."[96]

The multiplicity of dreams

As noted, through the ascendancy of psychoanalysis, the late nineteenth-century classificatory project in dream research died out. In a significant contemporary study, the cognitive psychologist Harry Hunt argued that as a consequence "Dream psychology, in haste for its own Darwin, has bypassed the necessary foundation of a Linneaus" (1989, 97). By contrast, Hunt develops an agenda for contemporary dream research that attempts to continue the classificatory project of nineteenth-century research.

---

[95] *Psychological Interpretation of Children's Dreams*, 71.
[96] *Ibid.*, 78. Lincoln's work has also been critiqued by contemporary anthropologists of the dream. See Barbara Tedlock, 1992b, 21.

In Jung's dream theory, one witnesses the legacy of the classificatory project. The following is his strongest statement in this respect:

There are, it is true, dreams which manifestly represent wishes or fears, but what about all the other things? Dreams may contain ineluctable truths, philosophical pronouncements, illusions, wild fantasies, memories, plans, anticipations, irrational experiences, even telepathic visions, and heaven knows what besides.[97]

His differentiation between compensatory dreams, diagnostic dreams, archetypic dreams, collective dreams, telepathic dreams, and "Adlerian" and "Freudian" dreams has already been noted. The following are further categories of dreams which he recognized. He nominated certain dreams as reaction dreams, which he described as dreams "in respect of which certain objective events have caused a trauma that is not merely psychic but at the same time a physical lesion of the nervous system."[98] In addition,

There are also affect dreams, usually affects which have failed to reach consciousness during the day, and there are warning and informatory dreams . . . Then there are philosophical dreams which think for us and in which we get the thoughts we should have had during the day.[99]

In psychology, the period within which Jung wrote can be characterized as the heyday of monocausal explanations of dreams. He was trying to establish a psychology of dreams that was both historically and anthropologically inclusive, as the only means of establishing a theory that could have universal validity. It was this attempt to validate the multiple ways in which dreaming has been regarded and the traditional valorization of dreams, historically and anthropologically, that accounts for the popular success of Jung's work on dreams.

As pointed out earlier, in the latter half of the nineteenth century, interest in the dream shifted from the dream itself, to utilizing the dream as a psychoscope, or as the basis for a general psychology of the unconscious. Paradoxically, this elevation of the dream had the effect of canceling out its privileged status: for if other phenomena were analogized to the dream and could be regarded in the same way, the specific value of dreams correspondingly decreased. Within psychoanalysis, the number of articles explicitly on dreams increasingly declined. Among Jungian analysts, the prominence that Jung (and those attracted to Jungian therapy) attached to dreams assured their continued utilization as tools in clinical practice,

---

[97] "Practical use of dream analysis," 1934, *CW* 16, § 317.
[98] "General standpoints on the psychology of dreams," *CW* 8, § 499.
[99] *Modern Psychology: Notes on Lectures given at the Eidgenössische Technische Hochschule*, vol. 1, 1934–1935, 135.

but there was little specific interest in the psychology of dreams as a subject, and few attempts to further Jung's work in this domain, either by elaboration or criticism.[100]

While Freudian and Jungian theorists promoted a psychogenic understanding of dreams, divorced from any physiological underpinning, the physiological approach to dreams came back with a vengeance. In the 1950s, Aserinsky and Kleitman's claim to have demonstrated a correlation between the occurrences of dreams and REM [rapid eye movement] sleep was much heralded, and accorded a totemic status by the burgeoning experimental research in dreams. This was because it seemed to provide observable correlates for the process of dreaming, and hence enabled their reinstallation within the agenda of experimental psychology. This was coupled with the resurgence of physiologically based models of dreaming. In this literature, one frequently finds psychological factors accorded a similar secondary position as in the physiological dream theories of the nineteenth century.

Meanwhile, the most venerable tradition of dream literature, that of the dream keys, continues to flourish. Centuries-old texts continue to be reissued in popular editions. While the psychological and psychoanalytic investigation of dreams attempted to supersede this literature once and for all, current dream keys have simply accommodated Freudian and Jungian dream theories, and mined them for a new stock of symbolic meanings: penis envy, castration, anima-animus, and so on, have taken their place alongside traditional symbology.[101] Rather than supplanting traditional symbology, Freud and Jung's work on dreams has been incorporated into it, giving it a new lease of life. This development seems ironically to indicate the extent to which the contents of the Freudian unconscious and the Jungian collective unconscious have become familiar features of our conscious preoccupations, rather than necessarily indicating deep and hidden factors.

Finally, in the eighties, there took place the emergence and rapid growth of the dreamwork movement, which fostered the non-clinical exploration of dreams (see Krippner, ed., 1990). Dream groups, dream workshops and dream sites on the internet abound. Proponents of this movement speak of these developments as "deprofessionalizing the dream," taking it out of the exclusive preserve of the professional clinician. While

---

[100] For the exception to this, see Hillman, 1979.

[101] For example, in Eric Ackroyd's *A Dictionary of Dream Symbols*, we learn that "a spear may be a sexual symbol, representing the penis" (1983, 277) and that "Blue may sometimes symbolize the universal or collective unconscious . . . the blue sea may also symbolize the unconscious or the feminine (anima, mother or Great Mother)" (94). In 1951, *La Nouvelle clé des songes* written by two authors bearing the name "le vingtième Artemidore" bore an epigraph by Jung on the first page.

freely drawing from Freudian and Jungian dream theories, the dream-work movement represents a significant shift in social practice, from an allo-interpretive to an auto-interpretive model. While the work of Freud and Jung dominated the dream in Western societies for much of the twentieth century, with these developments, one finds the locus of dream investigation significantly shifting. Will the psychological investigation of dreams in psychotherapy find itself displaced by a pincer movement, from the experimental physiology of dreams on one side, and the popular symbolic traditions on the other? It is at present too early to draw conclusions as to how these changes will affect the dream cultures of Western societies.

3   Body and soul

At the end of the nineteenth century, the question of man's place in the natural order was paramount. Evolutionary thinking had revolutionalized long-standing conceptions concerning the origin of species and their interrelation. In so doing, man's relation to his ancestry appeared in a new light. Questions concerning the nature of inheritance, memory, instincts, life, and energy were critical issues in the sciences of the body – biology, ethology, physiology, zoology – as well as in the attempts to form a new scientific psychology.

Proponents of the new scientific psychology called their field "physiological psychology" to differentiate it from the older philosophical psychology, and to associate it with the contemporary revolutions in the sciences of the body. They sought to replace the static mind of the philosophical tradition with a mind that had evolved, and was adapted to the environment. For psychologists, the critical issue was one of linking their field with developments in the sciences of the body, while maintaining the disciplinary autonomy of psychology.

One means by which this was effected was through the concept of the unconscious. This provided a new formulation of the relation between the soul and the body. Conceptions of life, memory, and instincts became transfigured by the unconscious. This in turn became a new touchstone of self-knowledge, which came to signify knowledge of what was unconscious, in some shape or form, to the self.

Any study of the history of the unconscious is indebted to Ellenberger's monumental *Discovery of the Unconscious*, and this is no exception. Ellenberger's text marked the constitution and delineation of a new field of inquiry. While one may depart from a number of Ellenberger's theses, such a move nevertheless remains within the field of inquiry that he inaugurated.

Ellenberger's central assumption is embedded in the title of his work. As Mark Micale aptly notes, for Ellenberger, "the unconscious mind was not invented, or formulated, it was 'discovered'" (1994, 127). For Ellenberger, the reality of the unconscious as a natural object was unquestioned. Different conceptions of the unconscious figure as competing maps to a pre-existing terrain. A singular reality was supposed to underlay the multiple depictions. However, to grasp the historical constitution of the unconscious, such naturalism needs to be set aside. Without this suspension, the modes in which the unconscious came to be conceived of as a natural object, whose existence could simply be taken for granted, cannot be grasped.

For the new dynamic psychologies in the nineteenth century, the concept of the unconscious served to separate their field from the domains of philosophy, physiology, and biology. At the same time, this separation was far from straightforward, as philosophy and physiology had their own concepts of the unconscious and unconscious mental functioning. Reconstructing these complex series of appropriations enables one to assess to what extent they succeeded in this.

This section commences by considering Jung's views on his relation to philosophy, and then maps out the constitution of concepts of the unconscious in German philosophy. It then sketches conceptions of life, memory, and instincts in physiology and biology, and how these led to biological and physiological concepts of the unconscious. Finally, it shows how Jung attempted to synthesize these competing notions under an overarching concept of the collective unconscious.

Genealogies of the unconscious

In the 1950s, an increasing number of works expounding and discussing Jung's work began to appear. One of the earliest academic studies which came out was written by an American scholar, Ira Progoff. This work was brought to Jung's attention, and we are fortunate to have his detailed responses to it, in the form of an interview conducted by Ximena de Angulo. This forms an important correction as to how his work was generally being perceived. Against the Freudocentric reading of his work, Jung stated that his own conceptions were "much more like Carus than Freud" and that Kant, Schopenhauer, Carus, and von Hartmann had provided him with the "tools of thought" (Ximena de Angulo, 1952, 207). While Nietzsche and Burckhardt had influenced him, they were indirect "side influences." It was as a "phenomenon" that Nietzsche impressed him the most (*ibid.*). In his dissertation, Progoff had claimed that Jung had derived his concept of the unconscious from Freud. Jung denied this, adding, "I had these thoughts long before I came to Freud. *Unconscious* is an *epistemological* term deriving from von Hartmann" (208). In a similar vein, in his 1925 seminar, he recounted that his idea of the unconscious "first became enlightened through Schopenhauer and Hartmann" (1925, 5). Before considering their work, and their significance for Jung, it is important to reconstruct and draw together Jung's accounts of the philosophy of the unconscious.

In the 1930s, Jung became increasingly interested in the history of psychology, going so far as to deliver a series of lectures on the subject at the Swiss Federal Institute of Technology. At the same time, an increasing number of comparative works on Freud and Jung began to appear, which accentuated the Freudocentric account of the origins of Jung's psychology.[1] As a corrective, he made several statements concerning his intellectual lineage. His accounts of the historical development of concepts of the unconscious in philosophy broadly paralleled von Hartmann's account of the same. Indeed, while von Hartmann's sequence culminated in his own conceptions of the unconscious, Jung's correspondingly culminated in his own (von Hartmann, 1900, 16–42).

Jung claimed that Freud was uninfluenced by this philosophical background. His own avowed affiliation to this trajectory constituted one of the crucial differential factors between his work and Freud's. In 1934, he noted that "There had been talk of the unconscious long before Freud."[2] He stressed the fact that the idea had been introduced into philosophy by Leibniz, and that Kant and Schelling had expressed views on it. It had subsequently been elaborated into a system by Carus, and then by von Hartmann, who had been significantly influenced by Carus. In his 1933 lectures on the history of psychology at the Swiss Federal Institute for Technology, he noted that it was Schelling's insight that the unconscious constituted the absolute foundation of consciousness. Schelling had also realized that the unconscious was the same for all intelligences, in other words, that "The primeval foundation is not differentiated, but universal."[3]

Within this historical sequence, he gave especial importance to the work of his namesake, Carl Gustav Carus. In 1940 he wrote that though philosophers such as Leibniz, Kant, and Schelling had drawn attention to the "problem of the dark soul," it was Carus, a physician who had been impelled "to point to the *unconscious* as the essential ground of the soul."[4] In 1945, he went so far as to say of Carus that if he had

---

[1] Kranefeldt (1930); Heyer (1932); Adler (1934). Jung wrote prefaces to the works by Kranefeldt and Adler and reviewed Heyer's work. Such endorsements of works by his pupils was critical for their success.

[2] "A review of complex theory" (1934), *CW* 8, § 212.

[3] *Modern Psychology*, vol. 1, 15.

[4] "The psychology of the child archetype" (1940), *CW* 9, 1, § 259, trans. mod.

been living today, he would have been a psychotherapist.[5] Indeed, the psychology of the unconscious began with Carus, who did not realize that he had built the "philosophical bridge to a future empirical psychology."[6] However, Carus' and Hartmann's philosophical conceptions of the unconscious "had gone down under the overwhelming wave of materialism and empiricism."[7] It was only after this that the concept of the unconscious reappeared "in the scientifically orientated medical psychology" (*CW* 9, 1, § 1.). In comparison with the philosophical tradition of the unconscious, the significance of modern psychology was that it discarded the metaphysics of the philosophical psychologists "and restricted the idea of psychic existence to the psychological statement, in other words, to its phenomenology."[8]

The philosophical genealogy of the psychology of the unconscious that Jung developed here raised the question of the significance of Romanticism for him. In 1935 Jung wrote a preface to a work by Rose Mehlich on Fichte. Mehlich had argued that Jung's psychology was romantic. In his preface, he stated that while he was familiar with the work of Leibniz, Carus, and von Hartmann, "I never knew until now that my psychology is 'Romantic'" (*CW* 18, 1732). The rest of his preface was taken up with distancing his work from Romanticism. Mehlich's linking of Jung to Romanticism was cited in Olga von Koenig-Fachsenfeld's work of the same year, *Transformation of the Dream Problem from the Romantics to the Present*, for which he also wrote a foreword. Curiously, this time he responded quite differently to the linkage of his work with romanticism. He stated that it was undeniable that certain premises of modern psychology were a restatement of romantic ideas. He focused upon their experiential approach, which he claimed was the hallmark of their attitude to the psyche. He then noted:

> The parallelism with my psychological conceptions is sufficient justification for calling them "Romantic." A similar enquiry into their philosophical antecedents would also justify such an epithet, for every psychology that takes the psyche as "experience" is from the historical point of view both "Romantic" and "alchemystical." Below this experiential level, however, my psychology is scientific and rationalistic [wissenschaftlich-rationalistisch], a fact that I would beg the reader not to overlook. (*CW* 18, § 1740, trans. mod.)

Several years later, he again addressed this issue in a seminar on November 22, 1938. Commenting on a presentation of Philip Lersch's work, *The Dream in German Romanticism*, he said:

[5] "Medicine and Psychotherapy," *CW* 16, § 204.
[6] *Mysterium Coniunctionis*, *CW* 14, § 791, trans. mod.
[7] "Archetypes of the collective unconscious" (1934), *CW* 9, 1, § 1, trans. mod.
[8] "Transformation symbolism in the mass," *CW* 11, § 375, trans. mod.

von Hartmann is the connecting bridge between modern philosophy and roman-ticism. He was most deeply influenced by Carus . . . His metaphysical ideas were essentially those of Carus, and Carus is decidedly a romantic. That we speak of the unconscious at all is a direct inheritance of the romantic spirit.[9]

In his accounts, he sometimes refers to Carus and von Hartmann as philosophers and sometimes as psychologists. The weighting of the signif-icance of their work compared with subsequent developments in medical psychology also varies. These equivocations indicate tensions within his relation to philosophy. In his comments on Progoff's dissertation, he con-sidered the misunderstanding of his work as actually being philosophy was due to the fact that he utilized philosophical concepts to make clear his presuppositions and to formulate his findings (Ximena de Angulo, 1952, 203). Throughout his career, he railed at being called a philosopher, and insisted on his status as an empirical scientist. To his translator Richard Hull, he wrote: "Don't forget: I am definitely no philosopher and my concepts are accordingly *empirical* and *not speculative*."[10]

At different junctures, he gave varying descriptions of the relation of philosophy to psychology. In 1928, he argued that due to the fact that the thinking that underlay philosophy was a psychic activity, psychology held a superordinate position: "I always think with psychology of the whole extent of the soul, and that includes philosophy and theology and many things besides."[11] In 1931, he stated that the difference between philosophy and psychology was that while the former took the world as its subject matter, the latter took the subject. This definition might have been derived from a similar distinction made by Johann Herbart in 1814, who had claimed that "the work of psychology is . . . to make the total of inner experiences comprehensible, while it is the work of the philoso-phy of nature to accomplish the same in regard to outer experience."[12] Jung claimed that "Both disciplines cannot do without one another, and the one always supplies the mostly unconscious presuppositions of the other."[13]

At first glance such statements appear to be saying different things: for while in the former, psychology encompasses philosophy, in the lat-ter, they are both granted a coequal status. It is possible to provide an

---

[9] *Psychological Interpretation of Children's Dreams* (1938–1939), 47.
[10] February 9, 1951, LC.
[11] "General aspects of dream psychology" (1928/1948) *CW* 8 § 525, trans. mod.
[12] Jung discussed Herbart in the course of his lectures on the history of psychology in 1933 (*Modern Psychology* 1, 21). There are a few references to Herbart in Jung's work, indicating an interest in his conception of the relation of representations to the thresh-old of consciousness, "Theoretical reflections on the essence of the psychical" (1946) *CW* 8, § 350.
[13] "The basic problems of contemporary psychology" (1931) *CW* 8, § 659.

interpretation of these statements that reconciles them. It can be said that Jung's "philosophical presuppositions" included a psychologizing reading of philosophy that enabled philosophy to be subsumed by psychology. Finally, it should be noted that the "philosophy" he attempted to distance himself from was precisely that to which he was closest, that is, the philosophy of the unconscious, extending von Hartmann's title to designate the sequence of development that Jung sketched above.

The philosophy of the unconscious

In a landmark study, Michel Henry has studied the generation of the concept of the unconscious in the philosophical tradition, and its prolongation in psychoanalysis. As Henry argues, the concept of the unconscious made its appearance in Western thought *"simultaneously with and as the exact consequence of the concept of consciousness."*[14] The progressive expansion of the concept of the unconscious in philosophy was made possible by a progressive delimitation of the concept of consciousness. In Henry's reading of the modern philosophical tradition from Descartes onwards, the philosophy of consciousness, in which the essence of consciousness was conceived in terms of representations, consisted in a failure to take up precisely the path opened up by Descartes' *cogito*, namely that "'I think' means anything but thought. 'I think' means life" (3). Henry concludes that Freud's conception of the unconscious, far from breaking with the philosophy of consciousness, paradoxically prolonged it, through conceiving of the unconscious as consisting in hidden representations – the defining characteristic of consciousness in the modern philosophical tradition. To follow these developments, we now turn to developments in eighteenth and nineteenth-century German philosophy.

Kant

To a student at the Jung Institute in the 1950s, Jung exclaimed, "Kant is my philosopher."[15] Immanuel Kant (1724–1804) was born in Königsberg and spent his life there. After working as a private tutor, he was given a chair of philosophy at the university in 1770. It was with his so-called critical philosophy that Kant inaugurated a new era in philosophy. He commenced his preface to the first edition of *The Critique of Pure Reason* (1781) by highlighting the fact that it was a peculiarity of human reason that it took up questions which, by its very nature, it was unable to solve. Attempting to supersede what was presented by

---

[14] 1985, 2. On Henry, see Borch-Jacobsen, 1989.
[15] Jung to John Phillips, personal communication, John Phillips.

experience led metaphysics into error. In his preface to the second edition of the *Critique*, Kant stated that it had been hitherto assumed that our mode of cognition must conform to objects of experience. This assumption, he claimed, had been responsible for the failure of metaphysics. By contrast, he proposed to suggest the reverse, that is, that objects of experience have to conform to our mode of cognition. This reversal, he famously claimed, corresponded in philosophical terms to Copernicus' replacement of a geocentric with a heliostatic model of the universe. For Kant, the question was determining the form that cognition had to take to make the experience of the world possible. At the outset, he distinguished between pure and empirical knowledge. He claimed that while it was indubitable that all knowledge commenced with experience, it was by no means the case that it was all derived from experience, as the empiricists such as Locke and Hume claimed. Pure knowledge consisted in the universal *a priori* notions which were not derived from experience. Such notions he termed categories. An example of such a category was the law of causality. He claimed that the law of causality must have an *a priori* basis in the understanding, as it could not be derived from experience alone. Empirical rules could not be strictly universal, as induction could only lead to comparative universality and extensive utility (Kant, 1787/1930, A 92). The categories constituted the conditions for the possibility of experience. Only through representation was it possible to know something as an object.

Coupled with the categories, he introduced a distinction between things as they were experienced, which he termed phenomena, and things as they were in themselves, which he termed noumena. Phenomena were representations of things which were unknown in themselves (A 249ff.). The concept of the noumenon was a "borderline concept" that served to limit "the pretension of the sensibility" (B 311). Hence it was only posited negatively, to set limits to the understanding, which could only conceive of things through the categories.

For Kant, in the "contest of the faculties," psychology occupied a lowly place, as it could not be a natural science. He maintained that for any discipline to be a science, it had to be founded upon mathematics, which constituted its *a priori* basis. He claimed that mathematics was "inapplicable to the phenomena of the internal sense" (1786/1985, 8). In addition, psychology was not an experimental discipline. This was due to the difficulty of self-observation. As inner experience constituted a temporal flux, it lacked the permanence necessary for observation. In strident terms, he cautioned against the practice of self-observation: "to wish to play the spy upon one's self . . . is to reverse the natural order of the cognitive powers . . . The desire for self-investigation is either already a disease of the mind (hypochondria) or will lead to such a disease and ultimately to the madhouse" (8). Thus Kant's strictures upon self-observation went as far as a nascent psychopathology of psychologists. The observation of others was also beset with difficulties, and observation distorted the state of the objects observed. Thus psychology could only aspire to being a natural description of the soul, as opposed to a science.

Kant's *Anthropology from a Pragmatic Point of View* (1798) covered much of the subject matter that was later to be claimed for psychology. He stated that in contrast to Locke, who had claimed that it was not possible to have ideas without being conscious of them, "we can be indirectly conscious of having an idea although we are not directly conscious of it" (18). He called such ideas obscure. Kant's recognition of these obscure ideas followed Leibniz (1646–1716). In his *New Essays on Human Understanding*, Leibniz put forward his thesis of the existence of "petits perceptiones," or perceptions that were too small to be noticed. As an example, he noted that when we hear the sound of the waves, it follows that we are affected by the parts that constitute it, that is, the sounds of each wave, which, by themselves, are too faint to be heard (1703–1705/1981, 55). These perceptions, which determined our behavior without our thinking of them, were responsible for the sense of temporal continuity. Kant speculated on these small perceptions, or as he called them, obscure ideas, in his lectures on psychology in the mid 1770s:

If through a supernatural revelation we were to become immediately conscious of all our obscure representations and of the whole extent of the soul at once, then we might be astonished at ourselves and at the treasure in our soul, of what abundance it contains of cognitions in itself. When we cast our eyes through a telescope upon the furthest heavenly bodies, then the telescope does nothing more than awaken the consciousness of countless heavenly bodies which cannot be seen with the naked eye, but which already lay obscurely in our soul. Were a human being able to be conscious of all that which he perceives of bodies through microscopes, then he would have a great knowledge of bodies, which he actually has now, only that he is not himself conscious of it. Further, everything that is taught in metaphysics and morality, every human being already knows; only he was not himself conscious of it; and he who explains and expounds this to us actually tells us nothing new that we have not already known, rather he only makes it that I become conscious of that which was already in me. Were God suddenly to bring light immediately into our soul, that we could be conscious of all our representations, then the most learned will get no farther than the most unlearned; the only difference is that now the learned is already here conscious of something more. But if a light will go on in each soul, then they are both equally clear and distinct. There thus lies in the field of obscure representations a treasure which constitutes the deep abyss of human cognitions which we are unable to reach.[16]

---

[16] "Metaphysik L$_1$, psychology," in Kant, 1997, 47.

David Leary notes that in setting strictures on psychology, Kant had inadvertently set out prescriptions that were to be taken up in the nineteenth century by figures who wished to establish psychology as a science:

[Jakob Friedrich] Fries [1773–1843], argued that psychology can evolve a set of rational concepts to guide its theoretical work; [Johann Friederich] Herbart [1776–1841] devised a mathematical psychology . . . and [Friederich Eduard] Beneke proposed a set of experiments and ardently advocated the establishment of a truly experimental psychology. (1982, 35)

The abyss that separated us from the treasure of obscure ideas was to prove no less inviting. In his introduction to his edition of Kant's lectures on psychology, the spiritualist and philosopher Carl du Prel argued that dreams, somnambulism, and mediumship showed the simultaneity of Kant's transcendental subject with our earthly being. As a consequence, "the theory of the soul will now be directed to wholly new paths. Its stress will move from consciousness into the unconscious" (1889, 42).

Schelling

Friedrich Schelling (1775–1854) studied philosophy in Tübingen, where he was on close terms with Hegel and Hölderlin. For a number of years, he was a disciple of Johann Fichte. In 1798, he obtained a chair in philosophy at the University of Jena, and subsequently held positions at Würzburg, Erlangen, Munich, and Berlin. Kant had claimed that his demonstration that the concepts of the understanding were not applicable to the supersensuous realm had ended metaphysics. Schelling countered that if the former were true, the supersensuous realm could not only not be known, it could not be thought. Kant had fallen into a contradiction. For Schelling, philosophy had two tasks: to explain the genesis of nature, and to elucidate the metaphysical world. While Kant had failed in these, and unwittingly preserved metaphysics, his contribution lay in redirecting philosophy to the subjective. It was this aspect that J. H. Fichte had developed. In his *Philosophy of Nature* (1797) Schelling attempted to demonstrate the possibility of the existence of the outside world. Ultimately, the resolution lay "in the absolute identity of Mind *in us* and Nature *outside us*" (42). In his *System of Transcendental Idealism* (1800) he sought to reconcile this with Fichte's philosophy. Subsequently Schelling turned away from Fichte and developed a philosophy of identity. He mounted a critique of Hegel, and worked out a philosophy of mythology and religion, and Christianity in particular. In a fundamental study, Odo Marquard characterizes Schelling's work as a "depotentiating" of transcendental philosophy in which the historicizing of nature and the naturalizing of history went hand in hand. He identifies the following ambivalent components of this process:

on the one hand: to recognize nature as the basis of reason; on the other hand: to understand this nature itself as 'rational'; or – on the one hand: to show the not-I as the fundament of the I; on the other hand: to understand this not-I as an I; or – on the one hand – to identify the historical through the other to the historical, through nature; on the other hand: to define this nature as the other of nature, through history.[17]

The aspect of Schelling's work that concerns us here is his notion of the unconscious. He conceived of the unconscious as a productive force or ground of consciousness. In this, he was following Fichte's attempt to determine the "Act which does not and cannot appear among the empirical states of consciousness, but rather lies at the basis of consciousness and alone makes it possible" (Fichte, 1794, 93). As Marquard remarks, Schelling's emphasis on the unconscious and the "becoming conscious of the unconscious" stems from his depotentiating of Fichte's transcendental "I" (1987, 158). Another aspect of this depotentiating of the "I" was increasing stress on the significance of the drives. In his *System of Transcendental Idealism*, Schelling argued that the fundamental activity which produces the world is both conscious and unconscious (1800, 12). While the self-determination of the individual was conscious, the original act of self-consciousness itself was not. Thus there existed an unconscious region of the mind: "that which exists in me without consciousness is involuntary; that which exists with consciousness is in me through my willing" (204). Art – which included mythology – was par excellence the activity that revealed the concurrence of conscious and unconscious activity. The production of art consisted in two factors: one consisted of thought and reflection and was conscious, and could be learnt and handed down. The other was unconscious and inborn. In his work on mythology, he frequently referred to the Gods as primordial images [Urbilder] (1857). In his later work, he posited an irrational principle which formed the basic ground of the existence of the world, and identified this with the unconscious.

As for psychology, he held that its problem was that it saw everything in terms of cause and effect and degraded everything rare and sublime: "The great deeds of the past, once they have been dissected with psychological knives, appear as the natural result of a few quite understandable motives" (1803, 65). Thirty years later, he was somewhat more positive. While stating that psychology still lacked a real scientific basis, it did "open

---

[17] Marquard, 1987, 153. I thank Jean Starobinski for recommending this work.

up to the human spirit a new region of itself," in particular, the border between the physical and psychological (1827, 93).

Schopenhauer

Arthur Schopenhauer (1788–1860) was born in Danzig. He studied at the University of Göttingen, and attained a doctorate in philosophy from the University of Jena. In 1811, he briefly attended Fichte's lectures in Berlin. In 1813–1814, he was in Weimar, in close contact with Goethe. It was during this period that he was introduced to Eastern thought, which had a profound effect on him. His philosophical masterpiece, *The World as Will and Representation* appeared in 1819. With the opening lines, Schopenhauer proclaimed that:

"The World is my representation": that is a truth valid with reference to every living and knowing being, although man alone can bring it into reflective abstract consciousness . . . It then becomes clear and certain to him that he does not know a sun and an earth, but only an eye that sees a sun, a hand that feels an earth; that the world around him is there only as representation, in other words, only in reference to another thing, namely that which represents, and this is himself. (3)

At the same time, the world did not present itself to a pure knowing subject, but to one that was corporeal. For this aspect, he used the term will: "This and this alone gives him the key to his own phenomenon, reveals to him the significance and shows him the inner mechanism of his being, his actions, his movements" (100). His usage of the term "will" must be distinguished from everyday usage of the term. Michel Henry aptly states that for Schopenhauer, "*Will means life's will to live*, so that all the essential determinations of Schopenhauer's central concept (will to live) are explained by life" (1985, 134). Thus Schopenhauer introduced a radical delimitation of the provenance of representation. The will constituted not only one's innermost nature, but also of animals and all of existence. The will was blind, that is, it was not guided by representations. He claimed that

In outer as well as inner teleology of nature, what we must think of as means and ends is everywhere only *the phenomenon of the unity of the one will so far in agreement with itself*, which has broken up into space and time for our mode of cognition. (1819, 161)

Thus there existed "a self-adaption of what exists according to what is yet to come. Thus the bird builds the nests for the young it does not yet know" (160). The blindness of the will gave rise to the pathos of suffering and tragedy that pervaded his philosophy, commonly termed his pessimism.

His work initially attracted little attention. From the 1850s onwards, it became increasingly renowned, reaching a peak in the period between 1880 and the first world war, which was the period in which Jung first read his works (Magee, 1987, 262).

Carus

Marquard argues that Schelling's depotentiating of transcendental philosophy established the philosophical significance of medicine. With history being understood as nature, difficulties of history were conceived of as difficulties of nature, in other words, as illness (1987, 170). Hence custodianship of nature shifted from artists to doctors. Thus the fact that many of the philosophers of nature were doctors or had explicit relations with medicine, and that physiologists such as Karl Friedrich Burdach and Johannes Müller engaged with the philosophy of nature, was no accident. The disenchantment of transcendental philosophy's concept of nature gave philosophical value to the therapeutic attitude, a development which culminated in Friedrich Nietzsche's conception of the philosopher as a physician of culture. The medicalizing of philosophy depotentiated rationality, and led to an increased stress on the question of the genesis and development of rationality itself.

An exemplary figure in this regard was Carl Gustav Carus. Carus (1789–1869) was born in Leipzig. He studied medicine, and was appointed a professor of gynecology at the University of Dresden in 1814. He wrote on a wide variety of subjects, including comparative anatomy, physiognomy, physiology, symbolism, cranioscopy, comparative psychology, and Goethe. He had contact with Oken, Reil, von Humboldt and Goethe. Alongside his theoretical and scientific work, Carus was a painter. In 1829, he attended Schelling's lectures in Dresden. His *Psyche* of 1846 was his best-known work. This opened with the following frequently cited line: "*The key to an understanding of the nature of the conscious life of the soul lies in the sphere of the unconscious*" (1846, 1). This was because "the greatest part of the soul's life rests in the realm of the unconscious. While we are consciously aware of only a few ideas at a given moment, we create continuously thousands of ideas which we are completely unconscious of" (1). Thus consciousness was dependent upon the unconscious, from which it arose. Consequently, he claimed that the key to any genuine psychology lay in the study of the unconscious. He was combining the Leibniz–Kant thesis concerning the existence of unconscious representations with Schelling's notion of the unconscious as the primary ground of consciousness. Carus' unconscious had several layers. The first layer was the absolute unconscious, which was completely inaccessible to

consciousness. This consisted in an originary general level, which prevailed in embryonic development. After the development of consciousness, the formative processes take place in the partial level of the absolute
unconscious, which governed physiological processes. The relative layer
of the unconscious contained representations which were sometimes conscious. Given how little one is conscious of at any given time, this constituted the largest region of the soul. The unconscious was the primordial
source of life. The development of life was teleological: "a certain goal,
a foresight, must exist unconsciously towards which life develops and as-
pires" (22). He conceived of this goal in terms of the mimetic replication
of a primordial image: "something in our soul unconsciously produces a
copy of the primordial image (Urbild)" (23). The primordial image was
responsible for maintaining and expanding the species, as well as the life
of the individual. The unconscious was characterized by the fact that it
knew neither fatigue, nor disease. The healing power of nature worked
through the unconscious. It possessed "promethean" and "epimethean"
properties, in that it was oriented towards the future and the past. It was
through the unconscious that individuals were connected with the rest of
the universe.

Von Hartmann

The development of concepts of the unconscious in German philosophy,
which were not taken up in British and French philosophy, culminated
with the work of Eduard von Hartmann (1842–1906).[18] Von Hartmann
was born in Berlin. He graduated from the University of Rostock, and
thereafter pursued a military career, and subsequently lived as a private scholar. His major work, *The Philosophy of the Unconscious* appeared
in 1868, and was widely acclaimed. It went through ten editions in his
lifetime. It has been claimed that it was the most widely read philosophical work of its time. In this work, he attempted to reconcile the tradition of German idealism with the natural sciences. The unifying concept
was the unconscious, and his work consisted in presenting a taxonomic
plan incorporating virtually every conceivable phenomenon under this
rubric.

Von Hartmann presented his work as the culmination of eighteenth and
nineteenth-century German philosophy, which he refigured through the
problematic of the unconscious. He reformulated Schopenhauer's will in
terms of the unconscious, stating that as it was free of self-consciousness,
it was an unconscious will (1868, Book 1, 29).

---

[18] An exception being William Hamilton (1865).

Over the years, he revised his model of the divisions of the unconscious. Successive editions of *The Philosophy of the Unconscious* grew considerably in size, and so did the unconscious. In his final version of 1900, he differentiated between the epistemological unconscious, the physical unconscious, the psychic unconscious, the metaphysical unconscious, which had a relative and an absolute layer, and finally, the unconscious absolute spirit. The unconscious, rather than consciousness, was primary. Consciousness was viewed as a product of the unconscious (Book 2, 81). The emergence of the unconscious was not accidental, but represented an inherent teleological striving towards a higher state of consciousness (Book 3, 255). This ultimately had as its goal the redemption of the world, which consisted in a return to its originary state prior to its commencement.

The unconscious formed and preserved the organism, and through instincts, preserved the individual and the species. There existed a plurality of instincts: the instinct of self-preservation, of shame, of disgust, of modesty, of gratitude, of maternal love, and the sexual, sociable, and acquisitive instincts (Book 1, 205ff.). The principal characteristic of instinct was purposiveness: "*Instinct is purposive action without consciousness of the purpose*" (Book 1, 79). This purposiveness reached as far as what he termed the clairvoyance of instinct, which was present both in humans and animals (Book 1, 106–107). The unconscious was atemporal and aspatial, and never erred. In the psychological sphere, the unconscious provided guidance through providing hints. All artistic activity depended upon the "intrusion" of the unconscious (Book 1, 286). The same was true of mysticism, the essence of which he defined "*as the filling of consciousness with a content (feeling, thought, desire) through involuntary emergence of the same from the Unconscious*" (Book 1, 363).

For von Hartmann, a principal question concerning the nature of the unconscious was, one or many? Did a plurality of individual unconsciousnesses exist? (Book 2, 223). On this question, he opted for a monism, claiming that there existed an "everywhere identical unconscious" (Book 2, 226). Thus his concept of the unconscious was ultimately transindividual and collective: "When we, however, view the world as a whole, the expression 'the Unconscious' acquires the force not only of an *abstraction* from all unconscious individual functions and subjects, but also of a *collective*" (Book 1, 4). Consequently, this unconscious formed the substratum of all individual consciousnesses (Book 2, 230). Following from the overriding significance that he attributed to the unconscious, human development was dependent upon paying close attention to it. If one was unable to hear its inspirations, one would lose vitality, and the same fate beheld a rationalistic age which suppressed it (Book 2, 42). He proposed contact with nature and the arts as counterpoints to maintain the connection with the unconscious. The ultimate goal of individuality should be *"the complete devotion of the personality to the world-process for the sake of its goal, the general world-redemption . . .* TO MAKE THE ENDS OF THE UNCONSCIOUS ENDS OF OUR OWN CONSCIOUSNESS" (Book 3, 133). By the *philosophy* of the unconscious, he meant a speculative metaphysical system that subsumed the phenomena of biology, psychology, and even theology under its provenance. The philosophical conceptualization of the unconscious was made possible through a progressive delimitation of the attributes of consciousness. What had been understood to be conscious activity was increasingly transferred to the unconscious.

At this time, psychologists were attempting to separate psychology from speculative metaphysics and to establish it as a natural science. Consequently, von Hartmann's philosophy of the unconscious – in which the unconscious stood for a principle that completely subsumed the domain of psychology under the umbrella of philosophy – came in for extended criticism from psychologists. Physiologists were also at pains to differentiate their conceptions of the unconscious from von Hartmann's. In 1889, the American psychologist James Mark Baldwin dismissed von Hartmann's work as metaphysical. He concluded:

Phenomena called "unconscious mental states" may be accounted for partly from the physical side, as excitations inadequate to a mental effect, and partly from the mental side, as states of least consciousness. Where, in the progressive subsistence of consciousness, these two classes of fact come together we have no means of knowing . . . As Binet says, if there be unconscious mental phenomena, "we know absolutely nothing about them." (1890, 58)

Similarly the German experimental psychologist Oswald Külpe (1862–1915), argued that von Hartmann's system, like that of Schopenhauer, "may be styled a half mythological speculation, like the myths of *Plato*, rather than an extension and completion of scientific knowledge" (1913, 189).

In 1890 William James devoted an extended section of *The Principles of Psychology* to a critique of the concept of the unconscious. In his chapter on the "mind-stuff" theory, he dealt with the existence of unconscious mental states. In a characteristically prescient manner, he stated that the distinction between the consciousness and unconsciousness of a mental state was "the sovereign means for believing what one likes in psychology, and of turning what might be a science into a tumbling-ground for whimsies" (vol. 1, 163). He set out ten supposed proofs of the unconscious, which were "most systematically urged" by von Hartmann, and then subjected them to a detailed point by point refutation. In each case, while recognizing the existence of the particular phenomenon in question, he demonstrated that they were amenable to other forms of explanation, which were in turn quite distinct from one another. In place of the monistic appeal to the unconscious, what was required was a pluralistic account of diverse phenomena. James dismissed von Hartmann's work: "Hartmann fairly boxes the compass of the universe with the principle of unconscious thought. For him there is no nameable thing that does not exemplify it . . . The same is true of Schopenhauer" (169).

James' stricture concerning the term "unconscious" by no means indicated a disinterest in the states it was used to designate – far from it. In 1901 he described the discovery of the extra-marginal field of consciousness in 1886 as "the most important step forward that has occurred in psychology since I have been a student of that science" (1902, 233). The extra-marginal realm:

is the reservoir of everything that is latent or unobserved. It contains, for example, such things as all our momentarily inactive memories, and it harbours the springs of all our obscurely motivated passions, impulses, likes, dislikes, and prejudices. Our intuitions, hypotheses, fancies, superstitions, persuasions, convictions, and in general all our non-rational operations come from it. It is the source of our dreams, and apparently they may return to it. From it arise whatever mystical experiences we may have, and our automatisms, sensory or motor; our life in hypnotic and 'hypnoid' conditions, if we are subject to such conditions; our delusions, fixed ideas, and hysterical accidents, if we are hysteric subjects; our supra-normal cognitions, if there be, and if we are telepathic subjects. (483–484)

Critically for James, such phenomena were regarded as "conscious facts of some sort."

In his later work, James developed a metaphysics of radical empiricism. A critical notion that came in for re-examination was that of consciousness itself. In 1904, he published an essay entitled, "Does consciousness exist?" his resounding answer was no. Consciousness is "the name of the nonentity, and has no right to a place among first principles. Those who still cling to it are clinging to a mere echo, the faint rumour left behind by the disappearing 'soul' upon the air of philosophy" (1904, 2). James was denying that consciousness stood for an entity. Thoughts undoubtedly existed, and they had the function of *knowing*. He recommended replacing the appeal to consciousness with "its pragmatic equivalent in realities of experience" (3). Thus ultimately for James, if there was no unconscious, there was no consciousness either. The development of the concept of the unconscious had done nothing to resolve fundamental problems associated with the concept of consciousness, such as mind–body dualism.

The 1880s were characterized by attempts to put forward limited, restricted notions of the unconscious, typified by Janet's concept of the subconscious.[19] For such psychologists, their concept of the unconscious

_____
[19] See above, 122–124.

had to be radically differentiated from the philosophical concepts of the unconscious that anteceded them, to legitimate their scientific status. In most cases, this was simply accomplished through a denial of affiliation, and the claim that such conceptions were simply derived from clinical observations.

Alongside these developments in philosophy and philosophical psychology, transformations were taking place in biology and the life sciences which were to have a critical effect on the shape of the new psychologies. It is to these developments that we now turn.

Soul and life

In medicine and biology since antiquity, there has been a great deal of discussion concerning the nature of living organisms, and as to whether there exists a soul or life principle that inheres in them. Positions positing the existence of a specific life-force have been described as animist or vitalist. Definitions of the life-force have taken a positive or negative form. "Positive" definitions assert the existence of a specific principle of life. In the former, it is held that there is some external principle which endows the body with its vital properties. In the latter, it is held that living organisms possess non-reducible characteristics due to the organization of matter. With the rise of scientific materialism in the nineteenth century, the term vitalism became frequently used in polemics as a synonym for error and as a term of opprobrium, and this usage is still prevalent today.

In the nineteenth century, arguments concerning the existence of a vital principle were inextricably bound up with metaphysical and religious issues. An example of an early nineteenth-century proponent of vitalism, who would later be important for Jung, was Karl Friedrich Burdach (1776–1847). Burdach, sometimes described as a romantic physiologist, held chairs in anatomy at the Universities of Dorpart and Königsberg. Between 1826 and 1840, he produced a six-volume work, *Physiology as a Science of Experience*. He claimed that as the goal of physiology was the knowledge of the human spirit, the whole of nature had to be studied. *Physiology* incorporated contributions from his notable assistants, such as Karl Ernst von Baer, Heinrich Rathke and Johannes Müller. His work demonstrates the theological significance of the positing of a specific life force. This force was

an eternal, ideal principle throughout the world which has created every individual thing and harmonised them, in such a manner that nature as a whole is a living thing . . . It is also the same force which has created the whole world and produced each living thing. (1840, vol. 1, 307)

The basis of organic formation was not a pre-existent substance but a formative force [Bildungskraft]. No mechanical or chemical theory could fully explain organic formation, so one had to evoke the existence of a vital principle. This was not a transcendental entity, but a natural creative force. Its existence was taken to constitute evidence of divine design, as something blind and unintelligent could not create beings directed towards ends (309). Consequently the laws of nature were a direct revelation of God.

It was this theological implication of the positing of life force to which proponents of scientific materialism, such as Karl Vogt, Jacob Moleschott, and Ludwig Büchner, were most opposed (Gregory, 1977, 168). Prominent in the critique of vitalism were the physiologists Emil du Bois-Reymond (1818–1896) and Carl Ludwig (1816–1895). In 1847, together with Hermann von Helmholtz and Ernst von Brücke, they swore to base physiology on a purely chemico-physical foundation, banishing all recourse to vital forces. In 1848, in his "Researches on Animal Electricity," du Bois-Reymond set out his criticisms against the existence of the vital force. As all changes in the material world were reducible to motions, the concept of a specific life-force [Lebenskraft] separate from matter resulted from an "irresistible tendency to personification" and "a rhetorical artistic concept of our intellect" (1912, 14).

In the course of the nineteenth century, vitalistic theories declined. The development of cell theory was seen to provide the basis of a mechanistic analysis of living functions. The existence of a vital principle was said to contravene the principle of the conservation of energy, and both Robert Mayer and Hermann Helmholtz were resolutely opposed to it.[20] Darwin's theory of evolution was taken to obviate the recourse to the argument for design in the development of species, and the adaptation of living organisms to their environment was explained by natural selection, as opposed to an inherent teleological principle. In the neovitalist Hans Driesch's view (1867–1941), vitalist theories underwent an immanent collapse or self-extermination, through complacency and dogmatism (1914, 125).

Entelechy

Towards the end of the nineteenth century, varieties of vitalistic theories re-emerged. Hans Driesch became the principal proponent of what was known as neovitalism. Driesch studied under August Weismann and Ernst Haeckel. Initially a committed mechanist, he announced his conversion to vitalism in 1899. In experiments with sea urchins, he

[20] Robert Mayer (1845, 115). Helmholtz (1861, 120).

demonstrated that if blastomeres (the initial subdivision of an egg) were separated at the two-cell stage, each blastomere could still form a whole larva. His theoretical interpretation of these experiments went through a series of developments; in essence, he took their significance as indicating the existence of some innate teleological developmental factor (see Churchill, 1969).

He presented his views in a systematic form in his Gifford lectures in 1907 and 1908. Organic individual development could not be accounted for in purely physical and chemical terms, nor by means of causality alone. This necessitated the recourse to an additional factor, which, in honor of Aristotle, he termed entelechy. The existence of this principle at the same time secured the autonomy of life, and the disciplinary autonomy of biology (1908, 142–143). Entelechy underlay the origin of organic bodies and particular actions, and its work was inherently teleological. He differentiated entelechy – "the natural agent which forms the body" – from "the elemental agent which *directs* it" – the psychoid. He had established the irreducibility of biology to physics and chemistry, but its borders with psychology were less clearly demarcated. He used the term psychoid to avoid falling into the "pseudo-psychology" that would follow the use of the terms soul, mind, or psyche. The psychoid designated a form of agency irreducible to purely physical terms. It was "something which though not a 'psyche' can only be described in terms analogous to those of psychology" (82). Clarification of the question of instinct should eventually show that the psychoid constituted the basis of instincts, and that the difference between the "conscious" and "unconscious" was really a difference between two kinds of psychoids (83). Driesch was annexing psychology to neovitalistic biology.

He considered the question of whether entelechy should be thought of as a form of vital energy. It wasn't, principally because all known energies were quantitative and measurable. At an introspective level, entelechy was discernable through the category of individuality. Individuality came about through a process of individualization, and the agent of this process was entelechy (314, 317).

Driesch held that both Darwinism and Lamarckism were unable to explain evolution adequately. This was because natural selection was a negative principle, which could explain the elimination of particular forms, but not the creation of new diversities. Most critically, Darwinism was unable to explain organic restitution (262, 267). In conclusion, he correlated the "unknown principle" operative in descent with entelechy.

Alongside these debates concerning the existence of a life energy and its role in evolution, there arose new conceptions of memory and its relation to inheritance.

The memory question

I have more memories than if I had lived a thousand years.

> A great chest of drawers stuffed with accounts,
> verses, love letters, lawsuits, romances,
> with heavy plaits of hair rolled into receipts,
> hides fewer secrets than my sad brain.
> It is a pyramid, an immense vault,
> which contains more dead than the common grave.
> Charles Baudelaire, "LXXVI Spleen," *Les Fleurs du Mal*

In the philosophical tradition, questions concerning memory were closely linked to questions of personal identity. As a consequence, if the new scientific psychology of the nineteenth century were to establish itself, it had to be capable of annexing memory. There were three main ways in which psychologists attempted to do this: first, through subjecting memory to experimental study; second, through studying the variations of memory in individuals and establishing a psychology and pathology of memory (a new science of psychopathology sought to base itself on the pathologies of memory); and third, through developing physiological and biological conceptions of the understanding of memory. The new configurations that these developments gave rise to transformed the task of psychotherapy into one of memory management, and led to techniques for recovering, obliterating, and manipulating memories which are still with us (see Hacking, 1995).

Our relation to our past has been transformed by psychology and psychotherapy. This holds not only for our personal history, and the manner in which we view it, but for cultural history as well. The distinctiveness of Jung's work was the manner in which he conceived of the embeddedness of the individual in cultural history, or rather, the inherence of cultural history within the individual. Through introspection, an individual could review not only his personal history, but his cultural and ancestral history, and that of the human race as well. At the same time, through this vision, cultural history, appeared in a new light. Interpreted anew, it was to form the basis of a new psychology. Such a view was made possible by the development of expanded notions of memory in the second half of the nineteenth century.

Ancestral memories

In his *Biographia Literaria*, Samuel Taylor Coleridge narrated a remarkable incident which occurred shortly before his arrival in Göttingen in

1799. It concerned a young woman who could neither read nor write, who was taken ill with fever in a small town. In her delirium, she spoke incessantly in Latin, Greek, and Hebrew, and was said to be possessed. A young physician became interested in the case, and began investigating it. Her statements were taken down, and they were found to consist of intelligent statements with no apparent connection. The physician traced her past life, and learnt from an uncle of hers that the patient had been taken in by a Protestant minister at the age of nine, and had stayed with him till his death. From the niece of this pastor, he found out that it was a habit of the pastor to walk up and down in his house while reading out passages from his favourite books. Investigating the pastor's library, the physician managed to identify many of the statements of the patient.

For Coleridge, this episode furnished "Proof and instance, that reliques of sensation may exist for an indefinite time in a latent state, in the very same order in which they were impressed" (1817, chapter 6, 65). As it was likely that the feverish state simply acted as a stimulus, he reasoned that all thoughts were imperishable. This led him to speculate:

if the intelligent faculty should be rendered more comprehensive, it would require only a different and apportioned organization, *the body celestial* instead of the *body terrestrial*, to bring before every human soul the collective experience of its whole past existence. And this, this, perchance, is the dread book of judgment, in whose mysterious hieroglyphics every idle word is recorded! Yea, in the very nature of a living spirit, it may be more possible that heaven and earth should pass away, than that a single act, a single thought, should be loosened or lost from that living chain of causes, to all whose links, conscious or unconscious, the free-will, our only absolute *self*, is co-extensive and co-present. (65)

For Coleridge, the existence of an underlying self or soul which accorded with a traditional Christian viewpoint finds its support through memory. Shorn of its theological and cosmological elements, Coleridge's view of the powers of memory became quite widespread among psychologists in the late nineteenth century. For the Scottish philosopher, William Hamilton, Coleridge's story provided striking evidence for the existence of unconscious mental activities (1865, vol. 1, 345).

The last quarter of the nineteenth century saw the flourishing of the theory of organic memory, principally through the works of Samuel Butler, Ewald Hering, Richard Semon, Théodule Ribot and the ethnopsychology [*Völkerpsychologie*] of Moritz Lazarus, Heymann Steinthal, and Wilhelm Wundt (see Gasser, 1988 and Otis, 1994). This theory rested on two principal conceptions: Jean-Baptiste Lamarck's theory of the inheritance of acquired characteristics and Ernst Haeckel's biogenetic law, that ontogeny recapitulated phylogeny. Laura Otis claimed that proponents of the theory of organic memory theory identified memory with heredity, and located history in the body: "by envisioning history as something accumulated by a race and stored within an individual, they rendered it potentially accessible" (1994, 2). As we shall see, theories of organic memory left an important legacy in Jung's work, and informed his vision of psychology and psychotherapy.

The thesis that ontogeny, or individual development, recapitulates phylogeny, or species development, was put forward by the German biologist Ernst Haeckel. Haeckel's early work had been on marine animals, known as radiola. He became an apostle of Darwinism, and claimed that Darwinian theory provided the key to a unified monistic view of the cosmos. In 1866, he published his *General Morphology*, which presented the main outlines of his theories. Haeckel wrote that phylogeny designated the science which described the ascent of man from the lower animals. The history of the foetus recapitulated the history of the race. In other words,

The series of forms through which the individual organism passes during its development from the ovum to the complete bodily structure is a brief, condensed repetition of the long series of forms which the animal ancestors of the said organism, or the ancestral forms of the species, have passed through from the earliest period of organic life down to the present day. (1903, 2–3)

The chief source of information concerning phylogeny was ontogeny, the science of the development of the individual organism. This led him to speculate on a possible phylogeny of the soul. The chief support for this lay in the study of the ontogeny of the soul. He saw the works of William Preyer, James Sully, and Milicent Washburn Shinn on the psychology of child development as constituting the origin of this discipline (8).

Haeckel expounded a social philosophy of monism. The human spirit or soul was "merely a force or form of energy, inseparably bound up with the material substratum of the body" (356). Consequently, he was opposed to vitalistic theories and the neovitalism of Driesch.

In 1870, the German physiologist Ewald Hering gave a much cited lecture, "On memory as a general function of organised matter." He explored the functional interdependence of matter and consciousness. He proposed an extension of the concept of memory to include "involuntary reproductions of sensations, ideas, perceptions, and efforts" (1870, 68). Memory was not only a faculty of our conscious states, but also of our unconscious ones. The unconscious was identified with matter, which served to separate his physiology of the unconscious from von Hartmann's philosophy of the unconscious. Hering argued that human memory originated in the reflexes and instincts of primitive organisms. Accepting the inheritance of acquired characteristics, he claimed that the repeated actions of each generation became a "second nature" to the race (81). Thus instinct arose from memory. His extension of the concept of memory led him to differentiate between one's conscious memories, which ended at death, and the "unconscious memory of Nature," which was ineradicable (86).

Independently of Hering, the British physiologist Thomas Laycock published a paper in 1876 on the theme of ancestral memory. Laycock commenced by arguing that the origin of acquired habits, instincts, and capabilities, together with their heredity transmission, was already well known. These processes would be better understood if they were classed with memory. There were two parts to organic memory. The first consisted in the changes in the brain following acts of attention, which left behind a record of mental states. The second consisted in the reversion to this process. Thus heredity could be seen as "an evolutionary reversion potentially to antecedent modes of activity, manifested in parents and ancestors" (156). Consequently, many of our reactions could be seen as ancestral reversions. The gasp we felt when cold water was thrown upon our bodies was brought about by the "ancestral substratum formed in an amphibious state of existence" (162) Similarly, mountains and hills were pleasing to descendants of highland ancestry. Personal memory was distinct from ancestral memory. The latter consisted in the "capability of reproduction or re-evolution of ancestral strata" (162). Thus while new experiences and knowledge altered the body, brain, and mind, there was always a tendency to revert to ancestral substrata.

In 1878, the English writer and amateur scientist Samuel Butler published a work entitled *Life and Habit*. He argued that consciousness and volition disappeared when practice had rendered a habit familiar. As the facts of heredity were so like memory as to be indistinguishable, instincts were in fact inherited memories. Instincts represented the ancestral memories of the race. In conclusion, he defined life as "that property of matter whereby it can remember" (299). After publishing his book, he read Hering's lecture, and was so struck by the parallelism with his own conceptions that he published a translation of it.

The linkages which Hering and Butler established between memory, heredity and the unconscious were also present in the theory of organic memory developed by the French philosopher-psychologist Théodule Ribot. Ribot was pivotal in the development of the new psychology in France, where he disseminated new trends in England and Germany. In 1888, he was given a chair in experimental and comparative psychology at the Collège de France. He founded the *Revue Philosophique*, which became the pre-eminent psychological journal in France.

In *Maladies of Memory* (1881), he argued that memory was first a biological phenomenon, and only secondarily a psychological one. This led him to differentiate psychological or conscious memory from organic or unconscious memory. The former was but a special instance of the latter, exactly as consciousness was related to unconsciousness (39). In his work on heredity, following Haeckel, he had equated the development of the individual with the development of the species, and claimed that in both, consciousness came out of the unconscious and presupposed it (1873, 319–320).

In 1896, Ribot further differentiated three levels of the unconscious. There existed a hereditary or ancestral unconscious. This consisted in "the influence of certain inherited and fixed ways of feeling in a race, which exercise a mastery over our associations without our knowing it" (1896, 173–174). The second level was constituted by the ensemble of internal sensations in the individual, which Ribot called the personal unconscious stemming from coenesthesia. Finally, there was the personal unconscious, which consisted in the "*residue of affective states linked to former perceptions or events of our life*" (175). The emotional residues in the personal unconscious remained latent, but nevertheless had effects, and could be "refound by analysis." His discussion of the personal unconscious is of great interest. Among these effects was the "law of transference" which consisted in "*directly* attributing a sentiment to an object which was not the cause of it" (175). He differentiated between transference by contiguity and transference by resemblance. It was in the latter which one found the secret of the "the sentiment of love, tenderness, of antipathy, of respect, that one has for someone, at first sight, without apparent reason" (175). If one analyzed one's consciousness, one would find in many cases "a more or less close resemblance with someone known who inspires us or whom we have inspired with love, tenderness, antipathy or respect" (177). Such cases could be explained by "an unconscious state which is not easily seized, but which, if it becomes conscious again . . . explains everything" (177). We see here the notion of transference – which has been taken to be one of the quintessential signature concepts of Freud and psychoanalysis – developed in very nearly the same language and understanding by Ribot, ironically, in the very year that Freud first used the term "psychoanalysis." This example is indicative of the manner in which much of late nineteenth-century psychology has come to be solely associated with Freud through the power of the Freudian legend. Finally, in 1900, Ribot argued that what one commonly called inspiration was an unconscious factor, and part of the creative imagination. Among the products of the creative imagination were myths. This form of imagination was non-individual, anonymous, and collective (1900, 107).

Hering's and Ribot's work was taken up by August Forel. Forel's interests ranged widely. After studying medicine in Zürich, he went to Vienna where he studied brain anatomy under Theodore Meynert. Thereafter, he went to Munich, where his work on brain anatomy was pivotal to the formulation of the theory of the neurone. In 1879, he was appointed as a professor of psychiatry at the University of Zürich, and as Director of Burghölzli Asylum. A dedicated entomologist, he published important works on insects. In 1884, he gave a lecture in Zürich on memory and its abnormalities which took up and developed Hering's and Ribot's conceptions of organic memory. Forel began with a consideration of unconscious processes. In his view, we could think, feel, and will unconsciously. Everything which is conscious could become unconscious. The conscious activity of the brain left behind memory traces. Conscious memory could become unconscious – in other words, fixed and automatic – through repetition. Like Ribot and Hering, he identified memory with heredity. The properties of plants and animals appeared in the next generation as inherited attitudes and latent potentials (Forel, 1885).

In 1887, after a brief study of hypnosis and suggestion with Hyppolite Bernheim in Nancy, he returned to Zürich and played a prominent role in promoting the practice of hypnotism and psychotherapy in Switzerland. He developed the conviction that a principal cause of insanity was alcoholism, and became an active proponent of the temperance movement. In 1898, he retired from the Burghölzli, where he was succeeded by his former student Eugen Bleuler, and dedicated himself to the cause of social hygiene.

Conceptions of organic memory were widely diffused. For many psychologists, Haeckel's conception of the ontogenetic recapitulation of phylogeny was taken as an established fact. It was often detached from the rest of Haeckel's system. Hence their use of it did not imply any commitment to Monism. Consequently, the biogenetic law was frequently referred to without any reference to or citation from Haeckel. An example of this approach was James Mark Baldwin. Without citing Haeckel, he claimed that this law took on a different form when applied to psychology. Whereas in biology the question was whether "the human organism and mind goes through stages which recapitulate the forms of the animal world," in anthropology, the question was whether "the human individual goes through the stages of culture which the human race as a species has gone through" (1897, 189). He went so far as to argue that the stages of development that the science of psychology had passed through paralleled the development of consciousness in an individual (1913).

Evolutionary thinking had a major impact on the development of the field of child psychology. In 1882, the physiologist and psychologist William Preyer published *The Soul of the Child*, which became a best seller. This work was based on close observations of the development of his son. Preyer (1841–1897) conceived his work as applying Darwinian evolution to psychology. At Jena, he had close contact with Haeckel. He accepted the biogenetic law as established. Discussing the issue of heredity, he claimed that the new-born child was not a *tabula rasa*, but contained "the traces of the imprint of countless sensuous impressions of long-gone generations" (1882, part 1, xiv). In the course of development, the individual filled out and reanimated "the remains of the experiences and activities of his ancestors" (xv). These ancestral remains revealed themselves in childhood fears, which were based in a "heredity timidity" (164). The same held true for courage. While the ideas themselves were not innate, they were inherited. Individuals possessed an "innate aptitude to perceive things and form ideas" (part 2, 211).

Similar views were put forward by the English psychologist James Sully. In *Studies of Childhood*, he claimed that the value of the biogenetic law was that it enabled the psychologist to "connect the unfolding of an infant's mind with the mental history of the race" (1896, 8). The child's first manifestations of rage were a survival from the life and death struggles of remote ancestors. Similarly, the impulse of obedience could be viewed as "a transmitted rudiment of a long practised action of socialised ancestors" (9).

In America, the notion of a phylogenetic unconscious was developed by Stanley Hall (1844–1924). He had studied with Wundt at Leipzig, and on his return to America, completed his PhD under William James. He founded the *American Journal of Psychology*, and was the first president of the American Psychological Association. Hall played a critical role in establishing the child study movement. For Hall, Haeckel's views on recapitulation marked the real beginning of a "truly genetic psychology" (1925, 369). Just as the body bore traces of its ancestry, so too did the soul (1897, 158). It was as "freighted with memories" of its development as the body. The soul was pervaded by traces of past ancestral experiences:

Our own soul is full in all its parts of faint hints, rudimentary specters flitting for an instant at some moment of our individual life and then gone forever, dim and scarcely audible murmurs of a great and prolonged life, hot, intense richly dight with incident and detail that is no more; a slight autonomism, perhaps, being the sole relic of the most central experiences of many generations, a fleeting fancy all that survives of ages of toil and blood, a feeling that only peeps out for a moment in infancy, the far-off dying echo of what was once the voice of a great multitude. Yet these psychopores, whatever they are, are wax to receive and marble to retain. (1904, vol. 2, 64–65)

These traces of ancestral experiences were present in the unconscious, which contained a record of the evolutionary experiences of the species. One area in which these vestiges resurfaced was in fear. In his study of fear in childhood, the fear of water and the fear of animals were the results of ancestral experiences. The fear of water was an instinctive vestige which developed when our ancestors left the sea and ceased to be amphibious (1897, 169). Such fears, which were out of proportion to their precipitating causes, were "like lapsed reflexes, fragments and relics of psychic states and acts which are now rarely seen in all their former vigor" (210). In adolescence, which was a second birth, the "flood-gates of heredity" were thrown open (1904, 70). The adolescent was a "neo-atavist" in whom the later acquisitions of the race became prepotent. Thus our consciousness was a superstructure built up from the "deeper unconscious and dispositional strata of Mansoul" (1922, 37).

By the 1890s, the thesis that every impression left a memory trace had become widespread. Coleridge's speculation that forgotten memories could spontaneously resurface, while not being recognized as such, was argued by Joseph Delboeuf in his account of his Asplenium dream in *Sleep and Dreams*.[21] Delboeuf accepted the biogenetic law and praised Hering's work. He argued for the permanence of memory traces:

All acts of feeling, of thinking or of volition, by virtue of an universal law, imprint in us a trace which is more or less deep, but indelible, generally engraved on an infinity of anterior traces, later overburdened by another infinity of outlines of all nature, but whose writing is nevertheless indefinitely susceptible of reappearing clearly and sharply. (1879–80, 147)

In 1899, Théodore Flournoy developed these notions in *From India to Planet Mars*.[22] In the case of Hélène Smith, what was presented as memories of her anterior existence, were in fact made up of memories of her life which had been subjected to subconscious elaboration. A major part of Flournoy's book was taken up with a detective style quest for the original impressions which were the sources of her spiritualistic fantasies, in the manner of the physician depicted by Coleridge.

Semon's engrams

In 1904 a work appeared that synthesized and developed the conceptions of the organic memory theorists. Its author was Richard Semon (1859–1918). He was born in Berlin, and went to Jena to study under Ernst Haeckel, where he obtained a medical degree. Haeckel became Semon's intellectual mentor, and he adopted Haeckel's monism, as well as his biogenetic law. In 1885, he converted to Christianity from Judaism. In 1899, he moved to Munich, where he worked as a private scholar.

---

[21] See above, 116–117. One dissenter was William James, who considered it a "completely extravagant opinion" (1890, vol. 1., 683).
[22] See above, 127–128.

Semon commenced his book by recounting the work on organic memory by Hering, Butler, Laycock, and Cope. All of these authors had attempted to connect memory, heredity, and habit. He attempted to develop a physiological theory to explain these phenomena. Instead of using these terms, he spoke of a mnemic principle. His basic theory was that excitation left behind traces. Repetition of the original stimulus led to the revival of the trace, and this process was inherited (1904, 12).

All organized or irritable matter had the property of retaining traces which could be revived. He called the capacity for this effect the mneme, and he called the traces engrams. Under certain conditions, these traces were revived. He called the influences which revived the engrams "ecphory." There were two mnemic laws, the law of engraphy and the law of ecphory. According to the first, all simultaneous excitations within an organism left behind an engram-complex. According to the second, the partial recurrence of the condition which had led to the engram-complex acted ecphorically on it, or revived it (273–274). The theory of the mneme supplied a fuller understanding of the biogenetic law, as it was the presence of the mnemic factor in ontogenesis which explained why the ancestral path of development had to be followed by each descendant (291).

Semon's work met with a mixed reception. It was hailed by Haeckel as the "most important advance that evolution has made since Darwin"[23] and was championed by Forel and subsequently by Bleuler. As we have seen, Forel shared Semon's assumptions and starting point. Forel attempted to demonstrate the relevance of Semon's work for psychiatry.[24] Forel described himself as having been "converted" by Semon's work to a "slow inheritance of acquired characteristics" (1907, 137). What in evolution could not be explained by the workings of natural selection alone could be explained by Semon's understanding of the process of mnemetic engraphy. In his *Textbook of Psychiatry*, Eugen Bleuler argued for the notion that "everything that has been psychically experienced leaves behind a lasting trace, or *engram*" (1916, 28). Whilst this could not be conclusively demonstrated, he considered it probable on the evidence of dreams, hypnosis, and disease. He utilized Semon's work to explain the conservation and revivification of such traces. As an example, he cited Coleridge's case, via W. B. Carpenter's citation of it (28–29). For Forel and Bleuler, Semon's theory provided them a monistic psychophysiology, in which psychic functions grew out of an underlying physiology, of which they were simply the continuation.

[23] Cited by Schacter, 1982, 139.
[24] Forel, 1907. An offprint of an article by Forel, "Eine Konsequenz der Semonschen Lehre der Mneme" (1905) bearing a dedication by Forel, was in Jung's library.

Semon's work was roundly criticized by August Weismann, who had been responsible for the first systematic attack on the Lamarckian notion of the inheritance of acquired characteristics. As Weismann saw, this notion formed a critical underpinning of Semon's work. The discrediting of this notion and the rediscovery of Mendel's work on inheritance led to the demise of his work. In 1912, he had a nervous breakdown, and he committed suicide in 1918, after his wife died.

One development of his theory was put forward by a Swiss philosopher, Hans Ganz. In 1917 he published a dissertation, *The Unconscious in Connection with Modern Theories*. Ganz studied the development of the concept of the unconscious in philosophy. He approached this via Semon's theories, which clarified the conception of the unconscious. There were two levels of the unconscious, the first consisting of acquired mnemes, which he called the underconscious [Unterbewußte], and the second consisting of inherited mnemes.[25]

The riddle of instincts

Discussions of the scope of memory and its relation to inheritance were linked with discussions of the nature of instincts. Given its nodal position in debates about man's relation to the animal world and the role of human freedom, it is not surprising that there has been a great deal of long-standing speculation concerning the nature of instincts in philosophy and psychology.

Before the nineteenth century, the predominant conception of instinct was what Karl Groos termed the transcendental–theological conception. According to this, the apparent intelligence of animals, the suiting of means to ends, was an innate factor of divine design, namely instinct. In Groos' view, there was a reaction against this in the second half of the nineteenth century. Some sought simply to do away with the term, while others sought to give it a non-supernatural meaning (1898).[26]

In German biology and philosophy, the term instinct was reserved for animals, and the term drive was used to designate analogous factors in humans. Philosophers speculated about the number and nature of the instincts and drives, and the role of the latter as motivational factors in human action.[27]

---

[25] At one point in his text, Ganz noted that "we find already in Agrippa von Nettesheim the suspicion of a collective unconscious [Kollektiv-Unbewussten] as world-soul." 1917, 29.

[26] Jung possessed the second edition (1907) of this work.

[27] For Schopenhauer and von Hartmann's views on instincts, see below, 198–9.

Further impetus to reformulations of notions of instinct was given by Darwin's theory of natural selection. In *The Origin of Species*, he argued that instincts arose out of natural selection, and hence the existence of instincts could not be counted as an objection to the theory. Instincts developed through the "slow and gradual accumulation of numerous, slight, yet profitable, variations" (1859, 256). Darwin's theory of evolution redefined the relation of the human and the animal. By implication, this had critical bearings on the relation between psychology and biology. Before considering how psychologists attempted to deal with these issues, it is important to consider the work of Nietzsche. In critical respects, Nietzsche's concept of instincts and drives represents a confluence of the older philosophical tradition of theorizing about drives with the post-evolutionary considerations of the relation between the animal and the human.[28] Furthermore, in Nietzsche's writings, the concept of instincts figured in an historical critique of the malaise of Western civilization, which had important bearings on Jung's work.

The sick animal: Nietzsche's instincts

Nietzsche (1844–1900) studied in Bonn and Leipzig. In 1869 at the age of twenty-four, he was appointed to a chair in classical philology at the University of Basel. In 1872, he published his first masterpiece, *The Birth of Tragedy*. Initially drawn to the work of Schopenhauer and Wagner, whose circle he entered, he published a series of essays of cultural criticism, *Untimely Meditations*. After a crisis that led to an estrangement from Wagner, he experienced a return to himself. As he subsequently put it, "I sensed a total aberration of my instinct of which the individual blunder, call it Wagner or my professorship at Basel, was merely a sign."[29] It was then that he realized the connection between an activity "contrary to one's instincts" and the need for "stupefaction through a narcotic art," such as Wagner's (*ibid.*). Due to deteriorating health, he resigned his professorship in 1879, and thereafter travelled in Europe. In 1890, he underwent a collapse, and after a spell at Jena asylum, he spent the last ten years of his life under the care of his mother and sister. It was during these years that his works suddenly began to have a widespread convulsive effect in Europe.

Human all too Human (1878–1880) marked the inception of a series of works that undertook a critique of modernity, Western thought, and the unmasking of Christian morality. A vital insight was the realization that the most cherished values in the West had in fact been against life, born of

---

[28] See Parkes (1994), chapter 7.   [29] *Ecce Homo*, ch. 6, § 3.

"ressentiment." The course of Western civilization ultimately culminated in nihilism, that "most uncanny of guests." Thus what was required was a "transvaluation of all values." At various moments, he styled himself as a physiologist and psychologist, going so far as declaring himself a *"psychologist* who has not his equal." He had some familiarity with contemporary work in physiology and psychology, and drew upon Ribot's conceptions of memory.[30] However, he radically reworked the elements that he took up, and his conceptions of psychology and physiology were quite unique. Fundamentally, this was because they feature as moments in the transvaluation of values and critique of metaphysics. Psychology, in Nietzsche's hands, was a name given to a means by which this could be accomplished. The "psychologists" whom he singled out for praise were Dostoevsky and Stendhal.

Nietzsche postulated a series of instincts and drives: a herd instinct, a social instinct, an instinct for freedom, a maternal instinct, a religious instinct, an instinct for cruelty, a scientific instinct, an instinct for rank, an instinct for cleanliness, a defensive and offensive instinct, and a causal drive.[31] All these drives and instincts, fundamentally considered, were manifestations of the will to power. All organic functions and effective energy were derived from this.[32] His postulation of a plethora of instincts and drives was in keeping with nineteenth-century German philosophy. The distinctiveness of his approach lay in his conception of the significance of the drives, and his view that man's relation to his drives was not constant, but historically shaped by the rise of Western civilization, and by Christianity in particular.

He maintained that "every psychologist" knew that states of consciousness and beliefs were matters of "complete indifference and of the fifth rank compared with the value of the instincts."[33] The largest part of conscious thinking was an instinctual activity.[34] The drives and instincts were in a state of conflict with one another. What we considered as our personal identity was a mask for this strife: "while 'we' believe we are complaining about the *vehemence* of a drive, at bottom it is one drive *which is complaining about another.*"[35] His revaluation of the significance of drives and instincts led him to assert that "most of a philosopher's thinking is secretly guided and channelled into particular tracks by his

---

[30] On Nietzsche and physiology, see Gauchet, 1992. On Nietzsche's relation to Ribot, see Lampl, 1989.
[31] *The Gay Science*, § 116; *Human, all too Human*, § 98; *On the Genealogy of Morals*, second essay, § 17; third essay, § 8; *Beyond Good and Evil*, § 53; § 207; § 263; § 271; *Ecce Homo*, ch. 11; ch 1, § 6; *Twilight of the Idols*, "The four great errors," § 5.
[32] *Beyond Good and Evil*, § 36.   [33] *The Anti-Christ*, § 39.
[34] *Beyond Good and Evil*, § 3.   [35] *Daybreak*, § 109.

instincts."[36] The drives and instincts practised philosophy, and the systems that portrayed themselves as the summits of rationality were in fact nothing of the kind. Each drive had a tendency to mastery. Thus "each of them would be only too glad to present *itself* as the ultimate goal of existence and the legitimate *master* of all the other drives. For every drive is tyrannical: as it is as *such* that it tries to philosophize."[37]

The misrecognition of the role of the drives in philosophy was part of a more pervasive relegation and subjugation of the drives by Christian morality. Christianity had waged war against the "higher type of man and excommunicated his vital instincts."[38] Such a war against the instincts was the hallmark of decadence.[39] Christianity was an anti-natural morality. All anti-natural morality, which constituted almost every morality, condemned the instincts.[40] Any animal or species which had lost its instincts was "depraved."[41] As a consequence, man was the sickest animal, as he was "the one most dangerously strayed from its instincts."[42] Thus one's relation's to one's drives or instincts had to be seen in the cultural–historical setting of the destructive effects of Christianity. The reaffirmation of the drives and instincts constituted a repudiation of decadence and an overcoming of metaphysics.

While for Nietzsche, instincts and drives had to be considered in a cultural-historical context, other psychologists who dealt with the riddle of instincts neglected to consider this.

The instincts of psychology

An influential formulation of instincts was put forward by William James in *The Principles of Psychology*. Instincts were generally defined as the "*faculty of acting in such a way as to produce certain ends, without foresight of the ends, and without previous education in the performance*" (1890, vol. 2, 383). Throughout this chapter, he commenced with a reflection on animal behaviour before passing on to consider man as a special case. A traditional assumption was that man differed from the animals through the almost total absence of instincts, whose place was taken by reason. He suggested that reason could be viewed as the tendency to obey certain impulses (which he used as a translation of the German *Trieb*), and that instinct should be broadened to cover all the impulses. What differentiated

[36] *Beyond Good and Evil*, section 3.   [37] *Ibid.*, section 6.
[38] *The Anti-Christ*, section 5.
[39] *Twilight of the Idols*, "The problem of Socrates," section 11.
[40] *Twilight of the Idols*, "The four great errors," section 5.
[41] *The Anti-Christ*, section 6.   [42] *Ibid.*, section 14.

man from the animals was that he had more impulses, that is, more instincts, rather than fewer.

In considering man's instincts, he began with a consideration of childhood. He called the following instinctive actions: sucking, biting, clasping objects, carrying to the mouth, crying, smiling, turning the head aside, holding the head erect, sitting up, standing, locomotion, vocalization, imitation, emulation. Considering adults, he nominated emulation, pugnacity, sympathy, hunting, fear, acquisitiveness, constructiveness, play, curiosity, sociability, secretiveness, cleanliness, modesty, love, jealousy, and parental love. The question of instincts was inseparable from that of emotions, as instinctive reactions and emotional expressions shaded into one another. Thus he asserted that every object that evoked an instinct evoked an emotion as well (442).

Ribot agreed with James that there were many instincts in man, but contested his list (1896, 202). He held that instincts were the roots of the emotions, and he used the term "tendency" as a synonym for needs, appetites, instincts, inclinations, and desires. For something to be an instinct, it had to be innate, specific, and fixed. Among the instincts or tendencies he nominated were nutrition, the instinct of preservation, the sexual instinct, the play instinct, the tendency to know, and egoistic tendencies (203–206). He later added a creative instinct (1900, 35).

The French philosopher Alfred Fouillée developed a psychology of force ideas (idées-forces) which had important consequences for the conceptualization of instincts. In 1893, he argued that the problem with psychology was that it had conceived images and ideas statically. Mental states had been falsely conceived as representations. As illustration, he argued that one's sensation of the sun did not copy or represent the sun; rather, it was "a means of passion and reaction in relation to the sun" (1893, vol. 1, viii). For Fouillée, ideas were not only forms of thought, but also forms of action – "Or rather, these are no longer forms, but acts conscious of their exertion, of their direction, of their quality, of their intensity" (*ibid.*). All acts of consciousness were accompanied by three terms. One first felt a change of state. One then felt a feeling of wellbeing or disquiet at this change. Finally, one reacted. When this process reflected on itself, it formed an idea. Consequently, the act of discerning was inseparable from the act of preferring, thinking and acting were indissoluble. States of consciousness and ideas were not endowed with a separate and detached energy – rather, a force was inherent in them. Instincts were fixed types of force ideas. In instincts, representations were not innate, "but only the aptitude to form them when the occasion presents itself" (1890, 207). While the ideas themselves were not inherited, the relation or association between them were, to a certain extent. The force ideas were not only individual, as collective force ideas also existed, which constituted the national consciousness or soul of a people (1903, xix).

The most far-reaching attempt to base social psychology upon instincts was that of William McDougall (1871–1938). After studying medicine, he became interested in psychology, inspired by James' *Principles of Psychology*. He taught for a while under James Sully at University College London, and in 1904, was appointed as a reader in Mental Philosophy at Oxford. He published numerous works on psychology, and became one of the most widely known psychologists in Britain. He established a system of hormic psychology, which placed particular emphasis on the dynamic and purposive aspects of the mind. In 1920, he emigrated to the United States, taking up William James' former post at Harvard University. In America, he found Behaviorism in the ascendant, and himself and his psychology "back-numbers" (1930, 213). He did not found a school, and was institutionally isolated.

In his *Introduction to Social Psychology*, he noted that it was widely held that the old static, descriptive, and analytic psychology had to make way for a "dynamic, functional, voluntaristic view of mind" (1908, 14). This move could be accomplished through the study of instincts as motivational factors. He held that each instinct conditioned one specific type of emotional excitation. This led him to differentiate between primary and derived emotions. Seven of the instincts were linked to the primary emotions: the instincts of flight (fear), repulsion (disgust), curiosity (wonder), pugnacity (anger), self-abasement (subjection), self-assertion (elation), and the parental instinct (tenderness). The remaining instincts played lesser roles in the emotions: the sexual instinct, the gregarious instinct, and the instincts of acquisition and construction.

James, Ribot, and McDougall all concurred in linking the issue of instincts to that of the emotions, and in deriving the latter from the former. For psychologists, the value of formulations of instincts was that they provided a means, albeit speculative, of linking psychology with biology. The continuity of man and the animal world was expressed through the term "instinct." Stressing the importance of instincts also had the significance of differentiating psychology from moral philosophy and philosophical psychology. James, Ribot, and McDougall were taking generally recognized emotions and redescribing them as instincts, or as being derived from instincts. The plasticity of the term "instinct" meant that it could both carry many metaphorical connotations as well as appear to be rooted in biology. Where they disagreed was in deciding precisely what to class as an instinct. This problem was compounded by the fact that the other psychologists proposed quite different lists of instincts.

Jung's philosophical education

When Jung was a medical student at the University of Basel, he engaged on extensive extra-curricular reading. Indication of this is given by the checking records at the University of Basel Library together with lectures that he presented before a student fraternity, called the Zofingia Society. These lectures present his early philosophical, psychological, biological, and religious conceptions, and show his engagement with many of the leading issues of the day. During this period, he became acquainted with neovitalistic theories (Jung/Jaffé, 1963, 121). It was also during this period that he read Schopenhauer, whose work had a critical impact on him. The lasting effect of Schopenhauer on him is visible in the following statement in 1921: "Psychologically, 'the world' means how I see the world, my attitude to the world; thus the world can be regarded as 'my will' and 'my representation'" (*CW* 6, § 322, trans. mod.). Hence the psychological world was distinctly Schopenhauerian.

Jung read Kant, Schopenhauer, Carus, and von Hartmann in his youth (De Angulo, 203). To Aniela Jaffé, he recalled that "Schopenhauer was so to speak the first man I had encountered who spoke *my* speech."[43] To Jung, Schopenhauer was the first to speak of the suffering of the world – confusion, passion, and evil. He felt that Schopenhauer's vision confirmed his observations of nature and human beings. However, he was dissatisfied with Schopenhauer's solution to the problem. He felt that "with his 'Will' he meant God, the creator" (*Memories*, 88). His dissatisfaction with Schopenhauer's theory on the relation of the intellect and the will led him to study Kant, in particular, *The Critique of Pure Reason*. Here, he found what he took to be the major flaw in Schopenhauer's system, namely, that "he had made a metaphysical statement, he had hypostasised and qualified a mere noumenon, a 'thing in itself'" (Jung/Jaffé, 1963, 89, trans. mod). This was the charge which Schelling had made against Kant. Jung's copy of *The World as Will and Representation* bears his bookplate, dated 1897.[44]

It is not clear how quickly Jung perceived what he held was Schopenhauer's fallacy of hypostasizing the will, as in his 1898 lecture before

[43] MP, 303. The abiding significance of Schopenhauer for Jung is indicated by further comments he made to Jaffé. He stated that fundamentally, he had continued the Schopenhaurian idea. According to Schopenhauer, the intellect held a mirror up to the will, showing it to be full of suffering. However, Jung maintained that consciousness of suffering did not fully express life, and a consciousness that was not full of suffering was also possible (*ibid.*, 132.)

[44] On May 4, 1897, Jung took out a copy of Schopenhauer's *Parega und Parapilomena* from the Basel library (Basel library checking records).

the Zofingia Society, "Thoughts on the value and nature of speculative inquiry," he argued: "the Kantian critique of epistemology left the problem of the *Ding an sich* unsolved. The first of the post-Kantian philosophers to do an intelligent job of making this problem once again useful to philosophy was Schopenhauer" (1898, *CW* A, § 199). He followed this by praising the centrality accorded to suffering by Schopenhauer and von Hartmann, whom he described as the former's intellectual heir. His avowal of the pathos underlying Schopenhauer's work is indicated by the following statement: "Every genuine philosophy, every true religion is wrapped in the earthly garment of pessimism as the only accurate mode of reviewing the world befitting man in the awareness of his nothingness" (*ibid.*, § 229).

In the discussion following this lecture, Jung stated that he could not understand how a theologian could be an optimist. In his view, theologians considered the world sub specie aeternitatis, which provided more than enough proof for pessimism.[45] At the same time, he proposed a novel reinterpretation of Kant's thing in itself, namely, that at any given time, the dividing line between noumena and phenomena was provisional and not eternally fixed, and that science increasingly encroached upon the thing in itself (§§ 196–198). Thus before their discovery, X-rays represented a thing in itself (for Kant, they would have simply represented an unknown phenomenon).

In his 1925 seminar, Jung noted that contrary to his view on the blindness of the will in *The World as Will and Representation*, in *The Will in Nature* Schopenhauer

drifts into a teleological attitude . . . in this latter work he assumes that there is a direction in the creating will, and this point of view I took as mine. My first conception of the libido then was not that it was a formless stream so to speak, but that it was archetypal in character. That is to say, libido never comes up from the unconscious in a formless state, but always in images. (1925, 4)

The linkage that this passage establishes between Schopenhauer's will and the libido is also brought out in the following retrospective statement: "To Schopenhauer I owe the dynamic view of the psyche; the 'will' is the libido that is back of everything" (De Angulo, 1952, 204). These passages suggest that his initial conception of psychic energy was derived from Schopenhauer's concept of the will.

Schopenhauer's *The Will in Nature* was principally taken up with a survey of how developments in the sciences since the appearance of his *The World as Will and Representation* had confirmed the truth of his system. He noted that as the will was the "ultimate substratum of every

---

[45] Protocols of the Zofingia Society, 1898, Staatsarchiv, Basel, 376.

phenomenon," the organic body "is nothing but the will that has entered the representation, the will itself perceived in the cognitive form of space" (1836, 41). The suitability of every animal to its environment and the perfection of its organization presented a great deal of material upon which to consider the question of teleology. He critiqued the "physio-theological proof" by claiming that

the works of animal instinct, the spider's web, the honeycomb of bees, the structure of termites, and so on, are all of them constituted as if they had originated in consequence of an intentional conception, far-reaching and rational deliberation, whereas they are obviously the work of blind impulse, that is, of a will which is not guided by knowledge. (1836, 51–53)

He was attempting to free the concept of teleology from any theological implications. As an animal's body was "its will itself," "everything in it and pertaining to it must conspire to its ultimate purpose, the life of the animal" (1836, 64). In *The World as Will and Representation,* he noted that final causes were required to understand organic, as opposed to inorganic nature (1819, vol. 2, 329).

Contrary to Jung's statement, Schopenhauer's views on teleology in *The Will in Nature* are congruent with those set forth in *The World as Will and Representation.* However, his perception of a change in Schopenhauer's view is significant, for it denoted his own modification of Schopenhauer's understanding of the relation between will and representation. His modification of Schopenhauer's views on teleology and the blindness of the will may have occurred through his reading of von Hartmann. In his 1925 seminar, Jung stated that von Hartmann formulated Schopenhauer's ideas in a more modern way. He states he followed Hartmann, in contrast to Schopenhauer, in attributing "mind" to the unconscious. In *The Philosophy of the Unconscious,* von Hartmann stated that while Schopenhauerians had recognized the existence of the unconscious will, they had failed to recognize that it contained unconscious representations (1900, 125). The unconscious will was one which had unconscious representations for its content (136). Further evidence that Jung adopted von Hartmann's reformulations of Schopenhauer's philosophy is found in his lecture "Thoughts on the nature and value of speculative inquiry," where he stated that "Schopenhauer describes instinct as a stage in the objectification of the Will. So does Hartmann, adding the absolutely essential element of purposeful intention" (1898, *CW* A, § 182).

In Jung's Zofingia lectures, frequent allusions to Kant appear, whom he termed "our great master . . . the sage and prophet of Köningsberg who has, not unjustly, been called the last philosopher."[46] He presented himself as holding to Kant's epistemology, which he claimed had endured unaltered to the present day.

His sympathy with vitalist theories is apparent in these lectures. In his 1896 lecture, "Border zones of exact science," he embarked upon a determined critique of materialism, stating that "the standpoint which the skeptical materialist view of today takes is simply intellectual death" (*CW* A, § 63, trans. mod.). At one point in the discussion, M. Burckhardt criticized scientific research of hypnotism. To this, Jung replied that "one can also research exactly in a metaphysical field."[47]

In these essays, he took up debates between materialism and spiritualism and materialism and vitalism. These debates were critically linked. At this juncture, it was only through defending the existence of a vital principle, irreducible to physical and chemical terms, that he could provide an acceptable epistemology for spiritualism that squared the postmortem existence of the soul with biology.

Jung made several caustic comments against Du Bois-Reymond and other materialists. At one juncture, he prophesied that monuments to Schopenhauer would eventually be built, and that people "will curse Carl Vogt, Ludwig Büchner, Moleschott, Du Bois-Reymond, and many others, for having stuffed a parcel of materialistic rubbish into the gaping mouths of those guttersnipes, the educated proletariat."[48]

In "Some thoughts on psychology," the issue of the autonomy of life is connected with Jung's attempt to establish the immortality of the soul. He cited the following statement from Burdach, whom he described as "one of the much-despised vitalists": "Materialism presupposes that life which it sets out to explain. For the organization and the blend of components from which it derives the life processes, are themselves the product of a life process."[49]

Burdach's comment occurred in a general critique of materialism, which he had defined as "the assertion that life is nothing but the working of material force" (1826–1840, vol. 6, 526). For Jung, the vital principle was what endured in phenomena. It formed the scaffolding on which life was built up (§ 89). He conceived of this vital principle as an immanent, endogenous principle. He again approvingly cited Burdach, who had stated that:

[46] "Some thoughts on psychology," 1897, *CW* A, § 77.
[47] Protocols of the Zofingia Society, 1896, Staatsarchiv, Basel, 154. Jung's lecture was well-received, and a proposal by Brenner to send it for publication to the journal of the Zofingia Society, the *Centralblatt*, met with unanimous support. However, it was not published.
[48] "Some thoughts on psychology," 1897, *CW* A, § 136.
[49] *Ibid.*, § 88. The passage is found in Burdach's *Der Physiologie*, vol. 6, 526.

The matter of our bodies continually changes, whereas our life remains the same, remains on. Corporeal life is embraced in the continual, simultaneous destruction and formation of organic matter. This life is something higher, which dominates matter.[50]

Jung dismissively stated that physiologists were mistaken to attempt to explain life in terms of natural laws, as life existed *despite* such laws. He then criticized Darwin's theory of natural selection for being incapable of adequately explaining the development of new species, and claimed that in phylogeny, it was necessary to postulate a vital principle. This was "more or less equivalent" to the "life force" of ancient physiologists. It governed all bodily functions and consciousness, to the extent that the latter were dependent upon the cerebral cortex (§ 94–95). In a manner that recalled Stahl, he identified this vital principle with the soul.

This lecture was followed by heated discussion. The president of the session regretted Jung's polemical tone, though he understood the reasons for his anger against mean and lazy critics. Several in the audience defended Du Bois-Reymond. Jung replied that what he objected to in Du Bois-Reymond was the manner in which he had carried over natural scientific skepticism into the field of philosophy, which lay outside of his competence. To the charge that it was difficult to form theories on the facts which had been discussed, he replied that he thought the factual material was sufficient – it was simply a question of explaining it animistically or spiritualistically.[51]

Between Jung's Zofingia lectures and his first publications, there are considerable discontinuities in language, conceptions, and epistemology, as the far-reaching speculations on metaphysical issues characteristic of the Zofingia lectures largely disappeared. Following his discovery of his vocation as a psychiatrist, he appears to have undergone something like a conversion to a natural scientific perspective. Indication of this is given by a discussion following a lecture by Lichtenhahn at the Zofingia Society on theology and religion on June 20, 1900. Jung stated that he would stand in for the standpoint of the natural sciences, where "one is accustomed to operate only with clear firmly defined concepts." He then launched on a critique of theology, religion, and the existence of God, which led one person to remark on the fact that Jung had previously held so many positive views on these subjects, which he had now abandoned.[52]

---

[50] *Ibid.* The passage is found in Burdach's *Der Physiologie*, vol. 1, 550.
[51] Protocols of the Zofingia Society, 1896, Staatsarchiv, Basel, 227–230.
[52] Protocols of the Zofingia Society, 1900, Staatsarchiv, Basel, 257–258.

As a consequence of this transformation, his early researches at the Burghölzli were framed in terms of prevalent psychological and psychiatric methodologies, and this goes for his concept of energy. Before turning to this, it is necessary to sketch out how energy was taken up in psychology at this time.

Energy and fatigue

The development of thermodynamics had far-reaching effects on social, psychological and metaphysical thought in the later half of the nineteenth century. Anson Rabinbach argues that the significance of the principles of the conservation of energy and entropy was that the productive activities of humans, machines, or natural forces were not distinguished. Thermodynamics gave rise to a conceptual and metaphorical chain linking inorganic and organic nature, individual activity and society, which had as its outcome modern *productivism*: "the belief that human society and nature are linked by the primacy and identity of all productive activity, whether of laborers, of machines, or of natural forces" (1992, 3). This development was brought about by the advent of new sciences of work, which set out to measure the physical and mental expenditure of workers and calibrate them to maximal efficiency in requisite settings. Alongside these developments, the problems of fatigue became increasingly prominent. Rabinbach speculates that there was an epidemic of fatigue amongst workers and students (6). Following the constitution of fatigue as a principal social nemesis, the task of overcoming fatigue preoccupied social reformers, psychologists and psychiatrists.

The problem of fatigue and exhaustion were prominent in the American neurologist George Miller Beard's diagnostic category of neurasthenia, or nervous exhaustion, which had its heyday at the end of the nineteenth century. According to Beard, "Neurasthenia is a chronic, functional disease of the nervous system, the basis of which is impoverishment of nervous force" (1880, 115). Individuals were natively endowed with a fixed amount of nervous force, which obeyed the principle of the conservation of energy. Consequently, excess strain led to a deficit of nervous force, which resulted in a plethora of diverse symptoms.[53]

Experimental psychologists were anxious to demonstrate that the basic conceptions of psychology fulfilled general scientific criteria. In the case of concepts of energy, it would be obvious that psychologists would be concerned to demonstrate that their energy concepts fulfilled the principle of the conservation of energy. In 1860, in his founding text, *Elements of*

---

[53] See Gijswijt-Hofstra and Porter, ed., 2001.

Psychophysics, Gustav Fechner claimed that as the conservation of energy was a general law, psychophysical processes and the mind were bound by it (30–31). According to Wilhelm Wundt, muscular movements, together with the physical processes which accompanied sense perception, association and apperception obeyed the principle of the conservation of energy (1902, 366). This held despite the fact that the mental values represented by these energies differed. Psychical energy could be distinguished from physical energy:

> The ability to produce purely *quantitative* effects, which we designate as *physical energy*, is, accordingly, to be purely distinguished from the ability to produce *qualitative* effects, or the ability to produce values, which we designate as *psychical energy*. (Wundt, 1902, 366)

Thus Wundt's solution to this problem was nominalistic; psychic energy, which might appear to undergo increases, was merely the qualitative and hence unquantifiable aspect of physical energy.

It was Wundt's student the psychiatrist Emil Kraepelin who attempted to establish a quantitative measure of states of fatigue. Kraepelin constructed an experiment to measure the number of syllables that could be read in a given period of time as an indicator of mental efficiency. He expanded these experiments to measure the onset of fatigue in various tasks, which he depicted by means of "work curves." He claimed that these experiments enabled the quantification of fatigue.[54] The significance of this was that it was intended to enable the scientific understanding of the societal problem of "overburdening," the traumatic neuroses and psychopathic conditions.

In contrast to Wundt, one psychologist who postulated the existence of a specific psychic energy and asserted that its variations could be quantitatively determined was William Stern. In a chapter on "psychic energetics," Stern stated that psychic life represented a little understood energy system.[55] Drawing on Kraepelin's work, his interest focused on means of experimentally quantifying the fluctuations of levels of psychic energy through the course of the day.

Thus for psychology, the problem of energy was at once a critical theoretical, therapeutic, and social question: theoretical, in that the laws of

---

[54] Kraepelin, 1987, 45. Kraepelin and Gustav Aschaffenburg studied the effects of fatigue on individual performance in the associations experiment. Aschaffenburg explained the effect of fatigue on associations, and the similar patterns of association in states of mania, as due to increased motor excitation. Jung later provided an alternative psychological interpretation of their results in terms of disturbance of attention and suggestibility. Jung and Riklin, "Experimental researches on the associations of the healthy" (1904) *CW* 2, § 132.

[55] 1900, see also above, 42–43.

thermodynamics were taken to constitute the template for any scientific concept of energy; therapeutic, in that through the diagnostic category of neurasthenia (and later Pierre Janet's psychasthenia),[56] loss of energy was seen to characterize the clinical presentation, and the underlying explanation of the disease; and social, in that augmentation of the capacity for work would resoundingly establish psychology's social charter and mandate.

The energies of men

While Kraepelin and Stern attempted to quantify psychic energy, one prominent psychologist who critiqued these developments was William James. In 1906, James presented an address to the American Philosophical Association entitled "The energies of men." James commented on the gulf between structural and functional psychology – the former designating laboratory psychology, and the latter, the clinical approach, as exemplified by Janet's work. While clinical concepts were vaguer, they were more adequate, concrete, and practical. One significant problem of functional psychology which had been completely neglected by structural psychology and left to the "moralists and mind-curers and doctors," according to James, was that of the amount of energy available for mental and moral tasks. He noted:

Practically everyone knows in his own person the difference between the days when the tide of this energy is high in him and those when it is low, though no one knows exactly what reality the term energy covers when used here, or what its tides, tensions, and levels are in themselves . . . Most of us feel as if we lived habitually with a sort of cloud weighing on us, below our highest notch of clearness in discernment, sureness in reasoning, or firmness in deciding. Compared with what we ought to be, we are only half-awake. Our fires are dampened, our drafts are checked. We are making use of only a small part of our possible mental and physical resources. (1906, 130)

For the time being, the vagueness of such terms was unavoidable:

for though every man of woman born knows what is meant by such phrases as having a good vital tone, a high tide of spirits, an elastic temper, as living energetically, working easily, deciding firmly, and the like, we should all be put to our trumps if asked to explain in terms of scientific psychology just what such expressions mean. We can draw some child-like psychophysical diagrams, and that is all. (140)

In keeping with the concern for functional psychology, his interest was not one of providing a conceptual definition of such an energy, nor with

[56] See Shamdasani, 2001c.

spelling out its relation with physical and neural forces, but with studying the means of its evocation. Functional psychology should proceed independently of structural psychology. The phenomenon of the "second wind" took on an exemplary status for him, for he claimed that there existed untapped reservoirs of energy in all of us. In the clinical domain, the significance of this was indicated by Janet's cases of psychasthenia, which were characterized by feelings of fatigue, lassitude, and listlessness. He commented: The way to treat such persons is to discover to them more usual and useful ways of throwing their stores of vital energy into gear" (136). As examples of systems which focused upon the means to release untapped energy resources, he cited the spiritual exercises of Ignatius Loyola, the practices of yoga, and the practices of hypnotic suggestion. Suggestion was dynamogenic: "It throws into gear energies of imagination, of will, and of mental influence over physiological processes, that usually lie dormant" (139). His proposal was for an in-depth study and inventory of individual lives, through history and biographies, of the means that different types of individuals had employed to release such energies.

From the perspectives James outlined in this essay, the key task of psychotherapy lay not in determining the structure or cause of a neurosis, but in finding the means to unlock hidden resources of energy, principally through hypnosis and suggestion. Rather than developing a supposedly scientific vocabulary of energetics, he proposed articulating what lay implicit in the everyday terms of tiredness, elation, vigor, and so forth.

James' energetics were taken up by the Boston school of psychotherapy. This emerges from the presentations at the symposium of the American Therapeutic Society held at the beginning of May 1909 in New Haven, an event which has been posthumously eclipsed by the Clark conference in Worcester later the same year. In his presentation, Morton Prince highlighted the utilization of emotional energy as one of the principles of psychotherapy. He maintained that it was well known that depressive memories or ideas produced states of fatigue, while exalting ideas and memories released energy and brought about well-being. Referring to James' "brilliant illumination" of this principle, Prince stated that this principle accounted both for the development of neurosis, and of states of health. He claimed that it was easy to transform energy levels through hypnosis, by bringing certain ideas and memories into consciousness.[57]

Boris Sidis contended that contrary to the "Germans," tracing the psychogenesis of symptoms did not lead to cure, and had "no special therapeutic virtues." Rather, the therapeutic effect of psychotherapy rested upon the access to hidden reserves of energy provided by the hypnoidal

---

[57] 1910, 32–33. On Jung's relations with the Boston school, see Taylor, 1986.

state, which he described as a primordial state of sleep: "*The therapeutic value of the hypnoidal state consists in the liberation of reserve energy requisite for the synthesis of the dissociated systems*" (1910, 126). The theory of reserve energy which he and James had advanced could provide an alternative explanation of the therapeutic pretensions of other schools of psychotherapy: "it is highly probable that Freud's success in the treatment of psychopathic cases is not so much due to 'psycho-analysis' as to the unconscious use of the hypnoidal state" (132). For Sidis, in psychoanalysis, the couch had more therapeutic efficacy than the analyst, and the "talking cure" was really a reincarnation of the "rest cure." Rather than claiming to advance a supposedly unique method of treatment as Freud did, Sidis was attempting to account for the efficacity of different modes of psychotherapy.

Both Prince and Sidis used generalized concepts of psychological or emotional energy that did not have an exclusively sexual basis. While great attention was paid to the alteration of the levels of energy, in practical terms, this energy was not regarded as constant, as the untapped reserves of energy were regarded as being far in excess of energy generally used. With the eclipse of the Boston school of psychotherapy and the decline in the use of hypnosis, and the ascendance of psychoanalysis, such energy conceptions played an increasingly minor role in psychotherapy.[58]

Interest

A different attempt to relate psychology to biology was developed in Geneva, by the psychologist Edouard Claparède (1873–1940). Claparède was a cousin of Théodore Flournoy, who was nineteen years his senior. Like his friend William James, Flournoy had become uninterested in experimental work, and handed over his psychological laboratory to Claparède in 1904.

At the 1905 Congress of Experimental Psychology in Rome, Claparède delivered a paper on "Interest, fundamental principle of mental activity." In the proceedings of the congress, only an abstract was published. He argued that if we undertake to determine through introspection the reason for our actions or the active connections of our thought, we always arrive at the fact that such an action or connection of thoughts *interested* us. Consideration of the behavior of animals led to the same result, as a viable organism was one which adapted itself to the present situation through realizing the most useful action or "mental synthesis," and

---

[58] One exception was Pierre Janet. Inspired by James' essay, he developed a whole system of psychotherapy out of it. See Janet, 1919.

hence acted in the line of its greatest interest. This reaction consisted in a "dynamogenization" of appropriate processes. This explanation enabled one to dispense with an appeal to an intelligent faculty dominating the mind, such as the will or apperception, and allowed a reflexive, reactive conception to be substituted in its place. This concept of interest could explain various psychopathological phenomena (1905, 253). His concept of interest was part of an attempt to ground psychology and psychotherapy in biology. Only in such a way could one differentiate between normal and abnormal mental phenomena, determine the causes of disease, and apply appropriate "rational psychic treatment" (1906, 92).

He developed the application of his concept of interest to the understanding of sleep and hysteria in his "Outline of a biological theory of sleep." He observed that at a given moment, it was the most important instinct which dominated and controlled the activity of a living being. He formulated this as the law of the "supremacy of the instinct of the greatest momentary importance" or the "law of momentary interest" (1904, 280). He maintained that several instincts existed, and he referred to the instinct of feeding, the instinct of preservation, and the sexual instinct. For Claparède, interest was a characteristic of waking life. He characterized hysteria as a state of partial, systematized distraction towards certain objects. The hysteric was someone who escaped the law of momentary interest, and for certain stimuli, presented a "cramp of disinterest." Each time a particular object presented itself, it provoked an inhibitive reaction of disinterest. This reaction constituted a defence against something repugnant. In itself, such a reaction was perfectly normal – only its exaggeration and permanence could be regarded as pathological (338–342). He proceeded to use this model to explain the efficacy of psychotherapy, which lay in loosening the "reflexes of exaggerated mental defence." Psychotherapy worked by means of suggestion and persuasion, including under the latter term the confidence that the doctor inspired in the patient. Persuasion and suggestion worked through directly provoking a reaction of interest, which released the inhibitive reactions of mental defense.

Creative evolution

While Claparède was attempting to ground psychology in biology, the relation of biology to philosophy, and by extension, psychology, was being radically reworked by the French philosopher Henri Bergson. In retrospect, Bergson gave the following account of his intellectual trajectory. He came to realize that existing philosophical systems were not "cut to the measure" of reality: "examine any one of them . . . and you see that it could apply equally well to a world in which neither plants nor animals have existence, only men, and in which men would quite possibly do without eating and drinking" (1934, 11). Attempting to remedy this, he turned to Herbert Spencer's evolutionary philosophy. This led him to realize that accounts of evolution had failed to deal adequately with the question of time. Duration had been measured by the trajectory of a body in motion, i.e., spatially. However, "the line that one measures is immobile, time is mobility. The line is made, it is complete; time is what is happening, and more than that, it is what causes everything to happen" (12). What was thus measured was not duration, but isolated intervals of time. The measure of time was an abstraction. Hence, real time, or time as it was experienced, escaped mathematical treatment, as its essence was to flow. He claimed that it had been a prevailing turn of thought to conceive of time in spatial terms, and that the categories of Western thought had spatialized time. This tendency resided in a fundamental trait of the intellect.

In his 1889 *Essay on the Immediate Givens of Consciousness*, he put forward a detailed critique of the claims of psychophysics. In the last quarter of the nineteenth century, the Fechner–Weber law, which stated that the magnitude of a sensation could be mathematically derived by multiplying the logarithm of the strength of the sensation by a constant factor, was hailed as a great triumph for the experimental program in psychology. It was seen to have successfully demonstrated the possibility of quantifying qualitative states, and establishing law-like relations between them. Wundt held that the significance of this was that it "allows us for the first time in the history of psychology to apply principles of exact measurement to mental magnitudes" (1892, 59). Bergson claimed that Fechner's mistake had been to believe in an interval between two successive sensations "when there is simply a *passing* from one to the other and not a *difference* in the arithmetical sense of the word" (1889, 67–68). Consequently, psychophysics was caught in a vicious circle as:

the theoretical postulate on which it rests condemns it to experimental verification, and it cannot be experimentally verified unless its postulate is first granted. The fact is that there is no point of contact between the extended and the unextended, between quality and quantity. We can interpret one by the other, set up one as the equivalent of the other; but sooner or later . . . we shall have to recognize the conventional character of this assimilation. (70)

Bergson's *Creative Evolution* of 1907 was important for Jung. He commenced this work by stating that the intellect felt most at home with solids, and that logic was the logic of solids. Consequently, the intellect was neither able to grasp the nature of life, nor evolution.

Two predominant modes in which life was understood were through mechanism and finalism, which Bergson criticized in turn. The errors of both stemmed from an over extension of concepts natural to the intellect, which worked by thinking out mechanisms and adapting means to ends. Each failed to grasp the dimension of time. The essence of mechanical explanation was to "regard the future and the past as calculable functions of the present," which was only valid for systems artificially detached from the whole. Finalism in fact represented an inverted mechanism, with the simple alteration that it substituted "the attraction of the future for the impulsion of the past." In radical finalism, entities were the resultant of a previously established program. Consequently, "if nothing is unforseen, no invention or creation in the universe, time is useless again" (1907, 37–39).

His consideration of the shortcomings of radical finalism led him to criticize vitalistic theories, on the grounds that "in nature, there is neither purely internal finality nor absolutely distinct individuality" (42). However, the very rejection of a mechanism implied the acceptance of an element of finalism as:

The future then appears as expanding the present, it was not, therefore, contained in the present in the form of a represented end. And yet, once realized, it will explain the present as much as the present explains it, and even more. (52)

For Bergson, life possessed an element of finality, as it was directional, without being guided towards pre-existing ends. Science had to proceed on the basis that organic formation was mechanistic, as the aim of science was not to reveal the essence of things, but to supply a means of acting upon things. Philosophy, however, was not constrained by this imperative. The only means by which organic formation could be truly grasped as a whole was through positing "an *original impetus* [élan original] of life, passing from one generation of germs to the following generation of germs through the developed organisms" (87). This impetus which was responsible for variations in evolution, was the *élan vital*.

If the intellect was characterized by an inability to comprehend life, the same was not true of instinct, which was "moulded on the very form of life" and which "carried further the work by which life organizes matter" (165). One form that instinct took that was of special significance was intuition, which was "instinct that has become disinterested, self-conscious, capable of reflecting upon its object and of enlarging it indefinitely" (176). It was intuition that enabled one to grasp what surpassed the intellect. In the present day, intuition had been "almost completely sacrificed to the intellect" (267). The task of philosophy, however, was to seize upon and develop whatever fleeting intuitions were present and then develop them.

The publication of this work was greeted by much acclaim, and Bergson became a celebrity. William James hailed it as "the *divinest* book that has appeared in *my* life-time."[59] Its significance, James claimed, was that it "inflicts an irrecoverable death-wound upon Intellectualism" (619). While Bergson was against intellectualism, he was hardly against the intellect per se, as he was frequently misunderstood to be; he claimed that what was required was a complementary development of both principles. It was principally the critical aspect of Bergson's work that James appreciated, expressing some reservations concerning his notion of the *élan vital* and his positing of the "unconscious or subconscious permanence of memories."[60] With the publication of this work, Bergson became the most popular philosopher of his day.

Freud, Jung, and the Libido

Freud's concept of the libido may be briefly contextualized.[61] Ellenberger noted that prior to Freud, the term libido had been used by Theodore Meynert, Moriz Benedikt, Richard von Krafft-Ebing in the sense of sexual desire, and as indicating the sexual instinct in its evolutionary sense by Albert Moll.[62] In Freud's work, the field of application of the term libido far exceeded the domain mapped out by the sexologists, and indeed, encompassed human psychology and psychopathology as a whole. Peter Swales has shown the manner in which Freud's concept of the libido was principally derived from his experiences with cocaine, and specifically, from his attempt to understand psychoactive drugs in terms of putative sexual chemistry (Swales, 1989). Another important contextualization of Freud's libido theory has been put forward by Jean Starobinski, in an essay on the history of imaginary fluids. He argues that Freud's concept of the libido should be situated in the context of imaginary fluids, such as Descartes' "animal spirits" and Mesmer's "animal magnetism." Starobinski argues that the public success of Freud's libido theory, with its progression and regression through developmental stages, when compared with Liébault's static model of attention, was due to the fact that it represented a metaphorical convergence with contemporary, evolutionary language (1970, 212).

As noted above, Jung's initial conception of the libido was derived from Schopenhauer's concept of the will. In his *On the Psychology of Dementia*

---

[59] William James to T. S. Perry, June 24, 1907, ed. Henry James, 1920, 2, 294.
[60] James to Bergson, June 13, 1907, 619; February 25, 1903, 609, *ibid.*
[61] On the mimetic rivalry between Freud and Jung over the libido, see Borch-Jacobsen, 1982, 53–126.
[62] Ellenberger, 1970, 303.

Praecox, the term that Jung employed was psychic energy, in the manner of Stern. He argued that a strong complex had the effect of sapping the individual's energy.[63] In 1912, he stated that he had used the term psychic energy in this work as he felt that Freud's libido theory was inapplicable to dementia praecox (*CW* B, § 221).

In his preface to *On the Psychology of Dementia Praecox*, dated July 1906, Jung openly stated that he didn't grant sexuality the psychological universality that Freud did (*CW* 3, 4). At the inception of his correspondence with Freud, he immediately took up with Freud the possibility of reformulating the libido theory to bring it into closer alignment with contemporary biology and psychology. On October 23, 1906, he asked Freud: "But do you not believe, that one can take a number of border points as subspecies of the other basic drive [Grundtriebes] of hunger, for instance, eating, sucking (predominately hunger), kissing (predominantly sexuality)?" (*FJL* 7, trans. mod.). The following March, he wrote to Freud that Freud's broadening of the concept of libido had opened it to misunderstandings and made the following suggestion:

Is it not thinkable that one keeps the sexual terminology only for the extreme forms of your "libido" for the protection of the presently prevailing reduced concept of sexuality, and one incidentally establishes a less offensive collective concept for *all* "libidines"?[64]

The following year, he proposed to Freud a biological reformulation of hysteria and dementia praecox in terms of non-sexual drives. He stated that in dementia praecox or paranoia "the detachment and regression of the libido in an autoerotic form has its basis in the self assertion and psychological self-preservation of the individual."[65] While the former remained on the plane of self-preservation, he claimed that hysteria remained on the plane of the preservation of the species. He concluded that "The psychoses (the incurable ones) are probably to be understood as unsuccessful or rather over extended defensive encapsulations" (*FJL*, 123–4). The following year, he expressed himself to Ernest Jones in a similar fashion concerning the necessity of bringing the libido theory in line with general biology:

I share *your opinion entirely*, when you say that one must turn one's attention to biology. It will be one of our great future tasks to transfer the *Freud*ian metapsychology into biology. I am already gathering thoughts in that direction. Then we will render Freud an ever greater service than if we charge directly against

---

[63] Jung, *CW* 3, § 138. The same year, in "Psychophysical investigations with the galvanometer and pneumograph in normal and insane individuals", which he wrote with Frederick Peterson, noted that complexes resulted in fatigue. *CW* 2, § 1067.
[64] March 31, 1907, 25, trans. mod.   [65] February 20, 1908, 123–124, trans. mod.

the resistances of our opponents. The worst is undoubtedly the Freudian terminology. It is not only difficult but also misleading to many since it does not
originate from general, elementary biological insights but rather from the occa-
sional requirements of psychoanalysis, for instance, the entire sexual terminology.
By "*Libido*," for example is meant the instinct for the preservation of the species
and its derivatives (coerced assimilation, etc.), *repression*, defensive move, defense reflex etc., *phantasy wish* = preparatory *play* amongst animals and humans,
rehearsals for adaptation etc., *identification* = imitation drive (for the adoption of
defensive positions etc.)[66]

He went on to to say that they would meet with a better response if they
did not make the theme of sexuality so prominent. He added that since
he had "introduced sexuality as the instinct for the self preservation of
the species to Monakow, he at least in principle concedes the validity of
certain matters."[67]

While his letter to Jones makes clear his political identification with the
psychoanalytic cause, it also shows that in private he thought as little of
some of its fundamental theories and terminology as its opponents. These
letters also indicate that his allegiance to psychoanalysis, understood on a
contractual level, was predicated on the assumption that its basic theories
were flawed and could be thoroughly reworked.

Jung was not alone in his dissatisfaction with Freud's libido theory.
In 1909 James Jackson Putnam wrote that Freud and his colleagues had
for years unsuccessfully sought a wider term than the libido that "would
include the idea 'sexual' yet without making that word so prominent"
(1909, 25). To this end, Putnam proposed the term "craving." Two years
later, in a presentation before the American Psychopathological Association, he went further, and presented a vastly expanded conception of
the libido. The mind contained an element of the energy from which the
life of the universe was made, upon which all our striving and willpower
depended. He named this the *psyche generatrix* or *mens creative* (1911,
83–84). He claimed that this energy was in accord with the principle of
the conservation of energy.

---

[66] February 25, 1909, SFC.

[67] *Ibid.*, The neurologist Constantin von Monakow (1853–1930) formed the Psychiatrisch-
Neurologische Verein in Zürich with Paul Charles Dubois (1848–1918). Monakow
featured as an important opponent of psychoanalysis, and Jung gives several caustic descriptions of him in letters to Freud. Concerning psychoanalysis, Monakow later stated
that he had confirmed the correctness of the clinical facts observed by Freud and Breuer,
Bleuler, Jung and Adler, which were biologically important, without totally accepting
their explanations (Von Monakow, 1925, 82). Interestingly in the light of Jung's comments, he identified sexuality with the maintenance of the species (*ibid.*, 24). He gave
a critical account of the meetings of the Freud Society in Zürich that he attended in
his autobiography, (1928, 244–245). On the relation of his work to Jung's, see below,
269–270.

For Jung, his contact with Putnam was significant for him. In 1959, he wrote a brief recollection of Putnam, which was never published. For Jung, Putnam exemplified what was best about Americans of an academic background, and he admired his lack of bias, desire for objectivity, and integrity.[68] Jung met him in 1909, when his dissatisfactions with Freud's theories were taking shape. He added that "I am afraid that my enthusiasm on the one hand for what Freud had done in opening the way to recognition of the unconscious, and my criticism on the other hand – which kept welling up – confronted Putnam with a situation that scarcely furthered his understanding of the new ideas."[69]

Cryptomnesia and the history of the race

C. G. Jung's biological reformulation of psychoanalysis led him to attempt to place it on an evolutionary basis. In so doing, he embarked on an extension of the concept of memory, which consisted in taking up some of the themes of the organic memory theorists. Before turning to this, it is important to review his earlier work on cryptomnesia.

In his 1902 dissertation, he presented a remarkable example of this. Struck by the resemblance between a passage of Nietzsche's *Thus spoke Zarathustra* and a passage in Justinus Kerner's *Letters from Prevost*, he entered into a correspondence with Nietzsche's sister Elizabeth.[70] The latter confirmed that Nietzsche had been familiar with the work of Kerner in his adolescence. Jung also identified three ways in which the cryptomnesic image entered consciousness: intrapsychically, without the mediation of the senses (as in the example of Nietzsche), through the mediation of the senses, as in a hallucination, and through a motor automatism. For the last two categories, he gave Flournoy's Hélène Smith as an example. A few years later, he wrote a paper on "Cryptomnesia." Here, he commenced by noting that psychology differentiated between direct and indirect memory. The example he gave of a direct memory was that of seeing a house and recalling that one's friend lived there years ago. The example of an indirect memory he gave was that of walking past a house where a friend lived while thinking about other things, when an unexpected image comes forward of discussing such matters with his friend years ago, and not knowing why he was recalling this. He claimed that the

---

[68] An example of Putnam's even-handedness is the following letter to Alphonse Maeder: "I hope that the scientific differences between Jung and Freud will not lead to any breach between them" (December 11, 1912, Maeder papers).

[69] This tribute was incorporated into the manuscript of *Memories, Dreams, Reflections*, only to be deleted from the final text (CMS).

[70] *CW* 1, §§ 140–143. See Bishop, 1993.

memory of the friend attached itself to the nearest impression. What both of these examples had in common was the quality of being known. For Jung, all novelty arose from new combinations of existing elements. Every day, we had thousands of associations, without knowing where they were from. This was because consciousness was only part of the soul. Most of our psychic elements were unconscious (1905, *CW* 1, § 170). As he saw it, the unconscious could perceive and associate autonomously. All new ideas and combinations were premeditated by the unconscious. Accepting the view that every impression left a memory trace, it followed that these indirect memories resided in the unconscious.

In 1909, Jung devoted himself to an extensive study of mythology. Some indication of his evolving formulation of mythology is given in his letters to Freud. On November 8, 1909, he wrote to Freud that his readings in mythology and archeology provided "rich lodes" for the "phylogenetic basis of the theory of neurosis" (*FJL*, 258). A week later, he informed him that the "oldest and most natural" myths spoke of the "core complex of the neuroses."[71] These letters indicate that the search for the core complex and a phylogenetic basis for the neuroses were critical motivations for Jung's study of mythology. A phylogenetic basis was necessary if the theory of neurosis was to be placed on an evolutionary and developmental level. A few weeks later, these themes began to come together. Jung wrote to Freud,

I come always more to the feeling that a complete understanding of the psyche (if possible at all) will only come through history or with its help. Just as the understanding of anatomy and ontogenesis is possible only on the basis of phylogenesis and comparative anatomy. For this reason mythology appears to me now in a new and significant light. What we now find in the individual soul – in compressed, stunted or one-sidedly differentiated form – may be seen spread out broadly in the historical past.[72]

Biology here provides an analogy for understanding the significance of history and mythology in particular for psychology. The study of mythology and history are to psychology what the study of phylogenesis and comparative anatomy are to biology. Jung continued to develop this analogical parallel. On Christmas Day, 1909, he wrote to Freud:

It has become completely clear to me that we shall not solve the last thing of neurosis and psychosis without mythology and cultural history [Kulturgeschichte], for *embryology* belongs to *comparative anatomy*, and without the latter the former is still in the deepest a not understood play of nature. (279).

[71] November 15, 1909, 263.
[72] *Ibid.*, 269, November 30 – December 2, 1909, *Ibid.* 269. On Jung's use of the biogenetic law, see below, 299–300.

Here, individual psychopathology is analogically linked to embryology, and mythology and cultural history to comparative anatomy.

Around this time, the psychiatrist Adolf Meyer paid a visit to Jung and his assistant Johann Honegger (1885–1911) in Küsnacht, and made notes of their conversation.[73] He wrote:

> One of Honegger's patients (whom J. had analysed 3 years ago without any results in this direction) gave a splendid reproduction of a Ptolemaic conception of the world with interesting detail – which also have been crushed out from my mind in my Zustand der Gesundheit [state of health]. The patient made the world – very much as in the creation, flat with an edge . . . something about the ether . . .[74]

Honegger had finished his medical studies in Zürich in 1909. He was a voluntary doctor at Burghölzli from January 7 to March 12, 1910, and was never a permanent member of the staff.[75] Thus Meyer's visit was probably during this time.

At the end of March that year, Honegger presented a paper at the second International Psychoanalytic Congress at Nuremberg on paranoid delusion formation. Only an abstract was published. However, the original paper has survived, together with another unpublished paper on the same case, "Analysis of a case of paranoid dementia."[76] It emerges that the patient was the same one whom Jung and Honegger had discussed with Meyer. The patient, E. Schwyzer, was born in 1862. He was a store clerk, and had not had any higher education. He had lived in Paris and London, and after an attempt at suicide, he was committed to an asylum in London for one and a half years. After this, he went to Zürich, where he was committed to the Burghölzli on October 7, 1901. Honegger presented him as a case of paranoid dementia. He noted that the work had stemmed from a suggestion of Jung's, and that he had studied the case for two months. As Jung embarked on his mythological researches after leaving the Burghölzli, his access to clinical material from psychotic patients to substantiate his new hypothesis was no longer what it used to be. Hence the research of his students took on added importance.

Honegger noted that as word association experiments and free associations were not suitable for the patient, he asked the latter about points in his case history. Honegger stated that what was noteworthy about this case was that it showed the return to earlier phylogenetic levels, and included "a whole series of new creations of ancient mythological and philosophical ideas" which the patient "could not have had an inkling of."[77] Among these ideas were

[73] For information on Honegger, see Hans Walser, 1973, 1974.
[74] Adolf Meyer, diary, Johns Hopkins archive.
[75] "Index of directors, secondary, assistant and voluntary doctors at the Burghölzli since 1 July 1870," Burghölzli archives.
[76] Honegger papers, ETH.   [77] Cited in Walser, 1974, 253.

the idea of the rebirth of the world, the *aeqivoca generatio*, the complete identification of the universe with God (i.e., with the patient), the idea that the deity
was originally feminine (Near Eastern mother cult), the moon as seed preserver
(Asiatic mythology), the translation of the dead into stars in heaven, a variation
of the transmigration of souls, a modification of the vampire legend . . . despite
accurate knowledge of the modern theory of the world the patient returned to
the Ptolemaic system: the earth is flat and surrounded by infinite seas. (*Ibid.*)

The patient appeared to be a veritable textbook of mythology. Honegger
argued that the revival of such motifs indicated a regression to the childhood of the human race, caused by the regression of the libido. If one
studies closely the material which Honegger presents in his "analysis of a
case of paranoid dementia," the following question arises: to what extent
was the elaboration of the patient's fantasies the result of Honegger's questioning, of his suggestive procedure? From Honegger's perspective, his
questioning was simply uncovering a pre-existing delusional system. The
following are examples of some of these questions: "How do you know
that the seed body was always feminine?" "Can you also make wind?"
"How do you do it, when you want to make it rain?" "Could you now
alter the weather?"[78] Faced with Honegger's interest and sympathy, the
patient appeared only too willing to oblige, and elaborated cosmological
fantasies. If it is fair to say that the fantasies were a co-production stimulated by Honegger's suggestive procedure, it would explain why Jung
told Adolf Meyer that he had analyzed the patient three years ago (that is,
around 1907) "without any results in this direction." Honegger's analysis
would then be an example of a "folie à deux."

Jung held that the study of mythology could put the theory of the
neuroses on a phylogenetic basis. This was the subject of his presentation at a meeting of Swiss psychiatrists in Herisau later that year.
On January 30, 1910 he wrote to Freud that in this lecture, he had
tried to place symbolism on the foundation of developmental psychology [Entwicklungspsychologischen]. His claim was the conflict in an individual could be considered to be "mythologically typical" (288–289).
This led him to provide the following definition of the nuclear complex:
"The 'nuclear complex' seems to be the profound disturbance – caused
by the incest prohibition – between libidinal gratification and propagation."[79] In evolutionary terms, the notion of a nuclear complex could be
described as a form of psychological monogenism: the thesis that all neurosis stemmed from a common origin. This psychological monogenism
underlies Jung's *Symbols and Transformations of the Libido*, and as such,

[78] Honegger, "analysis of a case of paranoid dementia", 125–126.
[79] June 2, 1910, 326.

should be clearly differentiated from the subsequent psychological polygenism of his theory of archetypes.

While continuing his study of mythology, he increasingly noted the incidence of myth-like themes in his practice. On September 29, 1910, he reported to Freud that he noted the presence of a fragment of a Peter-Antichrist legend which surfaced in the childhood of a now eighteen-year-old Jewish girl (356). In another case of a woman with dementia praecox, he noted the presence of a redemption mystery composed of liturgical imagery.

While Jung was in the United States in March 1910, Honegger had taken on his patients. He had wanted to take on Honegger as his assistant, and Honegger's fiancée, Helene Widmer, was working as Jung's secretary. Efforts were made to find suitable offices for Jung and Honegger in Zürich (Walser, 1974, 247). Jung subsequently informed the American psychiatrist, Trigant Burrow, that Honegger was ambitious, and began to consider his fiancée as an obstacle, and broke off his engagement. He had an affair with a female patient, and gave up his position with Jung, and stopped writing to him.[80] At the beginning of February 1911, Honegger took up a post at the Rheinau asylum as an assistant doctor. On March 28, 1911, he committed suicide, through a morphine overdose. The next day, he was due to return to military service. His father, who had been a psychiatrist, had been interned in the Burghölzli, where he died. According to Ris, the director of Rheinau, Honegger feared that he would meet a similar fate. Patients in the hospital were informed that he had died of a heart attack.[81] Jung informed Freud that he had committed suicide to avoid a psychosis.[82] Jung informed Burrow that Honegger had committed suicide after realizing that he had made the wrong decisions and did not sufficiently believe in life. He added this was a great loss to him, as Honegger was his only congenial friend in Zürich.[83]

On June 12, 1911, Jung argued that in dementia praecox introversion did not only lead to a "renaissance of infantile memories" but also to a "loosening up of the historical layers of the unconscious." The historical layers of the unconscious consisted in racial memories (*FJL*, 427). In September, he presented a lecture on symbolism at the International Psychoanalytic Congress in Weimar. According to Otto Rank's abstract, he argued that in contrast to hysteria, historical parallels were necessary to understand dementia praecox, as the dementia praecox patient "suffers from the reminiscences of mankind" (*CW* 18, § 1082).

---

[80] June 28, 1911, JP.
[81] Ris to the Zürich medical administration, March 28, 1911, Staatsarchiv, Zürich.
[82] *FJL*, March 31, 1911, 412.   [83] Jung to Burrow, June 28, 1911, JP.

On October 13, he wrote to Freud "If there is phylogenetic memory in the individual, which unfortunately will soon be undeniable, this is also the source of the *uncanniness* of the "doppelgänger" (*FJL*, 449). The following week he put forward a bold thesis concerning the significance of such phylogenetic memories:

the so-called "early memories of childhood" are not at all individual memories but phylogenetic ones. I mean of course the *very early* reminiscences like birth, sucking . . . Just now my Agalthi is having such dreams; they are closely related to certain Negro birth-myths . . . I believe one will later see that unbelievably many more things than we now accept are phylogenetic reminiscences. (450)

In essence, what Jung was proposing was a radical extension of Flournoy's concept of cryptomnesia. He was claiming that it wasn't only memories of impressions gained during one's lifetime that reappeared in unrecognized forms, but also memories of the race. This concept forms an important stage in the development of his thinking. It could be termed "phylo-cryptomnesia." Flournoy's theory of cryptomnesia still provides an explanation of the storage and reproduction of memories – it is simply the scope of the memories which is extended to encompass those of the race. In making this extension, he was closely following the work of the organic and ancestral memory theorists, as well as the work of psychologists such as Stanley Hall and James Sully.

Jung's phylogenetic explorations raised the question of the relation of psychoanalysis to biology. To Freud, he criticized the overly biological views of Adler, Bleuler, and Sabina Spielrein.[84] He wrote that if he used biological arguments, he did so "*faute de mieux.*" While he thought that psychoanalysis should alone be "master of its field" he thought it was useful to attempt connections from other fields as they enabled one to look at things from a different perspective (*FJL*, 470).

In *Transformations and Symbols of the Libido* (1911–1912) he drew a parallel between the phantastic mythological thinking of antiquity, dreams, children and the lower human races. Such connections were not strange, but were well known through comparative anatomy and evolutionary history "which shows us how the structure and function of the human body are the result of a series of embryonic changes which correspond to similar changes in the history of the race" (*CW* B, § 37, trans. mod.). Consequently the supposition that ontogeny corresponded to phylogeny also in psychology was justified. As a result infantile thinking in children and in dreams was "nothing but a repetition of the prehistoric and

---

[84] *FJL*, November 29, 1910, 374; December 11, 1911, 470.

antiquity" (*ibid.*, trans. mod.). We all possessed this phantasy thinking. With adults, it entered in when directed thinking stopped. Just as the organs of the body kept the relics of old functions and conditions, "so our mind, which has apparently outgrown those archaic tendencies, nevertheless still bears the mark of the evolution passed through," which was repeated in phantasies (§ 47). This led Jung to envisage the soul geologically: "The soul possesses in some degree a historical stratification, whereby the oldest stratum of which would correspond to the unconscious" (§ 51, trans. mod.). Introversions in later life first went back to regressive infantile reminiscences. Stronger introversions, as in the psychoses, led to the revival of archaic mental products. One such example that he gave was the following hallucination that Honegger had observed in his case of paranoid dementia:

The patient sees in the sun a so-called 'upright tail' (i.e. much like an erect penis). When the patient moves his head back and forth, the sun's penis also moves back and forth and from this the wind arises. This strange delusionary idea remained unintelligible to us for a long time, until I became acquainted with the visions of the Mithraic liturgy.[85]

Honegger had referred to the patient conducting "a new sun experiment," viewing the sun with one eye, etc.[86] Jung became familiar with the Mithraic liturgy through Albrecht Dieterich's work, *A Mithras Liturgy*. This had been published in 1903, and Jung possessed the second edition of 1910 (which has numerous annotations).

In Jung's model, the soul was a historical formation, which contained its history within. If, as Otis has argued, organic memory theorists located history within the body, Jung's analogical transformation of that theory led him to locate history in the soul. While he would come to discard or revise much of the content of *Transformations and Symbols of the Libido*, this basic vision was maintained throughout his later work, where it forms one of the key leitmotifs.

During his psychiatric career, the import of his philosophical readings are not readily apparent. However, they began to re-emerge strongly during the period of his secession from the psychoanalytic movement. In 1912 he noted: "I have come to the realization that the religious and philosophical driving forces – what Schopenhauer calls the 'metaphysical need' of man – must receive positive consideration during analytic

---

[85] *Ibid.*, § 173, trans. mod. He also cited Honegger's example of the reproduction of the flat earth later on (§ 233).
[86] "Analysis of a case of paranoid dementia," 76.

work."[87] The same claim was made by James Jackson Putnam, who had argued in the previous year that unless such "metaphysical needs" were catered for, the therapeutic potential of psychoanalysis would remain limited, as it was precisely difficulties in this domain that brought many patients to analysis (Putnam, 1911). Jung's and Putnam's contentions ran directly counter to Freud's figuration of psychoanalysis as consisting in an outright replacement for metaphysics. For Jung, the problem was how to provide for such needs, and yet maintain psychology as a science. His answer to this took the form of his theory of the archetypes and the collective unconscious. As stated earlier, the dynamic psychologies of the 1880s and 1890s sought to distance themselves from the philosophies of the unconscious through providing restricted psychological models of the unconscious or subconscious that were supposedly derived purely from clinical observation, rather than metaphysical speculation. Such a model informs Jung's early work, up until *Transformations and Symbols of the Libido*. From that period onwards, Jung began to argue for an extension of the notion of the unconscious and the libido.

In 1912, in the second part of *Transformations and Symbols of the Libido*, he stated that while the term libido had been taken initially from the sexual sphere, it had become the most widely used term in psychoanalysis, due to the fact that its significance was wide enough to cover all the manifestations that Schopenhauer attributed to the Will.[88] He noted that since Freud's *Three Essays on the Theory of Sexuality*, the field of application of the libido concept had widened, and that both he and Freud had consequently felt the need to widen the concept of libido. To back up this assertion, he gave a lengthy citation of a section from Freud's study of the Schreber case, in which Freud raised the question as to whether the detachment of the libido from the external world was sufficient to account for the idea of the end of the world. Freud stated:

we should either have to assume that what we call libidinal cathexis (that is, interest emanating from erotic sources) coincides with interest in general, or we should have to consider the possibility that a very widespread disturbance in the distribution of the libido may bring about a corresponding disturbance in the ego-cathexes. But these are problems with which we are still quite helpless and incompetent to solve. It would be otherwise if we could start out from some well-grounded theory of instincts; but in fact we have nothing of the kind at our disposal. (1911, *SE* 12, 74)

---

[87] "General aspects of psychoanalysis," *CW* 4, § 554.

[88] *CW* B, § 212. He added that "Freud's original conception does not interpret "everything sexual," although this has been asserted by critics." Sixteen years later, Jung was to claim that the critics who had charged Freud with pansexualism were quite justified. "On the energetics of the soul" (1928), 19.

Freud concluded this passage by stating that it was most probable that the paranoiac's altered relation to the world stemmed from the loss of his libidinal interest. Jung took up this passage to argue that the loss of reality in dementia praecox could not solely be explained by the withdrawal of libidinal investments, which would suggest that what Janet termed the function of the real was sustained solely by erotic interests. Consequently, he claimed that the libido theory was inapplicable to dementia praecox.

However, Jung claimed that after Freud's *Three Essays*, a genetic concept of the libido had arisen, which had enabled him to replace the term psychic energy, which he had employed in *On the Psychology of Dementia Praecox*, with that of the libido. He then turned to evolutionary history, claiming that it demonstrated that many functions which presently lacked a sexual character were originally derived from the general propagation drive [Propagationstrieb]. Through evolution, part of the energy which had been previously required for propagation became transposed to create mechanisms for allurement and protection, which gave rise to the artistic drive [Kunsttrieb], which then attained a functional autonomy.

He noted that in nature, the instinct for the preservation of the species [Instinkt der Arterhaltung] and the instinct for self-preservation [Instinkt der Selbsterhaltung] were indistinct, where one only saw a life drive [Lebenstrieb] and a will to live [Willen zum Dasein].[89] He stated that this conception coincided with Schopenhauer's conception of the will. Consequently, libido was related to every form of desire.

After an excursus on ancient intuitions of this conception, Jung gave an account of ontogenetic development. He claimed that in childhood, the libido was present in the form of the drive of nutrition [Ernährungstriebes]. In nominating a drive of nutrition, Jung was following Ribot.[90] New applications of the libido opened up through bodily development, culminating in sexuality. Subsequently, this sexual primal libido [Urlibido] becomes desexualized into new operations. In the genetic conception, the libido contained not only the "Rezentsexuelle" but also what had widened into desexualized primordial libido.

While Jung had initially claimed that the libido theory needed to be widened to deal with the psychoses, he now added that his genetic conception of the libido was applicable to the neuroses as well. In his genetic

---

[89] Throughout his German publications, Jung utilized the standard German biological terminology, in using the term "Instinkt" to refer to animals and humans, and reserving "Trieb" specifically for the latter. These distinctions were not maintained in translations of Jung.

[90] See above, 195. Stanley Hall later argued that the study of the psychology of hunger could form the basis of a new psychology, which he held had been "dimly glimpsed" by Jung, who had given a place, though inadequate, to hunger (1923, 420).

model, there were three phases in the development of the libido: a pre-sexual stage, a prepubertal stage starting from around the age of three to five, and maturity. He recognized a multiplicity of drives and instincts, which were distinct from the libido. This uncoupling of the libido from sexuality and its reformulation as a general principle of psychic energy led him to claim that the concept of libido had the same significance in the biological realm as the concept of energy since Robert Mayer had in the physical realm (*CW* B, § 218). Analogously, in his Fordham lectures the same year he claimed that the movements of the libido had a close analogy with the principle of the conservation of energy. When a quantum of energy disappeared from a particular activity, it would reappear elsewhere (*CW* 4, § 254). He went on to claim that with his genetic conception of the libido, psychology fell in line with the conception of energy in other sciences, and publicly stated what he had earlier written to Jones, concurring with the critics of Freud's libido concept:

Just as the older natural sciences were always talking of reciprocal actions in nature, and this old-fashioned view was replaced by the law of the conservation of energy, so here too, in the realm of psychology, we are seeking to replace the reciprocal action of co-ordinated powers of the soul [Seelenkräfte] by an energy conceived to be homogeneous. We thus give space to those correct criticisms that reproach the psychoanalytic school by saying that it operates with a mystical conception of the libido. (§ 281, trans. mod.)

He took up the question of the relation of this new concept of the libido with vitalism. This was necessary, as both Mayer and Helmholtz had been resolutely opposed to vitalistic theories, which were supposed to have been repudiated by the principle of the conservation of energy. He argued that:

It cannot disturb us, if we are reproached with vitalism. We are as far removed from the belief in a specific life-force [Lebenskraft] as from any other metaphysics. Libido should be the name for the energy which manifests itself in the life process and is perceived subjectively as striving and desire. (§ 282, trans. mod.)

Here, he appears not to be denying the possibility of reducing life to physical and chemical processes, as he had done in the Zofingia lectures, but solely to be claiming that libido designated the subjective perception of such processes. No longer defending the autonomy of life or championing a vitalistic biology against the claims of materialistic biology, his concern became one of defending the autonomy of the psyche, and the irreducibility of psychology from biology, however the latter conceived of the processes of life.

Jung added that Freud's concept of libido "is understood in so innocuous a sense that Claparède once remarked to me that one could just as well use the word 'interest'" (§ 273). This substitution of interest for libido was itself far from innocuous, as the former term played an important role in Claparède's own work, as depicted above.

Claparède's model of a plurality of instincts which were momentarily motivated by a supplementary factor of interest, corresponded closely to how Jung was reformulating the libido theory. Jung's reference to Claparède indicates that they had personally discussed this matter.[91] In 1914, Jung stated the word interest could be used to designate the wider libido concept, as Claparède had suggested, "if this expression had to-day a less extensive application."[92] It is not clear whether Jung had in mind the widespread general use of the word interest, or Claparède's use of the term, or both, and hence whether the reason that he didn't use the term was to differentiate his concept from the former or the latter.[93]

As Jung had cited Freud's statements in the Schreber case to back up his genetic conception of the libido, the question arose as to what extent his views were to be regarded as divergent. The public response to his views took the form of Ferenczi's review of Jung's *Transformation and Symbols of the Libido*, Jones' and Abraham's reviews of Jung's Fordham university lectures, and Freud's rebuttals in "On the history of the psycho-analytic movement" and "On narcissism." The careful orchestration of these responses is evident from the letters that they exchanged between themselves. What also emerges is that the political significance of the theoretical difference between Freud and Jung was by no means constant. Rather, at moments of political significance, theoretical differences took on an importance that they didn't previously have.

On September 12, 1912, Ernest Jones wrote to Freud after a discussion with Jung's supporters Alphonse Maeder and Franz Riklin that while he

---

[91] In an undated letter to Claparède, who was planning to attend a congress in Aarau, Jung invited him to stay and to discuss problems of Freudian psychology (Claparède papers, BPU, Geneva).

[92] "On psychological understanding," *CW* 3, § 418. This sentence appeared in the German edition of Jung's presentation to the Psycho-Medical Society in London on July 24, 1914.

[93] Claparède's views on Freud's libido have a curious aftermath. In his autobiography, Claparède stated that in his introduction to the French translation of Freud's Clark University lectures, which was the first work of Freud to appear in French, "I thought that the best way to explain his *libido* would be to identify it with 'interest.' But Freud did not agree" (1930, 77). Freud was upset with Claparède's remarks concerning the libido in his introduction. Freud wrote to him on December 25, 1920 that "It is *Jung*, and not *I*, who has made the libido the equivalent of the drive power [Triebkraft] *of all* the activity of the soul [seelischen Tätigkeiten], and then who combats the sexual nature of the libido. Your assertion does not agree completely with my conception, nor with that of Jung, but constitutes a combination from us both. From me you have taken the sexual nature of the *libido*, from Jung its universal significance. And thus the pansexualist situation comes about, which only exists in the uncreative fantasies of critics, but which is not the case with myself nor Jung" (in Cifali, 1991, 299).

suspected that some of Jung's views were of "purely personal origin," nevertheless

much of this work is in striking agreement with the logical development of the *Sexualtheorie* that you yourself have gone through in the last years; especially the phylogenetic aspects, the inheritance of repression and perhaps already desexualised (sublimated) tendencies. (Paskauskas, ed., 1993, 158)

In his preface to the first edition of his papers on psychoanalysis, dated September 1912, Jones wrote that the strongest opposition to Freud's was due to the significance that he attached to the sexual instinct. However, he argued that Freud used this in a far wider sense than was usual, and that the importance he attached to it "does not greatly differ from that of Schopenhauer's and Nietzsche's *Wille zur Macht*, Bergson's *élan vital*, Shaw's 'life force,' and the 'vital impulse' of so many writers, all of which are equivalent to what Freud terms *Libido*" (1913, xi). This passage was deleted from all subsequent editions, along with a number of favorable statements about Jung. While Freud claimed that Jung had misunderstood his passage in the Schreber case, he initially did not accord much significance to this: "I never obliterated or changed the meaning of the libido, but stuck to my first definition all over . . . I hope we will have a good talk over it, but to be sure it is all discussable and highly interesting and there is no enmity in it."[94] This letter gives some indication of the fact that theoretical reasons played far less of a role in the split between Freud and Jung than has been generally maintained. Political developments led to a retrospective emphasis being given to theoretical differences. Again to Karl Abraham, Freud claimed that the question he posed had been asked "purely dialectically, in order to answer it in the negative."[95] Ferenczi publicly criticized Jung's reading of this passage in Freud in his review, which Freud also repudiated in "On the history of the Psycho-Analytic movement."[96]

Jung's new libido theory provoked an equivocal response in his former chief Eugen Bleuler. On October 30, 1912 Jones wrote to Freud citing a letter he had just received from Bleuler stating that he had always thought that the libido theory had lacked clarity, and that Jung's work was very important (ed. Paskauskas, 1993, 165). The following month Bleuler wrote to Freud that his difficulty with Freud's concept of the libido was the manner in which he subsumed under it the eating and sucking of

---

[94] Freud to Jones, September 22, 1912, 163.
[95] June 14, 1914, ed. Falzeder, 2002, 247.
[96] Ferenczi disputed Jung's claim that any widening had occurred in Freud's work, adding that he himself had once wanted to generalize the libido concept, which Freud had protested against (1913, 396).

little children, which he could not agree with.[97] After the appearance of Jung's Fordham university lectures, while he was not convinced by the "all powerfulness" of Freud's concept of the libido, he could not accept Jung's "sexless standpoint," which probably went too far the other way. Jung's concept really had nothing to do with the libido in Freud's sense, and should be separately developed and given a new name.[98] Finally, on reading Freud's "On the history of the Psycho-Analytic movement," Bleuler wrote to Freud that "inspite of the difference in basic psychological concepts and my doubts on pansexuality and your sexual development, I stand infinitely closer to your conception than to the modern Jungian one."[99] Thus between 1912 and 1914, Bleuler's judgment on Jung's genetic conception of the libido grew increasingly negative.

In his 1913 review of *Transformations and Symbols of the Libido*, Flournoy welcomed Jung's reformulation of the libido. He stated that in Jung's work, the libido became the equivalent of Schopenhauer's "will to live," Ostwald's "energy" and Bergson's "élan vital." It broke free of the pansexualism with which Freud's libido concept had been charged, and regained its legitimate place alongside the nutritive functions, without losing its capital role in evolution. While Flournoy found Jung's general account of human evolution "a little confused," he certainly felt that it marked an advance on the "not less entangled" attempts of the Freudians (1913). It is interesting to note that prior to Jung's official secession from the International Psychoanalytical Association, Flournoy did not regard him as a Freudian.

While Jung's widening of the concept of the libido appears to have been initially favorably received by Putnam,[100] he subsequently altered his opinion. In 1915 he stated that Jung had overstressed the significance of the conservation of energy, and argued that love and reason were not subject to this quantitative law (1915, 305). In the same year, Putnam wrote to Freud on August 13 that no one had demonstrated that mental forces were really subject to the law of the conservation of energy (ed. Hale, 1971, 194). In 1917, he stated that while he sympathized with Jung's desire for a broader formulation of the libido, he could not agree with Jung's rejection of Freud's concepts of regression, infantile sexuality, and fixation (1917, 363).

---

[97] November 20, 1912, Sigmund Freud archives, LC, originals in German.
[98] July 24, 1913.   [99] July 4, 1914.
[100] Putnam, 1913, 190. On September 11, 1912, Putnam had written to his cousin Fanny Bowditch, whom he had sent to be analyzed by Jung, "I am going to write one of the philosophic papers of which I am so fond & so few other people go for, in which I hope to show that Dr. Jung's widened conception of the libido can still be further widened, in another sense." Katz papers, CLM.

Jung's reformulation of the libido brought it into closer proximity with general psychology and psychotherapy, as represented by such figures as Stern, Lipps, Claparède, Sidis, James, and Prince, and hence overturned the disciplinary autonomy of psychoanalysis that Freud was attempting to establish. In addition, it was welcomed by Flournoy. In the psychological context at this time, it is important to note that figures such as James, Flournoy, Claparède, Stern, and Lipps had higher professional and institutional standings than Freud. Through altering the psychoanalytic emphasis on sexuality, he had also gone a long way towards meeting the charges of many of its critics. This linkage was not lost on Freud. On January 1, 1913, he wrote to Putnam, that "For me it seems like a 'déjà vu' experience. Everything I encounter in the objections of these half-analysts I had already met in the objections of the non-analysts" (ed. Hale, 1971, 153). The one crucial, and embarrassing difference was that these charges were now made by the president of the International Psychoanalytical Association, who had previously been, alongside Freud, its most well-known exponent. In terms of strategy, Jung's reformulation of the libido was hence a formidable move, which the psychoanalysts were clearly aware of. On April 25, 1913, Jones wrote to Freud, "I am deeply impressed by the success of Jung's campaign, for he appeals to formidable prejudices. It is, in my opinion, the most critical period that we will have to go through" (ed. Paskauskas, 1993, 199). On November 22, Freud wrote to Jones: "We know J.'s position is a very strong one, our only hope is still he will ruin it himself. You will have to fight him for influence in England and America and it may be a long and hard struggle" (242).

It is insufficiently realized that these fears initially proved to be quite well founded. In a comprehensive survey of the reception in the British press between 1912 and 1925, Dean Rapp showed that the works of Jung and his followers consistently received better reviews than the works of Freud and the psychoanalysts. An example of this is a review in the *Journal of Education*: "It is well known that Jung has broken away from the more extreme positions of his master, Freud, and is therefore more likely to appeal to English thinkers."[101] Rapp states that the most frequent charge against Freud was that he had exaggerated the role of sexuality (1988, 195). In the period between 1912 and 1919, Rapp notes that reviewers stated their preference for Jung's wider conception of the libido, which also benefited from the widespread appeal of Bergson's *élan vital* that already existed (1990, 233).

---

[101] Anon., *Journal of Education*, July 1916, Jung press archive, ETH.

In 1957, Jung retrospectively remarked on the subsequent development of Freud's theories. He stated that Freud "later started to work
on concepts that were no longer Freudian in the original sense . . . He
found himself constrained to take my line, but this he could not admit to
himself."[102] Indeed, a substantive part of Freud's reworking of his libido
concept, from "On narcissism" to *Beyond the Pleasure Principle*, which
delimited the sexual nature of the libido and its provenance, can justly be
regarded as extended attempts at damage control.

Libido, hormé, élan vital

Bergson's work had immediately attracted interest from figures involved
with psychoanalysis. In 1909, Putnam gave a talk comparing Freud's
and Bergson's views on the unconscious. Nathan Hale notes that in addition to Putnam, William Alanson White and Smith Ely Jeliffe also began
to view Freud's libido as one manifestation of Bergson's *élan vital* (ed.
Hale, 1971, 49). This shifted Freud's concept of the libido away from his
positivist epistemology, towards one that, while receptive to philosophical
and spiritual values, remained embedded within a coherent evolutionary
and biological framework.

After presenting his conception of the libido in *Transformations and
Symbols of the Libido* and his Fordham lectures, Jung drew a parallel between it and Bergson's *élan vital*. The indications are that he read Bergson
subsequent to developing his conception of the libido; the copy of Bergson's *Creative Evolution* in Jung's library is the 1912 German translation.
His first reference to Bergson occurs in a letter to Loÿ in March 1913.
Commenting on the shortcomings of causal and mechanistic explanations of organic formation, he stated "I would remind you of Bergson's
excellent criticism in this respect" (*CW* 4, § 665).

On October 8, 1912, in his presentation before the New York Academy
of Medicine, while announcing that he proposed to liberate psychoanalytic theory from "the purely sexual standpoint," he claimed that libido
could be understood as vital energy in general.[103] He presented a slightly
revised version of the same paper the following year before the 17th International Medical Congress, in London, held between August 6 and 12,
1913. There, after the sentence just quoted, he added the phrase "or as
Bergson's *élan vital*" (*CW* 4, § 568). On March 20, 1914, following a presentation by Adolf Keller on the relation of Bergson's work to the libido

---

[102] MP, 154.
[103] Jung, presentation before the New York Academy of Medicine, 5, JP.

theory, Jung said that "a gap has been filled by Keller's paper. Bergson should have long been discussed here. B. says everything which we have not said. He comes down from the unity, we have climbed up from the multiplicity."[104]

On July 24, 1914 in a lecture before the psycho-medical society in London, Jung stated that as the term libido, which he had used in his German publications seemed to be misunderstood in English, he proposed to rename it *hormé*, adding that "*Hormé* is related to *Bergson's* conception of the '*élan vital*'" (1915, 396). This would have served to differentiate clearly his concept from Freud. However, Jung continued to use the term libido in his German publications, and the term *hormé* was not used at all by his translators, or subsequently by Jung when he wrote or lectured in English.

However, *hormé* was subsequently used by one individual who attended Jung's lecture in London, William McDougall, who later characterized his psychology as "hormic."[105] Concerning the relation between *hormé* and *élan vital*, Jung stated:

I am conscious of the fact that, as the conception of *hormé* corresponds to *Bergson's* "*élan vital*," so the constructive method also corresponds to his intuitive methods. But I confine myself to psychology and to practical psychological work, realizing that every conceptual formula is psychological in its essence. (1915, 399)

In his German version, Jung called Bergson's *élan vital* a parallel concept [Parallelbegriff] to his concept of the libido. Also in the German version of his text, he added at this point: "When I read Bergson a year and a half ago for the first time, I found to my great pleasure everything which I had worked out in my practical work had been put in consummate language and in wonderfully clear philosophical style" (ed. Long, 1916, 351, trans. mod.). What he had discovered through clinical work had been confirmed by Bergson's philosophy, and specifically indicated two points of convergence: that between his concept of *hormé* and Bergson's *élan vital*, and between his constructive method and Bergson's intuitive method. Jung differentiated his concepts, by claiming that they were purely psychological. He indicated that his reading of Bergson, some

---

[104] MZP.

[105] Ernest Jones wrote to Freud on August 3, 1914, "Jung unfortunately had a great success in his London lecture, and McDougall was so impressed by that he is going to be analysed by Jung . . . The one progress is that he has a new word 'Horme' for Libido, and 'prospective psychology' for Ps-A, as conceived by himself." (Ed. Paskauskas, 1993, 298). Concerning the term *hormé*, McDougall, who commended Jung's concept of the term libido over Freud, stated that the use of the same word would inevitably lead to confusions. He stated: "I regret that Jung did not see fit to adopt this word in place of 'libido', when I urged it upon him many years ago in conversation" (1926, 27).

time around the beginning of 1913, provided him with a confirmation of the new views he had independently worked out.

Further indication of the impact of Bergson on Jung is provided in his letters to Hans Schmid concerning the formulation of psychological types. From these, it emerges that the area in which Bergson's work had the greatest impact on Jung was on the development of his psychological typology. On June 4, 1915, Jung wrote to Schmid that he got the concept of the irrational from Bergson, and that "the unmistakable hypostatisation of this concept in Bergson pleases me. With it we gain two principles intimately connected with one another, which are reciprocally conditioned, the *rational* and the *irrational*" (ed. Iselin, 1982, 39).

The following year, in a lecture in Zürich, Jung stated: "one owes Bergson special thanks for having broken a lance for the right of the irrational to exist" (*CW* 7, § 483, trans. mod.). In *Psychological Types*, he used the concept "irrational" "not in the meaning of *against reason* [Widervernünftigen], but in the sense of *outside reason* [Außervernünftigen], namely that which is not grounded on reason" (*CW* 6, § 775, trans. mod.). He added that the irrational consequently surpassed rational explanation. Bergson does not appear to have specifically used the term "irrational." However, it is clear that the aspect of Bergson's work that was significant for Jung in this regard was what James described as his critique of intellectualism. The charge of irrationalism (as Jung would have put it, in the sense of Widervernünftigen) is often made against Jung. What is not realized is the fact that for Jung, the concept of the irrational derived its philosophical justification in the Bergsonian delimitation of the provenance of the intellect, and the recognition that life exceeded representational consciousness. Using Jung's terminology seen from a Bergsonian perspective, the key task was one of not subsuming the irrational into the rational.

The discussions of Bergson's work in the correspondence between Jung and Schmid indicate that Bergson's work played an important role in informing Jung's understanding of the relation and opposition between a pair of psychological functions, in addition to providing the basis for his distinction between the rational and the irrational, and his notion of intuition as a cognitive faculty.

In *Psychological Types*, however, Jung put forward a critique of Bergson, in the context of his critique of James' pragmatism:

Bergson though has pointed out to us intuition and the possibility of an "intuitive method." But it remains a mere *indication*, as we know. A *proof* of the method is lacking and will also not be so easy to produce, although Bergson may point to his concepts of the "élan vital" and the "durée créatrice" as products of intuition.

Aside from these intuitively grasped basic views . . . the Bergsonian method is intellectual and not intuitive.[106]

In actual fact, Bergson had explicitly dealt with a form of this critique in *Creative Evolution*. To the argument that any attempt to go beyond intelligence remained within it, he replied that this vicious circle, which had nevertheless constrained other philosophies, was only apparent. This was because:

all around conceptual thought there remains an indistinct fringe which recalls its origin . . . we compared the intellect to a solid nucleus formed by means of condensation. This nucleus does not differ radically from the fluid surrounding it. It can only be reabsorbed in it because it is made of the same substance. (1907, 193)

There is indication that Bergson was aware of Jung's work. In 1922, Adolf Keller wrote to Bergson inviting him to write a preface for a French translation of a work of Jung. He declined, stating that he had made a general principle of not writing prefaces. However, he added: "I have great respect for the work of Jung, which isn't only interesting for the psychologist and psychopathologist, but also for the philosopher! It is here that psychoanalysis has found its philosophy."[107]

Finally, while tracing the impact of Bergson's work on Jung, it is important to note aspects of his *Creative Evolution* that ran directly contrary to the positions that Jung would subsequently adopt. This is starkly apparent in Bergson's critique of forms, which may be taken as a critique of Jung's archetypes, "avant la lettre":

The Forms, which the mind isolates and stores up in concepts, are then only snapshots of the changing reality. They are moments gathered along the course of time; and just because we have cut the thread which binds them to time, they no longer endure. They tend to withdraw into their own definition, that is to say, into the artificial reconstruction and symbolic expression which is their intellectual equivalent. They enter into eternity, if you will; but what is eternal in them is just what is unreal. (1907, 335)

Primitive energetics

Jung was not only trying to bring his energy concept into relation with contemporary biology and philosophy, he also sought to relate it to "primitive" conceptions. In 1914, he stated that his concept of *hormé* and Bergson's *élan vital* were ancient conceptions of primitive mankind, as

[106] *CW* 6, § 540, trans. mod. Jung added that it was Nietzsche who had made far greater use of the intuitive source in *Zarathustra*.
[107] June 15, 1922, Keller papers, Staatsarchiv, Winterthur.

primitives had the same conception of "a dynamic soul-substance or a psychic energy." Thus from a scientific standpoint, such a conception would be viewed as a regression into superstition. However, from the constructive standpoint, it was precisely the antiquity of the idea which "guarantees its practical usefulness," as it was one of the primordial symbolic images which had always helped the transformation of "our vital energy" (1915, 399). However, he did not rest content with this formulation of the non-scientific nature of his energy concept.

In 1917, he took up the problem of the psychogenesis of Mayer's conception of the conservation of energy. Taking his cue from Mayer's statements that his initial conception of the idea was not logically deduced, but arrived at in a state of inspiration, Jung claimed that *"the idea of energy and of its conservation must be a primordial image that lay dormant in the absolute unconscious."*[108] If these concepts were indeed primordial images, it should be possible to show their emergence in other epochs. He claimed that this indeed was the case, and that *"Primitive religions, in the most dissimilar regions of the earth, are founded upon this image"* (*ibid.*). He approvingly cited Arthur Lovejoy's conception of "primitive energetics."

Lovejoy had put this forward in 1906. Lovejoy criticized the concept of animism, claiming that "primitive philosophy" contained a more important and more pervasive element: "that there is in nature a diffused and inter-connected impersonal energy or vital force, some *quantum* of which is possessed by all or most things or persons; that the amount of this energy is more or less fixed or limited" (1906, 360). He argued that striking events were attributed to this energy, that it was possessed by persons and things in different degrees, that it could be transferred, controlled and regulated by various means, and that the aim of numerous rites lay in its transformation. This energy conception was "the most nearly ubiquitous, most all-pervasive and most influential of the notions characteristic of early man's thinking" (361). He then marshalled an array of ethnological data in support of his claim. The *manitou* of the Algonkins, the *oki* of the Iroquois, the *wakonda* of the Dakotas, the *mana* of the Melanesians, the *atu* of the Polynesians, the *mulungu* of the Bantu, and the *ngai* of the Masai were all adduced as but different linguistic and cultural expressions of the same fundamental conception of primitive energetics. As the North American names were most familiar, Lovejoy proposed adopting the term *manitou* as a generic designation for this energy concept, and *manitouism* for the belief in this energy (382). While he did not include the modern notion of the conservation of energy under *manitouism* as did Jung, the extension was a natural one, as the very terms which he used to describe

---

[108] "The psychology of the unconscious processes," 1917b, 412.

primitive energetics were contemporary ones, such as quanta of energy. What Jung did was simply to provide an explanation for the "ubiquity" that Lovejoy claimed to have demonstrated, through his theory of primordial ideas. Jung's conclusion was that the revival of a primordial idea in the case of Mayer's conception of the conservation of energy was by no means an isolated incident, but simply exemplified the fact that the "greatest and best thoughts" were founded on primordial images.[109]

Jung's phylogenetic unconscious

In 1916 Jung presented a lecture to the Association for Analytical Psychology entitled "The structure of the unconscious," which was first published in a French translation in Flournoy's *Archives de Psychologie*. Here, he differentiated two layers of the unconscious. The first he called the personal unconscious, which consisted in elements acquired during one's lifetime, together with elements which could equally well be conscious (*CW* 7, §§ 444–446). Interestingly enough, the term Jung used, as it appeared in French translation, was one that Ribot had used in his *The Psychology of Sentiments* (Ribot died that same year). Jung was familiar with this work, and cited it in 1921 in *Psychological Types* (*CW* 6, § 720n). Jung noted that the continued existence of primitive conceptions had led him to differentiate a further layer of the unconscious, the impersonal unconscious or collective psyche (*CW* 7, § 449). This consisted of a collective spirit and a collective soul. While consciousness and the personal unconscious were ontogenetically developed and acquired, the collective psyche was inherited (§ 459). Here again, his differentiation also closely followed Ribot's conception of a phylogenetically inherited layer of the unconscious.

At some subsequent point, he wrote an addendum to this essay, in which he made some additional definitions. Referring now to the impersonal unconscious as the collective unconscious, he stated that its contents consisted in unconscious perceptions of real external processes, together with "the residues of phylogenetic perceptual and adaptive functions" (§ 507, trans. mod.). Its most important contents were the primordial images, which he defined here as "the unconscious collective ideas and life drives (mythical thinking and living)" (§ 520, trans. mod.).

This conception of a phylogenetic unconscious was a direct descendant of such conceptions in the organic memory theorists and psychologists such as Hering, Butler, Ribot, Forel, Laycock, and Hall.[110] It formed one of the key constitutive elements of Jung's concept of the collective

---

[109] "The psychology of the unconscious processes," 1917b, 413–414.
[110] See also Otis, 1993, 181–213.

unconscious. As such, it was a strand of his thinking which was never abandoned, despite the radical new conceptions of the notion of inheritance in biology which took place at the beginning of the twentieth century. However, there were some shifts in Jung's conception of it.

The following year, in *The Psychology of the Unconscious Processes*, Jung defined the absolute or collective unconscious as the "residue of all experiences of the world of all times, hence also an image of the world, that has been built up since aeons" (1917b, 432, trans. mod.). He added that in this image of the world, certain traits, the dominants, had been built up in the course of time.

It has been noted earlier that the concept that everything that an individual experiences is registered and capable of being revived had become widespread at the end of the nineteenth century. What Jung was proposing was a bold extension of this conception beyond the individual's memory to encompass the memory of mankind. His supposition was that nothing that mankind had ever experienced was truly lost. The residues of past experiences had left behind their traces in the collective unconscious, which was nothing other than mankind's collective inheritance. At the same time, he was at pains to differentiate his conception of inheritance from a classically Lamarckian position. In 1918 he wrote that

It should on no account be imagined that there are such things as *inherited ideas*. Of that there can be no question. There are, however, innate possibilities of ideas, *a priori* conditions for fantasy-production, which are somewhat similar to the Kantian categories.[111]

Herein lies the importance of Jung's assimilation of these ideas to Kantian categories – it presented the possibility of the way out of the problem of positing the inheritance of ideas. This distinction between the inheritance of ideas, and the inheritance of the possibility of forming ideas was close to William Preyer's concept of inheritance and Alfred Fouillée's conception of the force ideas presented earlier.

For Jung, phylogenetic inheritance did not only consist of the residues of archaic human modes of functioning, but also of the residues of functions from animal ancestry. In this, he was following Laycock and Hall. He went on to identify these residues with Semon's concept of engrams. He referred to H. Ganz's book on the unconscious in Leibniz, writing that Ganz had used Semon's engram theory as an explanation of the collective unconscious.[112] In 1918, he stated that his concept of the

---

[111] "On the unconscious," *CW* 10, § 14.

[112] Ganz's book had come out in 1917, the same year as the first edition of Jung's, also from Rascher Verlag. There is a copy of the work inscribed and dated 1919 from Ganz to Jung, bearing a dedication to Jung "in esteem and gratitude for his extensive research work in the unconscious" (German in the original).

collective unconscious "essentially coincided" with Semon's concept of the phylogenetic Mneme (1918, 135). This proximity of Jung's phylogenetic conception of the unconscious with Semon's theory of the Mneme is hardly surprising – as we have seen, they both drew directly from the same tradition of organic memory theorists. Both Semon and Jung were developing modern forms of organic memory theory.

In 1921 in *Psychological Types*, Jung identified the collective unconscious with Semon's Mneme (*CW* 6, § 624). Semon's work in turn enabled Jung to clarify his own concepts. He now redefined the primordial image as a

mnemic deposit, an engram (Semon) which has arisen through a condensation of innumerable, similar processes. It is primarily a deposit, and therefore a typical basic form of a certain ever-recurring experience of the soul . . . The primordial image, then is the psychic expression of an anatomically and physiologically determined disposition.[113]

Thus Semon's work provided Jung with an account of the formation and revivification of primordial images.

Jung's phylogenetic conception of the unconscious bore close similarities to Stanley Hall's.[114] In this regard, it is interesting that his contact with Hall occurred at the Clark conference in September 1909, just as he was about to commence on his researches into mythology and phylogeny. As a result of this convergence, Hall was impressed by Jung's *Psychology of the Unconscious Processes*. He wrote to Jung:

It is such a remarkable and condensed statement that it ought at once to be put into English. I write to ask if you would allow a former student of mine, for whose competence I can vouch, to translate it into English . . . Permit me also to express my own very deep sense of indebtedness to the above little book, which I am just finishing, and which clears up so many interesting and important points.[115]

To Smith Ely Jeliffe, Hall wrote that it "seems to me one of the most important things in the psychoanalytic field for years, whatever we may think of it."[116] Hall welcomed his recognition of the phylogenetic factor, which he saw as representing "the belated advent of evolution into the study of man's psychic nature" (1923, 414). However, he was put off by

---

[113] Jung, *Psychologischen Typen*, 1st edition, 598. In 1949, Jung revised this passage, and distanced himself from Semon. This passage now began with the phrase "From the scientific-causal standpoint." A little further down, Jung now added, "In view of such questions Semon's naturalistic and causalistic engram theory no longer suffices." *CW* 6, § 748.

[114] Indication of some early interest by Jung in Hall's phylogenetic conceptions is found in his copy of Flournoy's *Des Indes à la planète mars*, which he read in 1900, where he has underscored the reference to Hall's "A study of fears" on 243.

[115] October 29, 1917, JP.   [116] Cited by Ross, 1972, 408.

what he saw as his mysticism, which "transcended the bounds of science" (411).

Significantly, one of the terms that Jung initially used to designate his new conception of the unconscious, as we have just seen, in his 1917 *Psychology of the Unconscious Processes* was the "absolute unconscious" – the term that Carus had used. Subsequently, this was discarded in favor of the collective unconscious. Like Carus' and von Hartmann's conceptions of the unconscious, Jung's collective unconscious was a transindividual domain that subsumed the physiological, psychological, metaphysical, and theological domains under its provenance. While he argued that the notion of the collective unconscious was a non-speculative, empirical notion, it is clear that in this concept, the nineteenth century philosophies of the unconscious came to their final and most lasting expression.

From the foregoing, we have seen that transindividual or collective conceptions of the unconscious were so widespread in philosophy, physiology and psychology in the latter half of the nineteenth century, that it could be considered accidental that no one, as far as I am aware, had actually used the term "collective unconscious" before Jung. Indeed, it is ironic that a conception that was congruent with so many elements of late nineteenth century European thought – to the extent that it could almost have been regarded as commonplace – has come to be so singularly identified with Jung. His collective unconscious was collectively constituted, through drawing together the various transindividual and collective conceptions of the unconscious which had been put forward at the end of the nineteenth century. It represents the culmination, rather than the inauguration, of collective conceptions of the unconscious.

As we have just seen, in 1918, he defined the primordial images as *a priori* conditions for fantasy-production, and likened the primordial images to Kantian categories. The following year, he noted how from the high valuation of archetypes as metaphysical ideas or paradigms, they were eventually reduced by Kant to a few categories of understanding. In *Psychological Types*, he refined his understanding of the relation between ideas, images and archetypes. In his use, idea had a close connection with image. Images could be personal or impersonal. These impersonal images, distinguished by their mythological quality, were the primordial images. When these lacked this mythological character and perceptible images, he referred to them as ideas. The idea was the meaning of the primordial image. Thus ideas were originally derived from primordial images. He held that for Plato, the idea was the "primordial image of the thing." He cited Kant's statements that the idea was the "primordial image [Urbild] of the use of reason," and a "rational concept whose object is not to be found in experience." These statements were used to support his view of the priority of the primordial image. The term "Urbild" was used on a number of occasions by Kant (in translations of Kant, it is generally rendered as archetype).

In a section of his *Critique of Pure Reason* entitled "On Ideas as Such," Kant discussed Plato's concept of ideas at length, noting that "For Plato ideas are archetypes [Urbilder] of things themselves, and not merely keys to possible experiences, as are the categories" (1787, B370). It is likely that this section was suggestive for Jung's linkage of Plato's "idea" with Kant's categories, and his assimilation of both to his primordial images.

The linkage and assimilation of the primordial image to Kant's categories served several functions. First, it gave the theory of the former a philosophical lineage, and hence legitimacy. Second, through this assimilation, the primordial image took on some of what Jung took to be the attributes of Kant's categories. Jung argued that epistemological criticism (ie., Kant) had shown that the mind was not a *tabula rasa*, as "certain categories of thinking are given *a priori*; they are antecedent to all experience and appear in the first act of thought, of which they are its preformed determinants" (*CW* 6, § 512). What Jung was proposing was a vast extension of the range of categories, claiming that "what Kant demonstrated in respect of logical thinking is true of the whole range of the psyche" (*ibid.*). While the concrete contents were lacking, potential contents were given *a priori* "by the inherited and preformed functional disposition. This is simply a product of the brain's functioning throughout the whole ancestral line, a deposit of phylogenetic experiences and attempts at adaptation" (*ibid.*). In this formulation, Jung's primordial image represented the marriage of Kantian categories with organic memory theory. If Semon's engram theory was used to show how primordial images were built up through a neo-Lamarckian process of the repeated experiences of ancestors, the linkage with Kant's categories showed how they functioned, as "*a priori* conditions for fantasy-production" (*ibid.*). It was in this assimilative and syncretic manner that Jung's theory of archetypes was built up.[117]

However, as a result of this, the concept was an unstable compound. We see this in the above passage. For Kant, the *a priori* categories, as what made experience of the world possible, were not and could not be derived from experience. On the other hand, Semon's engrams, which were built up through repeated experiences, were not innate categories.

In addition to the categories, Kant's notion of the noumenon as a negative borderline concept was important for Jung. On April 8, 1932, Jung wrote in a letter to August Vetter that

---

[117] Further aspects of this syncretistic development are mapped in the following section.

In a certain sense I could say of the collective unconscious exactly what Kant said of the *Ding an Sich* – that it is merely a negative borderline concept, which cannot however prevent us from framing . . . hypotheses about its possible nature as though it were an object of experience. (*Letters* 1, 91)

In 1935, he argued that his concept of the Self, as representing the totality of consciousness and the unconscious, was a borderline concept, similar to Kant's thing in itself.[118] A few years later, he noted that Western psychology regarded the unconscious as a noumenon, a negative borderline concept, as Kant put it.[119] Finally, in 1946, he distinguished between the "archetype in itself," which was irrepresentable, and its representations.[120] Thus key terms in Jung's lexicon: the unconscious, the collective unconscious, the Self, and finally the archetype are said to be negative borderline concepts, like Kant's noumenon. In terms of Kant's definitions, such descriptions would be illegitimate. There are two ways one can view Jung's use of Kant in this context: as flagrant misreadings or as deliberate transformations. In this regard, Jung once informed Michael Fordham that he often framed his thoughts by searching for authors who had said something which he considered close enough to what he wanted to say, and then cited them, instead of making a point directly.[121] This would suggest the second possibility. References to Kant thus served to lend legitimacy to his concepts.

In subsequent years, Jung continued to reflect on the issue of the phylogenetic layer of the unconscious. In 1924, in his lectures in London on analytical psychology and education, he noted that the inherited brain was the product of ancestral life. It consisted in "psychic activities which were repeated innumerable times in the life of our ancestors. Conversely, it is at the same time the ever-existing *a priori* type and the author of the corresponding activity" (*CW* 17, § 207). In this passage, two different conceptions of the contents of the collective unconscious come together. On the one hand, the contents are the results of repeated experiences. As such, they are historical products. In this sense, the collective unconscious represents the immanence of human history in the soul. On the other hand, the contents are said to be *a priori* types, and the authors

---

[118] *Psychology and Alchemy, CW* 12, § 247.
[119] "On the 'Tibetan Book of the Great Liberation'," *CW* 12, § 819.
[120] "Theoretical reflections on the essence of the psychical," *CW* 8, § 417.
[121] Personal communication. On Jung's reading of Kant, see de Voogd, "Fantasy versus fiction: Jung's Kantianism appraised" 1984, and Bishop, 2000. These authors have taken Jung to task over the errors in his reading of Kant. A number of their points accurately draw out differences between Kant's work and Jung's understanding of him. However, one question which is insufficiently addressed is the extent to which the "errors" were actually intentional assimilations.

of the activities in question. Here, the contents of the unconscious constitute timeless structural forms or *a priori* categories. Faced with this conundrum, Jung states in the next sentence, "Far be it for me to decide which came first, the hen or the egg" (*ibid.*).

On other occasions, however, Jung was less reticent about speculating on the problem of the chicken and the egg. In 1927, in a paper talk entitled "The structure of the soul," originally part of a presentation before Keyserling's School of Wisdom in Darmstadt, he argued that the psychological conditions of the environment left mythical traces behind them. Dangerous situations aroused affect-laden fantasies. The repetition of such fantasies gave rise to archetypes (*CW* § 334). The collective unconscious was "the deposit of all human experience right back to its remotest beginnings" (§ 339). This deposit was not inert, but formed a "living system of reactions and aptitudes that determine the individual's life in invisible ways" (*ibid.*). The collective unconscious contained the whole mental or spiritual heritage of mankind's evolution, which was "born anew in the brain structure of every individual" (§ 342). Thus the collective unconscious represented the eternal return of history in the soul. In a similar vein, in his seminars on Nietzsche's *Zarathustra* in 1934, he defined archetypes as images that represented "typical situations of great and vital importance, which have repeated themselves in the course of history innumerable times" (ed. Jarrett, 1988, 21). Consequently, the archetypes were originally real situations. In his lectures at the Institute of Medical Psychology in London in 1935, he drew an analogy between the development of the mind and that of the body:

Our mind has its history just as our body has its history . . . Our unconscious mind, like our body, is a storehouse of relics and memories of the past . . . it carries with it the traces of that history, exactly like the body, and if you grope down into the basic structure of the mind you naturally find traces of the archaic mind. (*CW* 18, § 84)

If one attempts to reconcile these statements, it would appear that the archetypes, as timeless structures, were themselves built up through history. How this process occurs was never specified.

On the therapeutic significance of this perspective, Jung is reported to have said in an interview in 1935 that when dealing with someone mentally unbalanced,

I look for the ancient man in him. I try to trace the strata of the human mind from its earliest beginnings, just as a geologist might study the stratification of the earth. The fear of ancient man crouching at the ford is in our unconscious mind, as well as all other fears and speculations born of man's experience through the ages.[122]

---

[122] "Man's immortal mind," *The Observer*, October 6, 1935.

The task of the psychotherapist lay in finding the ancient in the modern and reconciling the two. Theories of phylogenetic, ancestral, or organic memory, long discarded by biology in the early decades of the twentieth century, were preserved and institutionalized in psychotherapy.

According to his critics, Jung had failed to provide sufficiently convincing proof for his theories. In 1927, he remarked that up till then, he had not yet given any proof that satisfied all the necessary conditions for the existence of the supra-individual soul, or collective unconscious. He then gave as an example the episode of the patient who saw the solar phallus which he had cited in 1911 in *Transformations and Symbols of the Libido*. Much greater significance was now given to this example. He noted that the patient was an ordinary clerk and that he personally made this observation in 1906, and came across Albrecht Dieterich's *A Mithras Liturgy* in 1910. This ruled out the possibility of cryptomnesia or telepathy, and hence provided evidence for the collective unconscious. He also indicated the existence of analogous conceptions in classical and medieval philosophy, and referred to a classical painting which depicted the fructification of Mary with a tube descending from Heaven with a dove, representing the Holy Ghost, often conceived as a wind, flying down. The editors added that Jung subsequently learnt that the 1910 edition was the second edition, and that the original had actually been published in 1903. The patient had been committed prior to 1903.[123] This clerk was the same patient whom Honegger presented at the Nuremberg conference in 1910 and that Jung and Honegger had discussed with Adolf Meyer. Nine years later, Jung cited the case again, not to prove that the vision was an archetype, but to show his method of procedure.[124] As Flournoy had demonstrated, it is one thing to show the possibility of cryptomnesia. But it is considerably harder, if not impossible, to demonstrate its impossibility. One may conjecture that Jung's use of this as an example was due to its striking figurative elements. It presented him with an ideal type.

In 1959, when asked by John Freeman whether there was any particular case which was the turning point in his thought, Jung replied that there were many. He then cited his investigations with Negroes at St. Elizabeth's hospital in Washington, and his encounter with this patient.[125]

Following this interview, a controversy ensued in the pages of *The Listener*. Robert Hetherington pointed to the fact that in *Transformations and Symbols of the Libido*, Jung had attributed the observation to Honegger, and not to himself, and claimed there were inconsistences between Jung's account of the vision in this text and in the broadcast (such as whether

---

[123] "The structure of the soul," *CW* 8, §§ 319–321.
[124] "The concept of the collective unconscious," *CW* 9, 1, § 110.
[125] Freeman, 1959, 434. On his investigations at St. Elizabeth's, see below, 311–313.

the phallus was flaccid or erect). He concluded that Jung had falsified the "cornerstone of his hypothesis" and that he personally preferred his religion to stand "without the support of solar genitalia" (1959, 834).[126] This was replied to by Jung's translator, Richard Hull, who took issue with the alleged discrepancies. He suggested that the attribution to Honegger might have been an error, or that Honegger may have made use of Jung's observation in his work, and that the phallus was consistently erect (1959, 1041). E. A. Bennet entered into a correspondence with Jung about this issue. He drafted a letter to *The Listener*, which he sent to Jung for approval. Aniela Jaffé informed Bennet that Jung had read it and that it was correct.[127] In his reply, Bennet wrote:

> Dr. Honegger, then a very young doctor and a pupil of Jung's, was told the incident by Jung who suggested, out of kindness, that he might investigate the matter further and publish a paper on the subject. Jung passed on to Honegger his own observations. Unfortunately Dr. Honegger fell ill and died soon after and the paper was never completed. (1960, 133)

In 1970, Henri Ellenberger noted that the symbol of the phallic sun had been noted by Friedrich Creuzier in 1841, and that Dietrich had stated that a similar conception was popular in many countries (1970, 743). In 1977, C. A. Meier wrote: "I knew the patient personally and have his casebook, which is over 200 pages long, but so far I have never succeeded in finding out the function of the solar phallus in his hallucination. During my time he no longer remembered it" (1977, 78).

Instinct and the unconscious

We return to the issue of how Jung developed his conception of instincts and related it to his new conception of the unconscious. As we have seen, in *Transformations and Symbols of the Libido*, Jung critiqued Freud's concept of the sexual libido, and replaced it with a more general concept of psychic energy. The latter, in turn, was not tied to any particular drive, and Jung recognized the existence of the following drives and instincts: propagation drive [Propagationstrieb], artistic drive [Kunsttrieb], instinct for the preservation of the species [Instinkt der Arterhaltung], instinct for self-preservation [Instinkt der Selbsterhaltung], drive of nutrition [Ernährungstrieb], and the sexual drive. Thereafter in the text, the question of instinct took a subordinate role to that of the libido. He interpreted an encyclopedic panoply of myths as symbols of the libido. This left open the question of how instincts were to be understood, and how

---

[126] Robert Hetherington, letter to *The Listener*, November 12, 1959, 834.
[127] Jaffé to Bennet, January 6, 1960, JP.

they were related, if at all, to the primordial images. Around this time, he commenced work on a paper originally entitled "The conception of the libido." It wasn't until 1928 it was completed. In their translators' note Cary and Peter Baynes noted that Jung had laid aside the question of the libido due to the "greater importance" of the type problem.[128] It is also likely that one reason why he left the working out of the libido conception to one side was the fact that clarification was required concerning his conception of the instincts.

In 1919, he took part in a symposium on "Instinct and the Unconscious," jointly organized by the British Psychological Society, the Aristotelian Society and the *Mind* Association. Leading philosophers, psychologists and neurologists participated, including William Brown, Henry Head, G. E. Moore, Bertrand Russell, F. C. S. Schiller, and A. N. Whitehead.[129] The other participants in Jung's session were W. H. R. Rivers, C. S. Myers, Charles Drever, Graham Wallas, and William McDougall.

Jung's contribution contained his first use of the term "archetype," and it remained for many years his most extended treatment of the topic of instinct. Furthermore, it set out a series of issues which he would often return to over the next thirty years.

The symposium commenced with a contribution from Rivers. Borrowing from physiology and his work with Henry Head, he argued that instinctive reactions were of the "all or none" type.[130] The early forms of this experience were incompatible with the more gradated forms which developed later, and were consequently suppressed or dissociated. These reactions made up the unconscious.

Jung commenced his paper by noting that it was impossible to rely fully on Rivers' definition of instincts in terms of the "all or none reaction," as this did not admit of any gradations of intensity. In everyday language, "instinctive" was used to designate actions whose motive and aim we were not wholly conscious of. Whereas conscious acts were characterized by an awareness of motives, this was not the case with instinctive acts. Consequently, instinctive activity belonged to the unconscious processes. He defined it as actions which were characterized by uniformity and regularity, and were inherited and unconscious. This led him to specify his conception of the unconscious, as it was precisely instinctive processes which required an "enlarged conception of the unconscious" (*CW* 8, § 270, trans. mod.). Whereas the personal unconscious consisted

---

[128] "Translators' foreword," Jung 1928b, ix.

[129] *Proceedings of the Aristotelian Society*, 1919, 296–297.

[130] In a postscript added after the paper had been submitted to the other participants, Rivers qualified his position, and claimed that the "all or none" principle only designated one class of instincts (6–7.)

of the acquisitions of an individual life, there was another stratum which contained the inherited and non-acquired characteristics, such as the instincts. As well as the instincts, this stratum also contained "the *archetypes* of perception and apprehension." These were the "*a priori* determining constituents of all psychic processes" (*ibid.*, trans. mod.). Archetypes acted in an analogous way to instincts. Just as instincts compelled man to a specifically human conduct of life, archetypes compelled man's intuition and apprehension into specifically human ways. Thus the collective unconscious consisted of instincts on the one hand, and the archetypes of apprehension on the other. Agreeing with James that there existed a plurality of instincts, Jung maintained that human actions were influenced by instinct to a far larger extent than was commonly believed.

Just as there was a question as to how many instincts there were, the same question applied to the archetypes of apprehension. This led him into a short excursus on the history of philosophy. From Plato's high valuation of the archetypes in his theory of forms, which was maintained through to medieval philosophy, the archetypes had been reduced by Kant to a few categories. From being overvalued as metaphysical ideas, they had come to be undervalued as logical categories. The primordial image was frequently found in the mythologies of the primitives, in the great religions, and even in the exact sciences, where they formed the basis of concepts such as ether, energy, and the atom.

Jung defined instincts in terms of uniformity and regularity, and he defined the archetypes of apprehension in the same way. Any uniform and regularly occurring way of apprehension was an archetype. He concluded that it was not possible to decide whether apprehension or the impulsion to action came first. He suggested that they both belonged to the same activity, which, unable to be conceived as one, were viewed as two distinct processes.

Several critical features emerge from this paper. First, it indicates the manner in which the concept of the unconscious – and Jung's collective unconscious – was partially derived from the problem of instinct. Just as psychologists in the middle of the nineteenth century expanded concepts of reflex action to form the concept of unconscious cerebration, so in the twentieth century, psychologists expanded concepts of instinctive action to form concepts of the unconscious. The unconscious was where instinctive activity took place. As instincts were the same in everybody, then it followed that there existed a collective unconscious. This then constituted Jung's "argument from instinct" for the existence of the collective unconscious.

The second point that emerges from this paper is the development that the theory of primordial images – now renamed archetypes of

apprehension – has undergone. Jung conceived these archetypes of apprehension as being distinct from instincts, but acting in a similar manner.
The precise relation of the two remained unclear. Another manner of
expressing this would be to say that Jung added to the primordial idea
the attributes which had been accorded to instincts.

There is also indication that Fouillée's conception of the force ideas
shaped Jung's notion of the archetype. On a couple of occasions, he used
the term (in French) interchangeably with that of the archetype. The one
occasion that he referred to Fouillée explicitly was in 1912, in a list of
authors who recognized the significance of instincts (*CW* B, § 219n). In
1929, in an abstract for a lecture presented at a congress in Zürich titled
"Outline of Modern Psychotherapeutics," he wrote:

> The therapy does not consist of a negation and depreciation of the unconscious
> contents, as in Freud's doctrine, but of an addition of the instinctive forces to the
> conscious as a reinforcement of an individual attitude through collective ideas
> ("idées-forces").[131]

Similarly, in 1956, he argued that there was no ground for assuming the
fantasies of individuals in different epochs sprang from different "*idées
forces* from ours."[132] The function of myths, he claimed, had always been
to enable a bridge between "consciousness and the effective *idées forces*
of the unconscious."[133] The implicit reference is clearly to Fouillée. One
can conjecture that the significance for Jung of Fouillée's conception of
the force ideas was that it provided a dynamic conception of ideas as
compulsions to act in certain ways. At the same time, these compulsions
or drives were not blind, but linked to representations.

The energy of the soul

Jung attached great importance to his essay on energy.[134] In his view, it
was critical to establishing the scientific status of psychology. Retrospectively, he recalled that a question which lay close to his heart was that
of the nature of the libido, and the attempt to show that it: "could be

---

[131] Jung, "Outline of modern therapeutics" (JP).
[132] *Mysterium Coniunctionis*, *CW* 14, § 736.
[133] *Ibid.*, § 751. For another reference, see the below, 327.
[134] The original manuscript of "On the conception of the libido," dating from around 1913,
consists of 29 typewritten pages. In his revision of 1927, the text approximately doubled
in length. One copy of this manuscript contains his handwritten changes and additions,
which correspond to the final version of "On the energetics of the soul" (JP). Some of
the changes between these manuscripts have been noted in the following, which assists
in gaining an approximate date for Jung's formulations. Unless otherwise noted, the
passages cited occur in "On the concept of the libido."

an approximately quantitative concept – in contrast to the misty conceptions of other psychologies, that did not have any inner connection at all (for example, the psychology of Wundt) but only accumulations of single facts."[135] Other natural sciences had a common energy concept. Consequently, he wanted to achieve the same in psychology. It was this which led to his essay on the energetics of the soul.

He commenced this noting that as the concept of libido that he had advanced in *Transformations and Symbols of the Libido* had met with misunderstandings, it would be useful to take up its fundamental conceptions. In that work he had presented his libido concept as if it were a broadening of Freud's. Following this, it has generally been taken that his concept of the libido grew out of Freud's, of which it was the revision. However, in "On the energetics of the soul," Jung presented a different account of the antecedents of his concept of libido, and of the issues that led to it.

Physical events could be viewed from the mechanistic and energic standpoint. He termed the latter finalistic, noting that he avoided the term "teleological," to avoid the misunderstanding that it implied the idea of an anticipated end or goal.[136] This notion of a directedness without a predetermined goal echoed Bergson's conception in *Creative Evolution*. Jung claimed both the mechanistic and finalistic standpoints were necessary. Raising the question whether psychic events could be viewed from the energic standpoint, he concurred with von Grot, who had argued that it was valid to posit the existence of a specifically psychic energy. As to the relation of this energy to physical energy, which opened up the mind–body problem, he stated that this could be left to one side, and that the psyche could be considered as a "relatively closed system."[137]

This raised the question of the possibility of quantitative measurement in psychology, which he answered in the affirmative: "our psyches possess what is in fact an exceedingly well-developed evaluating system, namely, the *system of psychological values*" (7, trans. mod.). He defined values as "energetic evaluations of quantity." An objective means of evaluating value-intensities was provided by the associations experiment, implicitly diverging from Wundt's position on the unquantifiable nature of psychic energy.

In Jung's initial reports of his associations experiments, while he had on occasion employed the term psychic energy, there had been little evidence of an overt concern with energetics. Here, he reinterpreted the

---

[135] MP, 229.

[136] Jung, "On the energetics of the soul," 1928, 1. In the first manuscript, "On the concept of the libido," Jung equated these two standpoints to the psychological types – the mechanistic being extraverted, and the finalistic introverted (JP).

[137] *Ibid.*, 6. This statement appears only in "On the energetics of the soul."

significance of these experiments for the measurement of psychic energy. A complex consisted of a nuclear element and secondary associations. This nuclear element was in turn made up of a component determined by experience, and a component determined by innate disposition. The nuclear element was characterized by the emotional stress, which was an affective accentuation and that "this accentuation is, energetically ex-pressed, a *value quantity*" (10, trans. mod.). The nuclear element created a complex when it had a high energetic value: "*the constellating force of the nuclear element corresponds to its value-intensity, respectively to its energy*" (11, trans. mod.). This could be quantitatively determined from the num-ber of constellations that the nuclear element affected, the frequency and intensity of the complex indicators, and the intensity of the accompany-ing affective phenomena (the latter being experimentally determined by measuring the pulse, respiration, and the psychogalvanic reflex). In each case, Jung was referring to his prior work on the associations experiment, and reformulating the results in terms of a new energic model.

He then considered the concept of psychic energy, which he noted had already been advanced by Schiller, and then by von Grot, Theodor Lipps, and William Stern. He credited Lipps with introducing a distinc-tion between psychic force and psychic energy, though he criticized Lipps' distinction between different forms of psychic energy. Jung argued that just as much as physics, psychology had the right to build up its own con-cepts, as Lipps had claimed.[138] This right enabled psychology to utilize its own energy concepts, despite the fact that there was no clear way of separating biological and psychic processes. Consequently, he noted:

we may safely conceive a psychic process as simply a life process. With this we enlarge the narrow concept of psychic energy to a broader concept of a *life-energy* [Lebens-Energie], which subsumes so-called psychic energy as a specific form . . . *The concept of a life-energy has nothing to do with a so-called life-force* [Lebenskraft], for this latter, as force, would be nothing other than a specific form of a universal energy . . . In consideration of the psychological use we propose to make of it, I have suggested that we call the hypothetically assumed life-energy, *libido*, to differentiate it in such a manner from a universal energy concept, in accordance with the biological and psychological privilege of specific concept formation. With this I will in no way forestall the bioenergists [Bioenergetiker], but only openly show them the aim in which I have employed *our* use of the term libido. For their use a "bioenergy" or a "vital energy" may be suggested.[139]

[138] Jung did not give a citation to Lipps' statement, but it occurs in *Leitfaden der Psychologie*, 62.
[139] 17, trans. mod. In "On the concept of the libido" the first sentence, "a psychic process as simply a life process," was followed by the clause "as a specific function of the brain and of the nervous system in a wider sense." In deleting this, Jung was giving greater autonomy to the psychic process. Also in "On the concept of the libido," the initial term that Jung used was "biological energy," which he revised to "life energy" (JP).

Jung's differentiation between libido as a life-energy and as a life-force may be seen as an attempt to demarcate his libido concept from what he understood to be the hallmark of vitalistic theories. Hence in the following sections, he attempted to demonstrate the manner in which his concept of libido fulfilled the requirements of the principles of the conservation of energy and entropy. These sections form a significant attempt by Jung to provide his psychology with a scientific basis. While he shared with the neovitalists such as Driesch, the rejection of the mechanistic model and the emphasis on the necessity for a finalistic perspective, he differentiated himself from them, in resisting the reduction of psychology to biology.[140] Having established the autonomy of the psyche, the question of whether life was reducible to physical and chemical terms was no longer of vital importance, as it had been for Jung at the time of his Zofingia lectures. In contrast to Driesch, in "On the energetics of the soul," he restricted his considerations to human psychology, as opposed to considering organic life as a whole. While Driesch had claimed that his principle of entelechy wasn't a form of energy, as it wasn't quantifiable, Jung claimed that his concept of psychic energy was quantifiable, if to a limited extent.[141] He argued that an energic standpoint in psychology would not be possible unless the principle of the conservation of energy was applicable. He referred to Busse's distinction between the principles of constancy and equivalence, the former stating that the sum total of energy remained constant, and the latter stating that for energy spent or consumed, a similar quantity of energy appeared elsewhere. The former principle constituted a generalized inference of the latter, and hence it was this that was of importance for psychology.

He claimed that he had demonstrated the applicability of this principle in *Transformations and Symbols of the Libido*, and that it had also been demonstrated by Freud's work on sexuality: "Nowhere better than precisely in the relation of sexuality to the whole psyche, does one see so to speak how the disappearance of a quantum of libido is followed by the appearance of a corresponding value in another form" (19, trans. mod.).

---

[140] Here I concur with Marilyn Nagy, who states that Jung "chose the alternatives favored by vitalism – an energic or final view of the psyche, a relatively closed system, and the possibility of a causal relationship between psyche and soma – for his concept of libido or psychic energy" (1991, 55). Nagy presents an informed discussion of Jung's relation to vitalism. Interesting in this regard is Richmond Wheeler's statement in 1939 that Jung "has reverted to belief in the autonomy and independence of the human spirit, a view which stultifies mechanism as adequate for the science of human life and so at least keeps the door open for vitalism in general biology" (1939, 182).

[141] In his autobiography, Driesch recalled that he met Jung in the 1930s, which he valued, as they had found that they had much in common, especially in matters of parapsychology (1951, 274).

Freud's mistake was his overvaluation of sexuality and the inevitable onesidedness of the mechanistic standpoint.[142] Through Freud's causal conception, every interpretation was led back to sexuality, and even Freud had noted the monotony of this.[143] Jung maintained that the principle of equivalence had a great practical utility which was known to anyone who had practiced "in this field": "When some conscious value, such as a transference, diminishes, or even disappears, one looks immediately for the surrogate formation, in the expectation of seeing an equivalent value spring up somewhere."[144]

When such a surrogate formation was not immediately apparent, Jung held that it was nevertheless present, but unconscious, and that careful observation would soon reveal heightened unconscious activity, such as significant dreams or symptoms. While such a principle may well be a useful practical maxim in psychotherapy, his anecdotal evidence would have been unlikely to convince a physicist as a rigorous demonstration that the putative psychic energy fulfilled the laws of the conservation of energy. Sidis' work could be said to have been based on a contrary maxim – that through psychotherapy, the patient would experience an increase in the availability of energy.

The libido possessed a further analogy with physical energy, namely a factor of extensity "which cannot pass into a new structure without the transference of parts or characteristics of the previous structure with which it was connected" (21). This had been demonstrated in *Symbols and Transformations of the Libido*. He then turned to a consideration of entropy. After a description of Carnot's principles, he stated that as the psyche could be regarded as a "relatively closed system," the principle of entropy applied, and that "the transpositions of energy also lead to an equalization of difference."[145] According to Boltzmann, this process consisted in the transition from an improbable to a probable condition. Jung argued that this was exemplified in the development of a lasting

---

[142] In a letter to Smith Ely Jeliffe on April 2, 1920, Jung had written that Freud's over-extension of the concept of sexuality had resulted in an unscientific metaphysical concept "like 'matter' in the famous philosophical materialism of 1870–1880." By contrast, he claimed that sexuality should properly be regarded as a "subdivision of the creative energy." He characterized Freud's theory as being of a "morbide [sic] character, as it shows that the psyche of its originator only can conceive of a psychology where *one* instinct prevails to such an extent that it becomes an obsession, an 'idée obsédante,' a morbid religious concept." John Burnham, 1983, 201–202.

[143] 22. In "On the conception of the libido" Jung wrote here that if one was completely consistent in the Freudian school, one had to come to the conclusion that all culture was a neurosis. Even Freud in his personal life did not share this false and "life-weary" conception, otherwise he wouldn't write (JP).

[144] 19–20. These passages occur only in "On the energetics of the soul."

[145] 27. These passages occur only in "On the energetics of the soul."

attitude: "After violent oscillations at the beginning the contradictions balance each other, and gradually a new attitude develops, the final stability of which is the greater in proportion to the magnitude of the initial differences."[146] As the psyche was only a relatively closed system, one did not observe a "complete psychological entropy." Likewise, in instances where the isolation of the psychological system was more pronounced, the entropy was correspondingly more pronounced, such as was evident in the "dulling of affect" in dementia praecox or schizophrenia.

Jung contended that this manner of speaking was only giving a precise statement of what was generally known:

This way of looking at things has long been familiar. Everybody speaks of the 'storms of youth' which yield to the 'tranquillity of old age'. We speak too of a 'strengthened opinion' after 'battling with doubts', of a 'relief from inner tension', etc. This is the arbitrary energic standpoint shared by everyone. (29)

Thus his libido concept was intended to enable the transition from the "arbitrary energic standpoint" to a precise scientific psychological energetics. While James had argued for the independence of functional psychology from structural psychology, Jung was attempting to ground the practice of psychotherapy in the latter. The question raised by his attempt to claim that the concept of the libido fulfilled the requirements of the conservation of energy and entropy is whether what was involved was anything more than an analogy, and the metaphorical transposition of the language of physics to psychology, or that to speak of "psychological entropy" was any less metaphorical than to speak of "magnetic personalities." The effect of such metaphorical transpositions was the constitution of the psyche as an autonomous self-regulating system of energy transformations, and the modeling of psychotherapy as a form of thermostat. It is unclear to what extent Jung himself was satisfied by his attempt to demonstrate that the postulates of his psychology fulfilled the requirements of the physical sciences, nor to what extent he applied this thermostatic model in psychotherapy. For the moment, it suffices to indicate that the grand analogy that principally occupied Jung for the ensuing decades was not between the modern sciences and psychology, but between psychology and alchemy, and that his attempt to establish a conformity between his psychology and the modern sciences was the precursor to his alchemical endeavor.

In the next section on "energism and dynamism" he claimed that the theory of energy had a pure and an applied side: as a pure concept, energy was, like the concept of time, *a priori*. Here he was attempting to subsume

---

[146] *Ibid.* This passage occurs only in "On the energetics of the soul."

the concept of energy within a quasi-Kantian epistemology. By contrast, the applied theory of energy dealt with forces. Through its empirical application, a concretized or illustrated content enters into the concept, which gives the appearance that a substance has been posited. His use of the term libido was justified by the fact that it was Freud who "was the first to follow out these actual, dynamic, psychological relations" (31). Other parallel conceptions were Aristotle's *hormé*, Schopenhauer's Will, and Bergson's *élan* vital. He quickly added that "From these concepts I have only taken the concreteness of description, but not the definition of the concept."[147] It was his omission of this epistemological clarification in *Transformations and Symbols of the Libido* that had led to the misunderstanding that he had constructed a vitalistic concept.

There were four movements of the libido: progression and regression, and introversion and extraversion. While progression represented an adaptation to the environment, regression led to adaptation to the soul, and demands of individuation. Progression and regression could both take introverted or extraverted forms. Transformations of the libido were accomplished by symbols, which he defined as psychological machines for transforming energy (50). Consequently, the development of individual symbol formation took a pre-eminent place in Jung's conception of psychotherapy.

He concluded this essay with a section on the "primitive libido concept," which expanded his earlier discussion of Lovejoy's primitive energetics. Now, the primitive conceptions, such as that of *mana*, were regarded as a pre-stage of Jung's psychic energy concept and the energy concept in general. This developmental account enabled him to preserve both the kinship between the primitive and modern conceptions, without regarding the latter as simply designating a reversion to the former, as he had done in 1914. At the same time, this enabled him to maintain that his concept was scientific as well as anthropologically and historically normative.[148]

Instinct, Christianity, and animals

For psychology to stand the test of history, it was not sufficient to develop a static model of psychic functioning. It was vital for psychology to be able to explain historical changes which had taken place in man's relation to the natural order. To see how Jung addressed this problem, we

---

[147] 32, trans. mod. E. A. Bennet records Jung saying to him: "Bergson's élan vital is also too specific. What is élan. It is only energy, & so, said CG, why not call it energy" (Diary, September 18, 1959, Bennet papers, ETH).

[148] 75–76. This passage occurs only in "On the energetics of the soul."

return to *Transformations and Symbols of the Libido*. In this work, he not
only presented a theoretical reformulation of instincts, but also began
to put forward a historical argument concerning modern man's alienation from instinct. In this, he drew from Nietzsche's historical account
of the relation to instinct, and in particular, on his depiction of the negative effects of Christianity. Jung claimed that the meaning of Christianity
and Mithraism lay in the "the moral mastery of animal drives" (*CW* B,
§ 124, trans. mod.). Christianity weakened the "animal state" so that a
large amount of the force of the drives could be used for social preservation and fruitfulness (§ 127). These statements introduce an important
theme in Jung's work: that of the relation between humans, animals, and
the "animal within."

It is generally held that in comparison to Freud, Jung downplayed the
significance of sexuality. This is misleading. In a lecture on psychoanalysis
in Zürich in July 1912, he argued that

The intense sexual significance is often a surprise and a shock to people that the
analysts overestimate the importance of sexuality – it is however very rare to find
a neurotic case where a sexual disturbance is not the root of the trouble. Modern
life does not consider sexuality half enough.[149]

A few months later, in his New York lectures, he presented a critique of
Freud's theory of infantile sexuality, claiming that it was adultomorphic.
Jung's critique of the Freudian theory of the role of infantile sexuality in
the etiology of neurosis, and his stress that the causes of a neurosis are
to be found in the actual present, led him to provide a different account
of the importance of adult sexuality. That same year, he argued in "New
paths in psychology" that erotic conflicts were the fundamental causes of
neurosis. Characterizing neurosis as a self-division, he argued that in a
neurosis there were two erotic tendencies in conflict, one of which was
unconscious. This had to do with the significance of the "sexual question" today, employing the title of Forel's book. In Jung's view, "the process of culture consists in a progressive mastery of the animal in man"
(*CW* 7, § 427, trans. mod.). However, this domestication process could
not take place without a rebellion on the part of the "animal nature."
This rebellion had become acute after the industrial revolution. This was
because the development of towns and cities together with progressive industrialization had removed outlets for venting affective energies. Hence
individuals in towns and cities were endowed with surplus energy. However, this pent up sexual energy comes into conflict with the "somewhat
ascetic and especially hypocritically inclined sexual morality of our time"

[149] Fanny Bowditch Katz notes, Jung's lectures on *Psychoanalysis*, July 23, 1912, CLM.

(§ 430, trans. mod.). The result of this conflict is neurosis, which represented "an unsuccessful attempt on the part of the individual to solve the general problem in his own person" (*ibid.*). Jung characterized this general problem in the following way: "The 'question' which troubles the patient is – I can't help it – the 'sexual question', or more precisely said, *the problem of present-day sexual morality*" (*ibid.*). The practice of analysis liberated the animal drives with a view to putting them to a higher use, or sublimating them. The task of analysis was that of solving modern man's alienation from the drives.

For Jung, Nietzsche had correctly recognized the general significance of the drives. In 1917 in *The Psychology of the Unconscious Processes*, posing the question of whether anyone knew what it meant to affirm the drives, Jung noted that this was what Nietzsche desired and taught. This made the 'case' of Nietzsche especially critical, as "he who thus taught saying yes to the life drive, must have his own life looked at critically, in order to discover the effects of this teaching upon him who gave the teaching" (1917b, 381, trans. mod.). Here, he was folding back Nietzsche's comments about the confessional nature of philosophy onto himself. But the manner in which he did this was in the form of a pathography. Nietzsche, as Jung saw it, lived "*beyond the drives*" in the high altitude of heroic "grandeur" (*ibid.*). To maintain this, he required careful diet, climate, and opiates. Such living eventually shattered his brain. His failure was not recognizing the "animal life drive." Nietzsche had faithfully followed the drive for self-preservation (ego-drive), which he called the will to power, and neglected the drive of the preservation of the species (sexual drive). Due recognition needed to be given to each. What Jung saw as Nietzsche's error – championing one drive to the exclusion of all others – was also the error of Freud and Adler (however, for Nietzsche, the will to power was not one drive amongst others, but underlay all the drives).[150]

For Jung, it was the rise of Christianity together with industrialization that had led to a problem with the drives, animality, and sexuality. Over the next few years, he tried to characterize these developments in more detail. In 1918, he wrote that Christianity had suppressed the animal element.[151] However, with the questioning of the absolute validity of Christian faith, this element sought to break out again. The repression of the animal meant that when it resurfaced, it did so in an uncontrolled and unregulated manner. Such outbreaks led to catastrophe, as witnessed by the war. Official Christianity, in contrast to Buddhism, had no relation to

---

[150] For a critique of Jung's analysis of Nietzsche here, see Parkes, 1999, 210–211. See also Bishop, 1995.

[151] "On the unconscious," *CW* 10, § 31.

the animal. The repression of the animal led it to becoming "more animal like." However, if individuals had a better relation to their own "animal," they would set a higher value on life. Life would become the absolute moral principle, and the individual would instinctively react against any institution that sought the destruction of life. A few years later in 1923, he expanded upon the historical effects of Christianity in his seminar at Polzeath, in Cornwall.

In the course of these seminars, he spoke on the historical effects of Ecclesiastical Christianity upon the unconscious.[152] He commenced by differentiating Ecclesiastical Christianity from the real Christianity of Christ's teachings. Ecclesiastical Christianity had a specific attitude, which led to the repression of the world of nature and the flesh, the animal, the inferior man and creative fantasy. It is his understandings of the effects of the repression of the animal which are of importance here.

In contrast to Eastern religions, he noted that it was quite curious how little appreciation there was in the gospels for animals as living beings. With few exceptions, such as St. Francis of Assisi, the animal was excluded from Christian mentality. The exclusion of the animal had the further effect of repressing the parallels between the animal and the human. However in recent times, this exclusion was breaking down. Signs of this were in the rise of societies for the care and protection of animals in the latter half of the nineteenth century, and in the development of animal psychology.

The exclusion of the animal had its effects on man, as man had a certain amount of libido for relations with nature and other living beings. The modern custom of keeping pet animals was an attempt to satisfy this need. Once this libido was repressed into the unconscious, it took on more primitive forms. An example of this was the herd instinct of crowd psychology, which was aggravated by large numbers of people living together in cities. Large crowds constellated the animal, and large organizations were like beasts in search of prey. The loss of respect for "brother animal" generates the animal in us. A relation to animals was necessary for true humanness to be possible.

At the same time, the libido for relating to animals was still present in man, and produced symbols which appeared in dreams. As a consequence of this, the appearance of animals in dreams took on a particular significance. At the same time, dreams of flying or of swimming possibly

---

[152] The following account has been pieced together from several sets of notes of these seminars which were taken by Esther Harding, Kristine Mann, Cary Baynes, W. B. Crow and other unidentified attendees.

contained "racial deposits" of the times which our animal ancestors spent in the sea.[153]

From these remarks, it emerges that Jung regarded one of the critical cultural tasks as being that of coming into a right relation with the animal. In 1928, he contended that while an animal fulfilled the laws of its life [Lebensgesetz], men could lose themselves from their roots in "animal nature."[154] As the collective unconscious contained not only the residues of human evolution, but also of animal evolution, any attempt to come to terms with the collective unconscious necessitated a coming to terms with the animal. There could be no individuation without establishing a new relation to animals. What was required was a balance of civilization and animality: "Too much of the animal distorts the civilized man, too much civilization [Kultur] makes sick animals"(§ 32). One way of coming into a correct relation to animals was through attending to the appearance of animals in dreams, and overcoming one's prejudices in regard to animals. In his seminars on the interpretation of visions in 1930, he stated:

We are prejudiced in regard to the animal. People don't understand when I tell them they should become acquainted with their animals or assimilate their animals. They think the animal is always jumping over walls and raising hell all over town. Yet in nature the animal is a well-behaved citizen. It is pious, it follows the path with great regularity, it does nothing extravagant. Only man is extravagant. So if you assimilate the character of the animal you become a peculiarly law-abiding citizen, you go very slowly, and you become very reasonable in your ways, in as much as you can afford it. (1930–1934, 168)

Thus we see that Jung identified animals with drives or instincts. The animal in man would correspond to his animal nature, and animals in dreams were generally interpreted as representing the instincts. A critical task of analysis was that of "becoming animal."

Instincts and the autonomy of psychology

As we have seen, the question of instincts played a critical role in the relations between psychology and biology. In the 1920s and 1930s, Jung

---

[153] W. B. Crow noted: "Dr. Jung told me in private conversation that he thinks the collective unconscious images in animals are in great part of a similar nature to those seen in man. He has found very great similarities in the collective images of the most diverse human tribes and thinks the higher mammals have practically the same collective images. He thinks that many of them may develop into a human state and that the pig is particularly promising because of its undifferentiated dentition, although handicapped by its two-toed feet. (*Cum grano salis!*)" (1925).

[154] "On the psychology of the unconscious," 1928, *CW* 7, § 41.

presented further reflections on this subject, and attempted to bring his theory of instincts into closer relation to his other theories. In 1924, in his lectures in England on analytical psychology and education, Jung stated that whenever the discussion turned to the problem of instinct, a dreadful muddle ensued. Questions such as how many instincts, and what they actually were, remained unresolved. Consequently, he advised that one should restrict oneself to the psychological sphere, without making assumptions concerning the underlying biological processes. Collaboration between biologists and psychologists was a task for the future (*CW* 17, § 157).

In his contribution to the Harvard Tercentenary in 1936, Jung presented an extended discussion of the problem of instincts. He began by noting that as the human soul lived in an inseparable unity with the body, psychology could only be artificially separated from biological assumptions. These biological assumptions were valid not only for man, but for all living beings, and therefore had a wider reach than psychological judgments. Consequently, psychology had to recognize a far-going correspondence between its facts and biological givens, while rightfully asserting its autonomy. In this regard, the problem of instincts formed a critical connection between psychology and biology. If we accepted that psychic functions were a concomitant of a centralized nervous system, we would have to doubt that instincts originally had a psychical nature. Instincts acquired this through a process of "psychification."[155] While it is not clear how this process took place, its significance in Jung's argument is apparent. The process of psychification indicated how instincts became psychological factors determining human behavior. It led to the instincts losing their compulsiveness. For example, while the physical state of hunger might be unequivocal, its psychic consequences were variable. Seen in relation to his earlier discussion, it was through psychification that instincts lost their "all or none" character.

From the psychological standpoint there were five main groups of instinctive factors: hunger, sexuality, activity, reflection, and creativity.[156] Jung was unsure whether creativity was a drive, and suggested that it be regarded as a psychic factor of a drive-like nature. Jung made only one reference to the archetypes in this paper, describing them as "psychic forms, which, like instincts are common to all mankind" (*CW* 8, § 254). Thus while archetypes shared their commonality with instincts, he did not draw any direct connection between them here.

---

[155] "Psychological factors determining human behavior," *CW* 8, § 234.
[156] Fichte had posited the existence of a "drive to reflection" in his *Wissenschaftslehre*. Cited by Parkes, 1994, 265.

In other contexts, however, he came to increasingly identify instincts with archetypes. In 1936 in a paper on "The concept of the collective unconscious" he noted that as the archetypes formed such close analogies to the instincts, there were grounds for asserting that "the archetypes are the unconscious portrayals of the instincts themselves; in other words: they represent the *fundamental patterns of instinctual behaviour*" (*CW* 9, 1, § 91, trans. mod.). Consequently, he claimed the hypothesis of the collective unconscious was just as "daring" as the assumption that there were instincts. As it was generally agreed that human actions were highly determined by instincts, it was straightforward to assume that imagination, perception, and thinking were shaped by innate universal factors. The implication was that the concept of the collective unconscious simply extended the range of instinctive activity. On the one hand, we have seen that Jung posited a limited number of instincts, such as in his 1936 presentation at Harvard. On the other hand, through identifying archetype and instinct, the number of instincts had become virtually limitless.

It was precisely at this time that the assumption of instinct being a prime motivating factor was no longer widely held in psychology. The lack of consensus concerning the nature and number of instincts was one of the criticisms that was directed to such theorists. Other charges which were made were that explaining a response by appealing to a corresponding instinct fell into the same fallacy as faculty psychology. For the behaviorists, what psychologists had been calling instincts were really conditioned responses which had been acquired, and hence were not innate. Furthermore, with the increasing hegemony of experimentation, speculation concerning instincts was considered to be idle, as it did not lend itself to experimentation. In the psychology of personality, the language of instincts became increasingly replaced with conceptions of needs, motives, and drives.[157] "Instinct, the noun, is a word to be avoided," wrote the American psychologist Henry Murray (who was a pupil of Jung) in 1938, and by this time in psychology, it increasingly was (Murray et al., 1938, 74).

In 1937, the American social psychologist Gordon Allport launched a critique of instinct theories, arguing that the purposes of different people were too diverse to be traced to a few primal motives shared by the species (1937, 113). In this regard, psychoanalysts and instinct psychologies such as McDougall's shared the common fallacy of reducing every motive to a limited set of basic and supposedly universal factors. Allport argued that it would be more parsimonious to explain behavior through

---

[157] As Danziger notes, this had no connection with the earlier term in German biology, psychology, and philosophy (1997, 132).

the environmental and culture factors. Hence "Instincts evaporate. They would turn out to be nothing more than constellations of emotion, habit and foresight, better called *sentiments* or *interests*, and regarded as acquired rather than innate" (*ibid.*). For Allport, adult motives were infinitely varied. While they grew from antecedent systems, they were functionally independent of them. He named this thesis the "functional autonomy of motives."[158]

The avoidance of the term instinct in psychology, and in social psychology in particular, also signaled its disciplinary separation from biology, and the increasing assurance with which psychologists felt free to nominate their own constructs without directly aligning them with biology. Conceptions such as Allport's of the functional autonomy of motives could also be read as designating the functional autonomy of psychology. In other words, wherever it took its concepts from, it felt free to proceed with them in its own way. While discussion of instinct increasingly disappeared from psychology, it reappeared, however, in biology.

Archetypes in animals

Whilst Jung's conception of archetypes was generally dismissed in psychology, there was some interest in it on the part of biologists. In 1937, the German zoologist Friedrich Alverdes published a paper entitled "The effectiveness of archetypes in the instinctive actions of animals." He argued that most zoologists regarded biology and psychology as separate disciplines. However, if biology had no place for the psychical, it remained a torso. This was because each human and animal organism was an integrated whole, with a psychical and a bodily-physiological pole. In human and animal activities, the whole organism was involved. The aim of Alverdes' article was to show how one could make Jung's researches fruitful for animal psychology, as Jung's work showed the instincts of animals in a new light.

Alverdes argued that men and animals possessed "inborn readiness for specific forms of behaviour" which Jung termed archetypes (1937, 227). In addition to the archetypes studied by Jung, Alverdes claimed that further archetypes existed, including those of the family, parents, husband, children, society, group, fellow man, comrade and friend, enemy, food, prey, property, home, meaningfulness, and the holy. According to

---

[158] Allport dismissed Jung's collective unconscious along with Myers' subliminal self; stating that they were out of fashion with psychologists because "by assuming innate ideas and the existence of an over-individual mind, they deny the basic tenets of empiricism," 1937, 536.

Alverdes, Jung held that human actions were projections and symbols of inner psychic states. Alverdes held that the patterns of behavior in animals could be viewed in the same manner, and that they also possessed archetypes. The archetypes that Alverdes attributed to animals were mainly from his expanded list. An example was the nest-building of spiders. This formed the expression and symbol of an inner psychophysiological state of the spider. He argued that the archetype of the net was in the collective unconscious of the spider. If an insect got caught in the net, another archetype was induced to specific activity. He concluded that Jung's archetypes could form the basis for a synthesis of human and animal psychology.[159]

Renewed impetus to the study of instinct in psychology came from ethnology, through the work of Konrad Lorenz (1903–1989) and Niko Tinbergen (1907–1988). Lorenz, an Austrian zoologist, is seen as one of the founders of modern ethnology. He maintained that psychological discussions of instinct in the 1920s and 1930s had come to an impasse. Lorenz and Tinbergen studied the patterns of behavior of animal species, and did critical work in clarifying the concept and reintroducing the study of instinct. In no small measure, this was due to the manner in which they devised means of observing and experimenting with the learning behavior of animals. They argued the regularity of patterns of behavior could not be explained through learning alone, but was due to the existence of innate releasing mechanisms, which were brought into play through the encounter with an appropriate environmental stimulus.

On several occasions, Lorenz discussed the relation of his concept of instinct with Jung's archetype. Significantly, this occurred when he was in the process of developing the notion of innate release mechanisms. In 1939, Lorenz argued that only the simple and distinctive stimuli of the releasers were matched by innate sensory correlates. This ran counter to Jung's theory of archetypes, which, he noted, had been used by Alverdes to explain animal behavior. According to this theory, the innate behavior patterns were brought about by "innate gestalt images" (1939, 29). A few years later, he expanded upon this divergence. In Lorenz's view, Jung

[159] Alverdes sent Jung a copy of his paper. Jung thanked him for sending him his "interesting article" (Jung to Alverdes, September 16, 1937, JP). Jung's secretary sent Alverdes Jung's paper "Factors determining human behaviour" and a talk on the collective unconscious. Alverdes replied that he had received "valuable scientific stimulation" from this paper, as from Jung's earlier publications. However, he took issue with Jung's statements against the "new Germany," which he could not understand. (Alverdes to Jung December 8, 1937, JP). Jung wrote to Henry Murray: "I notice that you could establish the validity of my idea of archetypal pattern. May I call your attention to the German zoologist Alverdes, who came to the same conclusions on quite different lines" (November 21, 1938, Murray Papers, Houghton Library, Harvard).

had put forward the view that "organisms are born into the world with a species-specific heritage of images of specific, biologically significant objects, such as parents, sexual partners, prey, and so on" (1948/1996, 274). Lorenz's list indicates that he may have had Alverdes' paper particularly in mind. According to Lorenz, Jung regarded these archetypes as remembered images of some kind which had become differentiated through evolutionary history, though not in a naive Lamarckian sense. When an organism appropriately responded to a situation or object without prior experience, this represented "a response to a 'species-specific remembered image' that is definitely to be regarded as a holistic gestalt" (274). This view corresponded to what Lorenz himself had held in his earlier work, i.e., that the innate response of organisms was based on the "'recognition' of a total image that ipso facto possesses the character of a complex quality in the form of a Gestalt" (274). However, he had been led to revise this view, after many observations of cases in which animals responded erroneously to a few stimuli in the stimulus situation. For Lorenz, Jung's theory of archetypes was "an anticipatory explanatory principle" that would not lead to further knowledge.

However, in 1973, he was questioned concerning the relation of his work to Jung by Richard Evans. Lorenz stated that he was convinced that humans possessed innate responses, and that

this innate-releasing mechanism, as we call it, combining with the human faculty of visualising – dreaming about a situation, results in phenomenal reactions which are more or less identical with Jung's concepts of archetypes. I think archetypes are innate-releasing mechanisms invested in visualisation, in fantasy, of the individual.[160]

He added that initially he strongly objected to the work of Freud and Jung, but had come to appreciate their work in old age (59). Thus it is possible that Jung's concept played a greater role in genesis of Lorenz's work than he initially acknowledged. The critical divergence lay in the fact that Lorenz's concept was more restricted, specific, and based on experimental observations.

The essence of the psychical

In 1946, Jung embarked on his final major reconceptualization of his conception of archetypes, instincts, and the unconscious in "Theoretical

---

[160] Evans, 1975, 59. In a similar vein, Marie-Louise von Franz reported that "Konrad Lorenz assures me that he accepts Jung's theory of archetypes in principle" (1975, 127).

reflections on the essence of the psychical." Taking up the issue of instincts, he commenced by noting the difficulty of defining and enumerating instincts. All that was certain was that they had a physiological and psychological aspect. Here, Janet's views of the superior and inferior parts of a function were of great use (*CW* 8, § 374). He cited Janet's statement that when a function had been used for a long time, it contained parts which were old, worked easily, and were represented by particular organs. These were the inferior parts. When a function adapted to recent and novel circumstances, this represented the superior parts. Jung added that the drive base governed the former, while the latter represented the psychic part.

The inferior part had a compulsive and automatic character. In this regard, Jung cited Rivers' definition of the "all or nothing" character of instinct. In contrast, the superior part had lost its compulsive character, and could be subjected to the will. From this perspective, the psychical appears to be "an emancipation of function from the instinctual form and its compulsiveness" (§ 377, trans. mod.). Ultimately, this emancipation reached a point where the function ceased to be orientated by the drive, and took on a "so-called spiritual form."

The final section of Jung's essay was titled, "Pattern of Behaviour and Archetype." He was attempting to relate his archetype theory to the work of the new ethnologists. Referring to Freud's positing of archaic vestiges in the psyche, and his own archetype theory, he noted that the drive and the archaic mode "coincided" in the biological concept of "pattern of behavior." He defined each drive as containing the pattern of its situation within it. The drive fulfilled an image: "The instinct of the leaf-cutting ant fulfills the image of ant, tree, leaf, cutting, transport, and the little ant-garden fungi" (§ 398). He referred here to Lloyd Morgan's *Habit and Instinct*. The behavior of animals and man was determined by inborn patterns. The problem of determining these patterns in humans lay in the fact that the only means of apprehending them was through consciousness, which "is not only a reshaping but also the reshaper of the original image of the drive" (§ 399, trans. mod.). However, he claimed to have succeeded in finding an indirect way to approach the images of the drives, through the method he called active imagination. The material brought to light by active imagination could be arranged into types and motifs, which coincided with mythology. He described how such experiences led him to conclude that "there are certain *collectively present unconscious conditions* which act as regulators and stimulators of creative fantasy-activity" (§ 403, trans. mod.). These regulators, or archetypes, acted so much like instincts that he could find no argument against regarding them as identical.

He then put forward his revised model of the archetype and its relation to the drive, employing the image of a spectrum to illustrate it: "the dynamism of the drive is lodged as it were in the infra-red part of the spectrum, the image of the drive lies in the ultra-violet part" (§ 414, trans. mod.). Drives had two aspects: one the one hand they were experienced as physiological dynamisms, and on the other, they entered consciousness as images. While psychologists such as James, Ribot, and McDougall linked instinct with affects, Jung linked them with images.

He also differentiated between the archetypic representations, and the archetype itself, which was irrepresentable. The archetype itself was not capable of becoming conscious, and hence Jung designated it as psychoid. In his writings, he had treated archetypic phenomena as psychical. The conception of the psychoid added a further differentiation to this. At the "infra-red" end of the spectrum, the archetype passed over into physical and chemical conditions, and hence could not be regarded as purely psychical. The term, "the psychoid," as we have seen, was an important one for Driesch. Subsequently, it had been taken up by Eugen Bleuler. Bleuler took his point of departure from Semon's theory of engrams rather than from Driesch, and he criticised Driesch's concept as being too philosophical.[161] For Bleuler, the psychoid lay between matter and psyche, and his system attempted to establish the continuities between "the lifeless, the living and the psychic world" (1925, 152). The psyche and the psychoid had things in common, and couldn't be strictly differentiated. The former was an "independently developed branch of the primordial psychoid" (11). For Jung, Bleuler's system, which included such entities as the cortical soul and the medullary soul, was excessively organological. Thus while both he and Bleuler were attempting to indicate an intermediary term between matter and psyche, to explain how the latter could arise, the theoretical basis for his speculations was quite different.

At a therapeutic level, active imagination enabled the discovery of archetypes "without a sinking into the sphere of the instincts" (*CW* § 414, trans. mod.). Drives could not be assimilated at the red end of the spectrum. However, their images could be integrated at the other end of the spectrum. Hence analysis provided one with a means of transforming instincts, and one's relation to them, through the mediation of images.

In this paper, Jung also embarked on an extensive revision of his concept of the unconscious. The discovery of the unconscious, he claimed, had as thoroughly revolutionized psychology as the discovery of radioactivity had revolutionized classical physics. In support of this, he cited James' description in *The Varieties of Religious Experience* of the

---

[161] Bleuler, 1925, 11.

significance of the positing of an extra-marginal realm of consciousness in 1886. Jung added that the discovery which James was referring to was F. W. H. Myers' positing of the subliminal consciousness.[162] Intriguingly, Myers had used the analogy of the spectrum to describe consciousness:

At the inferior, or physiological end . . . it includes much that is too archaic, too rudimentary, to be retained in the supraliminal memory . . . at the superior or psychical end, the subliminal memory includes an unknown category of impressions which the supraliminal consciousness is incapable of receiving in any direct fashion, and which it must cognize, if at all, in the shape of messages from the subliminal consciousness. (1891, 306)

He argued that the spectrum of consciousness extended "at the red end into the deeps of organic life, and at the violet end into a world of suprasensory perceptions" (1892, 483). The closeness of Myers' spectrum analogy to Jung's suggests that if Jung did not draw it directly from Myers, it forms a striking example of cryptomnesia.

For Jung, the unconscious was the unknown psychical. In this regard, it consisted of contents which, if they were to become conscious, would not differ from known psychical contents. As such, it corresponded to James' transmarginal field (*CW* 8, § 382). While we knew "next to nothing" of how the unconscious functioned, since it was conjectured to be a psychical system, it was possible that it had everything that consciousness had, "namely perception, apperception, memory, imagination, will, affectivity, feeling, reflection, judgment, etc., but all of these in subliminal form" (§ 362, trans. mod.). In support of this, Jung cited the nineteenth century British psychophysiologist George Henry Lewes, who had argued that sentience had different modes, and could be conscious, sub-conscious, or unconscious.[163]

In addition to these elements, the unconscious contained the "Freudian findings" and the psychoid level. Addressing the question as to what state psychical contents were in when they were unconscious, Jung argued that the findings of Freud and Janet indicated that psychical contents functioned in the same way in conscious and unconscious states. For Jung, this, together with other considerations raised the paradox that there was

No conscious content of which one can with certainty assume that it is totally conscious . . . so we come to the paradoxical conclusion that there *is no conscious*

---

[162] *Ibid.*, § 356. On Myers, see above, 125–127.
[163] See Lewes, 1877, 360. This is the earliest use of the term "sub-conscious" that I have located. Lewes gave the example of an absorbed thinker walking in a street being unconscious or sub-conscious of many of the sights that made up his sentient excitation, while being able to bypass obstacles, and also subsequently recall objects passed in subconscious indifference.

content which is not in some other respect unconscious. Maybe, too, there is no unconscious psychical phenomenon which is not at the same time conscious. (§ 385,
trans. mod.)

As a consequence of this, he suggested that the unconscious be conceived
as a "multiple consciousness." The support for this view came from consideration of the "consciousness-like state of unconscious contents" together with certain symbolic images, notably in alchemy (§ 388ff.). The
implications of this view were far-reaching. As a consequence, the collective unconscious was no longer completely unconscious. Rather, it was
reconceived as a collective multiple consciousness. In this reformulation
of the unconscious, Jung was aligning it far more closely with Frederic
Myers' conception of the subliminal consciousness and William James'
conception of the transmarginal field.

Pathologies of modernity

Jung's conception of archetypes and instincts had important social and
political consequences. As indicated above, he regarded the loss of connection to instinct to be a symptom of the pathology of modernity. In 1941
in a paper on "Psychotherapy in the present," he described the therapeutic effects of religion as the manner in which it preserved the parental
imagos of the individual as well as the "childhood soul of mankind in
numerous living vestiges" (*CW* 16, § 216, trans. mod.). This protected
against one of the greatest dangers, that of uprootedness. Jung was concerned with the effects of the breakdown of traditions: "the life of instinct
as the most conservative element in man always expresses itself in traditional customs. Age-old convictions and customs are deeply-rooted in
the instincts" (*ibid.*). When traditions broke down, consciousness became separated from instincts and lost its roots. These instincts, having
lost their means of expression, sank into the unconscious, causing it to
overflow into conscious contents.

Thus the collective unconscious was culturally and politically conservative. However revolutionary the conscious attitudes of an individual
were, "we have to reckon with a patriarchally or hierarchically arranged
psyche which instinctively holds onto this order or at least seeks it"
(§ 217, trans. mod.). Thus for political and social transformations to succeed, they had to recognize the intrinsic and deep-seated conservatism of
the psyche.

In 1957 in *Present and Future*, he continued these reflections. Instincts,
he claimed, were highly conservative: "just as the instinct is original
and hereditary, so its form is also primordial, which means archetypic"

(*CW* 10, § 547, trans. mod.). Human knowledge consisted in the contemporary adaptation of "our *a priori* given primordial forms of representation." These required modification, as they originally corresponded to an "archaic way of life" (§ 548).

Man's learning capacity was based on the instinct for imitation in animals. It was this capacity which estranged man from his instincts and was consequently responsible for numerous psychic disturbances. The contemporary estrangement from instincts was exemplified by the manner in which modern man was identified with his conscious knowledge of himself, which was determined by the environment. The problem with mass movements such as communism was that they were themselves symptomatic of this pathology, and lacked an adequate psychological basis.

In contemporary societies, it was the city dweller who was most estranged from instincts: "he lacks contact with growing, living, breathing nature. What a rabbit or a cow is, one only knows from the illustrated paper, the dictionary or the movies . . ."[164] The danger was that "the whole of reality will be replaced by words" (*ibid.*). Psychotherapy's task was to provide a means for modern man to overcome his alienation from nature, through refinding the guidance and regulation of the archetypes of the collective unconscious.

Biological reformulations

As we have seen, in the mid-twentieth century, psychology and biology were moving away from the late nineteenth-century concepts which formed the presuppositions and building blocks for Jung's theory of archetypes and instincts. In the biological field, this brought a particular problem. If Jung's theory was to be based on sound biology, shouldn't it be more closely related to contemporary work in biology, rather than to discarded notions? Further, if the biological underpinnings were shaky, what was the status of the psychological conceptions which rested on them? Could conceptions generated in the age of organic memory theory, when Haeckel and Lamarck were still prominent, still have any scientific status in the mid-twentieth century and beyond? Two associates of Jung addressed these questions.

Adolf Portmann was the most important biologist who was interested in and sympathetic to Jung's work. In 1949, he made a presentation before the Eranos Tagung on "The mythical in natural research." In Portmann's view, Jung's work was critically related to biology. For the collaboration between psychology and biology to be fruitful, mutual confrontation and

---

[164] "Good and evil in analytical psychology," 1959, *CW* 10, § 882, trans. mod.

clarification was required. One concept in particular that required clarification was that of the archetype. Portmann claimed that a great service of Jung's work had been to give the old idea of inherited psychic structures in man, such as Adolf Bastian's idea of elementary thoughts, a new underpinning and richness.[165] However, there was the danger that the assumption of the hereditary nature of such archetypes was too easily assumed. Portmann noted that different things were assumed under the idea of the archetype. On the one hand, they were considered to be natural inherited structures, which determined the experience of the world. On the other hand, they were considered as customs which had been taken on from early social contact in different ways, and that had been reinforced through centuries of tradition. Finally, they were conceived as historical and tradition developments which had become inherited possessions of the collective unconscious in an unknown way. For Portmann, this last view was pure Lamarckianism, and consequently, shared the fate of the latter. The future would decide which of these concepts psychologists would continue to refer to as archetypes. What was certain was that the idea of the archetype had overcome the fatal view of the mind as a *tabula rasa*. What was now required was clarification of the idea.

Portmann attempted such a clarification at his presentation at the following Eranos Tagung, "The problem of the primordial image in biological perspective." The proceedings of this conference were dedicated to Jung's seventy-fifth birthday. Portmann commenced by setting out the different notions which had been collectively referred to as the archetype. The first form derived from the crypto-Lamarckianism which was present in psychology around the turn of the century. By this, he meant the view that in the psyche of man, just as the strata of the crust of the Earth through the centuries, the experiences of numerous generations had been deposited and influenced the actions of present day men as a common collective unconscious. Semon's theory of the mneme – which Portmann considered a pure speculation – played an important role here. Another notion, which was sometimes mixed with this Lamarckian one, was of the collective unconscious as an eternal presence, the sum of all latent possibilities of the human psyche. In this formulation, the question of the origin of the archetypes was considered differently.

He then turned to the field of biology, and gave an account of recent developments of the concept of instinct, such as the work of Lorenz and Tinbergen. In his view, such biological work could be a stimulus to researching "those mysterious structures" which became known through Jung as archetypes. Following this, he then considered the research by

[165] On Bastian, see below, 272–274.

René Spitz and others concerning innate structures in infants. Spitz was a psychoanalyst and child psychologist. He demonstrated that at the age of two months, the human face formed the privileged object for the human. The infant responds to the human face by smiling. However, Spitz demonstrated that a cardboard replica of a face was sufficient to elicit the same reaction. Thus he argued that it was the configuration of eyes, forehead, and nose, which he called a "sign Gestalt," that triggered the smiling response (1965, 191). Portmann argued that this conception corresponded to Jung's archetypes. Even here though, he held that the question of conclusive proof for inborn structures was a difficult one. He argued that one should be extremely careful in psychology concerning the assumption of the heritability of developed psychic structures. A crypto-Lamarckian form of thinking, through which it was assumed that something was capable of being inherited without the slightest proof, was a great danger here. Proofs of the working of primordial images come from so late an age, that we simply could not correctly take account of all the possible influences. Consequently, he recommended leaving to one side the question of heredity in relation to researching the archetypes, and focusing instead on early development. Here, research concerning the first five years of life indicated three groups that made possible the differentiating of archetypic structures.

The first consisted of inherited structures which give rise to conceptions of forms, such as the recognition of the human face. Given the difficulty of proof of inheritance, the number of such structures would remain small. The second group consisted of shaped forms which were not inherited, such as the archetypes of the home and house. He thought that there were a large number of such shaped archetypes. The third group consisted in the "psychical workings of the secondary complexes," such as Gaston Bachelard had called "cultural complexes," or the representations which Jung had studied in his alchemical researches.[166] In these cases, the inborn layer was so general, that one wasn't really entitled to stress it anymore.

In these papers, Portmann had proposed a far-reaching overhaul of the theory of archetypes, which would have brought them into relation with current biology and child development, and opened up possibilities of interdisciplinary research. However, Jung did not like Portmann's paper. Ximena de Angulo wrote to her mother, Cary Baynes, that Jung

---

[166] In 1938 Gaston Bachelard sent Jung his book, *The Psychoanalysis of Fire*. Jung replied: "It is exactly this genre of books that we have need of, that is to say, writings on symbolic motifs, since we encounter these symbolisms in our daily work with our patients" (December 12, 1938, JP, original in French).

was building up animosity against Portmann and muttering that it was hopeless trying to explain archetypes to people who had no direct experience of the material, and that he wished scientists would sometimes ask *him* before plunging in blithely in fields they didn't know anything about.[167]

This was a critical juncture. For the theory of archetypes to find any credence in the field of biology and the natural sciences, it would have been critical to take up Portmann's recommendations. Otherwise, the concept would remain a local one, within the domain of analytical psychology, which has, indeed, been its fate.

In retrospect, Portmann gave the following reflections on the question of the biological aspects of Jung's work:

I was under the strong impression that not many of the biological and physical chemical experiences of our modern time entered into his thinking . . . He had come from the first great adventure of Darwinism; he had turned, as I see it, away from the extreme forms of Darwinism to a more Lamarckian way of thinking, and this was, I think, a more or less ever-present background he never discussed . . . A discussion about a notion like "archetype" is impossible when you do not consider the new biological facts of hereditary connections with the environment, or of the instinctive life of animals, and of the instinctive residuums in man. To find out exactly what the thinking of Jung was in this respect seems to me of a very great importance, but the work has not yet been done.[168]

The foregoing may in some measure have fulfilled this task.

Portmann's attempt to reformulate the concept of the archetype to bring it into line with contemporary biology failed. One final attempt in this vein in Jung's lifetime took place a few years later. In 1957 Michael Fordham attempted to clarify the relation of the theory of archetypes to biology. As he saw it, this was necessitated by the fact that analytical psychologists unnecessarily violated biology. After giving an account of the development of modern views of inheritance, Fordham noted that Mendel's theory of genes and Weismann's theory of the continuity of the germ plasm had demonstrated that there was no inheritance of acquired characteristics. This demolished the notion that archetypes were deposits of racial experience. Fordham argued that Jung's claim that archetypes were deposits of the constantly repeated experiences of mankind was contradicted by modern biology (1957, 20). Turning to the question of the origin and the development of the archetypes, he considered the status of the biogenetic law. This had been invoked recently by Erich Neumann in

---

[167] August 26, 1950, Cary Baynes papers.
[168] Adolf Portmann interview, CLM, 5. On May 2, 1947, Jung had written to Portmann requesting clarification of some statements in Schrödinger's *What is Life?* He noted that he was "no longer at home in modern biology" (JP).

his grandly titled 1949 *The Origins and History of Consciousness* as forming the basis of psychological development in the individual and the species. Indeed, in his glowing preface to this work, Jung credited Neumann with placing "the concepts of analytical psychology . . . on a firm evolutionary basis" (*CW* 18, § 1236). Fordham pointed out how the notion of the biogenetic law had been discredited in biology. If this were the case, he claimed, it was even less valid when it came to psychology (1957, 30).

Fordham was attempting a reformulation of the theory of the archetype, dissociating it from its roots in organic memory theory, the biogenetic law, neo-Lamarckian theory, and Semon's engram theory. The following year, he took this a step further. He noted that he had omitted the concept of heredity from his definition due to the developments in biology since Jung defined the archetypes (1958, 17).

Finally, he wrote to Jung on May 30, 1958 to clarify what his views were on heredity.[169] Fordham classified theories of heredity into three categories: the widely accepted genetic theory, the rejected theory of the inheritance of acquired characteristics, and the theory of transmission by verbal and other means. Jung's views did not seem to fit into any of these, as the first did not allow for the inheritance of experience, and the second dealt only with characteristics. He noted that Jung's biological references, with the exception of a reference to Alverdes' paper, were scanty, and consequently wondered if the sources of Jung's theory were more philosophical than biological.

Jung replied that he shared the ordinary views about heredity (June 14, 1958, *Letters* 2, 440). It was correct to say that he had set aside general biology, as far too little was known about human psychology to establish a biological basis for it. For the purposes of the psychologist, it was indifferent whether the archetypes were "handed down by tradition or migration, or by inheritance" (*ibid.*). This was because comparable biological phenomena, such as the instincts of animals, were inherited, and he saw no reason not to assume that this was also the case for the archetypes.

However, it was precisely this last question – tradition, migration or inheritance? – which was of paramount importance for biologists and anthropologists. The implication was that the inheritance of archetypes was established by analogy rather than by proof. With the exception of his own work, Fordham's reformulation made no further headway in analytical psychology than Portmann's.

[169] CMAC.

Energy and holism

Jung's energy concept did not fare better in biology and psychology than his concept of instinct. Despite his efforts to bring his concept of psychic energy into conformity with what he took to be the requirements of a scientific energy concept, outside of the circle of his followers, it did not seem to meet with much interest, even critical, with one principal exception. In 1934, William McDougall claimed that Freud and Jung were justified in postulating the existence of a "mental or psychophysical energy," just as they were correct in affirming Lamarckian inheritance (1934, 200). He justified this by putting forward a psychogenesis of notions of power and energy. While Jung claimed that his conception of psychic energy legitimately fulfilled the necessary criteria to be regarded as a scientific concept, such as the conservation of energy and entropy, McDougall challenged the status of such concepts themselves. He began with primitive conceptions, claiming that conceptions of power were far older than modern physics. Commencing with terms such as mana, McDougall argued that the attribution of powerfulness to beings was an abstraction from each man's experience of exerting power, in everyday actions (102). Hence modern concepts of power could be traced back to a psychological origin. He claimed that in talking of energy as an entity or substance, physicists were as guilty of hypostasizing as primitives with their notion of mana. This reading established the priority of psychology over physics, and hence legitimated the utilization of energy concepts in psychology. McDougall supported Jung's argument in "On the energetics of the soul" that conceptions of power could be regarded as archetypic. He went further though, claiming that the success of his own experiments on Lamarckian inheritance had substantiated Jung's claim.[170] McDougall's energy concepts, however, did not receive any more interest than Jung's.

Biology and neurology during this period saw the development of organicism and holism.[171] The organicists shared with the neovitalists such as Driesch a rejection of the reduction of biology to physics, together with a concern for wholes and teleology. They differed over the necessity

---

[170] McDougall wrote: "in the light of the positive results of my own prolonged experiment on this question [Lamarckian inheritance], I have little doubt that Dr. C. G. Jung is right in regarding our thinking of power or energy as one of the archetypal modes of thinking determined by racial experience and memory," (1934) 110. McDougall had attempted to prove the existence of the inheritance of acquired characteristics through experiments with generations of rats. Interestingly enough, despite his public disclaimers distancing himself from Lamarckianism, Jung liked these experiments of McDougall (Jung to Smith Ely Jeliffe, June 7, 1932, Burnham, 1984, 236).

[171] See Harrington, 1996.

for an additional agency. One figure who featured in these developments was Kurt Goldstein. In *The Organism*, he put forward views concerning the importance of the principle of the conservation of energy to clinical work which resemble Jung's. Goldstein claimed that "*The available energy supply is constant, within certain limits. If one particular performance requires especially great energy expenditure, some other performance suffers thereby*" (1939, 56). Consequently, he argued that "this aspect of differential energy distribution must be taken into full consideration in every symptom analysis" (59). His energy concept overlapped with Jung's. It is not clear to what extent Goldstein was familiar with Jung's concept of psychic energy; he was clearly well versed in psychoanalytic theory, putting forward a detailed critique of its main concepts, particularly the unconscious (307–355). Interestingly enough, in his presentation on psychoanalysis before the General Medical Congress for Psychotherapy in 1927, he specifically critiqued the concept of psychic energy. He stated that this concept played a great role in the psychoanalytic literature. He argued that the observation of organic illness had taught the importance of an energic view, and that a constancy in the amount of disposable force could also be observed. He claimed that this depended upon the "prevailing bodily constitution of the whole organism." Consequently, he contended that it was not useful to speak of psychic energy, because the "psychic" only existed in the abstract, and that it was always only a question of an "alteration of excitation in the excitation field of the milieu of the organism" (1927, 48–49). He did not cite Jung in this paper, though it is likely that he had him in mind.

In Zürich, similar developments were represented by the work of Constantin von Monakow. In a work published with R. Morgue in the same year as Jung's essay "On the energetics of the soul," they argued that living beings were distinct from machines in that they possessed a compensatory, creative principle of auto-regulation, which they termed *hormé*.[172] They argued that Freud and most of his disciples had not fully broken away from the intellectualism of academic psychology. Indicative of this was the anthropomorphic character of their concepts, including that of libido. The two figures they singled out for praise were Hughlings Jackson and Bergson. The latter, they claimed, had put forward three notions that were critical for biology: the importance of time for living beings, the duality of instinct and intelligence, and the notion of creative evolution (4). They defined *hormé* as:

---

[172] Von Monakow and Morgue, 1928, x. They cited Jung on two occasions in reference to his concept of psychological types and his association studies, 91 and 257.

the propulsive tendency of the living being, with all its potentialities acquired by heredity, towards the future . . . One must understand under the expression *hormé*, the tendency towards a creative adaptation of life in all its forms to its conditions of existence tending to assure the maximum of *security* to the individual, not only for the present moment, but for the most distant future. (33)

They did not discuss Jung's energy concept, and it is not clear whether they realised that he had used the same term.

In psychology during this period, the attempt to critique the "machine theory" and reintroduce a concern for wholes was represented by the Gestalt psychologists (see Ash, 1995). In doing so, they argued for the recognition and significance of "dynamic factors." Köhler's discussion of the proximity and distance of these to vitalism carries a resemblance to Jung's:

the concepts to which we have referred . . . are not in the least related to Vitalistic notions. On the contrary, in the future our dynamic concepts may serve to deal with objections which Vitalism has raised against the scientific interpretation of life. If this happens, the machine theories of life will lose ground – after all, Vitalistic arguments against these theories have sometimes been fairly convincing. But Vitalism will not profit – for from its objections against the machine theory it has wrongly concluded that the main problems of biology cannot be served in terms of natural science. (1947, 134–135)

The paucity of citations to similar conceptions in Jung in the work of organicist biologists, neurologists, and Gestalt psychologists is an index of the discredit that his work had fallen into in academic circles by the 1920s, from which it did not recover.

In this section, we have seen the manner in which Jung's conceptions of the archetypes, libido, and the collective unconscious represented a confluence and synthesis of a number of philosophical, physiological, biological, and psychological conceptions at the end of the nineteenth century. Since then, the increasing autonomy and fragmentation of psychology together with the diversification and specialization of sciences of the body has unraveled even the possibility of such a synthesis.

4   The ancient in the modern

The birth of the human sciences

The last quarter of the nineteenth century and the first quarter of the twentieth century saw the emergence of the modern disciplines of anthropology, sociology, and social psychology, as well as the short-lived disciplines of crowd psychology and ethnopsychology (*Völkerpsychologie*). Through studying prehistoric, primitive, or modern societies, these disciplines attempted to surpass the limitations of individual psychology. Each sought to establish the pre-eminent science of the social. Yet the very attempt at disciplinary differentiation and hegemony was bound up with numerous intermeshings and mutual borrowings. This clustering provides one of the matrices for the emergence of Jung's complex psychology, which attempted to incorporate the subject matter of these disciplines under its purview, while differentiating itself from them. This section commences by sketching the development of these disciplines. It then reconstructs how Jung drew upon them to form a collective transindividual psychology, and how this in turn was to enable the reconciliation of the demands of the individual and society, and, through reconciling the ancient and the modern within the individual, resolve the malaise of contemporary Western societies. It concludes by showing the reception of this project.

We first turn to anthropology. On the left-hand side of Jung's library, by the window, may be found the hefty volumes of the *Annual Report of the Bureau of Ethnology to the Secretary of the Smithsonian Institution* from 1879 to 1919. These dates demarcate a critical period in the founding of modern anthropology and modern psychology.[1] Their presence may be taken as indicative of the significance that Jung accorded to anthropology. The disciplinary separation of anthropology and psychology in the twentieth century obscures the extent of their intermingling at the end

---

[1] On Jung's acquisition of this set, see below, 323.

of the nineteenth century and the beginning of the twentieth. The very identity of these terms was by no means fixed, and the term anthropology also covered what would today be classed as psychology, and vice versa. What anthropology meant for Jung may be succinctly stated. Psychology needed anthropology if it was to attain the cross-cultural and transhistorical universality deemed necessary for a science; and anthropology in turn needed psychology in order to be based on a true understanding of human nature. Each was to be mutually dependent. This double necessity framed his encounter with anthropology, and indicates that what was at stake was nothing less than the possibility of both psychology and anthropology. It was from this mutual conjunction that his theory of civilization was born. A consequence of this is that debates in the history of anthropology came to have a critical role in the constitution of his theories, without always being overtly indicated. What needs to be traced then, is the history of anthropology, and in particular, German, English, French, and American developments, from the angle of how Jung came to utilize it.

Elementary thoughts

A prominent figure in the development of German anthropology whose theories were to have a critical significance for Jung was Adolf Bastian. Bastian (1826–1905) took his doctorate in medicine at Würzburg. He was the extraordinary professor for ethnology in Berlin from 1873 to 1900. During the course of his life, he undertook many voyages around the world and did much fieldwork. His voyages were in part motivated by a desire to salvage as much information as possible concerning primitive cultures before they were permanently transformed by modernization and imperialism. In 1867, he founded the Berlin Society of Anthropology, ethnology, and ancient history with Rudolf Virchow.

His major work, *Man in History*, was published in three volumes in 1860. At the outset, he proclaimed that psychology was "the science of the future" (1860, vol. 1, xiii). He thought that ethnology was the basis for finding the psychological laws of the mental development of groups. In 1893 he described the goal of modern ethnology as one of finding an adequate methodology for scientific psychology.[2] The psychology that Bastian had in mind was close to the ethnopsychology of Lazarus and Steinthal, whose work he admired, since he had attended the lectures of the former (Koepping, 1983, 55).

---

[2] Bastian, *Controversen* (1893–1894), selected translation in Koepping, 1983, 170.

The leitmotifs of his work were his concepts of the elementary thoughts [Elementargedanken] and the ethnic thoughts [Völkergedanken]. The former were held in common by all mankind:

we will find the same tight core of ideas in all places and all times. There are definite analogies in mythological thoughts and the world views amid both the fetishism of the savage and the aesthetics of the civilized . . . *in all these, after removing the cloak of local and temporal variations in language and idiom, we encounter the same small number of psychological kernels.* (in *ibid.*, 180)

These psychological kernels were the elementary thoughts. While the positing of such analogies was not by itself particularly contentious, his claim that they had a common and universal intrapsychic origin was. It was when the elementary thoughts of savages came into contact with outside stimuli that they developed their intrinsic potential in the historical form of cultural development (*ibid.*, 172). Thus historical change was itself explained as consisting in the developmental unfolding of elementary thoughts. The actualization of the latter in specific cultures led to the formation of ethnic thoughts. These were rooted in specific geographical areas, and represented developments of the psychologically determined elementary thoughts. Thus the ethnic thoughts were shaped by geographical and environmental conditions. The totality of ethnic thoughts comprised the thoughts of mankind (*Menschheitsgedanken*). The study of ethnic thoughts was to be the foundation of psychology, and through collecting and comparing them, one arrived at the underlying elementary thoughts. It was among natural peoples (*Naturvölker*) that ethnic thoughts were most evident. As these had developed in specific ways in given cultures, one needed to compare materials from different cultures to accurately identify them.

A prime example of such an elementary thought was that of the cross, which he claimed could be found in a myriad of forms in diverse cultures (183–185). While he acknowledged that migration and diffusion played a role, it was clearly a subordinate one. This involved him in a lengthy polemic with Friedrich Ratzel, an ethnographer and ethnologist (1844–1904), who is credited with founding anthropogeography. Ratzel's focus was on the relation of humans to their environment, and he studied processes of migration and cultural borrowings. Ratzel strongly criticized Bastian's concept of elementary thoughts, and put forward explanations based on diffusion. For Ratzel, if similar traits were found in different people, this indicated a historical connection between them. He maintained that what was needed was the study of geographical distribution, an "anthropogeography." By contrast, Bastian's notion of the relation between ethnic and elementary thoughts had the effect of grounding anthropology in psychology. Ratzel's work proved more successful than Bastian's. Not least of the reasons for this lay in the impenetrability of his style of writing (Goldenweiser, 1949, 476).

Evolutionary anthropology

The development of evolutionary anthropology has been well documented.[3] In the following I intend to sketch some of the principal thematics of the evolutionary anthropologists that informed Jung: the doctrine of survivals, the equation of the primitive with the prehistoric, the relation between the modern and the primitive, and the use of the comparative method. It has been rightly stressed that it is mistaken to look upon Victorian evolutionary anthropologists as constituting a unitary body with shared doctrines. However, in the case of Jung, it is clear that his relation to their work may be adequately characterized with reference to certain general notions.

The best known of the evolutionary anthropologists was Edward Tylor (1832–1917). Tylor was the keeper of the Pitt-Rivers Museum at Oxford, and subsequently became a professor of anthropology at Oxford. For Tylor, culture was not a static entity. As the outcome of evolutionary development, the index of culture was temporality. The striking uniformity of civilization could be explained by the "uniform action of uniform causes," and the various grades could be regarded as the outcome of evolutionary stages (1871, 1). Due to the general likeness of human nature and the circumstances it confronted, little significance needed to be accorded to history or geography, and "the ancient Swiss lake-dweller may be set beside the medieval Aztec" (6). Indeed, a window into prehistoric conditions could be provided by considering modern savage tribes which possessed elements of civilization that appeared to be remnants of an early state of the human race. The stress on the fundamental identity of mental processes led to the positing of the psychic unity of mankind. This, rather than diffusion, was invoked to explain the similarities of customs in diverse cultures.[4]

For Tylor, the progress to modernity consisted in the evolutionary development from "savage through barbaric to civilized life" (26). Evolution partook of the moral order, and represented a transition from the lower to the higher.

"Primitives" were characterized by the belief in magic. This stemmed from the misapplication of the association of ideas. The error of magic

---

[3] See Stocking, 1986.
[4] This term had been employed by Bastian. It is important to note that concepts of the psychic unity of mankind were by no means unitary.

was that primitives behaved as Humeans in reverse: having made mental associations between connected events, they inverted this relation, and falsely believed that mental association was sufficient by itself to indicate connection in "reality" (116). Under the heading of magic Tylor included practices such as palmistry, astrology, divination, and the interpretation of dreams. "Primitives" personified, believing in the animation of nature. "Primitives" were anthropomorphic, attributing events to the beneficent or maleficent volition of gods, humans, animals. In short, in that notorious phrase, "primitives" were children. If modernity was the obverse of primitivism, it constituted a fragile balance that was always threatened by a reversion to superstition. The danger of reversion was indicated by the continued presence in modern society of supposedly primitive practices and beliefs, which he termed survivals. These were processes, customs, and opinions that had been carried over by habit into a new state of society from that in which they originated. They were remnants of an older condition of culture. An example of a menacing survival whose popularity was on the increase was spiritualism.

Tylor's characterization of the primitive as magical and civilization being constantly menaced by a reversion to barbarity was reiterated by James Frazer (1854–1941) in *The Golden Bough*. Frazer typified the history of civilization as consisting in the transition from the age of magic, to the age of religion, through to the age of science. His graphic depiction of this transition reads like a modern creation myth of culture, as this excerpt from his depiction of the transition from the age of magic to the age of science demonstrates:

He [the primitive] had been pulling at strings to which nothing was attached. He had been marching, as he thought, straight to the goal, while in reality he had only been treading in a narrow circle . . . cut adrift from his ancient moorings and left to toss on a troubled sea of doubt and uncertainty, his old happy confidence in himself and his powers rudely shaken, our primitive philosopher must have been sadly perplexed and agitated until he came to rest, as in a quiet haven after a tempestuous voyage, in a new system of faith and practice, which seemed to offer a substitute, however precarious, for that sovereignty over nature which he had reluctantly abdicated. If the great world went on its way without the help of him or his fellows, it must surely be because there were other beings, like himself, but far stronger, who, unseen themselves, directed the course and brought about all the varied series of events which he had hitherto believed to be dependent on his magic. It was they, as he now believed, and not himself, who made the stormy wind to blow, the lightning to flash, and the thunder to roll; who laid the foundations of the solid earth and set bounds to the restless sea that it might not pass.[5]

---

[5] 1911–1915, vol. 1, 238–239. Jung had a set of this work.

Evolutionary anthropology was a comparative enterprise. As commentators have noted, general references to a "comparative method" obscure the fact that this term encompasses different forms of comparison. Joan Leopold differentiates three types of comparative method. She describes the first as the general method of comparing cultural phenomena with the intention of showing structural or functional similarities, as opposed to ancestral relations (1980, 58). The second, she terms the comparative-genetic method, was employed in comparative anatomy and Indo-European comparative philology, which consisted in the comparison of cultural traits thought to be genetically related. Finally, she argues that the comparative method in evolutionary anthropology consisted in a combination of the first two, and aimed at getting information on stages of development of less known ancient societies from existing and more observable societies" (59).

Franz Boas

A figure viewed as one of the fathers of modern anthropology is Franz Boas (1858–1942). Boas initially studied physics and geography. He worked for a time in Berlin under Bastian, who supported Boas' turn to anthropology. In the 1880s he did fieldwork amongst the Eskimos. At the invitation of Stanley Hall, he took up a lectureship in anthropology at Clark University, after which he held appointments at the Field Museum in Chicago, the American Museum for Natural History, and at Columbia University. Boas' critiques of the comparative method, of evolutionism and racism in anthropology together with his advocacy of the in-depth investigation of societies did much to set the tenor of modern anthropology. It is useful to look at these aspects of his work, as he elaborated it contemporaneously with Jung's work, and Jung had some familiarity with it. Further, these issues were critical in the anthropological reception of Jung's work.

In 1896, Boas launched a highly influential attack on the use of the comparative method in anthropology. He claimed that this method, as used by Bastian and others, presupposed that the occurrence of similar phenomena in different cultures supplied proof of the "uniform working of the human mind" (1896, 270). The fundamental assumption upon which the comparative method was based was that "the same ethnological phenomena are always due to the same causes" (273). This enabled the explanation of diverse phenomena in different cultures and epochs through a single set of laws. For Boas, this axiom was mistaken, as he held that the same phenomenon could develop in different ways in different settings. Correspondingly, the scope of comparison should be rigorously delimited, and that comparisons be limited "to those effects which have been proven to be effects of the same causes" (275). The implication was clear: rather than appealing to the occurrence of similar phenomena in different cultures to buttress a given theory, the very basis of the comparison had first to be established. He nominated such an investigation the historical method, which came to set the tone for the larger share of twentieth-century anthropology. Studies were required which limited themselves to a well-defined geographical territory. Comparisons were not to be extended beyond the cultural area in question.

In 1909, Boas was present with Freud and Jung at the Clark conference. He presented a paper entitled "Psychological problems in anthropology" in which he reiterated and expanded his criticisms of the comparative method. He commented on the relationship between anthropology and psychology, and claimed that anthropologists were also trying to determine the "psychological laws which control the mind of man everywhere, and that may differ in various racial and social groups" (1910, 371).

The fundamental problem of anthropology was the question as to whether all races were "mentally equally endowed or do mental differences exist?" While there appeared to be evidence that suggested that the composite features of races differed, he held that there was no justification for hierarchies. While Tylor and Bastian had shown the existence of similar ideas throughout the world, Boas argued that the psychological processes that produced them had not been sufficiently explained. Attempts to explain such process through the comparative method were doomed, due to the lack of adequate comparability. For instance, he claimed that totemism did not constitute a single psychological problem and that anthropological phenomena which were outwardly alike were entirely distinct from a psychological angle. What was necessary was to discover common processes as opposed to focusing on external similarity. Such an investigation was an area where anthropological data could be profitably used by psychologists.

In terms of the history of psychoanalysis, his paper could hardly have been more timely, or as the case may be, untimely, coming shortly before Freud and Jung embarked upon their colonization of anthropological material. For Boas had critiqued in advance what constituted the presuppositions of their endeavors. Given the subsequent development of anthropology, it is not going too far to say that had they heeded his recommendations for the negotiation of the interdisciplinary relation of anthropology and psychology, the fate and reception of their work in anthropology would have been totally different.

Boas' critique of the comparative method went hand in hand with his critique of evolutionary and physical anthropology. He argued that evolutionism was founded on the unproved premise that the historical changes in the cultural life of mankind followed definite universal laws (1920, 281). Having undercut the evidential basis for such an assumption, he concluded by discarding the Eurocentrism it was coupled with, namely, the view that modern Western European civilization represented the peak to which all more primitive types were orthogenetically developing.

One aspect of his work which was to have special significance for Jung was his critique of racial physical anthropology. In nineteenth-century physical anthropology, the constancy of the cephalic index in different races – the ratio of width to the length of the skull – was taken as axiomatic. The assumption of this constancy was a critical component which enabled various races to be arrayed in hierarchies. Between 1908 and 1910 Boas undertook an investigation for the United States immigration on the bodily form of descendants of immigrants in America. He initially expected that the headform of immigrant children would remain the same (Stocking 1968, 176). In a summary account of his report, he put forward his findings that "American-born descendants of immigrants differ in type from their foreign-born parents" (Boas, 1912, 60). The skull sizes of the descendants differed, and the width of their skulls was smaller. While he claimed that the changes could only be explained by environmental factors, he did not put forward a definite explanation. Elazar Barkan notes that Boas gave a talk on "The history of the American Race" in which "he speculated on the European's growing resemblance to the Indians in America" (1992, 82). Stocking notes that due to the fact that the changes in headform that Boas observed tended to move towards an intermediate form, journalists utilised this to support the popular notion that a new American "race" was developing through the assimilation of immigrants. Boas disavowed the idea that the distinct European types became the same in America, solely due to environmental influence (1968, 179).

Ethnopsychology

Alongside these anthropological developments, psychologists were attempting to stake their claims to the same terrain. Wilhelm Wundt has been canonized as the father of experimental psychology. However, there is a sense in which, in his own estimation, his achievements in ethnopsychology took pride of place.[6] In 1920, he recalled that he had conceived the idea in 1860 of adding a superstructure to experimental psychology.

[6] Various translations of the term *Völkerpsychologie* have been given. The closest would be 'ethnopsychology', which is used here throughout. On Wundt, see above, 31–33.

The latter had to limit itself to studying the mental life of the individual. The task of ethnopsychology was to study the phenomena of communal life. He held that this was ultimately more important and represented the proper conclusion of psychology (1921, 201).

For Wundt, ethnopsychology, while being based on experimental psychology, represented its culmination. The need for a separate discipline to study social life arose because of the restricted scope of experimental psychology, which was unable to study the "higher" mental functions. The term itself was initially coined by Moritz Lazarus (1824–1903) and Heymann Steinthal (1823–1899), and they were responsible for its initial conception.

Both Lazarus and Steinthal studied under Johann Friedrich Herbart at Berlin, and in terms of psychology, considered themselves as Herbartians. Steinthal was a privatdozent in Berlin, and in 1861, Lazarus was given a chair at the University of Berne in psychology and ethnopsychology. The term itself they coined in 1851, and in 1859 they formed the *Zeitschrift für Völkerpsychologie und Sprachwissenschaft*, which ran until 1890.

Analogies between the individual and society have been longstanding. In Johann Herbart's (1744–1803) view, individuals in every society were related to one another like concepts in the soul of an individual.[7] Hence the social could be conceived of as a supra-individual. For Lazarus and Steinthal, the term they used for this entity was the collective spirit (*Gesamtgeist*) or spirit of a people (*Volkgeist*) (the term had been coined by Herder). The spirit of a people was the principal subject of ethnopsychology, which had two components – ethnohistorical psychology and psychic ethnology. While the former dealt with the general psychological functioning of the spirit of a people, the latter dealt with its concrete embodiment. This spirit obeyed general psychological laws. In 1862 Lazarus wrote that it manifested itself in mental events, such as views, convictions, thoughts and feelings, and that these exerted an influence on the individual spirit.[8] While the only place of manifestation of the spirit was in the individual, it was a supra-individual factor. Crucially, it could be regarded as a unitary factor, that functioned like a single individual. As Danziger notes, for Lazarus and Steinthal, "the individuals whose common activity created the objective reality of cultural forms were themselves to be seen as the product of these forms" (1983, 305). The materials that ethnopsychology studied were primarily textual: languages, mythologies, religions, customs, and so forth. They viewed myth as the "collective world of representations of the *Volk*,"[9] and as the original form

[7] Herbart, 1816, cited in Jahoda 1992, 142.   [8] Cited in Kalmar, 1987, 679.
[9] Lazarus and Steinthal 1870, cited in Ingrid Belke, 1971, cxxii.

of representation of religious feeling. Lazarus and Steinthal were both Jewish, and their ethnopsychology was developed against the backdrop of rising German nationalism. They were at pains to separate the concept of a people from that of race, and to distance themselves from any notion of a hierarchical order of different peoples. Thus individuals of different races could belong to the same people. As Lazarus pithily stated, "To me blood means bloody little."[10]

What did psychology mean to Lazarus and Steinthal, and why did they use it to designate their new discipline? According to James Whitman, the use of the term psychology by Steinthal, Lazarus, Noack, Waitz, and Lotze, each of whom had a background in philological disciplines, was in part out of opposition to the materialism of Moleschott, Vogt, and Büchner. He argues that their utilization of the term, at the same moment when Weber, Fechner, and Wundt were putting forward programs for an experimental scientific psychology,

enabled philologists and their partisans to reformulate their old practices in terms more in tune with the new understanding of "scientific" without seeming faithless to their forebears within the tradition . . . the attempt was made to combine the old text-critical use of *Psychologie* with the natural scientific use, and make of the two strands in the history of *Psychologie* one social science. (1984, 217)

If language featured prominently as subject matter for ethnopsychology, it also played an important role in its appellation. What the term psychology offered then, was, paradoxically, a new lease of life for the older philological disciplines, through laying claim to the rhetoric of scientific modernity. This was achieved through deliberately using the same term, psychology, to designate radically distinct pursuits.

Wundt's turn to ethnopsychology was at the same time a repudiation of Lazarus and Steinthal's conception of it, and polemical exchanges ensued. His critique of their work was principally directed against the Herbartian psychology that underwrote it, and which he had challenged in his experimental psychology. In this context I plan to consider his general conception of the subject, together with his views on history and myth.

In the same year in which Jung published his *Transformations and Symbols of the Libido*, Wundt published his *Elements of Ethnopsychology*. These works form an interesting contrast. Wundt claimed that history should be based on a psychological history of development (1911, xvi). He defined ethnopsychology as dealing with the mental products which were created by communities. As these presupposed the reciprocal action of

---

[10] Cited in Kalmar, 1987, 688.

many individuals, they were inexplicable in terms of individual consciousness alone. Thus ethnopsychology and general psychology presupposed
one another. The psychological laws discovered by ethnopsychology did
not represent an independent realm of operation, but represented applications of principles valid for individual psychology. If Wundt challenged Lazarus and Steinthal's conception of ethnopsychology, there was
a straightforward continuity in subject matter: languages, mythology, religion, and customs again taking pride of place. These latter, according to
Wundt, were not the product of an individual, but of the soul of a people
(*Volkseele*).

Wundt's approach may be illustrated by his conception of mythology.
He accorded mythology an especial significance in the life of a people.
A people's mythology contained their theory of the universe (1897, 55).
Thus mythology included theories of nature, religion, and morals alongside one another. This inherent plurality of mythology led him to reject
the prevalent explanation of mythology as consisting in a (failed) attempt
to interpret nature, and indeed, to reject all monocausal interpretations of
myth. As he saw it, any one-sided theory of historical phenomena could
not deal with the complexity of life. At the same time, he put forward a
psychological explanation of mythology. Myth-making had a single psychological source: personification. This consisted in objectifying one's
own consciousness. Thus whenever "primitives" perceived movement,
they assumed that it was the result of a will. In such a way, they personified the environment. It was through this process that myths were built
up. The psychological explanation of mythology dealt with the most fundamental processes at work there. Mythology represented the projection
of human psychology into external phenomena. The study of mythology
was significant because "certain fundamental resemblances" between all
races were more marked there, while at the same time, the differences in
mythologies designated the differences in "fundamental moral character"
between peoples (89).

In *Elements of Ethnopsychology*, he put forward a speculative psychological developmental history of mankind. Mankind went through three main
stages: the primitive, totemic, the heroic, and finally, humanity. The work
consisted in identifying the soul of a people of each stage. He reiterated
the anthropological equation between the primitive and the prehistoric,
and drew upon the former for his knowledge of the latter. The transition through these stages resulted in a progressive individualization. The
transition to the stage of humanity consisted in an appreciation of the
human personality as such, and represented a transcendence of more restricted associations, such as family, tribe or state. The highest form of
society was that in which an appreciation of human worth had become

normative. However, the transition to the higher stages did not entail the disappearance of the earlier stages, as witnessed by the continued existence of religions.

Wundt's ethnopsychology did not survive his death. Several reasons have been given for this. To begin with, his strictures concerning the use of experimentation in psychology were not adhered to by his students, who sought to expand its purview. From this perspective, ethnopsychology would appear to be a relic of the older speculative and metaphysical psychology.[11] Secondly, the subsequent identification of ethnopsychology with German nationalism and *völkisch* movements – which represented a complete negation of Lazarus and Steinthal's vision – led to the subsequent discredit of the former. In 1920, Wundt proclaimed ethnopsychology as a German science.[12] His ethnopsychology presented a psychological theory that encompassed history, linguistics, sociology, anthropology, and comparative religion. The progressive disciplinary development of each of these disciplines mitigated against their unification under a more fundamental psychological discipline. Significantly the development of psychoanalysis and analytical psychology, from *Totem and Taboo* and *Transformations and Symbols of the Libido* onwards, took over much of the project of ethnopsychology. Critically, they coupled it with an institutional form that ensured its survival, up to the present day.

For Wundt, ethnopsychology was to form the basis of history. This view was espoused by one major historian, Karl Lamprecht (1856–1915), who was the best-known German cultural historian at the turn of the century. Lamprecht had studied with Wundt at Leipzig, where he himself became a professor. His masterpiece was his twelve-volume *German History*, which appeared between 1891 and 1909. In this context, the significance of his work lies in the manner in which he attempted to approach history psychologically, which was significant for Jung.

History, Lamprecht proclaimed, was an ethnopsychological science, "nothing but applied psychology" (1905, 29). Psychology, having freed itself from metaphysics, and having established itself as a science, could provide the basis for a scientific approach to history, which would enable the depiction of the general laws that underlay historical changes. This he presented in his theory of *dominants*. From ethnopsychology, he took the analogy between the individual and the collective, which enabled him to apply individual psychological models to understand epochal historical changes. The character of a given epoch was determined by its *dominant*. The transition between epochs consisted in the rise and fall of particular *dominants*. This general process was universal. In the soul life of

---

[11] On Wundt's reception, see Danziger, 1990, 34–48.
[12] Whitman notes that it was only with the nationalism of the first world war that ethnopsychology became *völkisch*, 1984, 214.

the individual, a particular feeling governed and regulated all other feelings, sensations, and aspirations. This was the dominant. When epochs
changed, a new epoch created new forms of psychic experience. The old
dominant lost its sway, and another took its place. Certain epochs could
be characterized as epochs of dissociation. Under such circumstances,
individuality yielded to the overpowering influences of a new external
world. This gave rise to new conceptions and the transformation of the
ego. The previous harmony that governed the personality is sacrificed
and individuality becomes open to the suggestions of the external world.
At the same time, individuality was given over to the effect of the "broad
unconscious substrata of the new psychic life" (126). Consequently, new
forms of psychic life become conscious. To adapt to the surroundings,
a greater breadth of soul was required, which led to the development of
a new power of psychological assimilation, and a new *dominant* of the
personality:

the whole psyche is set free, and – a centre of the total personality being created –
regains its former self-mastery; it now seeks the highest pleasure of existence by
proceeding, considering carefully what is possible, to the most energetic activity
of a central *dominant*. (133)

The development of a new *dominant* ushered in a new epoch. Since 1890,
there had been a new *dominant* in Europe, which was represented by the
predominance of imaginative activity, the increasing importance of the
observation of the inner life and symbolism in painting.

The *dominant* that characterized an epoch was present in each individual, and historical change in the culture at large was at the same time
a change in the psychology of the individual. Lamprecht's nomothetic
approach created a controversy in the historical profession, and his reputation did not survive (Woodruff Smith, 1991, 191).

Crowd psychology

While German ethnopsychology was principally orientated to ancient
and "primitive" societies, in France and Italy, psychologists attempted to
study contemporary societies. In 1895, the French crowd psychologist
Gustav Le Bon famously proclaimed: "The age we are about to enter will
in truth be the ERA OF CROWDS" (1895, 15). If the age was to be the
age of the crowd, then correspondingly, the psychology that would be the
psychology of the age was the psychology of crowds.[13]

The last quarter of the nineteenth century has been viewed as the
golden age of hypnosis. One significance of the study of hypnotism and

---

[13] On crowd psychology, see van Ginneken, 1992. On its significance in Freud's work, see
Borch-Jacobsen, 1982 and 1991a.

suggestion was that it was presented as a psychology of the relations between people, and their effects upon one another. In experiments which were conducted, such as getting subjects to commit imaginary crimes, the possibility of the hypnosis-suggestion model for forming a template through which to understand wider social relations, and to provide the psychologist with the authority of a privileged vantage point from which to comment on social issues was clearly grasped. In the famous legal disputations between the Nancy and the Salpêtrière schools, not least of the issues was the attempt of proponents of each school to secure the pre-eminent right as spokesmen for public morals.[14] Few saw this more clearly than the Belgian psychophysicist, philosopher, and hypnotist, Josef Delboeuf, in his repeated attacks on the unwarranted arrogation of political power by physicians in these debates.[15]

For these reasons, the hypnosis-suggestion models readily lent themselves to the understanding of society at large. While these models formed the basic template for crowd psychology, this sphere of application was not simply a supplementary, exterior terrain to which a supposedly purely clinical model could be exported, as concerns with the social and the political were intrinsic to the models themselves.

Imitation

In 1890 in *The Laws of Imitation* Gabriel Tarde (1843–1904) rhetorically posed the question, "What is society?", to which he replied with one word – imitation (80). Tarde had studied law in Toulouse and Paris and became a judge in Sarlat in 1875. His early work was in criminology. He subsequently was appointed to a chair at the Collège de France.[16] For Tarde, imitation defined the specificity of the social, and demarcated it from the vital and the physical. In a further statement that was only slightly less brief, he proclaimed: "*Society, is imitation, and imitation, is a species of somnambulism*" (95). The new psychology of hypnotism provided a template for understanding society at large. Man in society, he claimed, was a somnambulist, and the social state, "like the hypnotic state, is only a form of dream, a dream of command and a dream of action"(83). The fabric of society consisted in a cascade of successive, mutual, and conflicting hypnotizations. Imitation was broadly understood: it could be both conscious and unconscious, and not only indicated the emulation of a model, but also, under the form of counterimitation, attempted to do the

---

[14] See Laurence and Perry, 1988.   [15] Joseph Delboeuf, 1891. See Shamdasani, 1997.
[16] Tarde was lecturing at the Collège de France when Jung went there to attend Janet's lectures in 1902–1903. There is no evidence that Jung heard Tarde lecture, but it is possible that he may have encountered his work at this time.

exact opposite. The processes of memory and habit were reformulated as forms of self-imitation. Imitation did not consist in exact replication, as it always introduced differences and hence ushered in new developments. A social group consisted of a collection of individuals who were engaged in imitation between themselves, or whose common traits were "ancient copies of the same model" (73).

Through placing imitation at the heart of the social, psychology, or as he sometime styled it, inter-mental psychology, became the pre-eminent discipline for comprehending the social. The key to understanding society lay in the explication of the forms of psychological relation between the individuals that made up society. Hence "Inter-mental psychology must be to the social sciences what the study of the cell is to the biological sciences" (1969, 181).

Collective psychology

In 1891 an Italian lawyer Scipio Sighele (1868–1913) published a work on the criminal crowd. Sighele called for a collective psychology, a term which had been coined by the criminologist Enrico Ferri (1856–1929), to study the behavior of individuals in groups. Sighele claimed that the behavior of a group could be considered as that of a single individual, citing Auguste Comte's statement that human society should be considered as a single man who has always existed. He derived his principal characterization of the psychology of groups from Alfred Espinas, who had stated on the basis of his study of societies of animals that it was a law of all intelligent life that "the representation of an emotional state provokes the birth of this same state in someone who witnesses it."[17] He termed this the law of psychic mimetism. As aspects of this, he included moral contagion, social imitation, and hypnotic suggestion. He stressed the low moral qualities of the crowd, stating that in crowds, behavior sank to the lowest common denominator and that "the crowd is a terrain where the microbe of evil develops very easily"(60). Drawing upon the work of the Salpêtrière school, Sighele held that strong-willed individuals could escape the suggestive effect of crowds. Concerning the morality of crowd behavior, he developed a notion of collective responsibility.

Collective behavior was not only the source of crimes, but also of creativity. In 1899, in an essay entitled "The moral problem of collective psychology," he stated that language as well as the legends of all countries were created by the crowd, and were "unconsciously born in the infantile

---

[17] Espinas, 1878, cited by Sighele, 1891, 54.

soul of a people" (260). The role of the creative individual or genius was to reveal what lay dormant in the unconscious.

Le Bon

Gustav Le Bon (1841–1931) became the most widely known of the crowd psychologists. It has been estimated that during his lifetime, his works sold half a million copies (Nye, 1975, 3). After training in medicine, he travelled widely and wrote works on anthropology and archeology. His interests then shifted to psychology. In 1894 he set out his psychological views in *Psychological Laws of the Evolution of Peoples*. In this, the linkage between individual and collective psychology was made through regarding each race as a single individual. Thus Le Bon claimed that each race possessed a fixed mental constitution. Adopting a Lamarckian position on inheritance, he argued that the members of each race possessed a set of common psychological traits, which were inherited, and which constituted the national character, or the soul (âme) of a people (Le Bon also used the terms "soul of a race" and "collective soul"). Following from his stress on the significance of heredity, he claimed that the soul of a people was largely determined by its dead:

> Infinitely more numerous than the living, the dead are also infinitely more powerful than them. They govern the immense domain of the unconscious, this invisible domain which contains under its empire all the manifestations of intelligence and character. It is by its dead, much more than by its living, that a people is led. It is by them alone that a race is founded . . . The extinguished generations do not solely impose on us their physical constitution; they also impose their thoughts. (1894, 13)

Le Bon's unconscious was a hereditary, racial, suprapersonal unconscious, and closely followed Théodule Ribot's conception.[18] Each individual was constituted by a set of unconscious racial characteristics. The various races were arrayed in rank order. As the constitutional psychological character of each race was fixed, so too, consequently, was their order of rank.

While in *Psychological Laws of the Evolution of Peoples*, Le Bon had stressed the significance of fixed, constitutional psychological traits, in his best known work *The Crowd* he also stressed a readily malleable transformative dimension. When individuals gathered in a crowd, new psychological characteristics developed, which consisted in the "substitution of the unconscious action of crowds for the conscious action of individuals" (1895, 5). The act of gathering into a crowd created a collective soul

---

[18] See above, 186–187.

into which the individual became submerged. In the crowd, it was the unconscious that dominated: "The part played by the unconscious in all our acts is immense, and that played by reason very small" (10). Hence to gain access to the unconscious required no prolonged and expensive one-to-one clinical encounter: one could simply walk out into the street.

One could with justice reverse Le Bon's statements, and say that for him, the concept of the unconscious was itself modeled after the crowd. Crowds had an inferior mentality, which represented an atavistic return to a primitive condition. Our destructive instincts were the inheritance from primitive ages. While it would be dangerous for a lone individual to gratify these instincts, his absorption in a crowd enabled him to do this with impunity. From the evolutionary anthropologists, he took over the equation of the primitive with the prehistoric. Crowds were typified by contagion, and no one was free from their sway: "Isolated, he may be a cultivated individual; in a crowd, he is a barbarian" (36). Finally, crowds ineluctably and instinctively placed themselves under a leader.

There were several priority disputes between the crowd psychologists.[19] The work of the crowd psychologists formed a predominant mode of the psychological understanding of society, and one which gave epistemological priority to individual psychology. Subsequently transformed, their work would in turn provide a principal template for Jung's collective psychology. Alexandre Métraux notes that the crowd psychologists were popular until around 1920. With the exception of Tarde, they were successfully excluded from the French university system by Émile Durkheim and his school (Métraux, 1982, 279). With the decline of the psychological concern with hypnotism and suggestion, social psychology increasingly sought to distance itself from the concerns of the crowd psychologists, though significant continuities continued to exist.

Baldwin

In early social psychology, social life was frequently explained in terms of the relations between the individual and the collective, envisaged as two competing actors. An example is the work of James Mark Baldwin (1861–1934). He played a significant role in the establishment of experimental psychology, founding laboratories at the Universities of Toronto and Princeton, and playing a key role in the establishment of *The Psychological Review* and *The Psychological Bulletin*. Baldwin's work is an example of the continuity between crowd psychology and social psychology. In *The Individual and Society*, he argued that the most cursory examination of

[19] See van Ginneken 1992, 119–126.

social life revealed two principal interests, that of the individual, and that of society. These principles were reflected in the disciplinary distinction between psychology and sociology. It was not the study of the externals of society that could reveal its workings, but the study of the mental life of individuals. Hence psychology took pride of place over sociology, which should be subordinated to it.

Human development could be characterized by the interplay of two impulses, those of individualism and collectivism, which were innate tendencies (1911, 18). These were represented by the self-preservative tendencies on the one hand, and social and gregarious tendencies on the other. Principal among the socializing tendencies were play and imitation. His stress on imitation was derived from Tarde, whose work he translated. It was through imitation that the child learns his capacities and limitations, acquires the riches of social traditions and gains access to culture, and learns to innovate.

The competition between individualism and collectivism led to the dangers of oversocialization and overindividualism. The former resulted in soft individuals and consequently a weak social life, and the latter produced individuals whose tendencies were destructive of social interest and the general good. The competing claims of individualism and collectivism were resolved in a specific type of character, which he described as a tempered individualism: "a tendency to competition, rivalry, self-assertion for personal advancement, *tempered by the requirements of the group life as a whole*" (85–86). The development of society and the progress of mankind depended upon the fostering of this.

Collective representations

In 1927 Daniel Essertier gave the following explanation of the disciplinary rivalry between psychology and sociology:

when nascent sociology wanted to delimit its domain, it recognized terrains which hadn't been seriously cultivated by anyone, and appropriated them. Now these terrains in reality belonged to psychology. Under the menace of invasion, the latter retook possession of them. (9)

In a 1945 tribute to Jung, the child psychologist Jean Piaget wrote:

The French-language reader cannot stop himself from making the connection – which seems perhaps artificial or surprising because the intellectual temperament of the two authors is so different – but which strikes us in reflecting on their work. One great French sociologist has also profoundly experienced this permanent action of the past on the present, and he also is "leaning on the tribal life of Australians" to clarify contemporary behaviour: Durkheim. But that which Durkheim, prophet and sociologist just as Jung is a prophet and psychologist, attributes to "collective consciousness," Jung searches in the "collective uncon-scious." And yet these antithetical entities come close more often than one be-lieves and it would be very interesting, in times to come, to analyse their possible interference.[20]

At first glance, few figures would appear to be as far apart as Émile Durkheim (1858–1917), self-proclaimed founder of scientific sociology, and C. G. Jung. Jung and Durkheim did not cite each other. Indeed, there appear to be few disciplines as distinct from each other as analytical psychology and modern sociology, given the almost complete absence of mutual references. Nevertheless, two central terms of Durkheim's soci-ology, which were critical to his attempt to establish the autonomy of so-ciology, found their way into Jung's psychology: collective consciousness and collective representations. Before tracing how these were taken up by Jung, it is first necessary to sketch out their significance for Durkheim.

Durkheim introduced the term collective representations in his 1897 study, *Suicide*, and in the following year provided an extended justification of it in "Individual and collective representations." What is of particular interest in this essay is the manner in which Durkheim marshaled psycho-logical arguments to argue analogically for the disciplinary independence of sociology. Just as psychology had "emancipated" itself from biology, he attempted to emancipate sociology from psychology. He claimed that collective life, like individual life, consisted of representations. Within psychology, there had been much debate concerning the nature of repre-sentations, in particular unconscious representations. He embarked upon an extended critique of William James' arguments in *The Principles* against the existence of unconscious representations, and affirmed the existence of unconscious psychic states.[21] Durkheim claimed that within each of us, many psychic phenomena occurred without our apprehending them, and that Janet had proven that many acts which had all the signs of being conscious, were not. Hence at every moment our judgments were influ-enced by unconscious judgments (1897, 20–21). If this was so within the individual, the possibility that it might be so outside of the individual was strengthened. As John Brooks comments,

> If the relation between collective representations and the social substratum is the same as that between individual representations and the physiological substratum, it follows that collective representations are relatively independent of individual minds. (1991, 226)

Durkheim further clarified his understanding of the term, and its rela-tion to the collective consciousness in *The Rules of Sociological Method*. Individual consciousness resulted from the nature of organic and psychic

[20] 170. On Piaget, See Vidal, 1994.   [21] See above, 177–178.

being taken in isolation. Collective consciousness resulted from a plurality of such beings (1895, 145). The aggregation of individuals had the effect of producing a distinct "psychical individuality" (129). Thus the collective consciousness was made up of collective representations, which expressed how the group thought of itself. These representations generally took the form of myths, legends and religious conceptions. Collective representations were not innate, but were the result of history and collective action. These concepts provided the key to the autonomy of sociology:

Social facts differ not only in quality from psychical facts; *they have a different substratum*, they do not evolve in the same environment or depend on the same conditions. This does not mean that they are not in some sense psychical, since they all consist of ways of thinking and acting. But the states of collective consciousness are of a different nature from the states of the individual consciousness; they are representations of another kind. The mentality of groups is not that of individuals; it has its own laws. The two sciences [sociology and psychology] are therefore as sharply distinct as two sciences can be. (40)

Not only were sociology and psychology distinct from one another, the latter was ultimately reducible to the former. In 1909, he argued that sociology ultimately arrived at a psychology that was more concrete and complex than that of the "pure" psychologists (237). Thus it is not surprising that he engaged in disputes with psychologists, notably with Gabriel Tarde.

Jung's knowledge of Durkheimian notions was based on his reading of Henri Hubert, Marcel Mauss and Lucien Lévy-Bruhl, all of whom were affiliated with Durkheim.

Primitive mentality

Durkheim's work had an important impact upon anthropology through the work of Lucien Lévy-Bruhl and Marcel Mauss. In 1910 Lucien Lévy-Bruhl (1857–1939) published his *The Mental Functions in Inferior Societies*. He had studied philosophy at the École Normale Supérieure, and in 1896 he took up an appointment at the Sorbonne, where he became a member of Durkheim's school. In retrospect, he recalled that his research into primitive mentality began when he read the work of an ancient Chinese historian. Being unable to see how the ideas of this historian connected together, he wondered if the logic of the Chinese was the same as "ours" (Mucchielli, 1998, 341). *The Mental Functions* began by taking up Durkheim's notion of collective representations, which Lévy-Bruhl sought to clarify through a consideration of anthropological material. He defined collective representations as being common to the members of a social group. They were transmitted through generations, and awakened sentiments of respect, fear, and adoration in individuals. Their existence did not depend on individuals, in that they could not be accounted for through considering individuals alone (1910, 13). The best place to elucidate the general functioning of collective representations was in uncivilized peoples. Dominique Merllié notes that while Lévy-Bruhl held, following Durkheim, that the collective representations were social, his interest was in studying their specific mode of functioning, as opposed to their social determination (1989b, 501). Lévy-Bruhl critiqued Frazer and Tylor's interpretation of primitive mentality in terms of animism. They were mistaken in believing that the functions of the mind were the same everywhere, and simply wrongly used by primitives. By contrast, he claimed that primitive mentality was fundamentally different from "our" mentality, as their social groups fashioned their minds in different ways. A mistake of the animist school was that it sought to base its explanations on the functioning of the individual mind, as opposed to the functioning of social processes.

"Primitives" were typified by having a different type of collective representations, which he described as mystical. By this he meant that they assumed the existence of invisible forces, influences, and actions. Despite his critique of the animist school, there were significant features of his account that mirrored theirs. First, as he assumed the unity of primitive mentality, he compiled his examples without concern for historical or geographical specificities. Secondly, while he disputed their explanations of primitive mentality, his account was no less condemnatory. No good word could be said for the primitive mentality.

Lévy-Bruhl stressed the disjunction between primitive and civilized mentality. Due to the nature of their collective representations, "primitives perceive nothing in the same way we do" (1910, 43). Not only were their collective representations different from those of the civilized, their representations were connected in a different manner. He formulated this as the law of participation. In the collective representations of "primitives," beings and things could both be themselves and something else. They also gave and received "mystic powers, virtues, qualities, influences, which make themselves felt outside, without remaining where they are" (76–77). Consequently, he characterized "primitives" as living in a state of mystical participation. They were indifferent to non-contradiction, less able to abstract and generalize, they neglected secondary causes for mystical ones.

While he described the collective representations of "primitives" as strange and peculiar, the British anthropologist Edward Evans Pritchard credited him with being the first to emphasize that primitive ideas were meaningful when seen as parts of interconnected patterns of ideas and behavior, which were intelligibly related (1981, 126–127).

One example that Lévy-Bruhl gave of primitive mystical participation that became particularly important for Jung was the significance of the sacred objects of the Arunta, drawn from Spencer and Gillen's *The Native Tribes of Central Australia*:

These things (pieces of wood or stone of an oblong shape, and generally decorated with mystic designs) are most carefully preserved and deposited in a sacred place which women and children dare not approach . . . from the standpoint of logical thought it would be very difficult to define exactly what *churinga* are, or are not. The external souls of individuals; the vehicles of ancestral spirits and possibly the bodies of these ancestors themselves; extracts of totemic essence; reservoirs of vitality – they are all of these in turn and simultaneously . . . I may note . . . the deep religious respect which surrounds the *churinga*, the care taken to preserve them, and the veneration and precaution with which they are handled . . . "A man who possesses such a *churinga* as the *churinga* snake . . . will constantly rub it with his hand, singing as he does so about the Alcheringa history of the snake, and gradually comes to feel that there is some special association between him and the sacred object . . ."[22]

When the individual began to become more aware of himself, there was less mystical symbiosis with the group. Consequently, participations come to be expressed by means of intermediaries rather than being felt directly. Through this process, collective representations began to approximate what we call ideas. Mystical participation was a permanent feature of the mind: as concepts had initially derived from collective representations, they retained a mystical residue. He argued that psychology and philosophy had hitherto assumed the homogeneity of the mind. The erroneousness of this assumption was demonstrated by a consideration of primitive mentality. Consequently, the unity of the thinking being posited by philosophers was something to be desired, rather than being given. Further, as rationality developed out of primitive mentality, it was only through studying this that the functioning of rationality could be truly grasped. These arguments lent his book a polemical cast: an adequate philosophy and psychology could only be arrived at on the basis of anthropology.

His work initially met with success. Merllié notes this had the unfortunate effect of leading to a spate of vulgarizations which contributed to his work becoming denatured, forgotten, and repressed. The main critiques emphasized the inadequacy of his armchair method, the questionableness of his radical differentiation of primitive and modern thought, his

---

[22] *Ibid.* The final quotation is from Spencer and Gillen.

assertion of the universality of the former, the tone of condescension, and his evolutionary assumptions (Merllié, 1989, 423). In particular, his positing of mystical participation as the defining characteristic of the primitive came in for much criticism. In his later works, he dropped the designation "mystical." Finally, the posthumously published notebooks of his last years strikingly revealed a repudiation of much of his earlier work:

> I was wrong, in *How Natives Think*, in wishing to define a character peculiar to the primitive mentality as far as logic is concerned, in believing that the facts, in certain cases, showed this mentality to be insensitive or at least more indifferent than ours to contradiction. Examined without prejudice, the facts say nothing at all, and participation itself involves, in essence, nothing incompatible with the principle of contradiction . . . (What I had not discerned at the period of *How Natives Think*) these minds do not differ from ours from the logical point of view, not only in the structure but also in the manifestations of their activity. (1949, 60)
> I see more and more clearly that the distinction between the two sorts of experience (although well founded on the feeling that primitive men very obviously have characteristics peculiar to the mystic experience) cannot be rigorously maintained, and that there is for the primitive mentality . . . only a single experience, sometimes mixed, sometimes almost entirely mystical, sometimes almost entirely non-mystical, but undoubtedly never exclusively one or the other . . . when I used to say that primitive men do not perceive anything as we do; I should rather have said: do not perceive anything entirely as we do. (188)

At the end of the day, Lévy-Bruhl himself was his most articulate critic.

Mana

Another member of the Durkheim school whose work was significant for Jung was Marcel Mauss (1872–1950). Mauss was Durkheim's nephew, and helped him in founding *L'Année sociologique*. After Durkheim's death, he was the leading figure in French sociology. Mauss' work can be approached through considering his work on magic. For Mauss, magic constituted a collective psychopathology. Mauss claimed that there were three laws of magic – contiguity, similarity, and opposition: that things in contact remain the same, that like produces like, and that opposites work on opposites. Fundamentally though, an originary notion underlay all these forms of magic, the belief in a magical power, which, after the Melanesians, he dubbed mana. This was not simply a force or a being, but could also be an act, quality, or state. Mana represented the essence of magic, in that it revealed "the confusion between actor, rite and object."[23]

---

[23] Mauss, 1902–1903, 108. This work was co-authored with Henri Hubert, though published under Mauss' name.

He proceeded to provide a lyrical compilation drawn from diverse societies, to demonstrate the omnipresence of the idea of mana, of which the following is a condensed abbreviation:

mana may be communicated from a harvest stone to other stones through contact . . . It may be heard and seen, leaving objects where it has dwelt. Mana makes a noise in the leaves, flies away like a cloud or flame . . . there is mana to make people wealthy and mana used to kill . . . Mana is the magicians' force . . . Mana is the power of a rite . . . Mana . . . causes the net to bring in a good catch, makes the house solid and keeps the canoe sailing smoothly . . . On an arrow it is the substance which kills . . . It is the object of a reverence which may amount to a taboo . . . It is a kind of aether, imponderable, Communicable which spreads of its own accord . . . It is a kind of internal, special world where everything happens as if mana alone were involved . . . Among the Straits Malays it is known by *kramât* . . . in French Indo-China is known by *deng* . . . In Madagascar, we have the term *hasina* . . . Among the Huron (Iroquois) it is called by the name *orenda* . . . The famous concept of manitou found among the Algonquins is basically the same . . . According to Hewitt, among the Sioux *mahope*, *Xube* (Omaha), *wakan* (Dakota) also mean magical power and magical qualities . . . Among the Shoshone the word *pokunt* generally has the same value . . . the term *naual* in Mexico and Central America seems to us to correspond to the same idea . . . The Perth tribes give it the name *boolya*. In New South Wales, the tribes use *koochie* to describe an evil spirit, personal or impersonal evil influences . . . again we find the *arungquiltha* of the Arunta . . . In India it crops up under such separate notions as brightness, glory, force, destruction, fate, remedy, the qualities of plants. And the basic idea of Hindu pantheism, contained in *Brahman*, seems to us to be profoundly connected with it . . . And indeed, the idea may well have existed without having been expressed. (1902–1903, 109–116)

kramat, deng, mahope, xube, pokunt, naul, boolya, orenda, koochie, arungquiltha, brahman, manitou, makan – Mauss's endless litany, retrieving the existence of *mana* everywhere, reads like a chant of exorcism – and one that claims not to believe in what it is exorcizing. It was not for nothing that the anthropologist Claude Lévi-Strauss noted:

We can see that in one case at least, the notion of mana does present those characteristics of mysterious power and secret force which Durkheim and Mauss attribute to it: it plays just such a role in their own system. There truly, mana is mana. At the same time one wants to know whether their theory of mana is anything other than an imputation to native thought of properties which were implied by the very particular role that the idea of mana was called upon to play in their own. (1987, 57)

Mauss claimed that *mana* was an unconscious *a priori* category of understanding. In 1909 Hubert and Mauss wrote of the categories:

Constantly present in language, without necessarily being completely explicit there, they ordinarily generally exist in the form of directing habits of consciousness, which are themselves unconscious. The notion of *mana* is one of these principles: it is given in language; it is implied in a whole series of judgments and reasonings, carrying attributes which are those of *mana*. We have said that *mana* is a category. But *mana* isn't only a special category of primitive thought, and today, by way of reduction, it is again the first form assumed by other categories always functioning in our mind, those of substance and of cause. (xxix–xxx)

Following Durkheim, they claimed that such categories were ultimately of a social derivation. Jung was to cite or refer to this passage on no less than eight occasions.

Manikins and *churingas*

Jung's library contains an annotated copy of an 1873 German translation of Tylor's *Primitive Culture*. As he did not comment on anthropological issues in his early writings, it is hard to gauge his initial views here. His reading of anthropology was taken up in earnest from 1909 onwards. In *Memories*, he recounted that his dream of descending into the cellars of a medieval house had awakened his old interest in archaeology, and that he subsequently began to read works on myths.[24] This consequently led him to see the close relationship between ancient mythology and the psychology of "primitives," which led him to take up the study of the latter.[25] As we have seen in the previous section, it was during this period that Jung turned to phylogeny to provide a basis for the understanding of individual development. These psychobiological researches were linked to his anthropological reading: for the assumption of phylogenetic inheritance led to the view that the "data" on what was inherited would be provided by anthropology. Thus anthropology could provide a window into mankind's collective inheritance.

His anthropological reading at this time led to a reminiscence to which he accorded a pre-eminent significance. In *Memories*, he narrated an experience which he described as having marked the climax of his childhood. At age of ten, he carved a manikin on his pencil case, and made a coat and bed for him. He also painted a stone, which "belonged" to the manikin. He hid this figure in the attic, and it provided a great sense of solace for him. At times, he would write letters to him in a secret language that he had invented. He did not understand why he did this, but it gave him a

---

[24] See above, 137–138.
[25] Memories, 1963, 186. In the Countway manuscript, this was followed by the following statement: "Freud's simultaneous interest in this field gave me moments of uneasiness, for I thought I saw again on his part that predominance of theory over facts which I was already familiar with," CLM, 179.

sense of security. However in 1910, in the course of preparatory reading for *Transformations and Symbols of the Libido*, he came across accounts of the Australian churingas and of a cache of soul-stones near Arlesheim. This reminded him of his manikin and stone: "Along with this recollection there came to me, for the first time, the conviction that there are archaic permanent components of the soul which can have penetrated the individual soul from no tradition" (*Memories*, 38, trans. mod.). He added that at a much later date, he examined his father's library, which did not contain a single work from which this could have been derived, and his father knew nothing of such matters. At this unspecified date, he was clearly investigating whether there could have been a cryptomnesic source for his actions, as Théodore Flournoy would doubtless have suspected. He concluded that as a child, "I performed the ritual in the same way as I later saw done by the natives of Africa, they act first and do not know at all what they are doing" (*ibid.*, 39, trans. mod.) reiterating the stereotypical equations between modern "primitives," prehistoric man, and children. It is useful to look closely at this experience, given its prototypical and auto-exemplary character.

As Jung narrates it, this recollection constituted the dawning recognition of the existence of the archetypes. It gives the impression that his conviction was a spontaneous inspiration. While this may well have been the case, there are grounds for suggesting that it may also have been informed by his prior readings. Fortunately, preparatory reading notes for *Transformations and Symbols of the Libido* have survived, which contain citations from Lévy-Bruhl's *The Mental Functions*, including the passages concerning the *churinga* cited above.[26] In addition, his own copy of the work contains numerous annotations. Lévy-Bruhl drew his information on the *churinga* principally from Spencer and Gillen's *The Central Tribes of Northern Australia*, a work which he also possessed, and cited in "On the energetics of the soul" (1928). In his reading notes, the passage from Spencer and Gillen which Lévy-Bruhl cited is copied, together with the reference to their work.[27] In his citation, he underscored the following statements:

a man who possesses a churinga like the *churinga serpent protects it with his hand in an uninterrupted manner* . . . [he] comes to feel *that a quality of a special sort passes from the object to him and from him to the object* . . . *he is intimately united with the ancestor.*[28]

---

[26] JP. It was part of Jung's working method to at times write out quotations and page references from specific works.

[27] See above, 292.

[28] There is also a stroke in the margin by this passage in Jung's copy of *Les fonctions mentales*, 97. I have here retranslated Lévy-Bruhl's French rendition of Spencer and Gillen.

This indicates that it was Lévy-Bruhl's work that was the initial source of Jung's information concerning the *churinga*. This being the case, it poses the question as to the relation of his interpretation of this episode to Lévy-Bruhl's. For Lévy-Bruhl, the practices around the *churinga* were examples of mystical participation, which, as we have seen, he claimed was present in modern societies in an attenuated form. For Lévy-Bruhl, what was at issue here was the survival of a particular form of mentality. This would seem to fit in with Jung's statement that he acted in the same way as the natives in Africa. However, Jung also claims that what was important was the similarity of the content of the act, and not just how it was done. He did not interpret this as a spontaneous reinvention of a particular practice, but as indicating the existence of an atemporal component of the soul. This would correspond to Bastian's elementary thoughts. One can conjecture that it was through combining key concepts of Bastian and Lévy-Bruhl that Jung came upon the conviction of the existence of that which he would subsequently call archetypes.

The history of thought

In *Transformations and Symbols of the Libido: A contribution to the history of the development of thought*, Jung first attempted to extend psychology to encompass prehistoric, primitive, and modern man. He commenced the work by speaking of the powerful impression made by Freud's reference to the Oedipus legend, likening it to one's first impressions of antique monuments. Its significance was that it demonstrated the living presence of the past, and bridged the "abyss" which separates us from antiquity. This insight taught an identity of elementary human conflicts, independent of time and space. It held out the prospect of the mutual illumination of modernity and antiquity. The study of the individual soul could enable one to grasp the living meaning of antique culture, as well as providing a firm point of view outside of our own culture, which would enable one to objectively understand it (*CW* B, 2). While psychoanalysis had concentrated on the problems of individual psychology, the time had now come to turn to historical materials, and study how they might illuminate the problems of individual psychology. Jung was proposing to rework individual psychology radically on the basis of ethnopsychology. In a similar manner to Lazarus, Steinthal, and Wundt, he focused on mythology. Like Wundt, he viewed mythology psychologically. Where he differed from Wundt's apperceptive theory of myth was in the nature of the subjective contents involved: for Jung, myths were symbols of the libido. He claimed that there had to be typical myths, which corresponded to the ethnopsychological development of complexes: "Jacob Burckhardt seems to have suspected this, since he once said, that every Greek in classical times carried a piece of Oedipus in him, and every German a piece of Faust" (§ 56, trans. mod.). In a footnote, he cited a letter of Burckhardt in which the latter wrote:

> What you intend to find in Faust, you will have to find in an intuitive way. – Faust is namely a genuine and legitimate myth, i.e., a great primordial image [urtümliches Bild], in which everyone has to intuit *his* own being and destiny again in his own way. Let me make a comparison: whatever would the ancient Greeks have said, if a commentator had planted himself between them and the Oedipus saga? For the Oedipus saga there lay an Oedipus chord in every Greek that longed to be directly touched and to vibrate after its own fashion. And so it is with the German nation and Faust.[29]

This passage was of exceptional significance for Jung. He referred to it on several occasions, in a manner which affirmed and augmented Burckhardt's statement. He subscribed to Burckhardt's reading of the significance of Faust for Germany. In 1945, he stated: "When Jacob Burckhardt says, Faust strikes a chord in the soul of the Germans, Faust must have gone on sounding."[30] He took this to its penultimate conclusion: "Now Germany has suffered the pact with the devil and its unavoidable consequences."[31] Secondly, he adopted Burckhardt's usage of "primordial image" [urtümliches Bild] as a conceptual term. Werner Kaegi notes that the term urtümliches Bild or Urbild did not originate with Burckhardt, as it stemmed from the seventeenth century, hence Jung's attribution of it to the latter is significant (1947–1982, 4, 464). Indeed, the term "Urbild" was also used by another figure that was significant for Jung – Carl Gustav Carus, who, interestingly enough, referred to the figure of the "mothers" in Goethe's *Faust* as "Urbilder" (1868, 15). Kaegi notes that Burckhardt didn't use the term often, but that when he did, it featured in an important art historical context. What appears to have been most significant for Jung was the reference to Faust, given its overpowering importance for him.

It was through his theory of the different types of thinking that Jung articulated the ongoing dynamic relation between the ancient and the modern. In *The Principles of Psychology* (1890), William James had contrasted

---

[29] *Ibid.*, trans. mod. In 1802, Schelling stated apropos Goethe that "We Germans owe him a particular debt, since we have acquired from him our most important mythological figure: Doctor Faust. Whereas we share other mythological figures with other nations, this one is ours alone, since he is cut straight from the middle of the German character and its basic physiognomy" (69). Incidentally, Burckhardt had attended Schelling's lectures in Berlin.

[30] "After the catastrophe," *CW* 10, § 434, trans. mod.

[31] *Ibid.*, § 436, trans. mod. Jung again referred to Burckhardt's comment concerning the relation of Faust to Germany in "Psychology and poetry" (1930), *CW* 15, § 153 and § 159, and in "Paracelsus as a spiritual phenomenon" (1942), *CW* 13, § 154.

associative thinking or empirical thought with reasoning or reasoned thought. He noted that much of our thinking was a spontaneous reverie, a sequence of images which suggested one another. In such thinking, the linkages were provided by contiguity and/or similarity, such that

a sunset may call up the vessel's deck from which I saw one summer the companions of my voyage, my arrival into port, etc., or it may make me think of solar myths, of Hercules' and Hector's funeral pyres, of Homer and whether he could write, of the Greek alphabet, etc. (1890, 2, 325)

James speculated on the historical relation between these two modes of thought, and claimed that reasoning by analogies preceded reasoning by abstract characters. He claimed that the historical transition from associative thinking to reasoning was far from complete, and that "over immense departments of our thought" we were all still in a savage state (365).

Taking his cue from James, whom he had recently met, Jung contrasted directed thinking and fantasy thinking.[32] The former was verbal and logical. The latter was passive, associative, and imagistic. The former was exemplified by science and the latter by mythology. In a similar fashion to James, he claimed that ancients lacked a capacity for directed thinking, which was a modern acquisition. Fantasy thinking, which was generally called dreaming or fantasizing, took place when directed thinking ceased, and to describe it, he cited the first passage from James above, emphasizing the second half of the sentence.

Jung reiterated the anthropological equation between the prehistoric, the primitive, and the child, speaking of the "parallel between the phantasticmythological thinking of antiquity and the similar thinking of children, of the lower races and of dreams."[33] Consequently, the elucidation of current day fantasy thinking in adults would at the same time shed light on the thought of children, savages, and prehistoric peoples.

It is important to grasp that he was not simply reiterating this equation, but endowing it with a new determination based upon this model of the two types of thinking. This equation was explained by the fact that the biogenetic law, that ontogeny recapitulated phylogeny, held good for

---

[32] Other figures Jung cited were Liepmann, Ebbinghaus, Külpe, Wolff, Nietzsche, Lotze, Baldwin, Hamman, Mauthner, Kleinpaul, Paul and Freud. However, Jung's general sequence bears closest resemblance to James'.

[33] CW B, § 36, trans. mod. In his 1952 revision of this text, Jung qualified this. He added that "one must certainly put a large question-mark after the assertion that myths spring from the 'infantile' soul life of peoples. They are on the contrary the most mature products that earlier humanity produced. . . . the man who thought and lived in myth was a grown reality and not a four-year-old child. Myth is certainly not a childish phantasm, but one of the most important requisites of primitive life." *Symbols of Transformation*, CW 5, § 29, trans. mod.

psychology, as well as comparative anatomy.[34] When affirming the validity of the biogenetic law, he was not primarily concerned with advancing a biological thesis: rather, his psychological reformulation of the biogenetic law enabled him to link individual psychology with ethnopsychology, collective psychology, mass psychology, and anthropology. Not only could the findings of individual psychology illuminate the latter disciplines, their findings could elucidate individual psychology, due to the persistence of collective, mythological, and primitive thought in the individual. Critically, these other disciplines were subordinated to psychoanalysis, as it was only through psychoanalytic interpretation that the true meaning of their material could be uncovered. Thus psychoanalysis would form a superordinate discipline, whose provenance reached into the prehistory of humanity.

To date, *Transformations and Symbols of the Libido* has only been considered from the perspective of the Freud/Jung break. However, around the same time, Théodore Flournoy was elaborating very similar ideas concerning types of thinking and the relation between prehistory and modernity. In his lectures on the history and psychology of the occult sciences in 1912–1913 (which were repeated in 1915–1916), Flournoy differentiated two attitudes of mind – the one orientated towards reality, the other towards the dream.[35] His distinction can be said to have formalized what had been one of the guiding themes of his work: the study of the workings of the creative imagination, and its contrast with rational thought. In a similar manner to Jung, he commenced by claiming that important indications as to prehistoric mental states could be furnished by the contemporary savages, the opinions of the masses, infantile mentality, pathological states, and dreams. Sleep was characterized by a regression to earlier stages:

> The summits of mental development break down each night and the scholar himself falls back into the state of the infant, of the dement, of the savage and of our primitive ancestors. Humanity made the same path that each of us makes between dreamless sleep and full consciousness. In this passage the banalities of which we think the least can be revelatory and permit us to grasp hold of the life of primitive mental states.[36]

What these conditions held in common was that they each partook of archaic thinking. He contrasted this with scientific thought:

---

[34] See above, 213–219.

[35] Flournoy presented his lectures from notes. In what follows, my account of Flournoy's lectures has been reconstructed from student notes taken for his 1912–1913 course by L. Baliassy, for his 1915–1916 course by Arnold Reymond (archives, University of Geneva), as well as from his own manuscript notes (private possession, Olivier Flournoy, originals in French).

[36] Lecture course, 1915–1916, notes of Arnold Reymond, BPU, 7–8.

scientific or moral thought is always voluntary; it is directed by ourselves; it is active and implies an effort on our part. When we abandon this latter, we fall into involuntary, automatic thought. The psychic mechanism functions by itself and calls forth anti-scientific, anti-real and anti-moral representations. (10)

The first, thought, was active, voluntary, teleological, rule bound; it required effort, took account of reality and consisted in abstract notions and words. The second, imagination, was passive, automatic, goalless, free, and spontaneous; it was playful and required no effort, took no account of reality and expressed itself in images, intuitions, and symbols. While the former required a state of rest, wakefulness, and possession of one's faculties, the latter was present in states of fatigue, sleep, hypnosis, and madness. Everyday, we found a mixture of both types of thinking, and that both were necessary: on the one hand, without imagination, science would make no progress, and on the other, artistic creation involved certain logical rules. He related these distinctions to Freud's contrast between the pleasure principle and the reality principle, and Janet's distinction between the function of the real and the function of the fictive.

In comparing Flournoy's account with Jung, the parallelism is quite striking. Jung's account of the two types of thinking appeared around August 1911. While in Jung's early work, one can straightforwardly trace the influence of Flournoy on him, in this case, it is hard to determine to what extent one is dealing with the influence of Flournoy on Jung, the reciprocal influence of Jung on Flournoy, or independent, converging elaborations. What is clear is that Jung's growing distance from Freud was at the same time an ever growing proximity to Flournoy.

Transformations and Symbols of the Libido was based upon an article published in 1905 by an American woman, Frank Miller, in Flournoy's *Archives de Psychologie*. For Jung, what was striking about her fantasies was the presence in them of mythological themes. As I have argued elsewhere, while Frank Miller herself interpreted these in the manner of Flournoy, through searching out the possible cultural sources for each element, Jung, by contrast discounted any external source, and instead argued that they had an endogenous origin, and represented the emergence of a phylogenetically antecedent mode of thought (Shamdasani, 1990). To demonstrate this, he attempted to establish parallels between her fantasies and a vast collection of myths and customs through utilizing a comparative method.

In two subsequent works, Jung explicitly commented on his method. In 1912 in his lectures on psychoanalysis at Fordham University, he stated that "in exploring the unconscious, we proceed in the usual way when conclusions are to be drawn by the comparative method" (*CW* 4, § 329). He further elaborated the rationale for this method in 1914 in his presentation before the Psycho-Medical Society in London, "On psychological understanding."[37] In describing the constructive method of interpretation, he noted that it contained an analytic part, which consisted in a "reduction to general types of phantasy," which were primarily supplied by mythology. The parallel between individual delusions and myths had become an important source for the comparative exploration of psychopathology. What legitimated this comparison was the fact that both were "products of the creative phantasy of the unconscious" (1915, 394–395). Boas would have raised the question as to whether the assertion of their common source was in fact derived from their surface similarities.

From this, it emerges that the comparative method served two purposes for Jung, which were interlinked. First, the comparative study of mythologies led to the thesis that what underlay them were certain universal invariant forms, akin to Bastian's elementary thoughts, which were called primordial images in 1911, dominants in 1917, and archetypes in 1919. Without the comparative method, the anthropological component of Jung's theory of archetypes would simply collapse.

Secondly, in Jungian analysis, the comparative method, renamed the constructive method, and later, amplification, furnished a mode of interpretation that enabled an individual to come into an appropriate relation with the archetypes. It was only the establishment of analogies with mythological material that enabled a comprehension of the non-personal images, and hence fostered the prospective development of the individual. At a theoretical level, this involved two comparative operations (though in practice, these were not always distinct). The first level of comparison led to the recognition of the archetypes (as indicated above), and the second consisted in a comparison of these with the specific images that appeared in analysis. With the use of mythological and anthropological material in the method of amplification, Jung introduced an interdisciplinary mode of interpretation into analysis. The psychic unity of mankind was not only the presupposition of the theory of the collective unconscious. The goal of analysis was to overcome individual alienation through revealing this unity.

The individual and the collective

What can one do . . . when, instead of educating a man for himself, people want to educate him for others? Harmony is then impossible. Obliged to fight either against nature or against the social institutions, one has to choose between making

---

[37] See above, 64–65.

a man or a citizen; for one cannot make the one and the other at the same time. (Jean-Jacques Rousseau, *Emile*)[38]

For centuries, philosophers, educationalists, and social commentators in the West had deliberated on the relations between the individual and society, frequently envisaged under the form of an antinomy of conflicting demands. As we have seen, these debates were reformulated in psychology through the language of crowd psychology. The implication was that psychology could find a solution to these moral and political debates through giving them a scientific basis. However, the ethical valuations by no means disappeared, as we have seen in the case of Baldwin's work. Rather, a moral discourse of rights and obligations was given a new lease of life through being recast in psychological terms.

In *Transformations and Symbols of the Libido*, Jung made his first attempt at providing a psychological model that encompassed the individual and society, linking individual and collective psychology. What he had yet to elaborate in detail was the mode of their interaction, and how an individual could resolve this conflict. The attempt to establish the normative relations between the individual and society occupied a central position in Jung's social and political vision.

It was in 1916 that he broached these issues at greater length, in several talks presented in Zürich. The first of these, "The structure of the unconscious," was published the same year in French in Flournoy's *Archives de Psychologie*.[39] Here, Jung set out how a resolution of the conflict between collective and individual interests could emerge through considering some of the typical phases of analysis. He commenced by differentiating the personal psyche and the collective psyche. Each individual possessed a personal unconscious, whose contents were acquired through

---

[38] Cited by Jung, "The structure of the unconscious" (1916), *CW* 7, § 455, note. In an unpublished manuscript dated September 1932, "The images of the goal in the psychology of the unconscious" (JP), Jung described himself as being "no friend" of Rousseau's philosophy.

[39] Flournoy was actively engaged in trying to introduce Jung's work into the French speaking world. In 1916, on hearing that Edith Rockefeller McCormick was willing to fund translations of Jung's work into French, he wrote to Maeder: "Mrs. McCormick will have made a great service to analytical psychology by having Jung's work translated. But this is so difficult! Where will one find the man qualified for such a delicate task! A translation is something impossible, – what is necessary is a paraphrase which will give the equivalent (in good French) of the text of Jung adapted to our language; this involves a great knowledge not only of the two languages, but also of psychology and mythology . . . It is a considerable work for which I do not see anyone capable" (29 June 1916, Maeder papers, original in French). (The work was *Transformations and Symbols of the Libido*.) A number of years later, Jung wrote to Charles Baudoin that a work of his that he had sent showed that the Latin mentality could understand his conceptions. He recalled that his dead friend Flournoy had reproached him with having an "excessively teutonic mentality" (original in French, September 11, 1933, JP).

one's life, together with psychological factors which could just as well be conscious. Alongside such factors, individuals held collective contents in common. He argued:

just as certain social functions or drives are, so to speak, opposed to the interests of the single individual, so also the human mind has certain functions or tendencies which, on account of their collective nature, stand opposed to the individual contents. (*CW* 7, § 455)

In this initial formulation, the positing of collective mental functions occurs precisely under the sign of their opposition to individual interests. These collective functions stemmed from the fact that every individual was born with a highly differentiated brain, which served to explain the similarity of people in different races, as represented by the uniformity of myths. The collective psyche consisted in a collective spirit and collective soul (the terminology here indicating the connection to the ethnopsychology of Lazarus, Steinthal, and Wundt). Like a Russian doll, this collective psyche contained within it limitless smaller collective psyches: "In so far as there are differentiations corresponding to race, descent, and even family, there is also a collective psyche limited to race, tribe and family over and above the 'universal' collective psyche" (§ 456). However at this juncture, Jung did not lay much emphasis upon these differentiations, and tended to consider the relations of the individual to the collective *per se*. The implication was that one's relation to the universal collective psyche was of more determining power than one's relation to familial or racial collectives.

Drawing upon Janet, he claimed that the collective psyche contained the inferior parts of the mental function, which, as it was inherited and omnipresent, was impersonal. The personal psyche contained the superior parts, which had been ontogenetically acquired. In "primitives," mental functioning was essentially collective. Progressive individual differentiation resulted in an increased consciousness of oppositions, such as that between good and evil. Individual development proceeded through the repression of the collective psyche, as "collective psychology and personal psychology exclude one another in a certain sense" (§ 459, trans. mod.). Thus collective movements were always a threat to the individual. Psychologically, individuals were menaced by their propensity for imitation (under which Jung subsumed suggestion and mental infection):

Human beings have a capacity which is of the utmost use for purposes of the collective and most prejudicial to individuation, and that is *imitation*. Collective psychology cannot at all dispense with imitation, without which the organization of the mass and the regulation of the state and society would simply be impossible. (§ 463, trans. mod.)

The centrality given to imitation immediately recalls Gabriel Tarde's *The Laws of Imitation*. Jung was clearly subscribing to Tarde's account of society as structured by imitation. His one qualification was that imitation hindered individuation. Yet at this juncture, he had not specified what individuation was, or how it could be attained.

Analysis of the collective psyche revealed several universal attributes, the first of which he termed the *persona*. This was "a mask of the collective psyche; *a mask which simulates individuality*, which makes others and oneself believe that one is individual, while it is only a part being played, through which the collective psyche speaks" (§ 465, trans. mod.). The analysis of the persona led to the dissolution of the individual in the collective. The identification with the collective gave rise to an experience of "Godlikeness," a term which Jung borrowed from Alfred Adler. Adler had stated that likening oneself to God or godlikeness (Gottähnlichkeit) was a motif frequently found in fantasies, fairy tales, and psychoses. He viewed this as the expression of the "masculine protest" – the desire to be a more complete man, to compensate for feelings of inferiority (1912a, 89). This dissolution also released a stream of fantasies of a mythological nature.

When confronted with this situation, there lay the option of attempting to restore the prior condition, which Jung claimed was the path taken by Freud and Adler. He contended that their reductive treatments of the unconscious in terms of sexuality and power represented false solutions. Thus the therapeutic limitations of Freud and Adler's analysis were due to their failure to resolve sufficiently the conflict between the individual and the collective. An alternative would be to identify with the collective psyche and be a prophet, which was also unsatisfactory. The failure of these approaches, Jung claimed, was that they respectively allowed the individual psyche and the collective psyche to predominate. The solution lay in a conscious assimilation of the contents of the unconscious. The constructive interpretation of fantasies led to the synthesis of the individual and the collective psyche, and hence to the recognition of the "lifeline" of the individual, which was a combination of the "individualistic and collective tendencies of the psychological process at a given moment" (*CW* 7, § 515). The lifeline of an individual defied scientific description. This was because: "It is necessarily always only the collective part of an individual psychology that can be the object of science . . . Every individual psychology must have its own textbook, for the general textbook only contains collective psychology" (§ 484, trans. mod.). In other words, it was only through reformulating collective psychology, crowd psychology, ethnopsychology, and anthropology that a scientific psychology would be possible.

Further manuscripts exist, dated October 1916, which were the basis of talks that were given at the Psychological Club in Zürich. These talks take up the issue of the relation of the individual to the collective, which had been discussed by Baldwin. More recently, these themes had been discussed in the summer of 1916 in the Psychological Club, in two presentations by Maria Moltzer (1874–1944).[40] In the first talk, "On the concept of the libido and its psychic manifestations," Moltzer argued that in addition to the introversion and extraversion tendencies, there existed an individualization tendency. As we have seen, Wundt had argued that the development of mankind consisted in a progressive individualization. The first two tendencies were mainly collective, in that they represented tendencies of the libido to create contact with collectivity. By contrast, the individualization tendency tried to create a form of its own, through a combination of personal and impersonal elements. This tendency was connected with the incest barrier, through the fact that a developing person could not find his life solely in connection with collectivity. This led to a need for differentiation. The individualisation tendency had to fight against the "polypus" of collectivity, and was symbolized by the hero.

Jung's talks were delivered to the Club a few months later, in October. The first is titled "Adaptation." This took two forms: adaptation to outer and inner conditions. However, within outer conditions, he included "conscious judgments which I have formed of objective things," and the "inner" was understood as designating the unconscious (*CW* 18, § 1085–1086). A neurosis consisted in a disturbance of adaptation. Under certain situations in analysis, a demand was raised by the unconscious, which was expressed in the form of an intense transference. This represented an overcompensation for an irrational resistance to the doctor which in turn arose from a demand for individuation. This demand was contrary to adaptation to others. The notion of individuation corresponded quite closely to Moltzer's concept of the individualisation tendency.[41] The answering of this demand and the corresponding break with conformity led to a tragic guilt, which required expiation, and called for a "*new collective function*" (§ 1095, trans. mod.). This was because the individual had to produce values which could serve as a substitute for his

---

[40] For the text of these talks, see Shamdasani, 1998b.

[41] The term "individuation" had been used by Schopenhauer. He defined space and time as the principium individuationis, noting that he had borrowed the expression from Scholasticism. The principium individuationis was the possibility of multiplicity (1819, 145–146). The term was taken up by Eduard von Hartmann, who saw its origin in the unconscious. It designated the uniqueness of each individual set against the "all-one" unconscious (1869, 519). In 1912, Jung wrote: "Differences arise through individuation. This fact gives a deep psychological justification to the essential part of the Schopenhauerian and Hartmannian philosophies" (*CW* 5, §180, trans. mod.).

absence from the "the collective personal atmosphere" (§ 1096, trans. mod.). These new values enabled the reparation of the collective. Individuation was for the few. Those who were insufficiently creative should rather reestablish collective conformity with a society. Not only had the individual to create new values, he had to create socially recognizable values, as society had a "right to expect *realizable* values" (§ 1097, trans. mod.).

The second manuscript is titled "Individuation and collectivity." Here, he commenced by stating that individuation and collectivity were a pair of opposites related by guilt. Society demanded imitation. Here, however, he provided a different estimation of the value of imitation for individuation than he had done in "The structure of the unconscious": "Through imitation, one's own values become *reactivated* . . . imitation is an automatic process that follows its own laws . . . Through imitation the patient learns individuation, because it reactivates his own values" (§ 1100). Here, the efficacy of analysis rested on imitation. He evaded the consequent charge of analysis simply being a process of cloning or indoctrination by claiming that imitation worked by awakening latent pre-existing values. Hence imitation was a form of platonic recollection. His reference to the existence of "laws of imitation" is again strongly suggestive of Tarde's *The Laws of Imitation*.

In his notes to the first publication of these papers, Richard Hull put forward a biographical explanation apropos the contradiction between Jung's statements on imitation:

This complete *volte face* points to the ferment of Jung's ideas at this time. It seems that the two equations, individuation = guilt and imitation = individuation, painfully reflect Jung's personal situation at that time. He was torn by opposite "destinies": the necessity to individuate and the necessity to conform and be of social value. (1970, 176)

To read such papers biographically, however justified, leaves out the fact that Jung clearly intended to describe the means by which any individual could achieve optimal relations with society. The impression of a "complete *volte face*" is lessened when one bears in mind that in the second account, the imitation that is valorized as fostering individuation occurs within the specific setting of analysis. Arguably, one could say that in social life, imitation hindered individuation through promoting conformity to collective values. Within the setting of analysis, since the desired "conformity" was itself individuation, imitation was beneficial – that is, if one held that individuation was indeed a universal intrapsychic process, and not simply a goal suggested by Jung and his co-workers. In either case, it is clear that he held that the process of analysis was the pre-eminent locus in which an individual could resolve the conflicting demands of individuation and collectivity. His model of individuation as a middle way came close to Baldwin's proposal of tempered individualism as a means of resolving the conflicting demands of the individual and society.

While Jung had attempted to forge a link between individual and collective psychology, he considered that solutions to collective problems were best approached through the psychological transformation of the individual. This was the great psychological conclusion that Jung drew from the first world war. In a preface to his 1917 *The Psychology of the Unconscious Processes: An Overview of the Modern Theory and Method of Analytical Psychology*, dated December 1916, he proclaimed:

The psychological processes, which accompany the present war, above all the incredible brutalization of public opinion, the mutual slanderings, the unprecedented fury of destruction, the monstrous flood of lies, and man's incapacity to call a halt to the bloody demon – are suited like nothing else to powerfully push in front of the eyes of thinking men the problem of the restlessly slumbering chaotic unconscious under the ordered world of consciousness. This war has pitilessly revealed to civilized man that he is still a barbarian . . . But the psychology of the individual corresponds to the psychology of the nation. What the nation does is done also by each individual, and so long as the individual does it, the nation also does it. Only the change in the attitude of the individual is the beginning of the change in the psychology of the nation. (*CW* 7, 4, trans. mod.)

War made visible the chaotic unconscious. While collective events could release the demons of the unconscious, the only resolution lay on an individual level. As Jung saw it, for many, this message had sunk in. In his preface to the second edition of this work, dated October 1918, he spoke of the growing interest in the problems of the human soul. The war had had the effect of forcing men to look within themselves. In a language that recalled William James' essay, "The moral equivalent of war," he asserted: "Every individual needs revolution, inner division, dissolution of the prevailing and renewal" (*CW* 7, 5, trans. mod.). This would be achieved through self-reflection and a return of the individual to the "ground of the human essence." Understood in this manner, analysis could furnish the basis for cultural renewal.

The Psychology of the Unconscious Processes provided an exposition of the collective, suprapersonal, absolute unconscious – these terms being interchangeably used. Frequently dismissed as an individual delusion, or embraced as a creation of creative genius, the concept of the collective unconscious is deeply interwoven with the development of anthropology, sociology, crowd psychology, collective psychology, and ethnopsychology, as well as with concepts of the unconscious in philosophy and physiology, as sketched out in the previous section.

The contents of this unconscious were what Jung in *Transformations and Symbols of the Libido* had called typical myths or primordial images. He wrote: "There are in every individual, beside personal reminiscences, the great 'primordial' images, as Jacob Burckhardt once aptly indicated" (§101, trans. mod.). Jung provided the following definition of them: "The primordial images are the most ancient and the most universal thoughts of humanity. They are as much feelings as thoughts; because of that one can name them *original feeling-thoughts* [ursprüngliches Fühldenken]."[42] He also called the primordial images, dominants:

The collective unconscious is the sediment of all the experience of the world of all time, and is also an image of the world, that has been forming for aeons. In the course of time certain features, the so-called *dominants*, have been brought out. These dominants are the ruling powers, the gods, that is, images of dominating laws and principles, average regularities in the sequence of images, that the brain has received from the sequence of secular processes. (432, trans. mod)

His reference to the "so-called *dominants*" suggests that he was referring to a usage that was well known. Lamprecht's dominants immediately come to mind. A sequence of references in Jung's works indicate that he was familiar with Lamprecht's work.[43]

If Jung adopted the term dominants from Lamprecht, certain reasons suggest themselves for it. Lamprecht's theory of dominants provided a psychological model of history which articulated a strong linkage between the individual and the collective. As seen earlier, for Lamprecht, the transition between epochs could be explained through the rise and fall of dominants. If one compares Jung's dominants with Lamprecht's, one sees that Jung utilized Lamprecht's general schema of the interrelation between the individual and the collective. For Jung, the dominants were located in the collective unconscious. This would be incompatible with Lamprecht's model, given his espousal of the unconscious, and the collective nature of the dominants. Where Jung differed was in his identification of these dominants with Burckhardt's primordial images, and more generally, with Mauss, and Hubert's categories and Bastian's elementary thoughts. Over and above all of these however, Lamprecht's work would have provided a fully articulated psychological theory of history, and that too, by a renowned German cultural historian. Unfortunately, the increasing discredit accorded to Lamprecht's work mitigated against any rhetorical gains to be made from any overt linkage. This may explain

---

[42] "The psychology of the unconscious processes," 1917b, 411, trans. mod.
[43] Jung, "On psychological understanding," *CW* 3, § 421; "Answer to Job," *CW* 11, § 576.

why, after the introduction of the term archetype, Jung dropped the term dominant. Curiously, however, after the war, he began to use it again.[44]

Jung and Bastian

On six distinct occasions between 1936 and 1946, the anthropologist whom Jung singled out for formulating the concept of archetypes *avant la lettre* was Adolf Bastian (1826–1905). Jung stated that what he called archetypes, "had long ago been called 'elementary' or 'primordial thoughts' by Bastian."[45] Bastian, he claimed, was "The first investigator in the field of ethnology to draw attention to the widespread occurrence of certain 'elementary ideas.'"[46] This proximity between his concept of the archetype and Bastian's ideas led Jung, in the following instance at least, to downplay his originality:

The theory of preconscious primordial ideas is by no means my own invention, as the term 'archetype', which stems from the first centuries of our era proves. With special reference to psychology we find this theory in the works of Adolf Bastian and then again in Nietzsche. In French literature Hubert and Mauss, and also Lévy-Bruhl, mention similar ideas. I only gave an empirical foundation of what were formerly called primordial or elementary ideas, "catégories" or "habitudes directrices de la conscience", "représentations collectives", etc., by setting out to investigate certain details.[47]

Here, he claims that his contribution simply consisted in putting ideas such as those of Bastian, Nietzsche, Hubert and Mauss, and Lévy-Bruhl on an empirical basis. Elsewhere, he claimed that it was Bastian's work that supplied some of the empirical support for his theory of archetypes.[48] By the time that he made these acknowledgments, Bastian's work had largely fallen into oblivion.

The breadth of Jung's anthropological reading makes it safe to assume that he would have encountered references to Bastian's work early on, such as in Edward Tylor's *Primitive Culture*. If he had not done so before, it is likely that he would have read Bastian's work during the course of his preparatory reading for *Transformations and Symbols of the Libido*.

As Jung indicates, the proximity of his concept of the archetype to Bastian's concept of the elementary thoughts is readily apparent.[49] Like

[44] See below, 350.
[45] "The concept of the collective unconscious," 1936, CW 9, 1, § 89.
[46] "The psychology of the mother archetype," 1938, CW 9, 1, § 153.
[47] "Psychology and religion," 1937, CW 11, § 89.
[48] "Medicine and psychotherapy," 1945, CW 16, § 206.
[49] The parallelism was also noted by Koepping, 1983, 118.

Bastian, he argued that the universality of mythic motifs could be explained only through supposing the existence of a common intrapsychic source. Similarly, he also claimed that through their actualisation, archetypes took on specific cultural and historical colorations. As against Bastian, explanations through migration and diffusion were used as counterarguments against Jung's concept of archetypes. In 1940 Jung claimed that the lack of recognition given to the universality of mythic motifs was due to disciplinary compartmentalization, and the hypothesis of migration, and that it was due to these factors that Bastian's ideas had met with little success in their time.[50] What was lacking then were the "necessary psychological premises." Thus he was aware that his theory went against the grain of anthropological orthodoxy, where it would have been viewed as a reversion to the "outmoded" Bastian. Indeed, diffusion was commonly appealed to as a repudiation of the existence of archetypes. Yet what enabled Jung to take this stance was the fact that while he drew upon Bastian's anthropological work as an empirical support for his theory of archetypes, it was ultimately psychology which held the key to the explanation of the genesis of cultural forms. Hence in the last analysis, anthropology was subordinated to psychology.

Racial inheritance or categories of the imagination?

In 1912 Jung investigated "Negroes" at St. Elizabeth's Hospital in Washington DC at the invitation of the American psychiatrist William Alonson White. In retrospect, he stated that the purpose of this visit had been to investigate the unconscious of "Negroes": "I had in mind this particular problem: are these collective patterns racially inherited, or are they 'a priori categories of the imagination' as two Frenchmen, Hubert and Mauss, quite independently of my work, have called them."[51] This indicates that Jung read Hubert and Mauss' *Miscellany of the History of Religions* sometime prior to 1912.[52] When asked in 1959 by John Freeman whether in retrospect there was any experience that Jung regarded as a turning point, one of the experiences he cited was his sojourn at St. Elizabeth's. To Freeman, he stated that he went there "in order to find out whether they have the same types of dreams that we have" (Freeman, 1959, 388). Directly after his trip, he reported to Freud that he "analysed" fifteen "Negroes."[53]

---

[50] "The psychology of the child archetype," 1941, *CW* 9, 1, § 259.
[51] "Symbols and the interpretation of dreams," 1961, *CW* 18, § 81.
[52] Jung's copy of Hubert and Mauss' work contains marks in the margin by the passage cited above, and particularly in the section dealing with sacrifice.
[53] November 11, 1912, *FJL*, 516.

A manuscript has survived, entitled "the psychology of Negroes," which corresponds to the abstract of a talk of the same title which Jung gave on November 22, 1912 to the Zürich Psychoanalytical Society. The notes consist of some general remarks concerning "Negroes," and in particular, their religious ideas, followed by brief notes on ten patients. According to the abstract, he stated that the psychoses of the "Negroes" were the same as those of whites. In light cases, diagnosis was difficult, as it wasn't clear whether one was dealing with superstition. "Negroes" were very religious, and their ideas of God and Christ were very concrete. Examining "Negroes" was difficult, as they did not understand what one wanted of them, and were generally ignorant. The "Negro" had a great inability to go into his own thoughts. On an earlier occasion, he had seen how some of the qualities of the American, such as self-control, arose from living together with the uncontrolled "Negroes." At the same time, the white man was a desired image for the "Negro." In the manuscript, a number of dreams are recorded. To some of the elements in them, he indicated mythological parallels, such as to the wheel of Ixion, a painting in the Musée des Beaux Arts in Geneva, the gnostic text "Poimandres," the crater of Zosimos and the Rig Veda. According to the abstract, he stated that there were many symbols of sacrifice in dreams, "exactly as the lecturer had mentioned in his work, *Transformations and Symbols of the Libido*" (*CW* 18, § 1285). The conclusion which he drew from this was that "this symbol is not only Christian, but finds its origin in a biological necessity" (*ibid.*). Thus symbols of sacrifice, rather than being culturally specific, were universal. He subsequently stated that his investigation convinced him that these patterns were not racially inherited, but archetypic (chronologically speaking, as Jung was not to employ the term archetype until 1919, it is likely that he would have initially regarded such patterns as *a priori* categories of the imagination in Hubert and Mauss' sense).

Jung's investigations appeared to have inspired White. He wrote to Jung informing him that he was busy reading Frazer's *The Golden Bough*, and that "the concepts which you gave me while here have enabled me to carry over the story from 'Primitive Man' and read it again in the psychoses."[54] In 1921, Jung stated he had been able to demonstrate "a whole series of motifs from Greek mythology in the dreams of pure-bred Negroes suffering from mental disorders."[55] However, he only gave one example of this. In 1935 he stated that an "uneducated" "Negro" from the south who was "not particularly intelligent" told him a dream of a man being crucified on a wheel. He stated that while it was quite probable for him to

---

[54] November 29, 1912, White papers, LC.   [55] *Psychological types*, *CW* 6, § 747.

dream of someone being crucified on a cross it was quite improbable for him to dream of someone being crucified on a wheel, which suggested that the image was not a personal acquisition:

Of course I cannot prove to you that by some curious chance the Negro had not seen a picture of sort and then dreamt about it; but if he had not had any model for this idea it would be an archetypal image, because the crucifixion on the wheel is a mythological motif. It is the ancient sun-wheel, and the crucifixion is the sacrifice to a sun-god in order to propriate him . . . In the dream of the Negro, the man on the wheel is a repetition of the Greek mythological motif of Ixion.[56]

While stating that this case by itself did not constitute proof, it was one of the critical experiences that gave him a clue that, as he wrote in 1952, "It is not a question of a specifically racial hereditary, but of a universally human characteristic."[57]

As quoted above, Jung claimed in 1936 that his achievement with his theory of archetypes was simply in giving "empirical foundation for what were formerly called primordial or elementary ideas, 'catégories' or 'habitudes directrices de la conscience,' 'répresentations collectives, etc.'[58] The "habitudes directrices de la conscience" were referred to by Mauss and Hubert, and Jung's spelling of "catégories" in French indicates that he was referring to their categories of the imagination. In 1928 he stated that the unconscious contained "impersonal, collective components in the form of inherited categories or archetypes."[59] However, there was no reference in Hubert and Mauss to categories being inherited, and they strictly refrained from biological speculation, stressing the sociogenesis of concepts and customs. At another juncture, he stated that he assumed that Mauss and Hubert called these a priori thought forms categories with reference to Kant.[60] (However, for the Durkheim school, these a priori categories were not timeless, but were socially constructed.) Jung added that "The authors assume that the primordial images are given through language. This assumption is certainly correct in individual cases, but in general it is contradicted by the fact that through dream

---

[56] "The Tavistock lectures" (1935), CW 18, §§ 81–82. In Jung's manuscript, "On the psychology of negroes," a dream of a woman was recorded (in English) with the following scene: "She is suspended over hell, down in hell. *revolving wheel*[1]) through which she was turned down, but the Christ child released her." In the margin, it is noted: "1.) Ixion" (2, JP).
[57] *Symbols of Transformation*, CW 5, § 154.
[58] "Psychology and religion," *CW* 11, § 89.
[59] "The relations between the ego and the unconscious," *CW* 7, § 220. In a note, he referred to the passage from Hubert and Mauss cited above.
[60] "On the archetypes, with special reference to the anima concept," 1936, *CW* 9 pt.1, § 136.

psychology as through psychopathology a mass of archetypic images and connections become extracted daily which would not even become communicable through the historical use of speech" (*ibid.*, trans. mod.). Hubert and Mauss referred to categories, not primordial images. This is illustrative of the manner in which Jung read other people's work through his own conceptions, which is particularly marked in his readings outside of psychology and psychiatry.

Jung cited Lévy-Bruhl's concept of collective representations, Hubert and Mauss's categories of the imagination, and Bastian's elementary or primordial ideas and concluded that the concept of the archetype "is not exclusively my concept, but is also recognized and named in other fields of knowledge" (§ 89, trans. mod.). This statement indicates the manner in which he regarded the concept of the archetype as the pivotal connection between psychology and the human sciences in general. If the concept was as widely recognized as he claimed, his own concept of the archetype would have met with little opposition, and would have been welcomed by those that utilized concepts of collective representations. Thus it could have become a key unifying concept of the human sciences, as it was intended to be. That this was not at all the case appears in part to have been due to the fact that apart from Bastian, whose work had fallen into discredit at this stage, the others whom Jung cited all belonged to Durkheim's school, and whether Jung realized it or not, their own understanding of categories and collective representations was quite different from what he took them to mean.

Mystical participation

The main anthropologist contemporary to Jung from whose work he drew was Lévy-Bruhl. On Jung's invitation, Lévy-Bruhl lectured at the Psychological Club in Zürich. There is little indication of the nature of their contact, but the evidence that there is indicates a level of cordiality at the very least. In 1935 Lévy-Bruhl sent Jung a copy of his *Primitive Mythology. The Mythical World of the Australians and the Papuans*, bearing the following dedication: "to Mr. Dr. C. G. Jung/in memory of his very friendly reception/L. Lévy-Bruhl."[61] Later that year, Lévy-Bruhl contributed an article, "Remarks on the initiation of medicine men," to the Festschrift volume for Jung's sixty-fifth birthday, *The Cultural Meaning of Complex Psychology*. On July 31 Jung wrote to him thanking him for this contribution and added: "I was very touched that you took the trouble to

---

[61] (Original in French.) In a letter of 21 February, 1935, Jung thanked Lévy-Bruhl for sending him a copy of this work. Lévy-Bruhl also sent Jung an offprint of his article, "The Cartesian spirit and history," with the dedication: "with the thanks and compliments of L. Lévy-Bruhl" (Seperata, JP, original in French).

write this article which is of a very special interest for me."[62] It is Jung's relation to Lévy-Bruhl's work that most clearly reveals his views on the interdisciplinary relation between psychology and anthropology.

He adopted two concepts from Lévy-Bruhl: mystical participation and collective representations. In 1929, he described Lévy-Bruhl's nomination of mystical participation as the hallmark of primitive mentality as a "stroke of genius."[63] He employed this term on numerous occasions, and his use of it may be characterized as consisting in an endorsement, a redefinition, and an extension of it. He wholeheartedly accepted Lévy-Bruhl's depiction of primitive mentality in *The Mental Functions*. Whilst Lévy-Bruhl had been criticized for his lack of fieldwork, after Jung's travels, the latter continued to affirm the basic outlines of Lévy-Bruhl's depiction of primitive mentality.

While Lévy-Bruhl had made no recourse to any concept of the unconscious, Jung argued that mystical participation was the same thing as projection and unconscious identity.[64] In 1921, after stating that he had derived the term from Lévy-Bruhl, he defined mystical participation as denoting:

a peculiar kind of psychological connection with objects. It consists in the fact that the subject cannot clearly distinguish himself from the object but is bound to it through a direct relationship which one can describe as a partial identity. This identity is founded on an *a priori* oneness of object and subject. The p. m. is a vestige of this primitive condition.[65]

Thus he subscribed to Lévy-Bruhl's claim that consciousness initially derived from a primary condition of mystical participation, and that the development of civilization could be characterized as consisting in an increasing individualization. While concurring that it was better observed in "primitives" than in civilized peoples, he argued that there was less difference than Lévy-Bruhl initially claimed, stating that it was "only a shade more characteristic of the primitive than of the civilised."[66] He added that Lévy-Bruhl was unaware of this, due to his lack of psychological knowledge. Jung claimed that with "primitives," mystical participation showed itself in their relationship with their environment, as well with each other; with civilized peoples, it was generally restricted to the personal form, such as in the transference relation, where one individual obtained a magical effect over another.[67]

---

[62] Jung to Lévy-Bruhl, July 31, 1935 (JP, original in French).
[63] "Commentary on 'The secret of the golden flower'," *CW* 13, § 66.
[64] "Archaic man," 1931, *CW* 10, § 131; "On the Tibetan book of the great liberation," 1939/1954, *CW* 11, § 817n.
[65] *Psychological types*, *CW* 6, § 781, trans. mod.
[66] *Mysterium Coniunctionis*, 1955–1956, *CW* 14, § 817n.
[67] *Psychological types*, 1921, *CW* 6, § 781.

If "primitives" behaved like children, it followed that the psychology of one could be transferred to the other. Consequently, Jung argued that the child lived in a state of mystical participation with his parents.[68] This position led him to draw a parallel between individual development and the development of mankind: both consisted in the transition from an originary condition of mystical participation to one of conscious individuality, and ultimately individuation:

Every advance, every conceptual achievement of mankind, has been connected with an advance in self-awareness: man differentiated himself from the object and faced Nature as something distinct from her. Any reorientation of a psychological attitude will have to follow the same road.[69]

This formed his psychological version of the biogenetic law. As in civilized people, mystical participation was principally present in relationships, an epochal significance was given to psychotherapy, whose "therapeutic effect par excellence" was the dissolution of mystical participation.[70] For the development sought at an individual level in psychotherapy corresponded with the development of the human race.

A psychologist at large

In contradistinction to Lévy-Bruhl, Jung did have first-hand experiences of the "primitives" that he talked about: in 1920 he visited North Africa, in 1925 he visited the Pueblo Indians in New Mexico and traveled in Kenya and Uganda, and in 1938 he was in India.[71]

In 1920, he accompanied his friend Hermann Sigg, who was on a business trip to North Africa. His intention was "to see for once the European from the outside, reflected by a milieu which was foreign in every respect" (*Memories*, 266, trans. mod.). He held that the only means of gaining an understanding of one's own national peculiarities was through becoming aware of how others viewed them. Hence traveling was the *via regia* to a comparative ethnopsychology.

His descriptions of his experience confirmed his prior convictions concerning primitive psychology. At the same time, a significant new element entered into these descriptions: while modern-day "primitives" were still seen to correspond to our prehistoric ancestors, and hence designated a prior stage in the development of consciousness, aspects of their life

---

[68] "Child development and education," 1928, *CW* 17, § 107.
[69] "General standpoints on the psychology of dreams," 1948, *CW* 8, § 523.
[70] "Commentary on "The secret of the golden flower'," 1929 *CW* 13, § 66.
[71] For Jung, Indians and "primitives" did not think, but perceived their thoughts. "On the unconscious," (1918) *CW* 10, § 15. "What India can teach us," (1939) *CW* 10, § 1007.

are valorised, as designating something that has been lost in the transition to modernity. Thus after watching the preparations for a festival in the Sahara, he noted that the people lived from their affects, and their consciousness was not reflective. We lacked their intensity of life.

His observations also "confirmed" French crowd psychology: simply being in such a crowd was sufficient to provoke a phylogenetic regression. The closeness to life of such people who lived from their affects had a suggestive effect upon "those historical layers in us which we just have overcome, or at least think we have overcome" (272, trans. mod.). He likened such an existence to the "paradise of childhood," which, like the latter, "thanks to its naiveté and unconsciousness, sketches a more complete picture of the Self" (*ibid.*). On reflection, he noted that aside from his conscious aim of wishing to observe the European from the outside, his unconscious aim had been to discover that part of his personality that had been obscured through being a European. Consequently, he felt that there was a danger that his European personality would be overwhelmed by an invasion from the unconscious, or that he would succumb to "going-black." The same phenomenon recurred five years later on his return to Africa. He dreamt of his barber in Chattanooga, Tennessee, curling his hair, to give him "Negro hair." He interpreted this as a warning from the unconscious, which indicated that "the primitive was a danger to me. At that time I was obviously "going-black" (302, trans. mod.). Consequently, he realized that he had gone to Africa to escape Europe with its problems, and that:

The trip revealed itself as less an investigation of primitive psychology . . . than much more to have as its object an embarrassing question: What is going to happen to Jung the psychologist "in the wilds of Africa"? A question I had constantly sought to evade, in spite of my intellectual intention to study the European's reaction to the conditions of the primeval world [Urweltsbedingungen]. (303, trans. mod.)

His geographical voyages were a form of phylogenetic time traveling. In 1925, he visited the Pueblo Indians in Taos, New Mexico. He thought that when he was in the Sahara, he had been with a civilization that had the same relationship to ours as Roman antiquity did. This led him to want to continue the historical comparison "by descending to a still deeper cultural level" (275, trans. mod.)

New Mexico

In the twenties, many artists and writers went to New Mexico, out of a recognition of a sense of bankruptcy of American civilization. The

Indians were viewed as people who had maintained their cultural integrity, and were rooted in communities with living traditions. Thus they were looked to as a source of renewal for white culture (Rudnick, 1984, 144). At the same time, they attracted anthropological interest. The anthropologist Ruth Benedict described them as: "one of the most widely known primitive peoples in Western civilization. They live in the midst of America, within easy reach of any transcontinental traveller" (Benedict, 1934, 57).

Jung's visit was arranged by Jaime de Angulo, and it is important to grasp their relation and collaboration to set it into context. De Angulo, described by Ezra Pound as the "American Ovid," was a linguist, ethnologist, ethnomusicologist, writer, and patron saint of the beat generation. His ex-wife, Cary de Angulo, had gone to live in Zürich to work with Jung at the beginning of the twenties (she later married Peter Baynes, and accordingly changed her name to Cary Baynes). In 1922, Jaime de Angulo wrote to her:

if you have Jung's ear you may try to make him realize that people who are thoroughly soaked in primitive thought . . . think he is all wrong about the anthropological part of his thesis. And a man of his intelligence cannot afford to ignore that criticism.

What I would do to take him with me among Indians – or even to only talk with him and make him realize what all these customs that have been so misunderstood are really like, and what the savages really feel!

I wonder how much real, scholarly study he has made in these fields. You see, it is simply too bad to erect a beautiful structure as Freud did in Totem and Taboo, and then find that the *basic facts* are wrong![72]

He also had sessions with Jung in 1923, and his initial impressions were very favorable. To Cary de Angulo, he wrote "my gratitude for him is boundless. He has liberated my mind, but above all given me the philosophical key which I had been groping for so long and was so vital to me."[73] The regard appears to have been mutual, for Jung provided funding for his fieldwork.[74] When he returned to Berkeley, he sent dreams to Cary de Angulo to read to Jung. She discussed them with Jung, and conveyed Jung's comments and interpretations to Jaime de Angulo. It was Jung who enabled him to realize the "paradoxical knife edge" of balancing the rational and irrational, which profoundly affected his ethnological work. He described this transformation to Cary de Angulo in the following way:

[72] April 20, 1922, Cary Baynes papers.   [73] November 9, 1923, Cary Baynes papers.
[74] On December 31, 1923, Jaime de Angulo wrote to Cary de Angulo conveying his joy at hearing from her that he would be getting 500 dollars for his fieldwork from Jung (Cary Baynes papers).

When I was with the Indians before, I called the spirits with them, and I *believed* in the spirits, altho I told no one I did. I knew I could not explain or excuse my belief, so I kept it secret. I talked with them about the rocks who spoke at night and the animals who are sorcerers, and I believed it, but I kept it secret . . . Well, now, I can talk both languages. I can speak about the rocks, the real rocks, with my Indians, and about the spirits, and I do know these rocks are the same thing as certain true facts in the world of psychology. They are the equivalents in the world of biology. I can talk either language, psychologically, in terms of biological facts (as the Indians do) or biologically in terms of psychological facts (as white men do, without knowing it).[75]

He planned to write his impressions on certain problems of primitive psychology, and to send them to Jung via Cary de Angulo, so that Jung could set him right at the start. In 1924, Jaime de Angulo visited Taos.[76] In Taos, he stayed with Mabel Dodge, who had married a Pueblo Indian, by name of Tony Luhan. On arriving in Taos, he narrated his conversations with Tony Luhan and his impressions to Cary de Angulo. In replying to Luhan's criticism that the whites simply wanted to know about the Indians to satisfy their curiosity, he replied, "I want to know because I think the whites have lost their soul and they must find it again. Some of the things the whites have lost, the Indians have kept."[77] He confirmed that he wouldn't tell anyone anything he managed to learn, "except that man in Switzerland and he will never tell, but he can do good with it" (*ibid.*). To Cary de Angulo, he added,

Even if I should ever get anything, even if I had permission to publish, I would not do it, I believe. I would not for this reason: because I begin to see clearly that the life of the pueblo community is inextricably tied to its ceremonies . . . Now the moment that that esoteric symbol is opened, revealed, published, it will become a dead sign, exoteric, a museum thing – and the Indians will die. . . . If I get any stuff that will help Jung I will give it to *him*, but I will not sacrifice the pueblo of Taos for the sake of museum anthropology. (39)

After his visit to Taos, he wrote to Cary de Angulo that he meant to write a résumé of his psychological impressions of the Pueblo Indians for Jung.

---

[75] January 26, 1924, Cary Baynes papers.
[76] An account of his time there is found in Mabel Dodge's *Lorenzo in Taos* (1933). Dodge's book focuses on D. H. Lawrence's sojourn there. Concerning Jung, Lawrence wrote to Mabel Dodge, "Jung is very interesting, in his own sort of fat muddled mystical way. Although he may be an initiate and thrice-sealed adept, he's soft somewhere, and I've no doubt you'd find it fairly easy to bring his heavy posterior with a bump down off his apple-cart. I think Gourdjieff would be a tougher nut," September 23, 1926, 310. For Lawrence, it was among the Pueblos that he found the strongest instance of living religion, "a vast and pure religion, without idols or images . . . A cosmic religion the same for all peoples, not broken up into specific gods or saviours or systems" (1928, 187).
[77] April 1924, G. de Angulo, 1985, 38.

He wrote to her concerning some of these, and asked her to read them to Jung, and to convey back to him any criticisms Jung might have. Jaime de Angulo conjectured that at the stage of culture which the Pueblo Indians were at, there was as yet no division into introverts and extraverts, and no division of the functions of thinking, feeling, sensation, and intuition. He thought that "there is no differentiation, or rather, there is differentiation but each man carries the whole burden equally balanced."[78] However, the overall psychological level was lower, that is, more diffuse, somnolent and less conscious. He conjectured that "Perhaps it was necessary, in order to obtain that keener degree, that intenser psychic life, to destroy the balance and develop each function separately" (*ibid.*). He criticized Lévy-Bruhl's depiction of the Indian mind as pre-logical, and claimed that it was logical as often as it was irrational. Rather it was post-Renaissance culture which was one-sidedly rational.

At the end of 1924, Jung visited America.[79] He cabled Jaime de Angulo, asking to meet in the Grand Canyon, offering to cover his expenses. Shortly after the trip, Jaime de Angulo wrote to Mabel Dodge about how he managed to take Jung to Taos, and of what ensued:

I made up my mind that I would kidnap him if necessary and take him to Taos. It was quite a fight because his time was so limited, but I finally carried it. And he was not sorry that he went. It was a revelation to him, the whole thing. Of course I had prepared Mountain Lake. He and Jung made contact immediately and had a long talk on religion. Jung said that I was perfectly right in all that I had intuited about their psychological condition. He said that evening "I had the extraordinary sensation that I was talking to an Egyptian priest of the fifteenth century before Christ."[80]

Thus it was due to Jaime de Angulo that Jung visited Taos. Jung's interest in the Pueblos had been stirred by Jaime de Angulo, who had given him ideas as to what he might find, as well as carefully preparing Jung's crucial conversation with Mountain Lake (Antonio Mirabel). Further indication of the importance of Jaime de Angulo's work for Jung is a letter from the former to the linguist Edward Sapir. Jaime de Angulo had sent some aphorisms on language to Jung, who had made comments, which he intended to forward to Sapir. Jaime de Angulo wrote:

The situation is this: Jung says to me, "all this psychological material which you are getting from the Indians as a result of your identification with them, and which you say cannot be given out to the world because that would destroy its mystic nature and value to the Indians, is of extreme importance to me for the work I am doing. However it is of paramount importance to yourself that you should have

---

[78] July 10, 1924, Cary Baynes papers.   [79] Concerning this trip, see McGuire, 1978.
[80] January 16, 1925, Dodge Papers, Beineke library, Yale University.

something to show to the world. Let your linguistic work be that. Now I will see to it that you get the necessary financial backing." Maybe you know that there are in Chicago some wealthy patients of his who will do anything for him.[81]

Jaime de Angulo did not publish anything on the religious life of the Pueblo Indians, and, as Jung suggested, only published on aspects of their language. The same year, he wrote a letter to Ruth Benedict, who asked for assistance concerning her proposed field trip to Taos. Benedict had asked him to introduce him to an informant who would tell her their ceremonials and tales. He replied:

do you realize that it is just this sort of thing that kills the Indians? . . . That's what you anthropologists with your infernal curiosity and your thirst for scientific data bring about. Don't you understand the psychological value of secrecy at a certain level of culture? . . . You know enough of analytical psychology to know that there are things which must not be brought up to the light of day, otherwise they wither like uprooted plants. . . . Of course if you promised that you would never publish the *actual* secrets, I would help you all I can. I would tell you a lot myself of the meaning of the whole thing.[82]

In his view, the significance of the Pueblos for contemporary Americans was that it was only through recognizing the Indians as their spiritual ancestors that Americans could find their spiritual stability.

Shortly after visiting New Mexico, Jung wrote to Cary de Angulo:

The trip was wonderful and Jaime was forced to behave. He did, with some reluctance. I saw Taos. I made friends with Mountain Lake and I talked to him sympathetically as if he were a patient in advanced analysis, it was a great time. The keynote of that country is secrecy.[83]

The significance of his time in New Mexico is demonstrated by a manuscript which Jung wrote, entitled "African voyage." Before turning to this, one needs to consider his trip to Africa which took place later that same year.

Africa

Given Jung's phylogenetic perspective, a journey to Africa, held to be the source of mankind, took on a particular significance. He traveled in the company of H. G. Baynes and George Beckwith. Their group was called the Bugishu psychological expedition. Later, they were joined by an

[81] April 15, 1925, cited in Gui de Angulo, *The Old Coyote of Big Sur: The Life of Jaime de Angulo*, draft chapter 11, 10.

[82] May 19, 1925, Gui de Angulo, 1985, 91–93, 550.

[83] January 19, 1925, Cary Baynes papers.

English woman, Ruth Bailey.[84] His trip led him to understand that "within the soul from the primordial beginning there has been a longing for light and an irresistible urge to rise out of its primordial darkness . . . The longing for light is the longing for consciousness" (*Memories*, 298–299, trans. mod.). His journey itself became an *imitatio* of the supposed origins of consciousness. Concerning his voyage up the Nile, he commented:

The myth of Horus is the story of the newly risen divine light. It would have been told after the deliverance out of the primordial darkness of prehistoric times through culture, that is to say through the revelation of consciousness. Thus the journey from the interior of Africa to Egypt became for me like a drama of the birth of light, which was intimately connected with me, with my psychology. (303, trans. mod.)

He did not elaborate on precisely how this drama was linked to his own psychology. He did however give some indication of the connection between his anthropological excursions and his own psychology in a passage which was omitted from the published version of *Memories*:

My experiences during the years 1913–1917 had burdened me with a tangle of problems whose nature demanded that I should study the psychic life of non-Europeans. For I suspected that the questions put to me were just so many compensations for my European prejudices. What I had seen in North Africa, and what Ochwiay Biano told me, were the first clues to an adequate explanation of my experiences.[85]

The years in question, which Jung dubbed his confrontation with the unconscious, were those during which he elaborated his theories of the collective unconscious and individuation. His statement here indicates that what he personally went through could also be conceived as a de-Europeanization. Extrapolating from this, the import for Westerners of the exploration of the collective unconscious could also be conceived of from this perspective. The task was one of reaching a synthesis of the Western and the primitive, without "going black." In a further passage that was also omitted from *Memories*, he reflected upon his impressions on returning to Europe:

---

[84] There is indication that Jung had some consultation with anthropologists in planning his trip. On June 12, 1925, Charles Seligman wrote to him, "I expect you are quite right to limit your trip to Uganda. You will be able to get about much more easily, see more natives, i.e., come into contact with more tribes sufficiently accustomed to white people to be useful to you – and of course the Uganda highlands are much more more healthy than the Sudan" (JP).

[85] CMS, 356. Ellenberger once asked Jung why he didn't publish his observations on the Elgoni, to which "Jung answered that being a psychologist he did not want to encroach upon the field of the anthropologist" (1970, 739).

It seemed to me that our conventional modes of conceiving and dealing with psychological problems were as inadequate as would be an attempt to use diamonds as road fill. No doubt this sounds exaggerated; but I employ this exaggeration with good reason because it reproduces my state of mind of that time. My modern self-assurance suffered a staggering defeat. Simultaneously richer and poorer, I returned from these travels to the task of my European existence. *"Tout cela est bien dit – mais il faut cultiver notre jardin,"* [all that is well said – but we must cultivate our garden] says Candide.[86]

Primitives and moderns

In 1926, Chauncey Goodrich, who had accompanied Jung on his trip to New Mexico, wrote to Walter Fewkes, the chief of the bureau of American ethnology at the Smithsonian Institution, informing him that he had received a request from Jung to obtain for him a set of the reports of the bureau. Goodrich wrote:

He has recently made a trip to Africa, spending several months among a primitive tribe on the slopes of Mt. Elgon. A year and a half ago with a party of which I was a member, he visited Arizona and New Mexico, spending some time at Taos, etc., and becoming much interested in the cultural and psychological aspects of the Pueblo Indians. At the moment he is writing on the subject of the more primitive culture with which he has been in more recent touch in Africa, but at the same time and in that very connection is anxious to familiarize himself more deeply with the available records on the American Indian.[87]

The volumes were duly shipped to Jung. The manuscript which Jung was writing was entitled "African voyage." This actually focused on general questions concerning psychology and anthropology, and on the Pueblos of New Mexico in particular. A few brief excerpts were taken from it and published by Aniela Jaffé in *Memories*. Unfortunately, the most important reflections were omitted.

The manuscript commenced with a reflection on the subjective conditioning of knowledge. Jung noted that the world was not only an outer experience but an inner one as well. While we assumed that what we called the world was the outer object, in actuality, this was a reflection and mental creation. This was because our "mental possibility of registration" was by no means a *tabula rasa*. Rather, it was constituted through presuppositions. Hence "registration is assimilation."[88] This was already indicated by the physiological process of perception. In everyday life, one often

---

[86] *Ibid.*, 392–393. These are the famous last lines of Voltaire's *Candide* – Candide's reply to his tutor Pangloss. (1759, 100). Jung kept a bust of Voltaire in his study.

[87] June 4, 1926, San Francisco Jung Institute Library.

[88] "African voyage" (JP, 1).

acted as if "the thing had forced its own interpretation" (2). However, the history of science indicated the extent to which inborn judgments had shaped our conceptions in such a way that they had little to do with the actual nature of things. The fear of subjectivity in scholarship led to thinking being forsaken in a quest for clear facts, and to the emphasis on amassing objective material records, the use of statistics, and photographic and phonographic registration. Presuppositionlessness had become an ideal – the assumption that "the material dictates and the thought orders itself under it" (2) However, he argued that it was only a short step from this ideal to mindlessness. What was left out of this was a consideration of the psychological factor of judgment, which was the "conditio sine qua non of knowledge" (3). This statement indicates his distance from the phenomenological movement.

An example of the playing down of the subjective factor was travel writing, in which one generally found depictions of outer facts and adventures, but little account of inner experiences. The same discounting of the subjective factor was present in scientific and ethnographic reports. This had serious consequences, as there were "many things in exotic peoples that we can only understand through subjective reactions in ourselves" (4). Without taking account of what happened to us when we came into contact with them, their world would remain incomprehensible to us. As an example, he cited the distinction that certain Indians made between ordinary coyotes and doctor coyotes, which is meaningless to us, for whom all coyotes were ordinary coyotes. What we failed to realize was that the difference was not to be seen outwardly, but inwardly. This raised the question of whether a white man who exposed himself to the effects of the exotic atmosphere would be psychically altered in such a way as to perceive differences of personality between animals of the same species. Enabling oneself to be psychically altered in such a way was the only means by which one could understand the mysteries and strangeness of the primitive mind. This formulation represented a further development of the notion of the personal equation: what was required was that one allowed oneself to be transformed by what one was trying to study, and to observe the changes in oneself. The problem, however, was that if one enabled oneself to be affected in such a way, one might lose the capacity of reportage. The best example of this was Dennett's book, *At the Back of the Black Man's Mind*, which bore the stamp of his having been overly exposed to primitive influences.[89]

---

[89] Dennett, 1906. The object of his work was to show that there was in Africa a religion giving a higher conception of God than is generally acknowledged, and to make clear the importance of the kingly office for African communities. This would have the effect of

Our own cultural spirit was a structure constructed from the relics of what our ancestors had built. The care which we accorded to the preservation of monuments from antiquity and the middle ages was an expression of their psychic power: the historical object affects the corresponding part of our historical personality. Such remnants, as we were connected to them through an uninterrupted historical tradition, affected conscious mental contents in us. This was not the case with prehistoric things, which affected our unconscious prehistoric mind.

Cultures could be differentiated as to whether they were marked by a historical or unhistorical spirit. The historical piety which marked the present was only about 150 years old. Times in which the unhistorical spirit ruled were those in which the present was given an absolute value, and for which the past was only a preliminary stage. By contrast, historical times doubted their own meaning. The concern with the past was prompted by the question of whether something valuable had been left behind, something which would lead to a new meaning in the present.

This explained the love/hate relationship which we have with the primitives, and the importance of studying the psychology of white settlers. Common speech had a term for the psychic alignment with the primitive: "going black." It wasn't only in Africa that the mutual influence of races coming into contact with one another was felt – such effects could be witnessed in America.[90]

The significance of anthropology did not only lie in the quest for knowledge of other cultures. He held that it was only through contact with other cultures that one could see one's own culture from the outside, just as one only became aware of one's own natural peculiarities through meeting people from other nations.

As indicated earlier, the most crucial episode in his stay in New Mexico was his encounter with Mountain Lake. It was through his conversation with Mountain Lake that his desire to see the European from the outside was fulfilled. In the manuscript, he reported some of the details of their conversation, which he referred to on several occasions. Two issues appeared to have particularly struck him. The first was Mountain Lake's view of the white man:

I asked him why he thought the whites were all mad.
He replied: "They say that they think with their heads."
"Why of course. Where do you think?" I asked him surprised. "We think here,"

----

facilitating the work of the missionaries and colonial government (v). Dennett described himself as "One who has lived so long among the Africans, and who has acquired a kind of way of thinking black" (233).
[90] The manuscript contains an extensive section on this topic. A number of these reflections found their way into Jung's 1930 paper, "Your negroid and Indian behaviour," *CW* 10.

326 Jung and the Making of Modern Psychology

he said, indicating his heart. I fell into a long meditation.
For the first time in my life, so it seemed to me, someone had drawn for me a
picture of the real white man. (*Memories*, 276, trans. mod.)

The second was the role of the sun in their religion and cosmology: "He
said, pointing to the sun, 'Is not he who moves there our father: How can
anyone say differently: How can there be another god. Nothing can be
without the sun' (279). Mountain Lake added that "We are the sons of
Father Sun, and with our religion we daily help our father to go across
the sky. We do this not only for ourselves, but for the whole world. If we
were to cease practising our religion, in ten years the sun would no longer
rise."[91]

Jung was impressed to encounter a solar monotheism, which he felt
corresponded to a spiritual disposition that lay several thousand years
behind us. By contrast, the mythic and cosmological embeddedness of
the Pueblo Indians showed us precisely what we had lost, and our spiritual
poverty. Of the Pueblo Indian, he said, "Such a man is in the fullest sense
of the word in his place" (282, trans. mod.).

As indicated in his letter to Cary de Angulo, Jung was impressed by
the importance of secrecy for the Pueblos. There would be no point in
asking about their religious practices. He grasped that the preservation
of their mysteries gave cohesion and unity to the Pueblos. Consequently,
ethnographic interest posed a great danger to them. He noted that despite
the fact that "every tourist is allowed to disturb the peace of the Egyptian
graves of the Kings and the solemn sight of the many thousand year
old regal dead with idiotic remarks," one didn't give the treasures of the
museums to fools ("African voyage," 26). However, this was precisely
what happened if one took the "most vital representations, which are
the spine of a whole collectivity" and published them (*ibid.*). Such an

---

[91] *Ibid.*, 280. The analytical psychologist Frances Wickes also befriended Mountain Lake.
In an unfinished autobiography, she narrated her first conversation with Mountain Lake,
which is strikingly close to what he said to Jung: "How does the white man keep his
partnership with a God who lives in a church or a far off heaven? An Indian must feel his
God always near him – He stretches out his hand and his God fills it with warmth. Then
he knows that his father is the Sun. Even at night, his god is there, living in the warmth
of the fire that burns upon his hearth How can there be any God but the Sun, and how
could he journey across the sky without the help of the Indian . . . The Indian does
not perform sacred dances for himself but for all the world. Without his partnership the
Sun would not move across the heavens and the world would sink into frozen darkness.
This the white man does not understand for he thinks with his head but the Indian
thinks with his heart" (Wickes collection, LC). As borne out by his correspondence with
Chauncey Goodrich, Mountain Lake was fluent in English, and actively campaigned
in defence of the Pueblos, who had been succumbing to moonshine whisky (Goodrich
papers, Bancroft library, UCSF).

act would destroy the mysteries. Jung's views on this matter were in full agreement with de Angulo's, cited earlier.

Concerning Mountain Lake's comments that the Pueblos think with the heart, Jung described this as a "prepsychological level" (28). This phrase seems to have been an alternative for Lévy-Bruhl's conception of "prelogical mentality," as he added that the latter phrase overemphasized the logical element. At this level, the differentiation of the functions of thinking, feeling, sensation, and intuition had not yet begun. Consequently, no function could be an object for another function. Hence there could be no psychological criticism. It was this that gave primitive conceptions their specific character. With the "primitives," conceptions emerged from the totality of the psyche. With us, however, conceptions arose through the isolation of the thinking function above the other functions.[92] These reflections followed and extended Jaime de Angulo's comments on the psychology of the Pueblo Indians cited earlier.

Pre-psychological conceptions, as Lévy-Bruhl had already said of collective representations, had a high affective value. Such conceptions mastered the psyche of the "primitive" and induced him to corresponding action. Jung considered this probably to be the origin of cultic action. In the West today, our mentality was so identified with consciousness that the Church had to demand that one believe in God, which indicated that "one has to give this representation artificial value or pump life into it" (36). This indicated that our prepsychological conceptions had gone under. However, such prepsychological "idées forces" (force ideas) still existed today, though in absurd dress.[93]

The manuscript concluded with some reflections on the different approaches of the ethnologist and psychologist. In ethnology, so much material had been collected and published, that the psychologist was simply helpless before it. This was part of a wider problem, that beset the sciences in general, the fact that "the extent of our present day sciences is simply hopeless. The proliferation of facts has flooded everything" (59). The development of ethnographic collections had led to a museum culture, in which the items became curiosities which served the recreational needs of a public in search of education. What was lost in such collections was the meaning and significance of the objects. It was for this reason that

---

[92] Jung also remarked on the "contentless state of immersion" that the Pueblos seemed to be in during the preparations for the Buffalo dance, noting that de Angulo had also confirmed this to him. In subsequent years, de Angulo turned against Jung, and became sharply critical of him. To Ezra Pound, he wrote: "ai introdysed him to the Indians in Taos & the s-o-b queered things for me thru his tuetonic stupidity . . ." December 23, 1949, Jaime de Angulo papers, UCLA.

[93] On Alfred Fouillée's conception of force ideas, see above, 195–196.

while such collections were meaningful for the ethnologist, they were of little help for the psychologist. Jung's reflections here were in accord with Jaime de Angulo's critique of "museum anthropology" cited earlier.

Finally, he reflected on the character of accounts of "primitives." The general impression one got from the literature on the subject was that they were a completely different type of man to us, with strange thoughts, paradoxical customs, and incomprehensible emotions. However, this was due to the fact that travelers tended to report what seemed incomprehensible to them, as opposed to what wasn't. This heightened the impression of strangeness.

The task for the modern became one of regaining this mythic and cosmological embeddedness exemplified by the Pueblos, without sacrificing the gains of modern consciousness. Individuation was conceived as a conjunction which resolved the conflict between the primitive and the modern.

During this period, he reformulated his views on the task of analysis, setting it within a global and historical perspective. Neurosis was conceived as consisting in a conflict between the primitive and the modern. Not only did he claim that primitive mentality survived in the unconscious, he equated the two. Anthropology could be put to a new use – to provide knowledge of the modern unconscious. In a seminar, in 1925, he noted that the understanding of primitive mentality was essential for the analysis of dreams. He recommended the reading of Dennett's *At the Back of the Black Man's Mind*, adding that "one should, in fact, read this work several times, as the ideas therein are by no means easy to grasp on first becoming acquainted with them" (Crow, 1925, 9–10).

These comments demonstrate that the anthropology of "primitives" was a key element in the constitution of his concept of the unconscious, the primitive in the modern. The anthropological account of the primitive mind could also be read as a description of the contemporary unconscious. It is here that his avowal of the significance of phylogenetic inheritance takes on its significance. Transferring the anthropological account of the archaic and primitive into the soul of the modern was a critical element in the constitution of the concept of collective unconscious. However, at the same point in time, it was precisely these equations which were unravelling in anthropology itself.

Jung among the anthropologists

Jung's reliance on Lévy-Bruhl was criticized by specialists who were otherwise favourably disposed to his work. In 1924, the anthropologist Paul Radin, a former student of Franz Boas, wrote to Cary de Angulo:

What you say about Jung feeling that if anything, Lévy-Bruhl underestimated "participation mystique" among primitive people is bewildering; and it is all the more bewildering to me that he (Jung) makes this statement on the basis of impressions obtained after a short sojourn among half-mohammedanized regions.[94]

He went onto say that while no men like Aristotle, Hume, and Kant existed amongst "primitive" people, they did possess people like Plato and Hegel. Thus while they didn't separate mind and matter in an Aristotelian fashion, it didn't mean that they didn't distinguish them – rather, that they assumed an interaction between the two. Radin had been invited by Jung to lecture to the Psychological Club in Zürich about American Indian religion, and he also attended Jung's seminar in 1925. In *Psychological Types* Jung had cited the following anecdote:

A Bushman had a little son upon whom he lavished the characteristic doting affection of the primitives . . . One day he came home in a rage: he had been fishing and had caught nothing. As usual the little fellow ran eagerly to greet him. But the father seized him and wrung his neck on the spot. Subsequently of course he mourned for the dead boy with the same abandon and lack of comprehension as had before made him strangle him.[95]

In 1927 Radin critiqued Lévy-Bruhl's work and the equation of the primitive and the prehistoric in his *Primitive Man as Philosopher*. Concerning Jung's citation, he stated that no greater distortion could be imagined. This illustrated the "unconscious bias" that lay in our view of primitive mentality, namely, the assumption of its lack of differentiation and integration. Radin argued that Jung's errors were due to "a certain mistiness of vision due to that sentimentality from which the northern European finds it so difficult to free himself" (1927, 40). He added that the fact that such an example could be used by Jung to describe the reactions of "primitives" showed the depth of ignorance that still existed on the subject. Unconscious bias, mistiness of vision, sentimentality and plain ignorance were Radin's summations of Jung's views of the "primitive."

For Radin, Jung's reliance on Lévy-Bruhl was his downfall. In 1929, he expanded on this issue. He noted Lévy-Bruhl would view the incorporation of his work by Jung with perhaps not unmixed feelings. As Radin saw it, the psychological approach to ethnology suffered from nearly all the defects of Lévy-Bruhl's approach, while being less informed and less critical (1929, 24). In discussing Jung's theories, he highlighted their relation to a central issue in nineteenth-century anthropology, that of the

[94] 24 November, Cary Baynes papers.
[95] *CW* 6, § 403. This quotation has been given in H. G. Baynes' 1923 translation (295), which Radin used.

nature of similarities in culture and their origin. The English evolutionary school explained such similarities as being due to uniform action of the mind in similar conditions, while Bastian ascribed them to a limited number of innate elementary ideas. Both subscribed to the thesis of the psychic unity of mankind. In Radin's view, Jung's theories represented a synthesis of both positions. Like the evolutionists, Jung considered primitive society to be an undifferentiated whole, postulated a series of stages in the psychic development of mankind, and equated this with the psychic development of the individual. Just like Lévy-Bruhl, he committed the error of projecting the archaic elements of the contemporary individual into primitive mentality (29).

Radin argued that if it could be shown that "all but a negligible minimum of culture elements originated but once," then the theories of the evolutionists, Bastian, Lévy-Bruhl, and Jung would lose much of their validity. What was at stake was determining the precise role of cultural transmission and diffusion in the development of cultural elements. Jung's theories of types and the unconscious provided "a real psychological basis" for the independent origin of many cultural elements (32). However, the existence of widespread diffusion obviated the need for positing (and explaining) their independent generation. Consequently "Jung's collective unconscious would then conceivably only operate as a selective agency determining what elements are to be borrowed" (32).

In 1931 Jung wrote a foreword to a work by Charles Aldrich, *The Primitive Mind in Modern Civilization*, which was an attempt to develop a psychology of "primitives" based on Jung's work. Aldrich had studied with Jung in Zurich and also attended his seminar in 1925.[96] To Cary Baynes, Aldrich wrote that the function of his book had been to "be helpful in calling Jung's work to the attention of thoughtful people."[97] Jung took this opportunity to comment on the history of the relation between anthropology and psychology. He stated that in the nineteenth century, anthropology had employed the "collection method," which drew together a great deal of material that was, however, insufficiently analyzed. Adequate analysis required an interdisciplinary study, of which Frazer's *The Golden Bough* was a "splendid example" (*CW* 18, § 1297). However, the field which had been drawn upon the least was psychology. At the same time, each investigator had drawn upon his own psychology to understand "primitives":

---

[96] Jung informed Aldrich that he would recommend his book to his patients, as it was an excellent introduction to primitive psychology. (January 5, 1931, *Letters* 1, 80).

[97] October 4, 1931, Cary Baynes papers.

Seen from Tylor's point of view, animism is quite obviously his individual bias. Lévy-Bruhl measures primitive facts by means of his extremely rational mind. From his standpoint it appears quite logical that the primitive mind should be an "état prélogique." Yet the primitive is far from being illogical and is just as far as from being "animistic." He is by no means that strange being from whom the civilized man is separated by a gulf that cannot be bridged. The fundamental difference between them is not a matter of mental functioning, but rather in the premises upon which the functioning is based. (*CW* 18, § 1297)

Thus anthropologists had fallen victim to the personal equation, and the fallacy of anthropology lay in its inadequate psychology. However, psychology itself had been of little assistance to anthropology, due to the lack of an adequate psychology. Jung argued that the value of Freud's *Totem and Taboo*, despite its blatant inadequacies, had been that it showed the possibility of a rapprochement between psychology and the understanding of primitives. Prior to *Totem and Taboo*, however, he himself had tackled this subject in *Transformations and Symbols of the Libido*. Whereas Freud had applied a pre-existing theory, he had used a comparative method. He claimed that this yielded better results for both psychology and anthropology (as we have seen, his comparative method had itself been taken over from anthropology). In this account, an adequate anthropology could only come about if it was based on an adequate psychology, namely, Jung's.

In addition to Jung's foreword, Aldrich's work carried an introduction by Bronislaw Malinowski which forms an interesting counterpart. Before considering Malinowski's introduction to Aldrich's work, it is worth sketching his attitude to psychoanalysis, as represented by his 1927 *Sex and Repression in Savage Societies*. Malinowski stated that for a time, he had been "unduly influenced by the theories of Freud and Rivers, Jung, and Jones" (1927, vii). The value of psychoanalysis was that it opened up a dynamic theory of the mind, and forged a link between psychology, biology, and the theory of society. He viewed his own work as providing a partial confirmation of psychoanalysis through showing: "a deep correlation between the type of a society and the nuclear complex found there" (82). At the same time it presented a relativization, as the universal existence of the Oedipus complex could not be assumed. Thus in place of the universalism of the psychoanalytic theory, he was proposing a cultural relativism.[98]

---

[98] Like Malinowski, Jung also cited his anthropological experiences as a critique of psychoanalysis. "Three versions of a press conference in Vienna," McGuire and Hull ed., 1977, 57 & 60.

In his work, Aldrich cited Malinowski's anthropological critique of the Oedipus complex as providing confirmation of Jung's views. Aldrich argued that Malinowski had presented the case of a society governed by matrilineal descent in which the youth's animosity was directed towards the authority figure, the mother's brother, as opposed to towards the father. This indicated that the Freudian father complex was metaphorical, which was "exactly parallel" to Jung's view, contrary to Freud, that the incestuous longing for the mother was also metaphorical (1931, 6–7).

However, Malinowski's espousal of a form of cultural relativism led him also to reject Jung's theory of the collective unconscious, without citing him by name:

> We have developed a theory of the plasticity of instincts under culture and of the transformation of instinctive response into cultural adjustment. On its psychological side our theory suggests a line of approach which, while giving full due to the influence of social factors, does away with the hypotheses of "group mind," the "collective unconscious," "gregarious instinct," and similar metaphysical conceptions. (1927, 277)

In his introduction to Aldrich's work, Malinowski stated that "Between the spheres of psychology and anthropology, there is today a No-man's-land" (Aldrich, 1931, xi). However, in his view, until psychology solved its conflicts between rival schools, anthropology should regard them all impartially, and not ally itself with anyone. Like Jung, Malinowski held that anthropology and psychology could be of mutual benefit. Unsurprisingly, he stressed the potential values of anthropology for psychology: "It is possible, even, that anthropological criticism and evaluation of the excursions into the Science of Man made by these various schools will do something towards clarifying the psychological atmosphere" (xii). When it came to Jung's work, Malinowski claimed that the contributions of the "Zurich school for analytical psychology"

> cannot be ignored by any anthropologist. And the main concept of this School – Racial Unconscious – challenges anthropological criticism for, though it is put forward as a psychological principle, it is so dependent upon cultural evidence that it is perhaps not claiming too much to say that in its final establishment or rejection, the anthropologist will have the last word. (xiii)

Thus if for Jung, the psychologist was to have the last word concerning the validity of anthropological theory, for Malinowski, the situation was reversed. In Malinowski's view, the anthropological judgment of Jung's "main concept" was resoundingly negative.[99]

---

[99] On Malinowski's relation to psychoanalysis, see Stocking (1986b). Jung never cited Malinowski's work. He did, however, have an offprint of his 1916 article "Baloma. The spirits of the dead in the Trobriand islands."

In his publications, Jung did not overtly reply to the anthropological criticisms of his work, but he addressed himself to the criticisms that had been addressed to Lévy-Bruhl's work. As Lévy-Bruhl was Jung's main anthropological authority, it would be sufficient to show the weakness of the criticisms of Lévy-Bruhl's work to defend his own.

While in 1929, Jung had described Lévy-Bruhl's nomination of *mystical participation* to characterize primitive mentality as a stroke of genius (see above), and adopted it, in 1930 he criticized the term, in concurrence with Lévy-Bruhl's critics. In a lecture in Zürich, he stated the word "mystical" was not well chosen, as for the "primitives," it was a question of things quite natural.[100] The following year he noted that there were still some ethnologists who were against this "brilliant" idea, which was probably due to the "unfortunate expression 'mystique.' "[101] If Lévy-Bruhl came to drop this term, Jung *reversed* his criticism of it. In 1948 he regretted that Lévy-Bruhl had eradicated this "perfectly apt expression." He assumed that he had "succumbed to the onslaught of the fools who under the term 'mystical' think of their own rubbish."[102] He attributed this change to Lévy-Bruhl's fear of the terms "bad reputation in intellectual circles": "It is rather to be regretted that he made such a concession to rationalistic superstition, since 'mystique' is just the right word to characterize the peculiar quality of 'unconscious identity.' "[103] Not only did he side with Lévy-Bruhl against his critics, he finally defended the (early) Lévy-Bruhl against the (late) Lévy-Bruhl. He noted that the concept of *participation mystique*:

has been repudiated by ethnologists for the reason that primitives know very well how to differentiate between things. There is no doubt about that; but it cannot be denied, either, that incommensurable things can have, for them, an equally incommensurable *tertium comparationis*. One has only to think of the ubiquitous application of "mana", the werewolf motif, etc. Furthermore, "unconscious identity" is a psychic phenomenon which the psychotherapist has to deal with every day. Certain ethnologists have also rejected Lévy-Bruhl's concept of the *état prélogique*, which is closely connected with that of *participation*. The term is not a very happy one, for in his own way the primitive thinks just as logically as we do. Lévy-Bruhl was aware of this, as I know from personal conversation with him. By "prelogical" he meant the primitive suppositions are often exceedingly strange, and though they may not deserve to be called "prelogical" they certainly merit the term "irrational." Astonishingly enough, Lévy-Bruhl in his posthumously

---

[100] "Archaic Man," *CW* 10, § 130.
[101] "Introduction to Wickes's 'Analyse der Kinderseele'," *CW* 17, § 83.
[102] "General standpoints on the psychology of dreams," *CW* 8, § 508n.
[103] "Commentary to 'The Tibetan Book of the Great Liberation,' " 1939/1954, *CW* 11, § 817n.

published diary, recanted both these concepts. This is the more remarkable in that they had a thoroughly sound psychological basis.[104]

Even if the anthropologist came to reverse his opinion, the psychologist need not follow suit, as his valuation was based upon the psychological validity of the ideas. Hence psychology was not in a dependent relation to anthropology, even in the interpretation of anthropological material. Consequently, subsequent developments in anthropological theory could in no way invalidate the anthropological assumptions of Jung's psychological theories. Given this, it is perhaps not surprising that modern anthropologists have generally completely ignored his work.

In the response to Jung's work by the anthropological community, a clear pattern emerges. On the one hand, his anthropological excursions were ignored and his theory of archetypes was criticized. The former were seen as being closely bound up with the late nineteenth and early twentieth-century "armchair" anthropology that anthropologists of the twenties and thirties were reacting against. The latter was out of keeping with the progressive valorization of historical and geographical particularities, and the emergence of modern concepts of cultures.[105] However, Jung *did* have a seminal influence on anthropology, through his *Psychological Types*.

When the English translation appeared in 1923, it became one of the main talking points among anthropologists. In 1924, the application of Jung's type theory to anthropology was the subject of Charles Seligman's presidential address before the Royal Anthropological Institute, "Anthropology and psychology: a study of some points of contact." Seligman had entered into correspondence with Jung before this presentation. He wrote to Jung informing him that he had become increasingly convinced of Jung's distinctions between the types. He was "trying to apply your [Jung's] ideas of the introvert and extrovert temperaments to savages, and if I can get enough facts even to make suggestions, I might go on to try and apply the ideas to the different non-savage races."[106] Seligman

---

[104] *Mysterium Coniunctionis*, *CW* 14, 1955/6, § 336n. On March 12, 1935, Jung wrote to Jolande Jacobi that "Lévy-Bruhl is a delightful relic, without doubt. The material that he brings in his books is of inestimable worth. It is just a pity that he didn't say anymore about it. One certainly misses the opinion, but I think that in this case the opinion would also not be interesting. So it at least remained intact" (JP).

[105] For example, Margaret Caffrey notes that in reply to Edward Sapir's question concerning the possibility of applying Jung's idea of primordial images to mythology, Ruth Benedict "rejected the archetypal approach to mythology largely because the idea of the archetype harked back to a closed system with fixed laws" (1989, 141). In relation to psychoanalysis more generally, Sapir noted in 1921 that anthropologists were reluctant to give up their sensitivity to the historical particularities of cultures, having but recently acquired it (Darnell, 1990, 140).

[106] September 22, 1923 (JP).

indicated how he was applying Jung's ideas, and wrote Jung a long list of questions concerning typology. Jung wrote Seligman a detailed reply, which has not come to light. However, in thanking Jung for it, Seligman informed him that he would recognize some of it in his presidential address before the anthropological institute.[107]

Seligman commenced by noting that his anthropological experience had demonstrated to him the greater suggestibility, tendency to dissociation, and resemblance to hysteria among "primitive" people, and yet it could not be stated that they were identical to modern hysterics. The explanation for this, he claimed, was found in Jung's distinction between extraversion and introversion. He accepted Jung's contention that such typological attitudes were innate, and set out about studying how various cultures could be classified into types. While Jung's interest in typology had been its utility as a means of developing a self-reflexive individual psychology, and while it was taken up by psychologists and the general culture as a characterological system, for Seligman and other anthropologists, the interest in Jung's type theory lay in its suggestion of the possibility of a differential typology of cultures.

In the West, Seligman claimed, there was a preponderance of extraverts. He cited a personal communication from Jung who disagreed with this. According to Jung, the apparent predominance of extraverts was because they were more conspicuous. In support of this, he supplied Seligman with the following figures, which indicate a concern with quantification which is absent from *Psychological Types*: "Of 77 friends, relatives and acquaintances, 34 are introverts and 43 extraverts, while of 70 patients treated during the past year, 39 were extraverts, 25 introverts, the type of the remaining 6 failing to be determined" (cited in Seligman, 1924, 23). Seligman, however, contended that this bore out his own view concerning the preponderance of extraverts. In contrast to this, the savages he had studied were extraverts. When it came to civilized peoples, he claimed that the Nordic races were introverted. Concerning the alpine races, he cited a letter from Jung in which he characterized the average Swiss as being "moderately introvert" (29), which seems to indicate some readiness on Jung's part to classify cultures typologically, though he did not write on this subject. The Mediterraneans, Seligman claimed, were extraverted, and "old speculative India" was introverted (30). In the far East, Japan was extraverted, while China was introverted.

Psychological Types was reviewed by Edward Sapir. He wrote of the work: "Its one idea is like the intense stare of a man who has found something, and this something a little uncanny" (1923, 529). While finding some of it

---

[107] January 3, 1924 (JP).

dry, impossible to follow and scholastic, he nevertheless lauded the work as contributing to the loss of "the serenity of an absolute system of values" (532). Sapir's biographer provides a psychobiographical explanation for his interest in *Psychological Types*:

Sapir was fascinated by Jung's concept of introvert and extravert as irreconcilable psychological types. Throughout his life, Sapir felt himself isolated from his fellow humans and failed to see why they did not perceive the world as he did. Jung's "explanation" released him from a previously unacknowledged sense of guilt.[108]

Whatever the validity of this explanation, one does find that no small part of the appeal of Jung's typology lay in its personal and interpersonal application. Thus Margaret Mead recalls that in her adolescence, "I was at that point supposed to be an 'intuitive introvert,' which everyone wanted to be because that was what Jung admired the most" (cited in Howard, 1984, 43). She recalled that there had been much discussion of Jung's *Psychological Types* among anthropologists:

The idea that there are systematic relationships between universal psychological types was one that she [Ruth Benedict] had been discussing with me and with Sapir ever since I had attended the Toronto meeting of the British Association for the Advancement of Science in 1924, where there had been discussions of Jung's *Psychological Types* (1923) which had recently been published in English.[109]

She also recalled that Sapir set about classifying the types of their fellow anthropologists. Like Seligman, in 1934 Sapir put forward a typology of cultures, based on Jung's types (1934, 563). Yet it is hard to see his schema as anything other than a restatement of typical racial stereotypes of warm-blooded Mediterraneans and otherworldly Indians, etc.

The impact of Jung's typology on Ruth Benedict may be found in her concept of Apollonian and Dionysian culture patterns which she first put forward in 1928 in "Psychological Types in the cultures of the Southwest," and subsequently elaborated in *Patterns of Culture*. Mead recalled that their conversations on this topic had in part been shaped by Sapir

[108] Darnell, 1990, 140. Sapir is often linked with Benjamin Lee Whorf (1897–1941) as joint articulators of the linguistic relativity thesis, the claim that languages structure our views of the world. Whorf was also impressed by Jung's *Psychological Types*, and his demonstration that through history, the opposition of the types had led to controversies and schisms. Around 1936, Whorf thought that Jung's work represented one of the clearest characterizations of thinking. Taking up Jung's functions, he speculated that the thinking function was distinguished from the other functions by containing a large linguistic element. Furthermore, Whorf thought that Jung's libido concept "may have significance for a 'linguistics of thinking' if it is true that the psychic energy available for linguistic processes (included in the thinking function) is a differentiated energy, entrained in a closed system" (ed. Carroll, 1956, 66).
[109] 1974, 42. In another reference to this same meeting, Mead stated that "we had all read Jung," 1977, 322.

and Oldenweiser's discussion of Jung's typology in Toronto in 1924 as well as by Seligman's article cited above (1959, 207). In *Patterns of Culture*, Benedict discussed Wilhelm Worringer's typification of empathy and abstraction, Oswald Spengler's of the Apollonian and the Faustian and Friedrich Nietzsche's of the Apollonian and the Dionysian. Conspicuously, she failed to cite Jung explicitly, though while criticizing Spengler, she noted that "It is quite as convincing to characterize our cultural type as thoroughly extravert . . . as it is to characterize it as Faustian" (1934, 54–55). One gets the impression that Benedict was attempting to distance herself from Jung, despite drawing some inspiration from his *Psychological Types*.

In her autobiography, Mead recalls that in the period that led up to her *Sex and Temperament*, she had a great deal of discussion with Gregory Bateson concerning the possibility that aside from sex difference, there were other types of innate differences which "cut across sex lines" (1973, 216). She stated that: "In my own thinking I drew on the work of Jung, especially his fourfold scheme for grouping human beings as psychological types, each related to the others in a complementary way" (217). Yet in her published work, Mead omitted to cite Jung's work. A possible explanation for the absence of citation of Jung by Benedict and Mead, despite the influence of his typological model, was that they were developing diametrically opposed concepts of culture and its relation to the personality to Jung's. Ironically, it is arguably through such indirect and half-acknowledged conduits that Jung's work came to have its greatest impact upon modern anthropology and concepts of culture. This short account of some anthropological responses to Jung may serve to indicate that when Jung's work was engaged with by the academic community, it was taken to quite different destinations, and underwent a sea change.

Another anthropologist who engaged with Jung's work in a sustained manner was John Layard (1891–1974). Layard had studied with W. H. R. Rivers and did his fieldwork in the New Hebrides. Subsequently, he underwent bouts of psychotherapy with many figures, including Rivers, Homer Lane, Wilhelm Stekel, H. G. Baynes, Jung, and R. D. Laing. In addition, he practiced as an analyst himself. His major anthropological work was his account of some of his fieldwork, *Stone Men of Malekula*, which was published in 1942, and ran to eight hundred pages. In this and subsequent articles, Layard set out to interpret the kinship patterns and social structures of the Vao in terms of analytical psychology. This aspect of his work, and in particular, his work on the incest taboo, was subsequently taken up by Jung. In 1945 he wrote a paper on "The Incest Taboo." On receiving it, Jung wrote to Layard: "It came in the right moment and gave me the key to a great puzzle in the psychology of the transference."[110] The following year Jung made use of Layard's work in his *The Psychology of the Transference*. Essentially, Layard's work provided Jung with a model of the interrelation of the endogenous and exogenous forms of the incest taboo. However, Layard felt that Jung had misused his work, and the second edition of Jung's work incorporated Layard's corrections. Evidently, even this wasn't enough, for in the English translation of Jung's work, which appeared five years after Jung's death, Layard had added yet more emendations, incorporated in square brackets, with the approval of the editors of the *Collected Works*.

The psychology of the political

In 1921 Jung defined collective psychic contents as "what Lévy-Bruhl calls the *représentations collectives* of primitives."[111] In 1924 Marcel Mauss argued that psychology only studied what took place within individuals, as opposed to the collective representations, which were the provenance of sociology. The overpowering significance of collective representations led Mauss to argue that "at times we seem to want to reserve for ourselves all investigations in these higher strata of the individual consciousness" (1924, 9).

Through adopting the term collective representations, Jung attempted the reverse operation of subsuming the domain of sociology through psychology. In 1928 he stated that the images of the collective unconscious were the collective representations.[112] However, a few years later, he noted that the archetypes only indirectly corresponded to collective representations, as they referred to unconscious contents which had not been submitted to conscious elaboration.[113] Thus archetypes formed the basis of collective representations. The latter designated the condition of the former after they had been subject to conscious elaboration.

Durkheim had used the supposed existence of the unconscious as one element in his argument as to the existence of representations outside of the individual, collective representations. Jung, interestingly enough, employed something close to a mirror image of the same argument. While stating that outer attractions like offices and titles belonged to society, or the collective consciousness, he argued that in the same way in which a society existed outside the individual, there was also a collective psyche outside the personal psyche.[114]

---

[110] Layard papers, University of California at San Diego.
[111] *Psychological Types*, *CW* 6, § 692.
[112] "The relations between the ego and the unconscious," *CW* 7, § 231.
[113] "On the archetypes of the collective unconscious," 1935, *CW* 9, 1, § 5–6.
[114] "The relations between the ego and the unconscious," *CW* 7, § 231.

While Jung referred to the collective consciousness on several occasions, he did not refer to it with anything like the frequency with which he referred to the collective unconscious, and it was with this latter term that his work became pre-eminently associated. However, the concept of the collective consciousness formed a counterpole to that of the collective unconscious, and without it, his concept of the latter, not to mention his social and political thought, are not understandable.

In his social vision, the individual was suspended between the collective consciousness and the collective unconscious. In 1947, he stated that ego consciousness was dependent upon the conditions of the collective or social consciousness, and the unconscious collective dominants, or archetypes.[115] This dual dependency resulted in a conflict, for there was an "almost unbridgeable" opposition between the "generally accepted truths" of the collective consciousness and the contents of the collective unconscious. From the standpoint of the former, the latter were rejected as irrational. The individual was caught this opposition (*CW* 8, § 423). Thus if subjective consciousness identified with the ideas and opinions of the collective consciousness, the contents of the collective unconscious became repressed. This tendency led ultimately to the absorption of the ego by the collective unconscious, which gave rise to the "mass man, who is always enslaved by an 'ism'" (§ 425, trans. mod.). The identification with the collective consciousness and the apotheosis of the masses inevitably led to a catastrophe. The only solution was the avoidance of identification with the collective consciousness, and the recognition of the "existence and importance" of the archetypes, as "these latter are an effective defence against the might of social consciousness and the mass psyche corresponding with it" (§ 426, trans. mod.). In this respect, contemporary religion failed the individual, due to the fact that

in as much as religion for the contemporary consciousness still essentially means a *denomination*, and hence a collectively accepted codified system represented in dogmatic precepts of religious statements, it belongs more to the sphere of collective consciousness, even though its symbols express the originally effective archetypes. (*Ibid.*, trans. mod.)

Curiously, this recognizes Durkheim's social definition of religion as descriptive of the *pathology* of contemporary religion, which had lost touch with the collective unconscious (Durkheim, 1912, 47).

These apocalyptic statements indicate why Jung prioritized the study of the collective unconscious over that of the collective consciousness. The dominance of the collective consciousness and the consequent development of "mass man" in the twentieth century, and the failure of religion to

[115] "Theoretical reflections on the essence of the psychical," 1945, *CW* 8, § 423.

form adequately a counterweight to it was *the* social pathology of modernity. The only solution lay in the collective unconscious, and ultimately in fostering of the process of individuation, which alone could enable an individual to differentiate himself from the collective consciousness and the collective unconscious, thus evading the dangers of totalitarianism on the one side, and psychosis on the other. These statements also indicate his understanding of the cultural significance of analytical psychology. Its cultural mission lay in establishing the existence and importance of the collective unconscious, which could save the West from catastrophe. While the collective consciousness found its spokesmen in social, political, and religious leaders, the collective unconscious found its spokesman in Jung.

His concept of the collective psyche and the collective unconscious drew together several different senses of the term "collective," corresponding to his different conceptions of the archetypes. On the one hand, collective was understood to designate the universally human attributes that everyone shared. On the other, collective referred to the functioning of supra-individual entities such as groups or nations. Thus he at times referred to the collective unconscious of nations. It was in this second sense that his understanding of the psychology of the political was embodied. Many of his statements concerning collective behavior in the thirties and forties were connected to the rise of Fascism and National Socialism. However, before one can grasp the interconnections between his thinking and the social and political events at that time, the development of the former needs to be reconstructed to a level which has not been sufficiently done to date.[116]

His comments concerning behavior in crowds closely followed the French crowd psychologists. Jung's citations were to Le Bon. In his Tavistock lectures in 1936, Jung noted that French psychologists had dealt with mental contagion, and written very good books on the subject. He singled out Le Bon's book, *The Crowd: A Study of the Popular Mind*.[117] On another occasion, he suggested that the best way of understanding some of his views on collective psychology was simply to read Le Bon: "One need only read what Le Bon has to say on the 'psychology of crowds' to understand what I mean: man as a particle in the mass is psychically abnormal."[118] Le Bon provided him with a ready made collective

---

[116] On the vexed issue of Jung's activities during this period, the best informed and most judicious account remains that of Cocks, 1997.

[117] "The Tavistock Lectures," *CW* 18, § 318. Jung possessed a copy of the 1912 German translation of Le Bon's book.

[118] Epilogue to "Essays on Contemporary Events," 1946, *CW* 10, § 477.

psychology. Some of his statements sound like a recasting of Le Bon into his own language:

A group experience takes place on a lower level of consciousness than the experience of an individual. This is due to the fact that, when many people gather together to share one common emotion, the total psyche emerging from the group is below the level of the individual psyche. If it is a very large group, the collective psyche will be more like the psyche of an animal, which is the reason why the ethical attitude of large organizations is always dubious. The psychology of a large crowd inevitably sinks to the level of mob psychology [footnote: Le Bon, *The Crowd*] . . . the presence of so many people together exerts great suggestive force. The individual in a crowd easily becomes the victim of his own suggestibility.[119]

To this classical depiction of the psychology of crowds, he grafted Lévy-Bruhl: "the mass is swayed by *participation mystique*" (§ 226). In crowds, the behavior of the "civilized" West reverted to the level of "primitives." For Jung, as for the crowd psychologists, the masses revolved around leaders: "the great liberating deeds of world history have sprung from leading personalities and never from the inert mass, which is at all times secondary and can only be prodded into activity by the demagogue."[120] Correspondingly, he came to a dire assessment of the resulting consequences: "the group, because of its unconsciousness, has no freedom of choice, and so psychic activity runs on in it like an uncontrolled law of nature. There is thus set going a chain reaction that comes to a stop only in catastrophe. The people always long for a hero" (§ 303). French crowd psychology provided a key template for his reading of the social and political developments in Europe from the 1930s onwards. In 1936 he observed: "Through Communism in Russia, through National Socialism in Germany, through Fascism in Italy, the State became all-powerful and claimed its slaves body and soul."[121] In each case, the state had come to embody itself in a leader. In the ensuing years, Jung increasingly generalized what had come to pass in these specific instances as designating a pervasive Western phenomenon. In 1941 he simply stated "the State is now making an absolute bid for totalitarianism."[122] This meant the total incorporation of the individual by the collective. As to the question of what the State consisted in, he stated that it "represents mass psychology raised to the nth power" (§ 223). These developments raised critical questions as to the location of psychology and psychotherapy. He claimed that science was increasingly being made to serve the practical ends of the social collective. In subsequent years, he became increasingly critical

[119] "Concerning Rebirth" 1939, *CW* 9, 1, § 225.
[120] "The development of the personality" 1934, *CW* 17, § 284.
[121] "Psychology and National Problems," *CW* 18, § 1324.
[122] "Psychotherapy in the present," *CW* 16, § 222.

of the role of science in the modern world (while nevertheless insisting upon the scientific status of his psychology). Not only was science increasingly an agent of the state, it itself contributed to the rising collectivism: "Under the influence of natural scientific assumptions, not only the psyche, but also the individual man, and indeed the individual event in general suffer a levelling and are made indecipherable. This distorts the picture of reality into a conceptual average."[123] He went so far as to claim that "one of the chief factors responsible for de-individualisation is natural scientific rationalism, which robs the individual of his foundations and therefore of his dignity" (§ 501, trans. mod.). His negative assessment of the effect of the natural sciences was his contention that they had no place for the individual, or rather, considered the individuals only to subsume them under the rule of generality.

He maintained that socio-political movements were inevitably opposed to religion, as the religious attitude maintained that the individual was ultimately dependent on higher powers. The State had come to take the place of God. However, the organized religions were of little help in this regard, as they too seemed to favor collective action: "They do not appear to have heard of the elementary axiom of mass psychology that the individual becomes morally and spiritually inferior in the mass" (§ 536). The churches then, required the instruction of Le Bon. As to psychotherapy, one option would be for it to turn into a handmaiden of the State. In this scenario, the State would insist that

psychotherapy should be nothing but a tool for the production of publicly useful assistants. In this way psychotherapy would become a goal bound technique [Technizismus], whose single aim can be the increasing social efficiency . . . psychological science would be degraded to just researches on the possibility of rationalising the psychic apparatus. As to its therapeutic aim, the complete and successful incorporation of the patient into the State machine would be the criterion of cure.[124]

While some social critics would contend that this is an accurate description of the actual role of psychotherapy in the twentieth century, Jung claimed that such an outcome would represent a complete negation of the developments of modern psychotherapy. Consequently, the social and political mission of psychotherapy lay in opposing the development of Statism through the only means of resistance possible – the promotion of psychological individuation and direct religious experience. He was at pains to distinguish this from individualism, which he saw as simply a morbid reaction to collectivism. The significance of individuation was

[123] "Present and future," 1957, *CW* 10, § 499, trans. mod.
[124] "Psychotherapy in the present," 1941, *CW* 16, § 225, trans. mod.

that it "produces a consciousness of human community precisely because it leads to consciousness of the common unconscious, which unites and is common to all men. Individuation is a becoming one with oneself and at the same time with humanity" (§ 227, trans. mod.). It was through individuation that the conflict between the individual and the collective could be brought to a resolution. It was only through individuation that the agglomeration of individuals could be, instead of an anonymous mass, "a conscious community"(*ibid.*). Hence in individuation, there lay the seeds of a new collectivity.

Interestingly enough, these views resulted in concrete suggestions being submitted by the newly founded Jung Institute in 1948 to Unesco. P. W. Martin was organizing a conference for Unesco on methods of attitude change. He approached Jung about this, and according to Martin, "he was interested but diffident as to his ability to make a short statement, feeling that a meeting of social scientists was rather outside his beat."[125] Martin consequently wrote a draft paper of the type the conference would be interested in. In a letter to Jung he proposed a testing of Jung's individuation hypothesis. Martin suggested getting together small groups of people with scientific training, such as sociologists and social scientists, to do an experiment, which he thought could be taken on by Unesco. Each would be given instructions over a few months for carrying out dream analysis and active imagination, and kept in touch with for a few years. Martin claimed that if between 20 and 30 percent of them experienced something of the individuation process, then it would have been placed on a scientific basis. As Martin recalls, "this, unfortunately, had the reverse effect to what I had hoped, drawing from Jung . . . a statement of the negative side of his work – the shadow, as he put it, of my paper." He found this completely unsuitable. Following this, he received a paper by Jolande Jacobi, which stitched together his paper and Jung's, and it was decided not to submit this to the conference.

Jung's paper took up and reformulated Martin's proposal. The element of providing statistical proof for his concept of individuation was completely dropped. His paper provides indication of his aspirations for the Jungian movement, and how he saw its significance for the fate of the West. He suggested that a number of individuals should undergo analysis, which would enable a change in attitude. This would form a "leading minority" whose numbers could be augmented by further individuals undergoing analysis and "by suggestion through authority."[126] The last

---

[125] P. W. Martin to William McGuire, August 17, 1962, McGuire papers, LC.
[126] "Techniques of attitude change conducive to world peace: Memorandum to Unesco," *CW* 18, § 1393.

was essential, as it was only through suggestion that the masses could be affected (as he saw it, 50 percent of the population did not possess either the intelligence or sense of morality required for analysis) (§ 1392). While the attitudes of the masses could not be changed, their behavior could, as this depended upon the authority of leaders. It was precisely in this manner that the ideas of modern psychology had spread, just like other religious and intellectual movements. Thus crowd psychology was not only a domain within psychology: it also explained the effects of psychology itself, and its societal impact. What was required was not a general assent to the truths of psychology – but a mobilization of influence of psychology through suggestive authority. The interest in psychology on the part of the general public had increased, despite the resistance of academic authority. This attested to the need for psychological knowledge.

This "leading minority" would form a psychological elite, upon whom the health of the collective would depend, since the nation's immunity depended upon there being a leading minority which was immune to the evil and which could combat "the powerful suggestive effect of seemingly possible wish-fulfilments" (§ 1400).

Given the fact that Jung's psychology had developed outside of universities and psychiatric clinics, it followed that the development of this "leading minority" would have taken place in separate institutions and associations.

From complex psychology to the Jungian School

From the 1940s onwards, a number of training societies and institutes bearing Jung's name began to develop from the network of non-professional analytical psychology clubs in various countries. While he had a strong sense of the possibility of a discipline of complex psychology, he expressed skepticism about the possibility of a school of Jungian psychotherapy. In 1924 he stated:

Since there is no horse that cannot be ridden to death, theories of neurosis and methods of treatment are dubious things. So I always find it amusing when businesslike fashionable doctors assert that they practise according to "Adler," "Kunkel," "Freud," or even "Jung." There simply is not and cannot be any such thing, and even if there could be, one would be on the surest road to failure.[127]

As a result of this position, he was opposed to the establishment of training programs. Fordham recalled that Jung "never liked followers it was quite clear . . . He was really very much against these societies starting

---

[127] "Analytical psychology and education," CW 17, § 203, trans. mod.

at all."[128] In a similar vein, Joseph Henderson recalled that Jung "hated the idea of promoting a school . . . he always advised us not to organise ourselves any more than we could possibly help."[129] While opposed to trainings in analytical psychology, he did not stand in their way. Joseph Wheelwright recalled that when he met Jung and informed him about the establishment of their training program in San Francisco, Jung looked as if "he had been hit by a Mack truck, and I said, 'I see you really don't want to hear about it.' He said 'To tell the truth I can think of nothing I would rather less hear about, Wheelwright.'"[130]

If organizations were to form, Jung held that it was incumbent upon them to represent accurately his ideas. In 1959, Joseph Henderson informed him of the establishment of a new organization by Ruth Thacker Fry. In his reply, Jung wrote: "As she calls her enterprise 'the C. G. Jung Educational Center of Houston, Texas' she is under the moral obligation to produce something that lives up to the name, otherwise the whole thing would be a mere advertising bluff."[131] It is an open question how many organizations that currently use Jung as their figurehead would have been regarded by him as perpetrating "a mere advertising bluff."

In 1948, the Jung Institute in Zürich was founded, and Jung presented an inaugural address.[132] According to one account, Jung began his address by stating that "My grandfather, Carl Gustav Jung once founded a home for retarded children: Now I am founding one for retarded adults."[133] His address gives the clearest indication of the directions Jung thought his students should explore. He stated that it was an honor to be present at the founding of an institute for complex psychology, and expressed the hope that he would therefore be allowed to say a few words about what had been achieved, and what it should strive for. He drew attention to the fact that Théodore Flournoy's contributions to psychological biography had yet to be sufficiently acknowledged. In his account of the achievements of complex psychology, he highlighted the interdisciplinary collaborations with Richard Wilhelm, Heinrich Zimmer, Karl Kérenyi, and Wolfgang Pauli in the fields of sinology, indology, Greek mythology, microphysics, and parapsychology respectively.[134] He

[128] Fordham interview, CLM, 27.   [129] Henderson interview, CLM, 24.
[130] Wheelwright interview, CLM, 34.   [131] June 24, 1959 (JP).
[132] Jung had been against the institute being named after him, but was overruled. On July 7, 1947, Jolande Jacobi wrote to him: "I have heard that you have chosen the name 'Institute for Complex Psychology' and had a resistance to connecting your name to it" (JP).
[133] Gene Nameche and R. D. Laing, *Jung and Persons: A Study in Genius and Madness*, Laing papers, University of Glasgow, 171. This work is the forgotten Jung biography.
[134] In a discussion in 1950, Jung remarked that if he was confronted with a case in which the archetypes played a role with which he was not familiar, such as in Greek mythology,

concluded by giving some programmatic suggestions for further work, in the form of a shopping list of about twenty specific points.

He noted that in the course of his work, he had left many unfinished beginnings.[135] The following are the issues that he singled out. He thought that further work needed to be done from the experimental aspect of complex psychology, and especially concerning the associations experiment. In particular, he highlighted the topics of the periodical renewal of the emotional stress of complex-stimulators, the problem of family patterns of associations, and the investigation of the physiological concomitants of the complexes. In the medico-clinical field, he stated that there was a dearth of fully elaborated case histories. In psychiatry, he thought that the analysis of paranoid patients with research into comparative symbolism needed to be undertaken. For psychotherapy, he held that casuistic dream research in connection with comparative symbolism would be of great practical value. In addition, he recommended the collection and evaluation of dreams in early childhood and those before catastrophes, such as dreams before accidents and death, as well as dreams during illness and under narcotics. He suggested the investigation of pre and post-mortem psychic phenomena. He held this to be particularly important, given the accompanying relativization of time and space. He thought that a difficult but interesting task would be the research into the process of compensation in psychotics and criminals and into the goal of compensation in general. In normal psychology, he urged the study of the psychic structure of the family in relation to heredity, as well as the compensatory character of marriage and emotional relationships. He also considered the behavior of the individual in the mass and its unconscious compensation to be a very timely problem.

Concerning further applications of complex psychology, he thought that much of the field of the mental sciences remained virgin territory. The same held for biography and the history of literature. Above all, he singled out the field of the psychology of religion for attention. He held that the study of religious myths would clarify questions of ethnopsychology as well epistemology. He recommended particular attention to the quaternity symbol, the alchemical axiom of Maria the Prophetess and

---

he would send the case to Kerényi, noting "this is a collaboration that one should make often. One can then make better headway with the patient." "Dozent-Einladung," June 10, 1950, Küsnacht, JP.

[135] Fifteen years earlier, Jung had written "I have been called a 'seeker'; I do not know whether this was a compliment. I thank the fate that graciously protected me from setting my ship on the sand of the barren beaches of a ghastly conclusiveness. He who seeks, finds, and he who *always* seeks, always finds. Because of this I am happy that I see conclusiveness nowhere, but much rather a dark expanse, full of mysteries and adventure." "On psychology," 1933, 106.

the proportio sesquitertia, the investigation and description of triadic and tetradic symbols and of the symbols of the goal and symbols of unity.

Jung could hardly have been more specific concerning the tasks confronting complex psychology. If any further indication were needed, it is clear that he conceived of complex psychology as a vast interdisciplinary enterprise. Fifty years after this was delivered, it is fair to ask how much of this agenda has been undertaken in analytical psychology. Clearly, very little. There are many points for which it is hard to recall a single article. In analytical psychology, much of what Jung saw as unfinished beginnings have simply been abandoned, unattempted. This is not to say that the topics he singled out have not met with any attention at all – it is significant that many of these topics have been extensively researched in other disciplines, such as parapsychology.

His agenda gives a clear indication of the wide gulf that lies between what he conceived to be the aims of complex psychology, and analytical psychology today. His words on that occasion have clearly carried little weight in influencing the future direction of research in analytical psychology. This is emblematic of the relation of contemporary analytical psychology to Jung.

One of the prime movers behind the Jung Institute, C. A. Meier, had actually conceived of it as a research institute. Meier was the first president of the Institute. In his presentation at the opening of the Institute in October, he argued that "there cannot be a training course for analysts, for the development of Jungian analysts must still be left to the integration of the individual. The movement is still so young that it needs outside help in the form of lecturers in many specialised fields."[136] Meier was strongly against it becoming "a conveyor belt for turning out ready-made analysts."[137] However, he was overruled by other members of the Curatorium. As he recalled:

In the course of time I had to realize that these people were not interested in anything else; they wanted to have their own trainees. Research or interchange with other psychologists was unimportant. Whenever I made an attempt at bringing in somebody who was not of the Jungian gang, but came from an entirely different field, they said, "Oh Meier has this damn resistance against Jung." So I finally gave up.[138]

It is hard to overemphasize the consequences of these changes of emphasis. According to Gene Nameche, Wolfgang Pauli, one of the founding

[136] Cited in the minutes of the Analytical Psychology Club of Los Angeles, November 12, 1948, C. G. Jung Institute of Los Angeles.
[137] Meier interview, CLM, 78.
[138] Ibid. Meier subsequently resigned from the Institute in 1957.

members of the institute, "had hoped that people there would collect 'archetypal' dreams and do mathematical analyses of them. When he discovered that no one knew or cared anything about scientific methodology, he resigned."[139] After Pauli's death, Cary Baynes wrote to Jung concerning Pauli: "He had the idea that doctors ruined the dreams of patients they handled, and he suggested that a lot of dreams from people not in analysis should be collected and then we would know what the unconscious was trying to say."[140] Thus for Pauli, complex psychology needed to utilize the mathematical and statistical methods to validate its findings. Only in such a way would interdisciplinary cooperation with the natural sciences be possible.

While having a strong sense of the research that future complex psychologists should do, Jung harboured no illusions about the role of institutes in safeguarding his work. Shortly after the foundation of the Jung Institute, he commented about this development to Cary Baynes:

The institute is flourishing in a modest way . . . There is of course the danger that living ideas are systematically killed by professional teaching. Most of the ideas will hardly escape this sad fate, but if one is careful enough with the choice of the teachers, one can keep the thing afloat for a while and if the central idea itself is really alive, then it will fulfill its lifetime either in the Institute or outside of it as long as it is really living.[141]

Laurens van der Post recalls Jung saying to him that

the Institute would be lucky if it did not outlive its creative uses within a generation . . . "I do not want anybody to be a Jungian," he told me. "I want people to be themselves. As for "isms," they are the viruses of our day, and responsible for greater disasters than any medieval plague or pest has ever been. Should I be found one day only to have created another "ism" then I will have failed in all I tried to do." (1976, ix–x.)

This comment is in line with his social and political thought – for if complex psychology resulted in another "ism" it would simply contribute to the mindlessness pervading European societies, rather than providing any point of resistance or capacity for reflection.

Preparing for the end

From the outbreak of the Second World War, Jung felt an increasing pessimism about the future of the world. In 1940, he wrote to the analytical

---

[139] Gene Nameche and R. D. Laing, *Jung and Persons: A Study in Genius and Madness*, 172.
[140] March 9, 1959, Cary Baynes papers, original in English.
[141] March 9, 1949, Cary Baynes papers, original in English.

psychologist H. G. Baynes that the year reminded him of the earthquake in 26 BC that destroyed the temple of Karnak.[142] The following year, he wrote to the analytical psychologist Esther Harding, "We are living in an incredible hellish time . . . it is just as if the very air were poisoned with the stench of hell."[143] After the war, he described his state of mind to her:

Things and exterior life slip past me and leave me in a world of unworldly thought and in a time measured by centuries. I am glad that you and others carry on the work I once began. The world needs it badly. It seems to come to a general show down, where the question shall be settled, whether the actual existing man is conscious enough to cope with his own demons or not. For the time being it seems to be a losing fight . . . Switzerland has become an island of dreams amidst ruins and putrefaction. Europe is a rotting carcass. Towards the end of the Roman Empire they have made attempts and had insights similar to mine.[144]

He came to see the problems of overpopulation and the hydrogen bomb as the foremost menaces.[145] The hydrogen bomb was first tested by the United States in 1952, and in the following year by the USSR (the United Kingdom followed in 1957). To Cary Baynes, he wrote in 1959 that the average man was right to be anxious, as he was bringing to the world the "fathers and mothers of all terrors," namely communism, the hydrogen bomb and overpopulation. Concerning the latter, he reflected

The white man will have to ask himself very thoroughly, whether he belongs to Africa or not. The menace of overpopulation will soon put such decisions before us, and the more urgent the problem becomes, the more the white man will be forced to regress to primitivity with its man-slaughter. This is the black cloud on our Western horizon.[146]

He saw the problems posed by the hydrogen bomb and overpopulation as being closely connected. In a passage deleted from *Memories*, he stated:

It is wonderful to save the lives of so many children; but what will become of them?   It is well known that the population of the globe is increasing by giant leaps. A reputable demographer has observed (with a benevolent smirk) that nature will undoubtedly find ways and means to stop the inexorable catastrophe. All natural ways, such as tremendous famines or continental epidemics, are being blocked by men. However, the H-bomb has been invented as an ideal means of extermination – invented by man who still unconsciously "follows the ways of nature" and therefore does not go astray.[147]

---

[142] August 12, 1940 (JP).   [143] March 1941 (JP), original in English.
[144] July 8, 1947 (JP), original in English.
[145] Jung to Adolf Keller, February 25, 1955 (JP).
[146] April 12, 1959, Cary Baynes papers, original in English.
[147] CMS, 377. Jung put forward the same position in "Symbols and the interpretation of dreams," 1961, *CW* 18, § 597.

Here, he considered the hydrogen bomb as a teleological compensation by nature for the failure to deal with the problem of over-population.

As Jung saw it, the West was faced with epochal changes. Around the time of the second world war, he began to utilize the term dominants again. Now, the dominants referred to archetypes that were in a super-ordinate role, in an individual, or in a culture. In 1944, he stated that when the collective dominants decayed, unconscious individuation processes developed. At such moments, many individuals were possessed by archetypes of a numinous character, that forced their way forward in order to form new dominants.[148] His most extensive treatment of the dominants occurred in 1955–1956 in his last major work, *Mysterium Coniunctionis*. There, he described the rise and fall of dominants in a manner which is strongly reminiscent of Lamprecht. In Jung's view, the ruling representations, the dominants, changed. This transformation was concealed from consciousness, and appeared only in dreams:

the aging of a psychic dominant is apparent in the fact that it expresses the totality of the soul in ever-diminishing degree. One can also say that the soul no longer feels wholly contained in the dominant . . . this loses its fascination and no longer possesses the soul as completely as before.[149]

This process led to a conflict between the old dominant and the contents of the unconscious, which was resolved through the arising of a new dominant. As an example of a collective dominant, he cited the Christian world view in Europe in the Middle Ages. The problem that confronted modern Europe was the inescapable need for a new dominant. Yet for Jung, this could only be founded upon the old dominant of Christianity. The ego always needed a mythical dominant. The problem was that such a dominant could not be invented, as many had tried to do (§ 520, trans. mod.). It was to this task, the psychological reinvigoration of Christianity, that he dedicated the final decades of his life. It need hardly be stated that such a collective revival as he envisaged has not come about, as he was clearly aware. On September 2, 1960, he wrote to Herbert Read:

I asked myself time and again, why there are no men in our epoch, who could see at least, what I was wrestling with. I think it is not mere vanity and desire for recognition on my part, but a genuine concern for my fellow-beings. It is presumably the ancient functional relationship of the medicine man to his tribe, the *participation mystique* and the essence of the physician's ethos. (*Letters 2*, 586–589)

---

[148] *Psychology and Alchemy, CW* 12, § 41.
[149] *Mysterium Coniunctionis, CW* 14, § 504–505, trans. mod.

In Jung's own estimation, his work supplied what was lacking in the West. On other occasions, he was more sanguine concerning its reception. In 1958 he said to Aniela Jaffé that the lack of resonance that his work had met with was not surprising, as his work was a compensation. He had said things which no one wanted to hear. Given this, he thought that the amount of success that his work had received was wonderful, and that he couldn't have expected more.[150]

Michael Fordham recalls that in 1960, Jung had written a letter to someone in London which was "an account of how he felt he had failed in his mission – he was misunderstood and misrepresented" (1993, 119).The letter appears to have been one that Jung wrote to Eugene Rolfe, which contained these statements:

I had to understand, that I was unable to make people see, what I am after. I am practically alone . . . I have failed in my foremost task, to open people's eyes to the fact, that man has a soul and there is a buried treasure in the field and that our religion and philosophy are in a lamentable state. Why indeed should I continue to exist?[151]

Consequently, Fordham flew out to see Jung, and assured him that the Jungians in London "were in a strong position to rebut open misunderstandings and were striving to further recognition of his work" (1993, 119). To this, Jung looked at Fordham "as if I were a poor fool who did not know a thing" and dismissed him. On reflection, Fordham stated that his comments had been on a superficial level, and that had he spoken more profoundly, he would have had to tell Jung "that it was the delusion of being a world saviour that made him feel a failure – I had not the stature to do that" (120).

However, more can be said than this. To begin with, these statements are linked with his general pessimism concerning the fate of the world. As he saw it, the ultimate value of psychology was whether it could prove to be of any significance in this regard. It is also possible to link his admission of failure to his letter to Herbert Read, which articulates the culmination of his understanding of the relation of the primitive to the modern, the individual to the collective and the import of complex psychology for the West. For Jung, in primitive societies, the relation of the medicine man to the tribe was not simply a contingent or arbitrary social arrangement, but corresponded to an archetypic necessity. What was required was to respond to the same necessity in a modern manner – the result being

---

[150] MP, 383–384.
[151] November 13, 1960, in Rolfe, 1989, 158. Fordham identified the recipient as a member of the Analytical Psychology Club in London, which Rolfe was.

complex psychology. For it to succeed in this task, it required the full-scale recognition of the West. No psychology has managed to achieve this. Judging by these late letters, in Jung's own estimation, complex psychology – and psychology as a whole – had failed to make sufficient social impact, and hence failed to provide adequate antidotes to the "fathers and mothers of all terrors." To Cary Baynes, he wrote,

Psychology like mine prepares for an end or even for the end. The question is only, what are we going to kill: ourselves or our still infantile psychology and its appalling unconsciousness.[152]

---

[152] April 12, 1959, Cary Baynes papers.

References

"Abstract of minutes of the joint session of the Aristotelian society, the British psychological society, and the mind association, at Bedford college, Regent's park, London" (1919) *Proceedings of the Aristotelian Society* 19, 296–297.

Abraham, Karl (1909) "Dreams and myth: a study in folk-psychology," ed. Hilda Abraham, *Clinical Papers and Essays on Psycho-Analysis* (London, Hogarth Press, 1955), 151–209.

Ackroyd, Eric (1993) *A Dictionary of Dream Symbols: With an Introduction to Dream Psychology* (London, Blandford).

Adler, Alfred (1912a) *Über den Nervösen Charakter*, ed. Karl-Heinz Witte, Almuth Bruder-Bezzel, Rolf Kühn (Göttingen, Vandenhoeck and Ruprecht, 1997).

(1912b) "Dreams and dream interpretation," *The Practice and Theory of Individual Psychology*, trans. P. Radin (London, Kegan Paul, Trench, Trubner, 1924).

(1935) "Complex compulsions as part of personality and neurosis," in Heinz and Rowena Ansbacher, eds., *Superiority and Social Interest: A Collection of Later Writings* (London, Routledge and Kegan Paul, 1965).

Adler, Gerhard (1934) *Entdeckung der Seele. Von Sigmund Freud und Alfred Adler zu C. G. Jung* (Zürich, Rhein Verlag).

Aldrich, Charles (1931) *The Primitive Mind and Modern Civilization* (London, Kegan Paul).

Allport, Gordon (1937) *Personality: A Psychological Interpretation* (New York, Henry Holt).

Angulo, Gui de (1985) *Jaime in Taos: The Taos Papers of Jaime de Angulo* (San Francisco, City Lights).

Anon. (1916) *Journal of Education*, July.

(1923) "Psychological Types," *Times Literary Supplement*, July 5, 1923, 448.

(1935) "Man's immortal mind," *The Observer*, October 6.

Ash, Mitchell (1995) *Gestalt Psychology and German Culture: Holism and the Quest for Objectivity 1890–1967* (Cambridge, Cambridge University Press).

Atmanspracher, H., H. Primas and E. Wertenschlag-Birkhäuser, eds. (1995) *Der Pauli-Jung Dialog und seine Bedeutung für die moderne Wissenschaft* (Berlin, Springer).

Baldwin, James Mark (1890) *Handbook of Psychology: Sense and Intellect* (London, Macmillan).

(1895) *Mental Development in the Child and the Race: Methods and Processes* (New York, Macmillan).

(1897) *Social and Ethical Interpretations in Mental Development: A Study in Social Psychology* (New York, Macmillan).

(1910) "Report on terminology," in Édouard Claparède, ed., *Vme Congrès international de psychologie, tenu à Genève du 2 au 7 août sous la présidence de Th. Flournoy* (Geneva, Libraire Kündig), 480–481.

(1911) *The Individual and Society, or, Psychology and Sociology* (London, Rebman).

Barkan, Elazer (1992) *The Retreat of Scientific Racism: Changing Concepts of Race in Britain and the United States Between the World Wars* (Cambridge, Cambridge University Press).

Barker, Dudley (1935) "He probes man's dreams: Professor Jung says he is a practical psychologist," *The Evening Standard*, September 30.

Bastian, Adolf (1860) *Der Mensch in der Geschichte. Zur Begründung einer psychologischen Weltanschauung*, 3 vols. (Leipzig, Verlag Otto Wiegand).

Baynes, H. G. (1927) "Freud versus Jung," in *Analytical Psychology and the English Mind* (London, Methuen, 1950), 97–129.

Beard, George (1880) *A Practical Thesis on Nervous Exhaustion (Neurasthenia): Its Symptoms, Nature, Sequences, Treatment* (New York, William Wood).

Béguin, Albert (1967) *L'Âme romantique et le rêve: essai sur le romantasisme allemand et la poésie française* (Paris, Jose Corti).

Belke, Ingrid, ed. (1971) *Moritz Lazarus und Heymann Steinthal: Die Begründer der Völkerpsychologie in ihren Briefen* (Tübingen, J. C. B. Mohr).

Benedict, Ruth (1928) "Psychological types in the cultures of the southwest," in Margaret Mead, *An Anthropologist at Work: Writings of Ruth Benedict* (London, Secker and Warburg, 1959), 248–261.

(1934) *Patterns of Culture* (London, George Routledge and Sons, 1961).

Bennet, E. A. (1960) Letter to *The Listener*, January 21, 133.

(1961) *C. G. Jung* (London, Barrie and Rockliff).

(1982) *Meetings with Jung: Conversations recorded by E. A. Bennet during the Years 1946–1961* (London, privately published).

Bergson, Henri (1889) *Time and Free Will*, trans. F. L. Pogson (New York, Macmillan, 1919).

(1901) "On dreams," in *Mind Energy Lectures and Essays*, trans. H. W. Carr (London, Macmillan, 1920), 84–108.

(1907) *L'Évolution créatrice* (Paris, Alcan); *Creative Evolution*, trans. A. Mitchell (London, Macmillan, 1954).

(1908) "Memory of the present and false recognition," in *Mind Energy Lectures and Essays*, trans. H. W. Carr (London, Macmillan, 1920), 109–151.

(1934) *The Creative Mind: An Introduction to Metaphysics* (New York, Citadel Press, 1992).

Bernfeld, Siegfried (1946) "An unknown autobiographical fragment by Freud," *American Imago* 4, 3–19.

Bertrand, Alexandre (1823) *Traité du somnambulisme et des différentes modifications qu'il présente* (Paris, J. G. Dentu).

(1826) *Du magnétisme animale en France* (Paris, J. B. Ballière).

Binet, Alfred (1886) *The Psychology of Reasoning: Based on Experimental Researches in Hypnotism*, trans. A. Whyte (Chicago, Open Court, 1899).

(1897) "Psychologie individuelle – la description d'un objet," *L'année psychologique* 3, 296–332.

(1903) *L'Etude expérimentale de l'intelligence* (Paris, Schleicher Frères and Cie).

(1905) *The Mind and the Brain* (London, Kegan Paul, 1907).

Binet, Alfred and Victor Henri (1895) "La Psychologie individuelle," *L'année psychologique* 2, 411–465.

Bishop, Paul (1993) "The Jung/Förster-Nietzsche Correspondence," *German Life and Letters* 46, 319–330.

(1995) *The Dionysian Self: C. G. Jung's Reception of Nietzsche* (Berlin, Walter de Gruyter).

(2000) *Synchronicity and Intellectual Intuition in Kant, Swedenborg and Jung* (Lewiston, Edwin Mellon Press).

Bleuler, Eugen (1916) *Textbook of Psychiatry*, trans. A. A. Brill (London, G. Allen and Unwin, 1924).

(1925) *Die Psychoide als Prinzip der organischen Entwicklung* (Berlin, Julius Springer).

Boas, Franz (1896) "The limitations of the comparative method of anthropology," *Race, Language and Culture* (New York, Macmillan, 1940), 270–280.

(1910) "Psychological problems in anthropology," *American Journal of Psychology* 21, 371–384.

(1911) *Changes in the Bodily Form of Descendants of Immigrants*, Senate Document 208, 1911, 61st Congress, 2nd session (Washington).

(1912) "Changes in Bodily Form of descendants of immigrants," *Race, Language and Culture* (New York, Macmillan, 1940).

(1915) "Modern Populations of America," *Race, Language and Culture* (New York, Macmillan, 1940).

(1920) "The methods of ethnology," *Race, Language and Culture* (New York, Macmillan, 1940), 281–289.

Borch-Jacobsen, Mikkel (1982) *The Freudian Subject*, trans. C. Porter (Stanford, Stanford University Press, 1988).

(1989) "The unconscious, nonetheless," in *The Emotional Tie: Psychoanalysis, Mimesis, Affect* (Stanford: Stanford University Press, 1993), trans. D. Brick and others, 123–154.

(1991a) *The Emotional Tie: Psychoanalysis, Mimesis, and Affect* (Stanford, Stanford University Press, 1993), trans. D. Brick and others.

(1991b) "The alibis of the subject," in *The Emotional Tie: Psychoanalysis, Mimesis, Affect* (Stanford, Stanford University Press, 1993), trans. D. Brick and others, 155–175.

(1997) "L'effet Bernheim (fragments d'une théorie de l'artefact généralisé)," *Corpus des oeuvres philosophiques* 32, 147–174.

Borch-Jacobsen, Mikkel and Sonu Shamdasani (2001) "Une visite aux archives Freud," *Ethnopsy: Les mondes contemporains de la guérison* 3, 141–188.

Borges, Jorge Luis (1939) "Pierre Menard, author of Don Quixote," trans. A. Bower, *Fictions* (London, Calder, 1965), 42–51.

Boring, Edwin (1929) *A History of Experimental Psychology* (New York, Century).

Breton, André (1932) *Communicating Vessels*, trans. M. A. Caws and G. T. Harris (Nebraska, University of Nebraska Press, 1990).

Brill, Abraham (1945) *Freud's Contribution to Psychiatry* (London, Chapman and Hall).

Brooks, John (1991) "Analogy and argumentation in interdisciplinary context: Durkheim's 'individual and collective representations,'" *History of the Human Sciences* 4, 223–259.

Burbridge, David (1994) "Galton's 100: an exploration of Francis Galton's imagery studies," *British Journal for the History of Science* 27, 443–464.

Burdach, Karl Friederich (1826–1840) *Die Physiologie als Erfahrungswissenschaft* (Leipzig, Leopold Boss), 6 vols.

Burnham, John and William McGuire, eds., (1983) *Jelliffe: American Psychoanalyst and Physician and His Correspondence with Sigmund Freud and C. G. Jung* (Chicago, University of Chicago Press).

Butler, Samuel (1878) *Life and Habit* (London, Trübner and Co.)

Cabanis, Pierre (1805) *On the Relations between the Physical and Moral Aspects of Man*, ed. George Mora, trans. M. Saidi (Baltimore, Johns Hopkins University Press, 1981).

Caffrey, Margaret (1930) *Ruth Benedict: Stranger in this Land* (Austin, University of Texas Press, 1989).

Carpenter, William (1876) *Principles of Mental Physiology*, 4th edn. (London, Henry King, 1876).

Carroll, John (1956) *Language, Thought and Reality: Selected Writings of Benjamin Lee Whorf* (Cambridge, MIT Press).

Carroy, Jacqueline (1999) "Le docteur gibert, ou le 'Breuer' de Pierre Janet," in P. Fédida and F. Villa, eds., *Le cas en controverse* (Paris, PUF), 213–230.

Carson, John (1994) "Talents, intelligence and the constructions of human difference in France and America, 1750–1920." PhD thesis, Princeton University.

Carus, Carl Gustav (1846) *Psyche: Zur Entwicklungsgeschichte der Seele* (Darmstadt, Wissenschaftliche Buchgesellschaft, 1975); *Psyche: On the Development of the Soul. Part One, The Unconscious*, trans. R. Welch (Zürich, Spring Publications, 1970).

   (1866) *Vergleichende Psychologie oder Geschichte der Seele in der Reihenfolge der Thierwelt* (Vienna, Wilhelm Braumüller).

Charcot, Jean-Martin (1889) *Clinical Diseases of the Nervous System*, trans. T. Savill (London, New Sydenham Society).

Churchill, Frederick (1969) "From Machine-Theory to Entelechy: Two Studies in Developmental Teleology," *Journal of the History of Biology* 2, 165–185.

Cifali, Mireille (1991) "Notes autour de la première traduction française d'une oeuvre de Sigmund Freud," *Revue Internationale d'Histoire de la Psychanalyse* 4, 291–305.

Claparède, Édouard (1903) *L'Association des ideés* (Paris).

   (1904) "Esquisse d'une théorie biologique du sommeil," *Archives de Psychologie* 4, 245–349.

   (1905) "L'intérêt, principe fondamental de l'activité mentale," in De Sanctis, Sante, ed. *Atti del V. Congresso di Psicoglia Tenuto in Roma dal 26 al 30 Aprile 1905* (Rome, Forzani E C. Tipografi del Senato, 253.

   (1906–1907) "The value of biological interpretation for abnormal psychology," *Journal of Abnormal Psychology* 1, 83–92.

ed. (1910a) *Vme Congrès international de psychologie, tenu à Genève du 2 au 7 août sous la présidence de Th. Flournoy* (Geneva, Libraire Kündig).

(1910b) "L'Unification et la fixation de la terminologie psychologique," in Edouard Claparède, ed., *Vme Congrès international de psychologie, tenu à Genève du 2 au 7 août sous la présidence de Th. Flournoy* (Geneva, Libraire Kündig), 467–479.

(1930) "Autobiography," in Carl Murchison, ed., *A History of Psychology in Autobiography*, vol. 1 (New York, Russell and Russell, 1961).

Cocks, Geoffrey (1997) *Psychotherapy in the Third Reich: The Göring Institute*, 2nd edition, revised and expanded (New Brunswick, Transaction).

Coleridge, Samuel Taylor (1817) *Biographia Literaria, Or Biographical Sketches of My Literary Life and Opinions*, ed. George Watson (London, J. M. Dent and Sons, 1975).

Coriat, Isador (1915) *The Meaning of Dreams* (London, William Heinemann).

Crow, W. B. (1925) *Notes of Jung's Polzeath (1923) and Swanage (1925) Summer Schools* (privately published, London).

D'Hervey De Saint-Denys, Jean Marie (1867) *Les Rêves et les moyens de les diriger* (Paris, Amyot); *Dreams and How to Guide Them*, ed. Morton Schatzman (London, Duckworth, 1982).

Danziger, Kurt (1980) "The history of introspection reconsidered," *Journal of the History of the Behavioral Sciences* 16, 241–262.

(1983) "Origins and basic principles of Wundt's *Völkerpsychologie*," *British Journal of Social Psychology* 22, 303–313.

(1990a) *Constructing the Subject: Historical Origins of Psychological Research* (Cambridge, Cambridge University Press).

(1990b) "Mid-nineteenth-century British psycho-physiology: a neglected chapter in the history of ideas," in William Woodward and Mitchell Ash, eds., *The Problematic Science: Psychology in Nineteenth Century Thought* (New York: Praeger), 119–146.

(1997) *Naming the Mind: How Psychology Found its Language* (London, Sage).

Darnell, Regna (1990) *Edward Sapir: Linguist, Anthropologist, Humanist* (Berkeley, University of California Press).

Darwin, Charles (1859) *Origin of Species* (London, Penguin, 1982).

Daston, Lorraine (1990) "The theory of the will versus the science of the mind," in William Woodward and Mitchell Ash, eds., *The Problematic Science: Psychology in Nineteenth Century Thought* (New York: Praeger), 88–118.

Davis, Miles with Quincy Troupe (1990) *Miles Davis: The Autobiography* (London, Picador).

De Saussure, Raymond (1926) "La psychologie du rêve dans la tradition française," in René Laforgue, ed., *Le Rêve et la psychanalyse* (Paris, Norbet Maloine).

De Saussure, René (1910) "Uniformigo de la scienza terminaro," in Edouard Claparède, ed., *Vme Congrès international de psychologie, tenu à Geneva du 2 au 7 août sous la présidence de Th. Flournoy* (Geneva, Libraire Kündig, 1910), 482–487.

De Angulo, Ximena (1952) "Comments on a doctoral thesis," in William McGuire and R. F. C. Hull, eds., *C. G. Jung Speaking: Interviews and*

Encounters (Princeton/London, Bollingen Series, Princeton University Press, 1977 / Picador, 1980), 202–213.

De Carpenteri, Albumazar (1822) *La Clef d'or ou l'astrologue fortuné devin* (Lyon, Matheron).

De Thèbes, Madame (1908) *L'Énigme du rêve: explication des songes* (Paris, Félix Juven).

Decker, Hannah (1975) *"The Interpretation of Dreams*: Early Reception by the Educated German Public," *Journal of the History of the Behavioral Sciences* 11, 2, 129–141.

Delboeuf, Joseph (1879/1880) "Le sommeil et les rêves," *Revue Philosophique* 8, 1879, 329–356, 494–520, 616–618; 9, 1880, 129–169, 413–437, 623–647; *Le Sommeil et les rêves et autres Textes* (Paris, Fayard, 1993).

(1890) *Magnétiseurs et médecins* (Paris, Alcan).

Dennett, Richard (1906) *At the Back of the Black Man's Mind, or Notes on the Kingly Office in West Africa* (London, Macmillan).

Descartes, René (1641) *Meditations on First Philosophy*, in *The Philosophical Writings of Descartes* vol. 1, trans. J. Cottingham, R. Stoothoff, and D. Murdoch (Cambridge, Cambridge University Press, 1984).

Dietrich, Albrecht (1903) *Eine Mithrasliturgie* (Leipzig, B. G. Teubner).

Dilthey, Wilhelm (1883) *Introduction to the Human Sciences: An Attempt to Lay a Foundation for the Study of Society and History* (London, Harvester Wheatsheaf, 1993).

(1894) "Ideen über eine beschreibende und zergliedernde Psychologie," *Gesammelte Schriften* 5 (Leipzig, Teubner, 1924), 139–240; *Descriptive Psychology and Historical Understanding*, trans. R. Zaner and K. Heiges (The Hague, Martinus Nijhoff, 1977).

(1911) "The types of world-view and their development in the metaphysical systems," in H. P. Rickman, ed. and trans., *W. Dilthey: Selected Writings* (Cambridge, Cambridge University Press, 1976), 133–154.

Dodge, Mabel (1933) *Lorenzo in Taos* (London, Martin Secker).

Dowbiggen, Ian (1990) "Alfred Maury and the politics of the unconscious in nineteenth-century France," *History of Psychiatry* 1, 255–287.

Driesch, Hans (1908) *The Science and Philosophy of the Organism*, 2 vols. (London, Adam and Charles Black).

(1914) *History and Philosophy of Vitalism*, trans. C. K. Ogden (London, Macmillan).

(1951) *Lebenserinnerungen: Aufzeichnungen eines Forschers und Denkers in entscheidender Zeit* (Munich, Ernst Reinhardt Verlag).

Du Bois-Reymond, Emile (1912) *Reden von Emil Du Bois-Reymond*, 2 vols., ed. Estelle Du Bois-Reymond (Von Veit, Leipzig).

Du Prel, Carl (1885) *The Philosophy of Mysticism*, 2 vols., trans. C. Massey (London, G. Redway, 1889).

(1889) *Immanuel Kants Vorlesungen über Psychologie* (Leipzig, Ernst Günther).

Duckyearts, François (1993) "Les références de Freud à Delboeuf," *Revue internationale de l'histoire de la psychanalyse* 6, 231–250.

Durkheim, Emile (1895) *The Rules of Sociological Method*, ed. Steven Lukes, trans. W. Halls (New York, Free Press, 1982).

(1897) "Individual and collective representations," in *Sociology and Philosophy*, trans. D. Pocock (London, Cohen and West, 1953).

(1909) "The contribution of sociology to psychology and philosophy," in *Sociology and Philosophy*, trans. D. Pocock (London, Cohen and West, 1953).

(1912) *The Elementary Forms of the Religious Life*, trans. J. Swain (London, Allen and Unwin, 1976).

Ellenberger, Henri (1970) *The Discovery of the Unconscious: The History and Evolution of Dynamic Psychiatry* (New York, Basic Books).

(1993) *Beyond the Unconscious: Essays of H. F. Ellenberger in the History of Psychiatry*, ed. Mark Micale (Princeton, Princeton University Press).

Ellis, Havelock (1911) *The World of Dreams* (London, Constance).

Elms, Alan (1994) "The auntification of Jung," chapter 3, *Uncovering Lives: The Uneasy Alliance of Biography and Psychology* (New York, Oxford University Press).

Espinas, Alfred (1878) *Des sociétés animales* (Paris, Alcan).

Esquirol, E. (1832) *Aliénation mentale. Des illusions des aliénés. Question médico-légale sur l'isolement des aliénés* (Paris, Crochard).

Essertier, Daniel (1927) *Psychologie et sociologie: essai de bibliographique critique* (Paris, Alcan).

Evans, Richard (1957) "Conversations with Carl Jung," in William McGuire and R. F. C. Hull, eds., *C. G. Jung Speaking: Interviews and Encounters* (Princeton/London, Bollingen Series, Princeton University Press, 1977 / Picador, 1980), 276–352.

(1975) *Konrad Lorenz: The Man and his Ideas* (New York, Harcourt Brace Jovanovitch).

Evans-Pritchard, Edward (1981) *A History of Anthropological Thought*, ed. André Singer (London, Faber and Faber).

Falzeder, Ernst (1994) "The threads of psychoanalytic filiations or psychoanalysis taking effect," in André Haynal and Ernst Falzeder, eds., *100 Years of Psychoanalysis: Contributions to the History of Psychoanalysis*, special issue of *Cahiers Psychiatriques Genevois*, 169–174.

(2000) "Profession – psychoanalyst: A historical view," *Psychoanalysis and History* 2, 37–60.

ed. (1993) *The Correspondence of Sigmund Freud and Sándor Ferenczi, volume 1, 1908–1914*, trans. Peter Hoffer (Cambridge, Mass., Harvard University Press).

ed. (2002) *The Complete Correspondence of Sigmund Freud and Karl Abraham* (London, Karnac).

Fechner, Gustav (1860) *Elements of Psychophysics*, vol. 1., ed. Davis Howes and Edwin Boring, trans. H. Adler (New York, Holt, Rinehart and Winston, 1966).

Ferenczi, Sándor (1913) "Kritik der Jungschen 'Wandlungen und Symbole der Libido,'" *Internationale Zeitschrift für ärztliche Psychoanalyse* 1, 391–403.

(1914) "Dr. C. G. Jung, 'Contribution à l'étude des types psychologiques,'" *Baustein zur Psychoanalyse*, vol. 4 (Bern, Hans Huber, 1939).

Feuchtersleben, Baron Ernst von (1845) *The Principles of Medical Psychology: Being the Outline of a Course of Lectures*, trans. H. E. Lloyd (London, New Sydenham Society).

Fichte, Johann (1794) *The Science of Knowledge*, ed and trans. Peter Heath and John Lachs (Cambridge, Cambridge University Press, 1982).

Flaubert, Gustave (1881) *Bouvard and Pécuchet*, trans. A. Krailsheimer (London, Penguin, 1976).

Flournoy, Théodore (1896) *Notice sur le laboratoire de psychologie de l'université de Genève* (Geneva, Eggiman).

(1900/1994) *From India to the Planet Mars: A Case of Multiple Personality with Imaginary Languages*, ed. Sonu Shamdasani, trans. D. Vermilye (Princeton, Princeton University Press).

(1908) "Automatisme téléologique antisuicide," *Archives de psychologie* 7, 113–117.

(1911) *The Philosophy of William James*, trans. E. B. Holt and W. James, Jr. (London, Constable, 1917).

(1913) Review of C. G. Jung, "Wandlungen und Symbole der Libido," *Archives de Psychologie* 13, 195–199.

Ford, Jennifer (1994) "Samuel Taylor Coleridge on dreams and dreaming," PhD thesis, University of Sydney.

Fordham, Michael (1957) "Biological theory and the concept of the archetypes," in *New Developments in Analytical Psychology* (London, Routledge and Kegan Paul).

(1958) "Development and status of Jung's researches," in *The Objective Psyche* (London, Routledge and Kegan Paul), 4–31.

(1993) *The Making of an Analyst: A Memoir* (London, Free Associations).

Forel, Auguste (1885) *Das Gedächtniss und seine Abnormitäten* (Zürich, Orell Füssli).

(1905) "Eine Konsequenz der Semonschen Lehre der Mneme," *Journal für Psychologie und Neurologie* 5, 200–201.

(1906) *Hypnotism, or Suggestion and Psychotherapy: A Study of the Psychological, Psycho-Physiological and Therapeutic Aspects of Hypnotism*, trans. H. W. Armit (5th edn.) (London, Rebman).

(1907) *Hygiene of Nerves and Mind in Health and Disease*, trans. A. Aikins (London, John Murray).

(1937) *Out of my Life and Work*, trans. B. Miall (London, George Allen and Unwin).

Fouillée, Alfred (1893) *La Psychologie des idées-forces*, 2 vols. (Paris, Alcan).

(1890) *L'Évolutionnisme des idées-forces* (Paris, Alcan).

(1903) *Esquisse psychologique des peuples européens* (Paris, Alcan).

Frazer, James (1911–1915) *The Golden Bough: A Study in Magic and Religion* (London, Macmillan).

Freeman, John (1959) "'Face to face' interview with Jung," in William McGuire and R. F. C. Hull, eds., *C. G. Jung Speaking: Interviews and Encounters* (Princeton/London, Bollingen Series, Princeton University Press, 1977 / Picador, 1980), 424–439.

Galton, Francis (1883) *Inquiries into Human Faculty and its Development* (London, J. M. Dent).

Gans, Hans (1917) *Das Unbewusste bei Leibniz in Beziehung zur modernen Theorien* (Zürich, Rascher).

Gasser, Jacques (1988) "La notion de mémoire organique dans l'œuvre de T. Ribot," *History and Philosophy of the Life Sciences* 10, 293–313.

(1995) *Aux origines du cerveau moderne. Localisations, langage et mémoire dans l'oeuvre de Charcot* (Paris, Fayard).

Gauchet, Marcel (1992) *L'Inconscient cérébral* (Paris, Editions du Seuil).

Gentile, Benedetto (1822) *Livre des rêves ou l'oneiroscopie* (Paris, Masson).

Geuter, Ulfried (1992) *The Professionalization of Psychology in Nazi Germany*, trans. R. Holmes (Cambridge, Cambridge University Press).

Giegerich, Wolfgang (1998) *The Soul's Logical Life* (Frankfurt, Peter Lang).

Gijswijt-Hofstra, Marijke and Roy Porter (2001) *Cultures of Neurasthenia: From Beard to the First World War* (Amsterdam, Rodopi).

Goldenweiser, Alexander (1949) "Adolf Bastian," in Edwin Seligman, ed., *Encyclopedia of the Social Sciences* (New York, Macmillan), 476.

Goldstein, Kurt (1927) "Die Beziehungen der Psychoanalyse zur Biologie," in Wladimir Eliasberg, ed., *Bericht über den II. Allgemeinen Ärztlichen Kongress für Psychotherapie in Bad Nauheim, 27 bis 30 April 1927* (Leipzig, Verlag S. Hirzel), 15–52.

(1939) *The Organism: A Holistic Approach to Biology derived from Pathological Data in Man* (New York, American Book Company).

(1940) *Human Nature in the Light of Psychopathology* (Cambridge, Mass., Harvard University Press).

Golinski, Jan (1998) *Making Natural Knowledge: Constructivism and the History of Science* (Cambridge, Cambridge University Press).

Goodman, Nelson (1978) *Ways of Worldmaking* (Hassocks, Harvester Press).

Gray, H. and J. B. Wheelwright (1945) "Jung's psychological types, including the four functions," *The Journal of General Psychology* 33, 265–284.

Gregory, Frederick (1977) *Scientific Materialism in Nineteenth Century Germany* (Dordrecht, Reidel).

Griesinger, Wilhelm (1867) *Mental Pathology and Therapeutics*, 2nd edn., trans. C. Lockhart Robertson and J. Rutherford (London, New Sydenham Society).

Groos, Karl (1898) *The Play of Animals: A Study of Animal Life and Instinct*, trans. E. L. Baldwin (London, Chapman and Hall).

Gurney, Edmund, Frederic Myers and Frank Podmore (1886) *Phantasms of the Living* (London, Trubner).

Hacking, Ian (1995) *Rewriting the Soul: Multiple Personality and the Sciences of Memory* (Princeton, Princeton University Press).

Haeckel, Ernst (1900) *The Riddle of the Universe*, trans. J. McCabe (New York, Harper).

(1903) *The Evolution of Man* (London, Watts, 1905).

Hakl, Hans Thomas (2001) *Der verborgene Geist von Eranos: Unbekannte Begegnungen von Wissenschaft und Esoterik* (Bretten, Scientia nova).

Hale, Nathan (1971) *Freud and the Americans: The Beginnings of Psychoanalysis in the United States, 1876–1917* (New York, Oxford University Press).

(1995) *The Rise and Crisis of Psychoanalysis in the United States: Freud and the Americans, 1917–1985* (New York, Oxford University Press).

ed. (1971) *James Jackson Putnam and Psychoanalysis: Letters between Putnam and Sigmund Freud, Ernest Jones, William James, Sandor Ferenczi, and Morton Prince, 1877–1917* (Cambridge, Mass., Harvard University Press).

Hall, G. Stanley (1897) "A study of fears," *American Journal of Psychology* 8, 147–249.

(1904) *Adolescence: Its Psychology and its relations to Physiology, Anthropology, Sociology, Sex, Crime, Religion and Education* (New York, D. Appleton and Co.).

(1922) *Senescence: The Last Half of Life* (New York, D. Appleton and Co.).

(1923) *Life and Confessions of a Psychologist* (New York, D. Appleton and Co.).

Hamilton, William (1865) *Lectures on Metaphysics* (Edinburgh, William Blackwood).

Handelbauer, Bernhard (1998) *The Freud–Adler Controversy* (Oxford, Oneworld).

Harms, Ernst (1967) *Origins of Modern Psychiatry* (Springfield, Charles Thomas).

Harrington, Anne (1996) *Reenchanted Science: Holism in German Culture from Wilhelm II to Hitler* (Princeton, Princeton University Press).

Harris, Ruth (1989) *Murder and Madness: Medicine, Law and Society in the Fin de Siècle* (Oxford, Clarendon Press).

Hartmann, Eduard von (1869). *Philosophie des Unbewussten: Versuch ein Weltanschauung* (Berlin, C. Dunker).

(1900) *The Philosophy of the Unconscious*, trans. W. Coupland (London, R. Paul, Trench and Trubner, 1931).

Haule, John (1984) "From somnambulism to archetypes: the French roots of Jung's split from Freud," *Psychoanalytic Review* 71, 95–107.

Hauser, Ronald (1992) "Karl Albert Scherner," *The Centennial Review* 36, 343–346.

Henry, Michel (1985) *The Genealogy of Psychoanalysis* (Stanford, Stanford University Press, 1993).

Herbart, Johann (1814) *A Text-Book in Psychology: An Attempt to Found the Science of Psychology on Experience, Metaphysics, and Mathematics* (New York, Appleton, 1891).

Hering, Ewald (1870) "On memory as a general function of organised matter," in Samuel Butler, *Unconscious Memory* (London, A. C. Fifield, 1910).

Hetherington, Robert (1959) Letter to *The Listener*, November 12, 834.

Heyer, Gustav (1932) *Der Organismus der Seele, eine Einführung in die analytische Seelenheilkunde* (Munich, J. H. Lehman).

Heynick, Frank (1993) *Language and its Disturbances in Dreams: The Pioneering Work of Freud and Kraepelin Updated* (New York, John Wiley).

Hillman, James (1979) *The Dream and the Underworld* (New York, Harper and Row).

Howard, Jane (1984) *Margaret Mead: A Life* (New York, Simon and Schuster).

Hubert, Henri and Mauss, Marcel (1909) *Mélanges d'histoire des religions* (Travaux de l'Année Sociologique) (Paris, Alcan).

Hull, R. F. C. (1959) Letter to *The Listener*, December 10, 1041.

(1970) "Translator's postscript," C. G. Jung, "Two posthumous papers," *Spring: An Annual of Archetypal Psychology and Jungian Thought*, 176.

Hunt, Harry (1989) *The Multiplicity of Dreams: Memory, Imagination, and Consciousness* (New Haven, Yale University Press).

Husserl, Edmund (1937) *The Crisis of European Sciences and Transcendental Phenomenology*, trans. D. Carr (Evanston, Northwestern University Press, 1970).

Iselin, Hans Konrad, ed. (1982) *Zur Entstehung von C. G. Jungs "Psychologischen Typen": Der Briefwechsel zwischen C. G. Jung und Hans Schmid-Guisan in Lichte ihrer Freundschaft* (Aarau, Verlag Sauerlander).

Isham, Mary (1923) "Dr. Jung expounds the psychology of individuation," *The New York Times Book Review*, June 10.

(1979) *Word and Image: C. G. Jung* (Bollingen Series, Princeton University Press, Princeton).

Jahoda, Gustav (1992) *Crossroads between Culture and Mind* (London, Harvester Wheatsheaf).

James, Henry Jr. (1920) *The Letters of William James*, 2 vols. (London, Longmans, Green and Co.)

James, Tony (1995) *Dream, Creativity and Madness in Nineteenth-Century France* (Oxford, Oxford University Press).

James, William (1890) *The Principles of Psychology*, 2 vols. (London, Macmillan, 1918).

(1892a) *Psychology: Briefer Course* (Cambridge, Mass., Harvard University Press, 1984).

(1892b) "A plea for psychology as a 'natural science,'" *Essays in Psychology* (Cambridge, Mass., Harvard University Press, 1983).

(1902) *The Varieties of Religious Experience* (London, Longmans).

(1904) "Does consciousness exist?" *Essays in Radical Empiricism* (Lincoln, University of Nebraska Press, 1996).

(1906) "The energies of men," in *Essays in Religion and Morality* (Cambridge, Harvard University Press, 1982).

(1907) *Pragmatism and Four Essays from The Meaning of Truth* (Cleveland, Ohio, Meridian, 1970).

(1909a) *A Pluralistic Universe* (London, Longmans, Green and Co.).

(1909b) "Report on Mrs. Piper's Hodgson-control," in Gardner Murphy and Robert Ballou, eds., *William James on Psychical Research* (London, Chatto and Windus, 1961), 115–210.

Janet, Pierre (1889) *L'Automatisme psychologique: essais de psychologie expérimentale sur les formes inférieures de l'activité humaine*, 4th edn., (Paris, Alcan, 1903).

(1893) *The Mental State of Hystericals: A Study of Mental Stigmata and Mental Accidents*, trans. C. R. Corson (New York, G. P. Putnam's Sons, 1901).

(1898) *Névroses et idées fixes*, 2 vols. (Paris, Alcan).

(1908) *Les Obsessions et la psychasthénie*, 2 vols. (Paris, Alcan).

(1914–1915) "Psychoanalysis," trans. W. G. Bean, *Journal of Abnormal Psychology*, 1–35, 153–187.

(1919) *Psychological Healing: A Historical and Clinical Study*, trans. E. and C. Paul, 2 vols. (London, George Allen and Unwin, 1925).

Jaspers, Karl (1919) *Psychologie der Weltanschauungen* (Berlin, Springer).

Johnson, Samuel, ed. E. L. McAdam and George Milne (1755) *Johnson's Dictionary: A Modern Selection* (London, Cassel, 1995).

Jones, Ernest (1913) *Papers on Psycho-Analysis* (London, Baillière, Tindall and Cox).

Jung, C. G. (1915) "On psychological understanding," *Journal of Abnormal Psychology* 9, 385–399.

(1916) "The conception of the unconscious," in Constance Long, ed., *Collected Papers on Analytical Psychology* (London, Baillière, Tindall and Cox, 1917, 2nd edn.), 445–474.

(1917a) Ed. Constance Long, *Collected Papers on Analytical Psychology* (London, Baillière, Tindall and Cox, 2nd edn.).

(1917b) "The psychology of the unconscious processes," in Constance Long, ed., *Collected Papers on Analytical Psychology* (London, Baillière, Tindall and Cox, 2nd edn.), 354–444.

(1918) *Die Psychologie der Unbewussten Prozesse: Ein Überblick über die moderne Theorie und Methode der analytischen Psychologie*, 2nd edn., (Zürich, Rascher).

(1921) *Psychologische Typen* (Zürich, Rascher).

(1925) *Analytical Psychology: Notes of the Seminar given in 1925*, ed. William McGuire, Bollingen Series XCIX (Princeton, Princeton University Press / London, Routledge, 1989).

(1928a) *Contributions to Analytical Psychology*, trans. C. F. and H. G. Baynes (London, Kegan Paul, Trench, Trubner).

(1928b) *Über die Energetik der Seele* (Zürich: Rascher).

(1928–1930) *Dream Analysis: Notes of the Seminar given in 1928–1930*, ed. William McGuire, Bollingen Series XCIX (Princeton, Princeton University Press, London, Routledge, 1984).

(1930–1934) *Visions: Notes of the Seminar given in 1930–1934*, ed. Claire Douglas, 2 vols. (Bollingen Series, Princeton University Press, 1997).

(1933) "Über Psychologie," *Neue Schweizer Rundschau* 1, 21–27 and 2, 98–106.

(1934) *Modern Psychology. Notes on the Lectures given at the Eidgenössische Technische Hochschule, Zürich by Prof. Dr. C. G. Jung, October 1933–February 1940*, compiled and translated by Elizabeth Welsh and Barbara Hannah (Zürich, 1959, privately published, 2nd edn.).

(1934–1939) *Nietzsche's Zarathustra: Notes of the Seminar given in 1934–9*, ed. James Jarrett, 2 vols. (Bollingen Series, Princeton University Press, 1988).

(1935–1936) *Notes of Jung's 1935/6 ETH Lectures*, compiled by Barbara Hannah, Una Thomas, and Elizabeth Baumann, privately published.

(1936) *Dream Symbols of the Individuation Process: Notes of a Seminar at Bailey Island, Maine, September 1936*, ed. Kristine Mann, Eleanor Bertine, and Esther Harding, privately published.

(1938–1939) *Psychological Interpretation of Children's Dreams: Notes on Lectures given by Prof. Dr. C. G. Jung at the Eidgenössische Technische Hochschule, Zürich, Autumn–Winter, 1938–9*, ed. Liliane Frey and Rivkah Schärf, trans. M. Foote, privately published.

(1939) *The Integration of the Personality*, trans. S. Dell (New York, Farrar and Rhinehart).

Kaegi, Werner (1947–1982) *Jacob Burckhart: Eine Biographie*, 8 vols. (Basel, Schwabe).

Kalmar, Ivan (1987) "The *Völkerpsychologie* of Lazarus and Steinthal and the modern concept of culture," *Journal of the History of Ideas* 48, 671–690.

Kant, Immanuel (1786/1985) *Metaphysical Foundations of Natural Science*, in James Ellington, ed., *Kant's Philosophy of Material Nature*, trans. P. Carus (Indianapolis, Hackett).

(1787) *Critique of Pure Reason*, trans. N. Kemp Smith (London, Macmillan, 1933).

(1790) *Kant's Critique of Teleological Judgement*, trans. J. C. Meredith (Oxford, Clarendon Press, 1928).

(1798) *Anthropology from a Pragmatic Point of View*, ed. Hans Rudnick, trans. V. L. Dowdell (Carbondale and Edwardsville, Southern Illinois Press, 1978).

(1997) *Lectures on Metaphysics*, ed. and trans. Karl Ameriks and Steve Naragon (Cambridge, Cambridge University Press).

Kern, Stephen (1975) "The prehistory of Freud's dream theory: Freud's master-piece anticipated," *History of Medicine* 6, 3/4, 83–92.

Kiell, Norman (1988) *Freud Without Hindsight: Reviews of his Work (1893–1939)* (New York, International Universities Press).

Kirsch, James (1975) "Remembering C. G. Jung," *Psychological Perspectives* 6, 1975, 54–63.

Klages, Ludwig (1929) *The Science of Character*, trans. W. H. Johnston (London, Allen and Unwin).

Koch, Sigmund (1975) "Language communities, search cells, and the psychological studies," in W. J. Arnold ed., *Nebraska Symposium on Motivation*, vol. 23 (Lincoln, University of Nebraska Press, 1976), 478–559.

(1993) "'Psychology' or 'The Psychological Studies'?" *American Psychologist* 48, 902–904.

Koepping, Klaus-Peter (1983) *Adolf Bastian and the Psychic Unity of Mankind: The Foundations of Anthropology in Nineteenth-Century Germany* (St. Lucia, University of Queensland Press).

Köhler, Wolfgang (1947) *Gestalt Psychology: An Introduction to New Concepts in Modern Psychology* (New York, Liveright).

Kraepelin, Emil (1987) *Memoirs*, trans. C. Wooding-Deane (Berlin, Springer-Verlag).

Krafft-Ebing, Richard von (1879–1880) *Lehrbuch der Psychiatrie auf klinischer Grundlage: für practische Ärzte und Studirende* (Stuttgart, Enke); *Text-Book of Insanity based on Clinical Observations* (Philadelphia, Davis, 1904).

Kranefeldt, Wolfgang (1930) *Die Psychoanalyse: Psychoanalytische Psychologie* (Berlin, Walter de Gruyter).

Kretschmer, Ernst (1934) *Textbook of Medical Psychology*, trans. E. B. Strauss (London, Oxford University Press).

Krippener, Stanley, ed. (1990) *Dreamtime and Dreamwork: Decoding the Language of the Night* (New York, Tarcher).

Külpe, Oswald (1913) *The Philosophy of the Present in Germany*, trans. M. and G. Patrick (London, George Allen and Co.).

Lacinius (1874) *La vraie clef des songes* (Paris, E. Guerin).

Lampl, Hans Erich (1989) "Flair du livre: Friedrich Nietzsche und Théodule Ribot," *Nietzsche Studien* 18, 573–586.

Lamprecht, Karl (1891–1909) *Deutsche Geschichte*, 12 vols. (Berlin).

(1905) *What is History? Five Lectures on the Modern Science of History*, trans. E. Andrews (New York, Macmillan).

Lanteri Laura, Georges (1968) "Le Rêve comme argument," *Cahiers Laënnec* 28, 2, 15–36.

Latour, Bruno (1993) *We Have Never been Modern*, trans. C. Porter (Cambridge, Mass., Harvard University Press).

(1996) *Pétite réflexion sur le culte moderne des dieux faitiches* (Le Plessis-Robinson, Les Empêcheurs de penser en rond).

Laurence, Jean-Roch and Campbell Perry (1988) *Hypnosis, Will and Memory: A Psycho-Legal History* (New York, Guilford Press).

Lavie, Perez and Allan Hobson (1986) "Origin of dreams: anticipation of modern theories in philosophy and physiology of the eighteenth and nineteenth centuries," *Psychological Bulletin* 100, 229–240.

Lawrence, D. H. (1928) "New Mexico," in *Selected Essays* (Harmondsworth, Penguin, 1981), 180–188.

Layard, John (1942) *The Stone Men of Malekula: Vao* (London, Chatto and Windus).

Laycock, Thomas (1876) "A chapter on some organic laws of memory," *Journal of Mental Science* 21, 155–187.

Le Bon, Gustave (1894) *Lois psychologiques de l'évolution des peuples* (Paris, Félix Alcan, 1898).

(1895) *The Crowd: A Study of the Popular Mind*, trans. anon. (London, Fisher Unwin, 1921).

Le Clair, Robert, ed. (1966) *The Letters of William James and Théodore Flournoy* (Madison, University of Wisconsin Press).

Le vingtième Artemiodore (1951) *La nouvelle clé des songes* (Monaco, Les documents d'art).

Leary, David (1982) "Immanuel Kant and the development of modern psychology," in William Woodward and Mitchell Ash, eds., *The Problematic Science: Psychology in Nineteenth Century Thought* (New York, Praeger), 17–42.

Leibniz, G. W. (1703) *New Essays on Human Understanding*, trans. P. Remnant and J. Bennett (Cambridge, Cambridge University Press, 1981).

Leopold, Joan (1980) *Culture in Comparative and Evolutionary Perspective: E. B. Tylor and the Making of Primitive Culture* (Berlin, Dietrich Reimer).

Lévi-Strauss, Claude (1987) *Introduction to the work of Marcel Mauss*, trans. F. Baker (London, Routledge and Kegan Paul).

Lévy-Bruhl, Lucien (1910) *How Natives Think* (*Les fonctions mentales dans les sociétés inférieurs*), trans. L. Clare (Princeton, Princeton University Press, 1985).

(1935a) *La Mythologie primitive. Le monde mythique des australiens et des papous* (Paris).

(1935b) "Remarques sur l'initiation des medicine men," in Psychologischen Club, ed., *Die Kulturelle Bedeutung der komplexen Psychologie* (Berlin, Julius Springer), 214–219.

(1936) "The Cartesian Spirit and History," in Raymond Klibansky and H. J. Paton, eds., *Philosophy and History: Essays presented to Ernst Cassirer* (Oxford, Clarendon).

(1949) *The Notebooks on Primitive Mentality*, trans. P. Rivière (Oxford, Blackwell, 1975).

Lewes, George Henry (1877) *The Physical Basis of Mind* (London, Trubner and Co.).

Leys, Ruth (1985) "Meyer, Jung and the limits of association," *Bulletin of the History of Medicine* 59, 345–360.

Lincoln, J. Stewart (1935) *The Dream in Primitive Cultures* (London, Crescent Press).

Lipps, Theodore (1906) *Leitfaden der Psychologie* (Leipzig, Wilhelm Engelmann).

Ljunggren, Magnus (1994) *The Russian Mephisto: A Study of the Life of Emilii Medtner* (Stockholm, Almqvist and Wiksell International).

Locke, John (1671) *An Essay concerning Human Understanding*, ed. Peter Nidditch (Oxford, Clarendon Press, 1975).

Long, Constance (1922) "Review of Beatrice Hinkle, 'A study of psychological types,'" *British Journal of Psychology* 2, 4, 229–233.

Lorenz, Konrad (1939) "The comparative study of behaviour," in *Motivation of Human and Animal Behaviour: An Ethnological View*, trans. B. A. Konkin (New York, Nostrand Reinhold, 1973).

(1948) *The Natural Science of the Human Species : An Introduction to Comparative Behavioral Research: The "Russian Manuscript" (1944–1948)*; edited from the posthumous works by Agnes von Cranach; trans. R. Martin (Cambridge, Mass., MIT Press, 1996).

Lovejoy, Arthur O. (1906) "The fundamental conceptions of primitive philosophy," *The Monist* 16, 357–382.

Macario, Maurice (1857) *Du Sommeil, des rêves et du somnambulisme dans l'état de santé et de maladie* (Paris, Perisse frères).

Macintyre, Alisdair (1958) *The Unconscious: A Conceptual Analysis* (London, Routledge and Kegan Paul).

Macnish, Robert (1834) *The Philosophy of Sleep* (Glasgow, W. R. M'Phun).

Maeder, Alphonse (1912a) "Sur le mouvement psychoanalytique: un point de vue nouveau en psychologie," *L'année psychologique* 18, 389–418.

(1912b) "Über die Funktion des Traumes," *Jahrbuch für psychoanalytische und psychopathologische Forschungen* 4, 692–707.

(1913a) "Zur Frage der teleologischen Traumfunktion. Eine Bemarkung zur Abwehr," *Jahrbuch für psychoanalytische und psychopathologische Forschungen* 5, 453–454.

(1913b) "Autoreferat, Ortsgruppe Zürich," "Korrespondenzblatt der Internationalen Psychoanalytischen Vereinigung," *Internationale Zeitschrift für ärztliche Psychoanalyse* 1, 621–622.

(1913c) "Über das Traumproblem," *Jahrbuch für psychoanalytische und psychopathologische Forschungen* 5, 1913, 647–686.

(1926) "De la psychanalyse à la psychosynthèse," *L'Encephale* 8, 1926, 577–589.

(1956a) "Mein Weg von der Psychoanalyse zur Synthese: Ein autobiographischer Beitrag zur Wandlung der Geisteshaltung seit 1900," in Elga Kern, ed., *Wegweiser in der Zeitwende* (Munich, Ernst Reinhardt).

(1956b) "Persönliche Erinnerungen an Freud und retrospektive Besinnung," *Schweizer Zeitschrift für Psychologie* 15, 114–122.

Magee, Bryan (1987) *The Philosophy of Schopenhauer* (Oxford, Clarendon Press).

Maine de Biran (1809) "Nouvelles considérations sur le sommeil, les songes et le somnambulisme," *Oeuvres Tome V: Discours à la société médicale de Bergerac*, ed. François Azouvi (Paris, J. Vrin, 1984), 82–123.

Malinowski, Bronislaw (1916) "Baloma. The spirits of the dead in the trobriand islands," *Journal of the Royal Anthropological Institute.*

(1927) *Sex and Repression in Savage Society* (London, Kegan Paul, Trench, Trubner).

Mandelbaum, David, ed. (1949) *Selected Writings of Edward Sapir* (Berkeley, University of California Press).

Marinelli, Lydia and Andreas Mayer (2000) "Vom ersten Methodenbuch zum historischen Dokument. Sigmund Freuds *Traumdeutung* in Prozeß ihrer Lektüren (1899–1930)," in Lydia Marinelli and Andreas Mayer, eds., *Die Lesbarkeit der Träume: Zur Geschichte von Freuds Traumdeutung* (Frankfurt am Main, Fischer Verlag), 37–126.

Marquard, Odo (1987) *Transzendentaler Idealismus, Romantische Naturphilosophie, Psychoanalyse* (Cologne, Verlag für Philosophie Jürgen Dinter).

Marx, Otto (1990–1991) "German Romantic Psychiatry," 2 parts, *History of Psychiatry* 1, 1990, 351–380; 2, 1991, 1–25.

Massey, Irving (1990) "Freud before Freud: K. A. Scherner," *The Centennial Review* 34, 567–576.

Masson, Jeffrey, ed. and trans. (1985) *The Complete Letters of Freud to Wilhelm Fliess, 1887–1904* (Cambridge, Mass, Belknap Press).

Maury, Alfred (1861) *Le Sommeil et les rêves: études psychologiques sur ces phenomènes et les divers états qui s'y rattachent* (Paris, Didier).

Mauss, Marcel (1902–1903) *A General Theory of Magic* (London, Routledge and Kegan Paul, 1972).

(1924) "Real and practical relations between psychology and sociology," in *Sociology and Psychology: Essays*, trans. Ben Brewster (London, Routledge and Kegan Paul, 1979).

McDougall, William (1908) *An Introduction to Social Psychology* (London, Methuen, 1950).

(1926) *An Outline of Abnormal Psychology* (London, Methuen, 1948).

(1929) "A chemical theory of temperament applied to introversion and extroversion," *Journal of Abnormal Psychology* 24, 393–409.

(1930) "Autobiography," in Carl Murchison, ed., *A History of Psychology in Autobiography*, vol. 1 (New York, Russell and Russell, 1961), 191–224.

(1933) *The Energies of Men: A Study of the Fundamentals of Dynamic Psychology* (London, Methuen).

(1934) *The Frontiers of Psychology* (Cambridge, Cambridge University Press).

(1938) *The Riddle of Life: A Survey of Theories* (London, Methuen).

McGuire, William (1978) "Jung in America, 1924–1925," *Spring: An Annual for Archetypal Psychology and Jungian Thought*, 1978, 37–53.

(1984) "American Eranos volume: introduction," *Spring: An Annual of Jungian Thought and Archetypal Psychology*, 57–9.

ed. (1974) *The Freud/Jung Letters*, trans. R. Mannheim and R. F. C. Hull (Princeton: Princeton University Press; London: Hogarth Press / Routledge and Kegan Paul).

McGuire, William and R. F. C. Hull, eds. (1977) *C. G. Jung Speaking: Interviews and Encounters* (Princeton/London, Bollingen Series, Princeton University Press).

Mead, Margaret (1959) *An Anthropologist at Work: Writings of Ruth Benedict* (London, Secker and Warburg).

(1973) *Blackberry Winter: My Earliest Years* (London, Angus and Robertson).

(1974) *Ruth Benedict* (New York, Columbia University Press).

(1977) *Letters from the Field 1925–1975* (New York, Harper and Row).

Medtner, Emil (1923) *Über die sog. "Intuition", die ihr angrenzenden Begriffe und die an sie anknüpfenden Probleme* (Moscow, Musagetes).

Meier, C. A. (1989) *The Psychology of Jung. Volume 3: Consciousness*, trans. D. Roscoe (Boston, Sigo Press).

(1977) *Personality: The Individuation Process in the Light of C. G. Jung's Typology*, trans. D. Roscoe (Einsiedeln, Daimon, 1995).

(1984) *The Psychology of Jung. Volume 1: The Unconscious in its Empirical Manifestations*, trans. D. Roscoe (Boston, Sigo Press).

(1986) *Soul and Body: Essays on the Theories of C. G. Jung* (Santa Monica, Lapis Press).

(1989) *The Psychology of Jung. Volume 3: Consciousness*, trans. D. Roscoe (Boston, Sigo Press).

ed. (2001) *Atom and Archetype: The Pauli/Jung Letters*, with a preface by Beverley Zabriskie, trans. D. Roscoe (Princeton, Princeton University Press).

Merllié, Dominique (1989a) "Présentation. Le cas Lévy-Bruhl," *Autour de Lucien Lévy-Bruhl, Revue Philosophique* 179, 419–448.

(1989b) "Lévy-Bruhl et Durkheim: Notes biographiques en marge d'une correspondance," *Autour de Lucien Lévy-Bruhl, Revue Philosophique* 179, 493–514.

Métraux, Alexandre (1982) "French crowd psychology: between theory and ideology," in William Woodward and Mitchell Ash, eds., *The Problematic Science: Psychology in Nineteenth-Century Thought* (New York, Praeger), 276–299.

Meyer, Adolf (1905) Review of Jung, ed., *Diagnostische Assoziationstudien, Psychological Bulletin*, 242.

(1906) "Application of associations studies," *Psychological Bulletin*, 280.

Micale, Mark. S. (1994) "Henri F. Ellenberger: The history of psychiatry as the history of the unconscious," in Mark S. Micale and Roy Porter eds., *Discovering the History of Psychiatry* (New York, Oxford University Press), 112–134.

Mucchielli, Laurent (1998) *La découverte du social: naissance de la sociologie en france (1870–1914)* (Paris, éditions la découverte).

Murchison, Carl, ed. (1930) *Psychologies of 1930* (Worcester, Mass., Clark University Press).

Murray, Henry et al. (1938) *Explorations in Personality* (New York, Oxford University Press).

Myers, Frederic (1891) "The subliminal consciousness, chapter 1. General characteristics of subliminal messages," *Proceedings of the Society for Psychical Research*, 298–355.

(1892) "Hypermnesic Dreams," *Proceedings of the Society for Psychical Research* 8, 333–404.

(1893) *Science and a Future Life* (London, Macmillan).

(1903) *Human Personality and its Survival of Bodily Death* (London, Longmans, Green and Co.).

Nagy, Marilyn (1991) *Philosophical Issues in the Psychology of C. G. Jung* (Albany, State University of New York Press).

Nicoll, Maurice (1917) *Dream Psychology* (London, Henry Frowde and Hodder and Stoughton).

Nietzsche, Friedrich (1880) *Human, all too Human: A Book for Free Spirits*, trans. M. Faber with S. Lehmann (Lincoln, University of Nebraska Press, 1984).

(1881) *Daybreak*, trans. R. Hollingdale (Cambridge, Cambridge University Press, 1982).

(1886) *Beyond Good and Evil*, trans. R. Hollingdale (Harmondsworth, Penguin, 1973).

(1882–1887) *The Gay Science*, trans. W. Kaufmann (New York, Vintage, 1974).

(1887) *On the Genealogy of Morals*, trans. D. Smith (Oxford, Oxford University Press, 1996).

(1888/1895) *Twilight of the Idols / The Anti-Christ*, trans. R. Hollingdale (Harmondsworth, Penguin, 1968).

(1908) *Ecce Homo*, trans. R. Hollingdale (London, Penguin, 1983).

Nye, Robert (1975) *The Origins of Crowd Psychology: Gustave Le Bon and Crisis of Mass Democracy in the Third Republic* (London, Sage).

Oppenheim, James (1923) "Watson on Jung – Jung on Watson," *The New Republic*.

(1931) *American Types: A Preface to Analytical Psychology* (New York, Knopf).

Otis, Laura (1994) *Organic Memory: History and the Body in the Late Nineteenth and Early Twentieth Centuries* (Lincoln, University of Nebraska Press).

Parkes, Graham (1994) *Composing the Soul: Reaches of Nietzsche's Psychology* Chicago, University of Chicago Press).

(1999) "Nietzsche and Jung: Ambivalent Appreciations," in Jacob Golomb, Weaver Santaniello, and Ronald Lehrer, eds., *Nietzsche and Depth Psychology* (Albany, SUNY Press), 205–227.

Paskauskas, Andrew, ed. (1993) *The Complete Correspondence of Sigmund Freud and Ernest Jones 1908–1939* (Cambridge, Mass., Harvard University Press).

Peck, John (1995) "Die Rezeption in den USA," *Du* 8, 1995, 88–96.

Perry, Ralph Barton (1935) *The Thought and Character of William James*, vol. 2, *Philosophy and Psychology* (London, Humphrey Milford / Oxford University Press).

Piaget, Jean (1945) "Hommage à C. G. Jung," *Schweizerische Zeitschrift für Psychologie* 4, 169–171.

Portmann, Adolf (1949) "Mythisches in der Naturforschung," *Eranos-Jahrbuch* 17, 475–514.

(1950) "Das Problem der Urbilder in biologischer Sicht," *Eranos-Jahrbuch* 18, 413–432.

Preyer, William (1888/1909) *The Mind of the Child*, 2 parts, trans. H. W. Brown (New York, Appleton and Co.).

Prince, Morton (1910) "The psychological principles and the field of psychotherapy," in Morton Prince and others, *Psychotherapeutics: A Symposium* (London, Fischer Unwin).

Putnam, James Jackson (1909) "Personal impressions of Sigmund Freud and his work," in *Addresses on Psycho-Analysis* (London, Hogarth Press, 1951), 1–30.

(1911) "A plea for the study of philosophic methods in preparation for psychoanalytic work," in *Addresses on Psycho-Analysis* (London, Hogarth Press, 1951), 79–96.

(1913) "Remarks on a case with Griselda phantasies," in *Addresses on Psycho-Analysis* (London, Hogarth Press, 1951), 175–193.

(1915) "The necessity of metaphysics," in *Addresses on Psycho-Analysis* (London, Hogarth Press, 1951), 297–311.

(1917) "The work of Sigmund Freud," in *Addresses on Psycho-Analysis* (London, Hogarth Press, 1951), 347–365.

Rabinbach, Anson (1992) *The Human Motor: Energy, Fatigue, and the Origins of Modernity* (Berkeley, University of California Press).

Radin, Paul (1927) *Primitive Man as Philosopher* (New York, Dover, 1957).

(1929) "History of ethnological theories," *American Anthropologist* 31, 9–33.

Raphael, Edwin (1886) *The Book of Dreams: Being a Concise Interpretation of Dreams* (London, W. Foulsham).

Rapp, Dean (1988) "The reception of Freud by the British press: general interest and literary magazines, 1920–1925," *Journal of the History of the Behavioral Sciences* 24, 191–201.

(1990) "The early Discovery of Freud by the British general educated public, 1912–1919," *Social History of Medicine* 3, 217–244.

Reil, Johann Christian (1803) *Rhapsodieen über die Anwendung der psychischen Curmethode auf Geisteszerrüttungen* (Halle, Prediger Wagnitz).

Ribot, Théodule (1873) *L'Hérédité: étude psychologique sur ses phénomènes, ses lois, ses causes, ses conséquences* (Paris, Libraire philosophique de ladrange).

(1885) *Diseases of the Memory: An Essay in Positive Psychology*, 3rd edn. (London, Kegan Paul, Trench).

(1896) *La Psychologie des sentiments* (Paris, Alcan, 1930).

(1900) *Essai sur l'imagination créatrice* (Paris, Alcan).

Rickert, Heinrich (1899) *Kulturwissenschaft und Naturwissenschaft: Ein Vortrag* (Freiburg, J. C. Mohr).

(1928) *Der Gegenstand der Erkenntnis: Einführung in die Transzendentalphilosophie*, 6th edn. (Tübingen, Mohr).

(1962) *Science and History: A Critique of Positivist Epistemology*, ed. Arthur Goddard, trans. G. Reisman (Princeton, Van Nostrand).

(1986) *The Limits of Concept Formation in Natural Science*, ed. and trans. Guy Oakes (Cambridge, Cambridge University Press).

Riklin, Franz (1908). "Wishfulfillment and symbolism in fairy tales," trans. W. A. White, *The Psychoanalytic Review* (1913–15), 94–107, 203–216, 322–332, 452–459, 102–105, 203–218, 327–340.

Ripa, Yannick (1988) *Histoire du rêve: regards sur l'imaginaire des français au XIXe siècle* (Paris, Olivier Orban).

Roback, A. A. (1927) *The Psychology of Character: With a Survey of Temperament* (London, Kegan Paul, Trench, Trubner).

Roelke, Volker (1994) "Jewish mysticism in romantic medicine? Indirect incorporation of kabbalistic elements in the work of Gotthilf Heinrich Schubert," *History and Philosophy of the Life Sciences* 16, 117–140.

Rolfe, Eugene (1989) *Encounter with Jung* (Boston, Sigo Press).

Rose, Nikolas (1996) *Inventing Our Selves: Psychology, Power, and Personhood* (Cambridge, Cambridge University Press).

Rosenzweig, Franz (1921) *The Star of Redemption*, trans. W. Hallo (London, Routledge and Kegan Paul, 1971).

Ross, Dorothy (1972) *G. Stanley Hall: The Psychologist as Prophet* (Chicago, University of Chicago Press).

Roudinesco, Elisabeth (1986) *La bataille de cent ans: histoire de la psychanalyse en France* (Paris, Seuil).

(1990) *Jacques Lacan and Co.: A History of Psychoanalysis in France, 1925–1985*, trans. J. Mehlman (London, Free Associations).

Rudnick, Lois (1984) *Mabel Dodge Luhan: New Woman, New Worlds* (Albuquerque, New Mexico, University of New Mexico Press).

Sand, Rosemarie (1992) "Pre-Freudian discovery of dream meaning: the achievements of Charcot, Janet, and Krafft-Ebing," in Toby Gelfand and John Kerr, eds., *Freud and the History of Psychoanalysis* (Hillsdale, New Jersey, Analytic Press), 215–229.

Sapir, Edward (1923) Review of Jung's *Psychological Types*, in David Mandelbaum, ed., *Selected Writings of Edward Sapir* (Berkeley, University of California Press, 1949), 529–532.

(1934) "Personality" in David Mandelbaum, ed., *Selected Writings of Edward Sapir* (Berkeley, University of California Press, 1949), 560–563.

Schaffer, Simon (1988) "Astronomers mark time: discipline and the personal equation," *Science in Context* 2, 1, 115–145.

Schelling, F. W. J. (1797) *Ideas for a Philosophy of Nature* (Cambridge, Cambridge University Press, 1988).

(1800) *System of Transcendental Idealism*, trans. P. Heath (Charlottesville, University of Virginia Press, 1981).

(1802) *The Philosophy of Art*, ed. and trans. Douglas Scott (Minneapolis, University of Minnesota Press, 1989).

(1803) *On University Studies*, trans. E. S. Morgan (Athens, Ohio, Ohio University Press, 1966).

(1827) *On the History of Modern Philosophy*, trans. A. Bowie (Cambridge, Cambridge University Press, 1994).

(1856–1857) *Philosophie der Mythologie*, Sämmtliche Werke, 2 vols. (Stuttgart, Cotta).

Scherner, Karl (1992) "The sexual stimulation dream," trans. Ronald Hauser, *The Centennial Review*, 347–360.

Schopenhauer, Arthur (1819) *The World as Will and Representation*, trans. E. J. Payne, 2 vols. (New York, Dover).

(1836) *On the Will in Nature: A Discussion of the Corroborations from the Empirical Sciences that the Author's Philosophy has received from its first Appearance*, trans. E. F. J. Payne, ed. David Cartwright (New York, Berg, 1992).

(1851) "Essay on spirit seeing and everything connected therewith," *Parega and Paralipomena*, vol. 1, trans. E. Payne (Oxford, Clarendon Press, 1974), 227–309.

Schubert, Gotthilf Heinrich von (1814) *Die Symbolik des Traumes* (Stuttgart, Besler Presse, 1968).

Schwartz, Joseph (1999) *Cassandra's Daughter: A History of Psychoanalysis in Europe and America* (London, Allen Lane).

Seligman, C. G. (1924) "Anthropology and psychology: a study of some points of contact," *Journal of the Royal Anthropological Institute of Great Britain and Ireland*, 54, 13–46.

Semon, Richard (1905) *The Mneme*, trans. L. Simon (London, George Allen and Unwin, 1921).

Shamdasani, Sonu (1990) "A woman called Frank," *Spring: A Journal of Archetype and Culture* 50, 26–56.

——— (1993) "Automatic writing and the discovery of the unconscious," *Spring: A Journal of Archetype and Culture* 54, 1993, 100–131.

——— (1994) "Encountering Hélène: Théodore Flournoy and the genesis of subliminal psychology," in Sonu Shamdasani, Théodore Flournoy, eds., *From India to the Planet Mars: A Case of Multiple Personality with Imaginary Languages* (Princeton, Princeton University Press), xi–li.

——— (1995) "Memories, Dreams, Omissions," *Spring: Journal of Archetype and Culture* 57, 115–137.

——— (1996) "De Genève à Zürich: Jung et la Suisse Romande," *Revue médicale de la Suisse Romande* 116, 917–922; "From Geneva to Zurich: Jung and French Switzerland," *Journal of Analytical Psychology*, 43, 1, 115–126.

——— (1997) "Hypnose, médecine et droit: la correspondence entre Joseph Delboeuf et George Croom Robertson," *Corpus des oeuvres philosophiques* 32, 71–88.

——— (1998a) *Cult Fictions: C. G. Jung and the Founding of Analytical Psychology* (London, Routledge).

——— (1998b) "The lost contributions of Maria Moltzer to analytical psychology: two unknown papers," *Spring: Journal of Archetype and Culture* 64, 103–120.

——— (1999a) Review of Robert C. Smith, *The Wounded Jung: Effects of Jung's Relationships on his Life and Work, Journal of the History of the Behavioral Sciences*, 35, 1, 66–68.

——— (1999b) "Of dream books," preface to David Holt, *A Common Eventuality: Fifty Years of Dreaming Remembered* (Oxford, Validthod Press), 3–7.

——— (2000a) "Misunderstanding Jung: The Afterlife of Legends," *Journal of Analytical Psychology* 45, 459–472.

——— (2000b) "Reply," *Journal of Analytical Psychology* 45, 615–20.

——— (2001a) "'The magical method that works in the dark': C. G. Jung, hypnosis and suggestion," *Journal of Jungian Practice and Theory* 3, 5–18.

——— (2001b) "Extrasensory perception," in Colin Blakemore et al., eds., *Oxford Companion to the Body* (Oxford, Oxford University Press), 265.

——— (2001c) "Claire, Lise, Jean, Nadia, and Gisèle: preliminary notes towards a characterisation of Pierre Janet's psychasthenia," in Marijke Gijswijt-Hofstra and Roy Porter, eds., *Cultures of Neurasthenia: From Beard to the First World War* (Amsterdam, Rodopi), 362–385.

——— (2002) "Psychoanalysis Inc.," *The Semiotic Review of Books* 13, 1, 5–10.

——— (forthcoming) "Psychologies as ontology-making practices: William James and the pluralities of psychological experience," in Jeremy Carrette, Robert Morris, and Timothy Sprigge, eds., *William James and the Varieties of Religious Experience* (London, Routledge).

Shapin, Steven (1994) *A Social History of Truth* (Chicago, University of Chicago Press).

Shulman, David and Guy G. Stroumsa, eds. (1999) *Dream Cultures: Explorations in the Comparative History of Dreaming* (New York, Oxford University Press).

Sidis, Boris (1910) "The psychotherapeutic value of the hypnoidal state," in Morton Prince and others, *Psychotherapeutics: A Symposium* (London, Fischer Unwin).

Sighele, Scipio (1891) *La foule criminelle: essai de psychologie collective* (Paris, Alcan, 1901).

Silberer, Herbert (1912) "Zur Symbolbildung," *Jahrbuch für psychoanalytische und psychopathologische Forschungen* 4, 607–683.

(1910) "Phantasie und Mythos," in Bernd Nitzschke, ed., *Ausgewählte Schriften Herbert Silberers: Miszellen zu seinem Leben und Werk* (Tübingen, Edition Diskord), 95–176.

Smith, Roger (1988) "Does the history of psychology have a subject?" *History of the Human Sciences* 1, 147–177.

(1997) *The Fontana History of the Human Sciences* (London, Fontana).

Smith, Woodruff D. (1991) *Politics and the Sciences of Culture in Germany, 1840–1920* (New York, Oxford University Press).

Spengler, Oswald (1918) *The Decline of the West*, trans. C. Atkinson (London, Allen and Unwin, 1926).

Spitz, René, in collaboration with W. Godfrey Cobliner (1965) *The First Year of Life: A Psychoanalytic Study of Normal and Deviant Development of Object Relations* (New York, International Universities Press).

Starobinski, Jean (1970) "Sur l'histoire des fluides imaginaires (des esprits animaux à la libido)," *L'Oeil vivant 2, La relation critique* (Paris, Gallimard), 196–213.

(1976) "The word reaction: from physics to psychiatry," *Diogenes*, 23, 1–27.

(1999) *Action et réaction: vie et aventures d'un couple* (Paris, Éditions du Seuil).

Stekel, Wilhelm (1943) *The Interpretation of Dreams: New Developments and Technique*, trans. E. and C. Paul (New York, Washington Press, 1967).

Stern, William (1900a) *Über Psychologie der individuellen Differenzen (Ideen zur einer "Differentiellen Psychologie")* (Leipzig, Barth).

(1900b) "Die psychologische Arbeit des neunzehnten Jarhunderts, insbesondere in Deutschland," *Zeitschrift für Pädogigische Psychologie und Pathologie* 2, 413–436.

(1905–1906) *Beiträge zur Psychologie der Aussage. Mit besonderer Berücksichtigung von Problemen der Rechtspflege, Pädagogik, Psychiatrie und Geschichtsforschung* (Leipzig, Barth).

(1930) "Autobiography," in Carl Murchison, ed., *A History of Psychology in Autobiography*, vol. 1 (Worcester, Clark University Press).

(1938) *General Psychology from the Personalistic Standpoint*, trans. H. Spoerl (London, Macmillan).

Stewart, Dugald (1808) *Elements of the Philosophy of the Human Mind* (Brattleborough, Vermont, William Fessenden).

Stocking, George (1968) "The Critique of Racial Formalism," in *Race, Culture and Evolution: Essays in the History of Anthropology* (New York, Free Press), 161–194.

(1974) "Some problems in the understanding of nineteenth-century cultural evolutionism," in Regna Darnell, ed., *Readings in the History of Anthropology* (New York, Harper and Row), 407–425.

(1986a) *Victorian Anthropology* (New York).

(1986b) "Anthropology and the science of the irrational: Malinowski's encounter with Freudian psychoanalysis," in Stocking, ed., *Malinowski, Rivers, Benedict and Others: Essays on Culture and Personality* (Wisconsin, University of Wisconsin Press).

Sulloway, Frank (1979) *Freud, Biologist of the Mind: Beyond the Psychoanalytic Legend* (New York, Basic Books).

Sully, James (1884) *Outlines of Psychology* (London, Longman, Green).

(1893) "The dream as revelation," *Fortnightly Review* 53, 354–365.

(1895) *Illusions: A Psychological Study* (London, Kegan Paul, Trench, Trübner, 4th edn.).

Swales, Peter (1982a) "Freud, Minna Bernays and the conquest of Rome," *New American Review: A Journal of Civility and the Arts*, 1, 1–23.

(1982b) "Freud, Minna Bernays and the Imitation of Christ," unpublished.

(1988) "In statu nascendi: Freud, Minna Bernays, and the creation of Herr Aliquis," unpublished.

(1989) "Freud, cocaine, and sexual chemistry: the role of cocaine in Freud's conception of the libido," in Laurie Spurling, ed., *Sigmund Freud: Critical Assessments*, vol. 1 (London, Routledge), 273–301.

Tarde, Gabriel (1890) *Les Lois de l'imitation* (Paris, Alcan, 1911), 6th edn.

(1969) *On Communication and Social Influence: Selected Papers*, ed. Terry Clark (Chicago, University of Chicago Press, 1969).

Taylor, Eugene (1980) "Jung and William James," *Spring: A Journal for Archetypal Psychology and Jungian Thought*, 20, 157–169.

(1984) *William James on Exceptional Mental States: The 1896 Lowell Lectures* (Amherst, University of Massachusetts Press).

(1986) "C. G. Jung and the Boston psychopathologists," in E. Mark Stern, ed. *Carl Jung and Soul Psychology* (New York, Haworth Press), 131–144.

(1996a) *William James on Consciousness Beyond the Margin* (Princeton, Princeton University Press).

(1996b) "The new Jung scholarship," *The Psychoanalytic Review* 83, 547–568.

Tedlock, Barbara, ed. (1992a) *Dreaming: Anthropological and Psychological Interpretations* (Santa Fe, School of American Research Press).

(1992b) "Dreaming and dream research," in Barbara Tedlock, ed. *Dreaming: Anthropological and Psychological Interpretations* (Santa Fe, School of American Research Press).

Tissié, Philippe (1898) *Les Rêves: physiologie et pathologie* (Paris, Alcan).

Tomlinson, Craig (1992) "C. G. Lichtenberg: dreams, jokes and the unconscious in eighteenth-century Germany," *Journal of the American Psychoanalytic Association* 40, 761–799.

Tridon, André (1919) *Psychoanalysis: Its History, Theory and Practice* (New York, Heubsch).

Tuke, Daniel Hack (1872) *Illustrations of the Influence of the Mind upon the Body in Health and Disease: Designed to Elucidate the Action of the Imagination* (London, J. and A. Churchill).

Tylor, E. B. (1871) *Primitive Culture: Researches into the Development of Mythology, Philosophy, Religion, Language, Art, and Custom*, 2 vols. (London, John Murray, 4th edn., 1903).

Van der Post, Laurens (1976) *Jung and the Story of our Time* (London, Penguin).

Van Eeden, Frederik (1893) "Les Principes de la psychothérapie," *Revue de l'hypnotisme* 7, 97–120.

Van Ginneken, Jaap (1992) *Crowds, Psychology, and Politics 1871–1899* (Cambridge, Cambridge University Press).

Vidal, Fernando (1994) *Piaget before Piaget* (Cambridge, Mass., Harvard University Press).

Volkelt, Johannes (1875) *Die Traum-Phantasie* (Stuttgart, Meyer and Beller's, 1875).

Voltaire (1759) *Candide and Other Stories*, trans. R. Pearson (Oxford, Oxford University Press, 1998).

Von Franz, Marie-Louise (1975) *C. G. Jung: His Myth in our Time*, trans. W. Kennedy (New York, C. G. Jung Foundation).

Von Koenig-Fachsenfeld, Olga (1935) *Wandlungen des Traumsproblems von der Romantik bis zur Gegenwart* (Stuttgart, Ferdinand Enke).

Von Monakow, Constantin (1925) *The Emotions, Morality and the Brain*, trans. G. Barnes and S. E. Jelliffe (Washington, Nervous and Mental Disease Publishing Co.).

   (1970) *Vita Mea, Mein Leben*, ed. Alfred Gubser and Erwin Ackerknecht (Bern, Hans Huber).

Von Monakow, Constantin and R. Morgue (1928) *Introduction biologique à l'étude de la neurologie et de la psychopathologie: intégration et désintégration de la fonction* (Paris, Félix Alcan).

Voogd, Stephanie de (1984) "Fantasy versus Fiction: Jung's Kantianism Appraised," in Papadopoulos, R. K. and G. S. Saayaman, eds. *Jung in Modern Perspective* (Bridport, Prism Press), 204–228.

Walser, Hans (1973) "Johann Jakob Honegger (1885–1911): Ein Beitrag zur Geschichte der Psychoanalyse," *Schweizer Archiv für Neurologie, Neurochirugie und Psychiatrie* 112, 107–113.

   (1974) "An early psychoanalytic tragedy: J. J. Honegger and the beginnings of training analysis," *Spring: An Annual of Archetypal Psychology and Jungian Thought*, 243–255.

Watson, John (1923) "Jung as psychologist," *The New Republic*, November 7.

Wheeler, Richmond (1939) *Vitalism: Its History and Validity* (London, Whiterby).

Wheelwright, Joseph (1972) Review of Jung, *Psychological Types, Journal of Analytical Psychology* 17, 212–214.

Whitman, James (1984) "From philology to anthropology in mid-nineteenth-century Germany," in George Stocking, ed., *Functionalism Historicized: Essays on British Social Anthropology, History of Anthropology*, vol. 2 (Madison, University of Wisconsin Press), 214–230.

Windelband, Wilhelm (1984) "History and natural science," *Theory and Psychology* 8, 1998, 5–22.

Witzig, James (1982) "Theodore Flournoy: A friend indeed," *Journal of Analytical Psychology* 27, 131–148.

Wolff, Toni (1935) "Einführung in die Grundlagen der Komplexen Psychologie," in ed. Psychologischen Club, *Die Kulturelle Bedeutung der komplexen Psychologie* (Berlin, Julius Springer), 1–170.

Woodworth, Robert (1931) *Contemporary Schools of Psychology* (London, Methuen).

Wundt, Wilhelm (1874) *Principles of Physiological Psychology*, vol. 1, trans. E. B. Titchener (London, Swan Sonnenschein, 1902, 5th edn.).

— (1892) *Lectures on Human and Animal Psychology*, 2nd edn., trans. J. E. Creighton and E. B. Titchener (London, Swan Sonnenschein, 1894).

— (1897) *Ethics: An Investigation into the Facts and Laws of Moral Life*, trans. J. Gulliver and E. B. Titchener (London, Swan Sonnenschein).

— (1900) *Völkerpsychologie: Eine Untersuchung der Entwicklungsgesetze von Sprache Mythus und Sitte*, 1, *Die Sprache* (Leipzig, Wilhelm Engelmann).

— (1902) *Outlines of Psychology*, trans. C. H. Judd (Leipzig, Wilhelm Englemann, 4th edn.).

— (1911) *Elements of Folk-Psychology: Outlines of a Psychological Development of Mankind*, trans. E. L. Schaub (London, Allen and Unwin, 1916).

— (1921) *Erlebtes und Erkanntes* (Stuttgart, Alfred Kröner Verlag).

Index